Manual of Internal Audit Practice

Manual of Internal Audit Practice

Edited by
JOCK STEARN AND KEN IMPEY

ICSA · Cambridge
IIA–UK · London

Published by ICSA Publishing Limited,
Fitzwilliam House, 32 Trumpington Street,
Cambridge CB2 1QY, England

First published 1990

British Library Cataloguing in Publication Data

Manual of internal audit practice.
1. Organizations. Internal auditing
I. Stearn, H. J. II. Impey, K. W.
657. 458

ISBN 0-902197-80-0

Designed by Geoff Green
Typeset by Pentacor PLC, High Wycombe, Bucks
Printed in Great Britain by Page Bros, Norwich

Contents

The editors

K. W. Impey, FCA

Ken Impey is by way of qualification a chartered accountant with extensive industrial management experience. As head of internal audit in Reed International Group through the 1980s, he developed and directed a highly respected operational audit service. This was a period of great change when Reed was being successfully transformed from an industrial conglomerate into a leading publishing group.

He had previously been company secretary of a public group in the textile industry for six years, commercial manager of the printed carton division of Reed for five years, and finance director of the Crown paint and wallcoverings division of Reed for seven years.

He is a member of the APC working party on internal audit guidance and joint author of a standard textbook, *Internal Audit*, by Venables and Impey, published by Butterworth and now in its second edition.

H. J. Stearn, BA MSc FCIS FIIA

Jock Stearn is a chartered secretary and a fellow of the Institute of Internal Auditors–UK, with a Master's degree from the City University Business School and a degree from the Open University, having originally studied engineering at Glasgow University.

He has been Technical Services Officer of the Institute of Internal Auditors–UK since 1984, where he has successfully developed and directed the Institute's distance learning courses for students.

He brought to this position a wealth of practical experience in systems development, internal audit, training and general management as a senior executive in a series of public-sector appointments. These included four years as an organisation and methods officer in H.M. Treasury, followed by three years as course director (Internal Audit) at the Civil Service College, leading on to H.M. Customs and Excise where he spent four years as branch head of internal audit and four years in general management.

He is a director of the charity 'Help The Homeless'.

The contributors

Contributions to the text of this manual are gratefully acknowledged from the following:

D. F. Bentley, BA(Hons) FCBSI FIIA MBCS, Chief Internal Auditor of Leeds Permanent Building Society, Past President of the Institute of Internal Auditors–UK.

A. Brazendale, FCA MBIM MIIM MInstAM, Consultant, formerly Senior Lecturer in management studies at Newcastle Polytechnic, Chairman of Gateshead Education Committee.

R. J. Ellison, FCIS, Group Internal Auditor of Express Newspapers Plc, Chairman of ICSA Internal Audit Group.

W. L. Ewing, FCIS, Deputy Director of the National Audit Office.

B. J. Green, MSc IPFA, Consultant, formerly Head of Department of Accountancy and Administrative Studies at Southampton Institute of Higher Education.

S. V. Hinde, FCA FIIA MIIA, Computer Audit Manager UK and Europe of Elders Plc, Chairman of Compacs, Past President of the Institute of Internal Auditors–UK.

P. Harvey, ACIS, Official of the European Commission, formerly Head of the Audit Division of East Dorset District Council.

K. W. Impey, FCA, formerly Head of Internal Audit for Reed International Group, joint author of *Internal Audit* (Butterworths), member of APC working party on Internal Audit; also a joint editor.

A. C. Mumford, ACIS ARCM, Internal Auditor, BET Plant Services Plc, member of ICSA Internal Audit Group.

S. Paul-Clark, BSc, Senior Computer Auditor, International Stock Exchange.

J. Ridley, ACIS FIIA CIA, Chief Internal Auditor of Kodak Ltd, Past President of the Insitute of Internal Auditors–UK.

J. Scott-Baird, FCA ACIS FBIM FIIA, Consultant, formerly Manager with Ernst and Whinney and Head of Internal Audit, Youghal Carpet Group.

M. J. Smallbone, FCA FIIA, formerly Chief Internal Auditor, Royal Dutch Shell Group, Past President of the Institute of Internal Auditors–UK.

H. J. Stearn, BA MSc FCIS FIIA, Technical Services Officer of the Institute of Internal Auditors –UK, formerly Internal Audit Course Director at the Civil Service College; also a joint editor.

W. P. Tickner, FIIA MIIA, Chief Internal Auditor at H.M. Treasury, formerly Internal Audit Course Director at the Civil Service College.

L. G. Westwood, FCCA IPFA FIIA, Training Consultant in Internal Audit, formerly Senior Auditor with Yorkshire Water Authority.

Foreword

The role of modern management continues to expand rapidly in response to technological development, changes in economic and social expectations, and the ever increasing complexity of organisations and their administration. These trends impose great reponsibilities upon directors and managers to maintain sound management control in order to safeguard the interests of the people who own the organisation, those whom it serves and, not least, those who work for it.

Effective internal audit is an invaluable tool of modern management. It provides positive assurance on the effectiveness and adequacy of control in a changing environment by identifying strengths and weaknesses and recommending any necessary remedial action. It also assists the achievement of management objectives by identifying opportunities

and threats and offering practical ideas for addressing them.

As an authoritative guide to good internal audit practice we commend this manual to you. It encapsulates the knowledge and experience of many years of practical and successful internal auditing.

In expressing our appreciation to all contributors we endorse the ethos of the internal auditing profession: 'progress through sharing'.

David O. Phyall, FIIA
President, 1990–91
The Institute of Internal Auditors–
United Kingdom

David W. R. Wright, FCIS FIPM MPIM
President, 1990
The Institute of Chartered Secretaries and Administrators

September 1990

Preface

The aim of this manual is to provide an authoritative reference book covering all aspects of the practice of internal auditing, with particular emphasis on the practical application of the principles involved. These principles are generally well established and have been comprehensively defined in the statements of standards and guidance published by the Institute of Internal Auditors. Appropriate extracts from these statements are quoted throughout the text.

This is essentially a practical book based upon sound theoretical principles. It is written by an exceptionally well qualified team of contributors selected from experienced practitioners who are acknowledged leading experts in internal auditing and in management, both in private and public sector operations. Consequently, the text draws on a great wealth of relevant practical knowledge and experience. It presents internal auditing throughout as a key management tool: a control function used to monitor the quality and effectiveness of other controls. This is internal auditing perceived from the viewpoint of general management and in the context of contributing to the achievement of management goals.

The main thrust of the text is, first, to explain the philosophy of internal auditing and the techniques developed for its practice; it then demonstrates the relevance of these techniques by analysing the requirements for effective control in all the critical areas of general management and in a range of specialist management areas. The final three chapters examine the role of internal auditing in the context of fraud, external audit and audit committees respectively.

The manual is intended primarily for use as a reference work, both by experienced internal auditing practitioners and trainees. It is likely to prove particularly helpful when tackling any internal audit assignment where unfamiliar circumstances occur or where fresh ideas are needed to resolve the problems encountered. It may not provide ready solutions to the problems: indeed, to have attempted to do so would, we believe, have been a disservice to the internal auditing profession. However, it will provide useful practical ideas for analysing the problems, so enabling the internal auditor to exercise sound, independent professional judgement which relates specifically to the circumstances found.

In adopting this approach we have also been concerned to make this manual a valuable guide for general managers who are in a position to benefit significantly from a sound understanding of internal auditing philosophy and practice. It should enable them to make best use of the function as a means for enhancing performance through improved control.

We are indebted to the contributors for the quality of the material provided, which we trust has lost none of its impact in the process of being welded into a single text.

Jock Stearn
Ken Impey

September 1990

Acknowledgements

The publishers wish to acknowledge the assistance of the following:

The Institute of Internal Auditors–United Kingdom for permission to quote from *Standards and Guidelines for the Professional Practice of Internal Auditing* throughout the manual.

The Standards are the same in every material respect as those published and adopted by the Institute of Internal Auditors, Inc., International Headquarters, 240 Mainland Avenue, Altamonte Springs, Florida 32701–4201, USA.

The Institute of Internal Auditors Inc., USA for permission to quote from the *IIA Inc. Statement on Audit Committees* in Chapter 10.

The Lockheed Aircraft Corporation and Publishers: The Institute of Internal Auditors Inc., for permission to reproduce extracts from sampling tables from the *Sampling Manual for Auditors* in Chapter 4.

The Institute of Chartered Accountants in England and Wales, for permission to quote and adapt from *Accountants' Digest No. 32: Flowcharting for Auditors* in Chapter 4.

The Chartered Institute of Management Accountants, for permission to quote from *CIMA Management Accounting Official Terminology*, first edition, in Chapter 6.

1 The nature of internal auditing

Introduction

Internal auditing is a developing profession which provides a service to assist managers to achieve corporate objectives. Consequently each internal audit unit must be designed to best serve its own organisation and will thus be unique with respect to its own environment. Nevertheless, as a profession, internal auditing must be identified with a common body of knowledge and recognised standards of practice.

Originally, internal auditing was primarily concerned with accounting accuracy and financial control but it subsequently developed to be equally applicable to appraising and evaluating the efficiency and effectiveness of all operational activity so that it now encompasses the entire field of management control.

Responsibilities

Internal auditing is an independent appraisal activity established within an organisation as a service to the organisation. It is a control which functions by examining and evaluating the adequacy and effectiveness of other controls.

The objective of internal auditing is to assist members of the organisation in the effective discharge of their responsibilities. To this end internal auditing furnishes them with analyses, appraisals, recommendations, counsel and information concerning the activities reviewed. The audit objective includes promoting effective control at reasonable cost.

The scope of internal auditing encompasses the examination and evaluation of the adequacy and effectiveness of the organisation's system of internal control and the quality of performance in carrying out assigned responsibilities.
(IIA–UK Statement of Responsibilities of Internal Auditing)

Analysis of the first paragraph of this statement enables us to clarify and crystallise our concept of what internal auditing now means.

Internal   Makes clear that the work is undertaken by members or employees of the auditee organisation. As employees, internal auditors can be expected to have significant knowledge of the organisation's staff and systems and they should be attuned to a mutual culture and have an identity of interest in the objectives of the organisation.

Auditing   Is defined in the Concise Oxford Dictionary as:

1. Official examination of accounts
2. Searching examination

Official examination of accounts is the role of external auditors appointed for such purposes. Searching examination of any or all activity of the auditee organisation is the function of the internal auditor.

Independent   Addresses the relationship and attitude required of an individual appointed from within the auditee organisation to carry out searching examination as an internal auditor. It relies upon the organisational status and the personal integrity and courage of the internal auditor all of which must be supported by top management.

Whilst no employee can be absolutely independent of the organisation which is the paymaster, internal auditors must be totally independent of all specific activities which they are required to examine.

Appraisal   Is an estimate of value or quality. The internal auditor has the responsibility to interpret the facts revealed by searching examination and to make known their purport and significance. This requires the application of professional judgement based upon knowledge and experience.

Established   Signifies the legitimacy and authority of the internal auditing function as prescribed by the top management of the auditee organisation.

Service   Defines the primary function of internal auditing to support and assist the management of the auditee organisation to achieve the organisation's goals.

Organisation   Is the corporate body which has established the internal auditing function within its organisational structure. This body is described as the auditee organisation because its activities are then subject to examination by the internal auditing function, it is the recipient of the internal auditing service, and it is entitled to benefit from it.

Control   Is defined in the Shorter Oxford Dictionary as:

The act of checking and directing action

This is a critical element in the cycle of management processes: planning – directing – controlling – planning. Control involves monitoring and corrective action; it has a forward influence related to backward review. Internal audit is a critical control tool for management because it focuses on the effectiveness of other controls.

Examining and evaluating   Describe the internal auditing tasks of collecting, analysing, interpreting and documenting information in support of audit conclusions and recommendations.

Adequacy and effectiveness   Mean that internal auditors must satisfy themselves both about the need for the control procedures in place and that such procedures are being properly applied so that they operate satisfactorily. Control procedures should be subject to cost/benefit analysis in the same way as other operational activities.

Other controls   Refers to the operation of all the control devices which the auditee organisation has adopted. They include all those functions, systems and procedures which have been established for the primary purpose of assisting the management of the auditee organisation to fulfil plans and achieve objectives. Internal auditing is one such function and it contributes by examining and evaluating the adequacy and effectiveness of any or all of the other control devices.

Definitions

Internal check

All functional units employing a number of people who undertake relatively routine tasks should have internal checks built into their procedures as a means of checking the quantity and quality of work and preventing error. The essential nature of internal check is that as each task is completed by one employee or group of employees the work is scrutinised, checked and approved by another employee or group of employees before the next task on that work can start.

Internal checking is particularly associated with accounting work as a means of ensuring accuracy and preventing irregularities. It is however equally applicable to all operational procedures which involve employees completing routine tasks. It is essentially preventative, ensuring that routine procedures are adhered to and that lapses are identified so that they can be promptly rectified.

Similar automatic checking routines must be built into computerised information processing systems.

This is a critical requirement in system design providing vital protection against misuse of the computer's high-speed processing power and its potential to corrupt vital information very fast. The data must be fully checked and validated at each stage of processing before it can progress to the next stage.

Control

A control is any action taken by management to enhance the likelihood that established objectives and goals will be achieved. Management plans, organises and directs the performance of sufficient actions to provide reasonable assurance that the objectives and goals will be achieved. Thus, control is the result of proper planning, organising and directing by management.

(IIA–UK, Guideline 300.06)

The overall system of control is conceptual in nature. It is the integrated collection of controlled systems used by an organisation to achieve its objectives and goals.

(IIA–UK, Guideline 300.06.4)

Internal control

The variant 'internal control' came into general use to distinguish controls within an organisation from those existing externally to the organisation (such as laws). Since internal auditors operate within an organisation and, among other responsibilities evaluate management's response to external stimuli (such as laws), no such distinction between internal and external controls is necessary. Also, from the organisation's viewpoint internal controls are all activities which attempt to ensure the accomplishment of the organisation's objectives and goals. For the purpose of this statement, internal control is considered synonymous with control within the organisation.

(IIA–UK Guideline 300.06.3)

The primary objectives of internal control are to ensure:

.1 The reliability and integrity of information.
.2 Compliance with policies, plans, procedures, laws and regulations.
.3 The safeguarding of assets.
.4 The economical and efficient use of resources.
.5 The accomplishment of established objectives and goals for operations or programmes.

(IIA–UK Guideline 300.05)

Internal control will usually mean all measures taken by management in order that the organisation's policies, plans and procedures succeed. It requires the setting of objectives, targets and standards so that performance deviations can be monitored and corrective action taken. The establishment of economic, efficient and effective systems of internal control is the responsibility of the management of an organisation. Management may set up an internal audit unit to assist members of the organisation in the effective discharge of their responsibilities.

2 Managing the internal audit department

The nature of management

'Management' is a term used generally for the managing process at many different levels in an organisation. Managing is perhaps the most important kind of work that is carried out in any organised human activity. This chapter is concerned with the practice of managing the internal audit function and how this relates to other levels of management, within an organisation and externally with other groups.

The theory and principles of management have been well researched this century. Many see management as a science based on a set of rational laws; others see management as more a set of values and style than a theory. The practice is almost certainly a mixture of established law with changing values and style influenced by time and a wide spectrum of events, internal and external to the organisation. It is this mixture which makes the managing process so predictable and yet so varied in its practice.

The established law governing the managing process is based on a series of rational steps which include the following:

> set objectives
> direct the process
> measure the results
> review the objectives

In this chapter each of these steps will be examined as it relates to managing the internal audit function. Each is a key to the success of any process, in any organisation. Each is strongly influenced by

values, style and organisation structure. Management never stands in isolation from an organisation's activities, nor indeed from changes in the environment whether social or technical. For the foreseeable future changes in values and style of the managing process will almost certainly continue to be influenced by the factors set out below.

Technology Increased information and the speed with which activities can be accomplished will accelerate.

World-wide operations International relationships, standards and regulations will increase.

Economic environment Results in home markets will react quickly across national boundaries. The drive for quality in both products and services will increase, forcing changes in organisations and operations.

Participation More open communication and participation by employees will be encouraged throughout organisations, prompted by improved education and a greater involvement by people in their situations within organisations.

Government influence Concurrent with an era of increased freedom for the individual there will continue to be increased regulation over the activities of organisations.

All of these changes will influence the development of management of the internal audit process. The remainder of this chapter will explore how these changes can be used to improve the service which internal auditing provides within organisations.

Independence

Achieving independence

Chambers, Selim and Vinten (1987) use the classical functional, administrative, task-oriented reporting lines to describe the responsibility relationships which can exist for an internal audit department. They provide examples of organisation structures using the services of an internal audit function and develop some general principles on methods of reporting.

John Child (1977) summarises organisation structure as a means for allocating responsibilities, producing a framework for operations and performance assessment and furnishing mechanisms to process information and assist decision making. The placing of the internal audit department in the organisation structure is therefore an important first step in managing the internal audit process. Each responsibility line added to the internal audit department enhances the independence of the function.

the only internal audit function in the organisation or it may form part of a larger organisation structure with national and international levels of audit management.

Responsibility lines created by the organisation structure can be extremely complex and can serve various purposes. It is important that these are all understood by those managing the organisation and by the chief internal auditor. The structure of reporting does not necessarily require the internal audit function to report directly to the chief executive of an organisation. In many organisations the line is to a financial manager and this can achieve the required objective provided it is at a senior enough level. A suitable structure as shown in Figure 2.1 is designed to achieve the following objectives:

Relationships	Objectives
1. Local internal audit to:	Authority of position
Corporate management	Broad audit scope
Local senior managment	Adequate consideration of
Operational management	audit findings
	Appropriate action
Audit committee	
Corporate internal audit	
2. Local internal audit to:	Co-ordination of audit
Corporate internal audit	activities
External authorities	Development of common
	audit techniques
Local external audit	Risk analysis
	Joint audits
3. Local internal audit to:	Audit assignments
Operational management	Internal consultancy role: prevention rather than detection

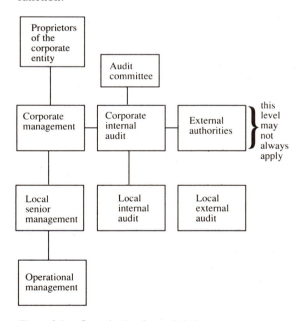

Figure 2.1   Organisation for audit independence

This can be seen more clearly by reference to Figure 2.1. The 'local' internal audit group may be

The responsibility for achieving these objectives should be written into the charter for the internal audit function which will then give considerable strength to the independent role of the chief internal auditor. Specific reporting lines should be developed from the responsibility lines.

The IIA Standards and Guidelines for the Professional Practice of Internal Auditing place the responsibility for seeking approval and acceptance for the independence of the internal audit function on the chief internal auditor. In some organisations, responsibility for the independence of the internal audit function has been assigned to an audit committee. There may also be a legal foundation for independence in certain organisations. There is some evidence that increasing regulatory laws may strengthen the independence of the internal audit function and encourage changes in the reporting lines to management and to those external bodies interested in an organisation's operations.

The tasks, responsibilities, and goals of audit committees and internal auditing are closely intertwined in many ways. As the magnitude of corporate accountability issues increases, so does the significance of the relationship of the internal auditing function to the audit committee. The audit committee has a major responsibility in ensuring that the mechanisms for corporate accountability are in place and functioning. A sound, well-orchestrated, co-operative relationship with the internal auditing function is critical to this responsibility.

Wherever the internal auditing function is placed in the structure of the auditee organisation, and whatever influences there are, the chief internal auditor has a clear responsibility to ensure that independence is written into the internal audit charter and that sufficient responsibility lines exist to achieve this. An example of an internal audit charter is given in Appendix 1.

Organising the internal audit department

Having established the responsibilities of the internal audit function, the next management step is to direct the internal audit process by establishing the department's resources and organising these in the most effective way. Size of the department and the nature of the auditee organisation's operations will play a significant part in the extent of internal audit coverage. It is rare for the size of a department to be based on any formulae calculated using the financial resources of the auditee organisation or the number and variety of operations to be audited, although all of these factors will have some influence.

It is the responsibility of the chief internal auditor to establish staffing plans and financial budgets consistent with the internal audit charter and the goals of the auditee organisation. The following factors must be taken into consideration when establishing an organisational structure for the internal audit department:

1. Scope of audit coverage – functions – frequency of audit.
2. Responsibility relationships with other audit groups, e.g. external audit, other control units in the organisation.
3. Geographic area occupied by the auditee organisation.
4. Risks involved in operations of the auditee organisation.
5. Quality of internal audit staff.
6. Other non-audit responsibilities, e.g. training, control.

Few internal auditing textbooks provide guidance on the organisation of internal audit departments. Heeschen and Sawyer (1984) outline some typical organisational structures for corporate audit departments based on specialist and generalist staffing. The tendency is for small departments to be single units which are generalist in staffing and structure, and the larger departments to be a number of units, possibly spread over a geographic area with generalist and specialist internal audit staff. Small departments usually recruit only professionally qualified staff and large departments have more levels of staff skills and responsibilities, which will influence the organisational structure adopted.

For certain organisations, there are statutory requirements to maintain an effective internal audit function and this can influence the size of the audit group and its structure. In the United States, the Treadway Commission report on fraudulent financial reporting issued an exposure draft (April 1987) which recommended that:

public companies should maintain an effective internal audit function staffed with an adequate number of qualified personnel appropriate to the size and the nature of the company.

Audit staff

Quantity and quality

The 1986 survey of internal auditing in the UK and Eire, published by IIA–UK, showed that the average number of internal auditors employed in an internal audit function was 15.8. There was, however, considerable variability in the averages for the different sectors surveyed; for example:

Nationalised industries	55.9
Private sector companies (turnover over £35m)	22.9
Government departments	20.3
Local authorities	87.1

However, the median figures produced for the different sectors are nearer to five in each case. The median is a more representative figure for the number of auditors employed, since it avoids the distortions introduced through large and small numbers. These statistics demonstrate the wide variety of recruitment processes that may be appropriate when staffing an internal audit department, from within the auditee organisation or externally.

The key to successful internal auditing is to staff the internal audit function with leaders. The practice of this maxim is essential to enable internal audit to achieve the status necessary to fulfil its responsibilities within the auditee organisation. Rose (1932) expressed the following view:

As to the qualifications of a management auditor these would obviously be firstly, the possession of at least fifteen years of management experience, which must be combined with a successful record of results obtained when in personal control of undertakings from the works manager's or general manager's position. Secondly, some form of diploma or certificate of qualification would be necessary and in this regard the fellowship of the Institute of Industrial Administration is indicated. The possession of these qualifications would ensure that the holder had received the approval of a qualifying body with regard to his theoretical knowledge of the subject and this, coupled with his personal experience, should be sufficient to give confidence to those who desire to make use of his services.

Rose goes on to say:

I would like to lay emphasis on the minimum of fifteen years experience. I am fully prepared to admit that a young man with comparatively few years of actual personal experience, a clever brain and an open intelligent mind, might perhaps be able to make a report which would be quite helpful, but management is certainly not a subject to be learnt through books.

The reader might argue that Rose was writing about the management audit and not internal auditing, which at the time was mainly concerned with transaction records and verification of assets.

Compare Rose's description of a management auditor with the role of the modern internal auditor:

Staffing

The internal auditing department should provide assurance that the technical proficiency and educational background of internal auditors are appropriate for the audits to be performed.

The chief internal auditor should establish suitable criteria of education and experience for filling internal auditing positions, giving due consideration to scope of work and level of responsibility.

Reasonable assurance should be obtained as to each prospective auditor's qualifications and proficiency.
(IIA–UK, Specific Standard 210 and Guidelines .01 and .02)

Despite being fifty years apart, the above statements identify the two key issues on staffing:

   qualifications
   experience

The nature and quality of the services that can be performed by the internal audit function depend on both. Each requires planning and direction by the chief internal auditor during the recruitment of staff if the internal audit responsibilities delegated by management are to be achieved.

In practice, most internal audit functions are staffed by some or all of the following types of staff, depending on the size of organisation and scope of work:

Management and supervisory staff Usually professionally qualified, with previous auditing or management experience in other parts of the organisation or in other organisations. In some cases there may be no or little auditing experience and this has to be acquired after appointment.

Professional staff   Either qualified before entry or preparing for a qualification whilst employed as an internal auditor. Usually in internal audit for a short period, although more now seek careers in internal audit.

Specialist staff   Usually with technical and specialist skills needed for specific types of audit, e.g. computing, engineering, finance, etc.

Support staff   Clerical and secretarial positions which require knowledge of audit administration and routine.

Seconded staff   These staff usually join internal audit assignments from other parts of the auditee organisation for a short period for a specific audit as part of their training. This is often an overlooked resource.

Recruitment

Recruitment of internal audit staff requires the following course of action which should be taken by the chief internal auditor:

1. **Prepare job descriptions**

   Each position should have a written job description which clearly represents the scope of internal audit work and level of responsibility and specifically sets out the requirements for performing the work. The job description communicates the status and standards of experience and qualification expected to perform the job satisfactorily. The job description is not only a useful guide for recruiting staff, it also provides the basis from which to develop personal objectives and training programmes for internal audit staff.

   It is also important that the status of internal audit job descriptions relate easily to job descriptions for other positions outside the internal audit

function and that they are not written in isolation from other career paths within the auditee organisation.

   An example of a typical job description for an internal auditor is shown in Appendix 2. This is one example of a level of seniority which should be able to operate effectively with little or no supervision.

2. **Establish a policy for qualifications**

   The need for qualifications is essential if the internal audit function is to receive the highest levels of support and carry out its scope of work effectively. What qualifications are needed will vary between organisations and sectors. Accounting, administrative and internal audit professional bodies all offer qualifications which require a formal period of training, examination and experience, covering areas of knowledge needed for internal audit work. It is unfortunately still possible to obtain some accounting qualifications with no internal audit experience.

   The professional qualification established by IIA–UK is seen as both a graduate and postgraduate qualification. It is the only qualification in internal auditing which requires relevant experience before being awarded. It requires a course of study covering three levels of learning and encompassing different disciplines. Among these are accounting, economics, management, statistics, computers, internal auditing principles and techniques.

   Many professional bodies providing education and training in disciplines outside accounting and auditing also recognise experience in internal auditing, e.g. banking, building societies, insurance. The internal audit departments in organisations in these sectors often require their own specialist qualifications. The Institute of Chartered Secretaries and Administrators recognises that its qualification provides a useful foundation for staff in internal audit and offers a post-qualifying education course leading to the IIA–UK qualification in internal auditing.

   Many organisations use the internal audit

function to train their accountants, or other professional staff, by recruiting staff who register as students with one of the accounting or other professional bodies. Internal audit can be a part of or all of the experience necessary to qualify for a career both within and outside the internal audit department.

3. **Establish a policy for experience**

The experience needed by internal audit staff can be classified as follows:

Organisational Experience of the auditee organisation, its polices, structure, products, services, customers, suppliers.

Technical Professional experience of internal auditing techniques as well as other skills related to past and future career paths.

Communication Experience in oral and written presentations and interviewing techniques.

Management Experience in planning, leadership and decision making.

Clerical and administration Experience in office routines, methods and procedures.

At the time of recruitment, the chief internal auditor should use these classifications to assess the level of experience and potential of new staff. To be an effective internal auditor eventually requires experience in all these areas. Without such experience, the internal auditor will not fully contribute to achieving his own or the internal audit function's objectives.

The need for experience can be overshadowed by an objective of the auditee organisation to use the internal audit function as a training unit for other disciplines within the organisation, particularly accounting. This can cause conflict and can weaken the effectiveness of internal audit as a service to management. Care should be taken when reviewing the experience needed for the internal audit function.

Training and development

How the chief internal auditor develops a training programme depends considerably upon the numbers and levels of staff in the internal audit function and on frequency of turnover. The leadership role of the internal auditor has been emphasised as a key skill for effective internal auditing. Koontz, O'Donnell and Weihrich (1984) explain a fundamental principle of leadership thus:

Since people tend to follow those whom they see as a means of satisfying their own personal goals, the more managers understand what motivates their subordinates and how these motivations operate and the more they reflect this understanding in carrying out their managerial actions, the more effective leaders they are likely to be.

It is not the purpose of this chapter to explore the considerable volume of theory and research concerning leadership, but to highlight its importance, both in relation to the process of managing the internal audit department and to the skills required by internal auditors. In their article, 'How to choose a leadership pattern', Tanenbaum and Schmidt describe a variety of styles in their concept of a leadership continuum, ranging from one that is highly 'boss'-centred to one that is highly subordinate-centred. They vary according to the degree of freedom a manager grants to subordinates. It is this aspect of freedom which the chief internal auditor must build into the training programme for internal audit staff in order that each one can be a leader, making decisions either alone or jointly as part of the internal audit team.

Internal auditors should be encouraged to view themselves as contributing to a team effort rather than as individuals working independently of the others. It is not an easy concept to adopt. By the very nature of the work and the short time some internal auditors spend in the department it can be difficult to develop team skills.

The identification and development of training needs require a number of basic steps to be followed regardless of the size of the internal audit function; these are set out below.

1. **Identify training needs for the individual**

Dialogue should always take place between the

manager and the subordinate with some consensus and understanding by both of the need for and the timing of appropriate training. Staff should always be encouraged to develop themselves and to discuss strengths and weaknesses in their performance. Individual development training plans are essential.

2. **Identify training needs for the group**

   There should also be dialogue with all staff, using the department objectives to identify training needs for the group. These may include team skills, knowledge of the auditee organisation, its policies and procedures. Equally important are comprehension of external guidelines, such as statutory regulations, internal auditing professional standards and standards issued by other professional bodies. Organising how these needs can be satisfied may be delegated within the department to provide training for individuals.

3. **Establish an annual training programme for all staff**

   Preparing an annual training programme for all staff assists in determining the cost of training, both in time and value. Much depends on the existing levels of knowledge and experience of the staff. Some internal audit functions will allocate as much as 10 per cent of time for off-the-job training.

4. **Counselling**

   Advising during an audit is a very important element of the training process and requires special skill. Motivation can easily be destroyed by insensitive communication of weaknesses identified in the audit process. Each audit should be seen as a learning process for the internal auditor, the auditee and the chief internal auditor. New methods and innovation should be encouraged and the results discussed and shared with others in the internal audit function. Internal auditing demands a high level of imagination if it is to be effective. Thus achievement should not be discouraged by badly prepared criticism of the audit work.

Managing the audit process

Preparing the audit plan

Establishing objectives and directing the audit process now enters the stage of preparing the internal audit plan, normally for a period of twelve months, but sometimes for more than one year. For most organisations this will require:

   internal audit staffing plans and costs
   detailed knowledge of the auditee organisation
   financial information for all operations
   systems information

It is important that these details are both current and future orientated to ensure that the plan is able to satisfy not only management's objectives for the internal audit function but also and very importantly, the goals of the auditee organisation.

It is clearly not possible to prepare a satisfactory internal audit plan without knowledge of planned or expected future changes in the auditee organisation. This knowledge may be at corporate, operation, systems and financial levels and, because of the dynamic nature of change in some organisations, it will usually be incomplete.

Nevertheless, it is very important for the audit plan to be reviewed with the appropriate operational management before it is established as the aim for scheduling future audit work. This review process also provides an opportunity for the auditee to participate in audit assignments at a very early stage, with the possibility of fostering general acceptance of the need for the audit.

Normally, unless the internal audit function is new, there will also be a history of auditing assignments and results which will influence the allocation of audit time. This task calls for wisdom and sound judgement since resources will normally be limited. Risk analysis adds an additional dimension which can improve the quality of the audit plan (see Chapter 4).

Developing an audit plan involves the following stages:

Charter and standards

1. The scope of the internal audit function should

Table 2.1   Depth of audit penetration

Primary objectives of internal control*	Type of audit review			
	Desk review	Transaction audit	System review	Operational audit
Reliability and integrity of information				
Compliance				
Safeguarding assets				
Economic and efficient use of resources				
Accomplishment of established objectives				

* IIA–UK Guideline 300.05

be outward looking within the auditee organisation and embrace all activities. The internal audit charter should identify restrictions. Each time a plan is prepared the chief internal auditor should identify and report to management all those areas and activities which have been excluded and the reasons for excluding them.

2. A formal record and history should be maintained for all areas and activities subject to audit.
3. The standards of quality to be maintained in the internal audit service to be provided should be clearly identified to be recognised and supported by all levels of management in the auditee organisation.

Audit process

1. The audit process can be represented by a matrix as shown in Table 2.1 One or more of the types of audit review listed may be selected as suitable for the appropriate category of primary control objective as shown. Moving from left to right on the grid, and from top to bottom, each type of review and each category of control include the previous stages progressively increasing both the penetration of the audit process and the time to be allocated for the audit.
2. Desk reviews are quick audits of available management information to establish leads for further reviews to be planned. This type of review can allow the audit plan to cover a wider scope in the time available.

Time

All internal audits should be future orientated even though much of the audit time may be allocated to present and past operations. Every internal audit assignment should consider past, present and future.

Teamwork

All audit planning involves teamwork, both in the internal audit function and externally with the managers of the operation to be audited. External teamwork also includes the relationship with external auditors and auditors working in associated companies within a group. This aspect of audit planning affects all others and has an important influence on the quality of the internal audit service.

When the audit plan is finally prepared it is important that it is shared with management and all the internal audit staff. It can provide an appropriate basis for measurement of departmental and individual performance against objectives. It should be used to report regularly the progress of internal audit work.

Policies and procedures

The form and content of written policies and procedures should be appropriate to the size and structure of the internal auditing department and the complexity of its work. Formal administrative and technical audit manuals may not be needed by all internal auditing departments. A small internal auditing department may be managed informally. Its audit staff may be directed and controlled through daily, close supervision and written memoranda.

In a large internal auditing department, more formal and comprehensive policies and procedures are essential to guide the audit staff in the consistent compliance with the department's standards of performance.

(IIA–UK Guideline 530.01)

Formal policy statements for internal auditing departments should cover:

> internal audit charter
> preparation of the audit plan
> allocation of responsibility for audit assignments
> filing of work papers during and at the end of an audit
> preparation, issue and follow-up of audit reports
> presentation of audit results to the chief executive and, if applicable, to the audit committee.

Establishing specific objectives for each internal audit assignment is an important aspect of planning that assignment. The internal auditor responsible must always recognise a leadership role in planning the work by relating the audit assignment to the objectives established for the internal audit function. A standardised format of assignment record is therefore a useful means of training internal audit staff in the managing process as well as providing a uniform control over each assignment.

Controlling audit activities

Every audit undertaken by the internal auditing department has key control elements which need to be monitored through the managing process, to ensure that it is the most effective use of the resources available. The twelve key control elements are:

> cost
> time
> staff resources
> objectives
> audit techniques
> working papers
> findings
> reports
> action on findings
> effect on other current audits
> effect on future audit plans
> quality assurance review after the audit process

The aim should be to measure all these control elements against standards defined in the established audit policies and procedures. However, not all of them have easily identified characteristics which are measurable. All the elements except the post-audit quality assurance review need to be measured as the audit process progresses.

'Objectives' is probably one of the most difficult elements to monitor and control during the audit process. Perry (1984) recommends four useful measures for audit objectives which should always be possible:

1. Number of audit objectives containing measurable numbers.
2. Percentage of audit objectives known to be complete at the end of an audit assignment.
3. Percentage of audits with clearly stated objectives.
4. Percentage of management workpaper reviews that disclose misunderstanding of the task to be accomplished.

Some of these measures may rely more on subjective assessment than objective calculation but in measuring the performance or productivity of any service-type activity this is often the case.

Perry goes on to say that in a real application to be investigated, an effective measurable objective has to be specific in the following characteristics:

1. **Area**: the objectives will be specific about what area is to be investigated.
2. **Concern**: evaluation of any known concern will be stated.
3. **Criteria**: the criteria for measurement will be stated.
4. **Quantitative measurement**: there will be a quantitative measure in the objective, stated as the measurable aspect of the audit.

For example, instead of 'audit of payroll' the objective will read:

> In the payroll application the auditor should evaluate overtime pay (audit area) to determine with 95% (quantitative measurement) confidence level (measurement criteria) that the overtime payments made to employees are properly authorised and worked (concern).

Table 2.2 Analysis of audit findings

Control weaknesses	Analysis of audit findings by year		
	19-- (this year)	19-- (last year)	19-- (previous year)
Organisational control weak			
Delegation inadequate			
Standards unsatisfactory			
Staff incompetence			
Accounting information unsatisfactory			
Operating information unsatisfactory			
Total audit findings			
Number of audit reports issued			

Annual report

Communication of audit results to management through the various responsibility lines is a critical part of the audit process. Jay (1970) emphasises two of the most important questions that should be asked when writing any report:

1. What am I trying to convey?

The aim should be to establish a clear reason why the report is being written.

2. To whom am I trying to convey it?

For this you have to get inside the reader's mind and identify their perception of the subject.

These questions must be asked when the internal audit annual report is written to the chief executive and the top management and, if it applies, to the audit committee.

The annual report is an opportunity to summarise the internal audit activity and, by presenting audit findings in a different form, to demonstrate control issues more forcibly – for example, by the use of statistics to analyse audit findings as a means to emphasise trends in weak control. Table 2.2 is an example of how this could be presented.

Examples of the content of the annual report include:

1. Staffing and costs of the internal audit department.
2. Percentage of audit plan completed during the year, with a list of significant areas not audited.
3. Significant areas audited during the year not included in the audit plan.
4. Non-audit work carried out by internal audit staff.
5. Significant audit findings.
6. Effectiveness of the policies and procedures of the auditee organisation to prevent weaknesses.
7. Weakness in the control environment of the auditee organisation which could encourage significant losses or risks in the future.
8. Any restrictions placed on internal audit work.
9. Relationships with other audit groups, e.g. external auditors and associated organisations.
10. Record of losses and frauds during the year, whether discovered by internal audit or otherwise.

Normally, the annual report is addressed to senior executives who have responsibility for directing the auditee organisation. It is usual for the report to go to a group of individuals with collective responsibility, e.g. the board of directors, audit committee, board of trustees or executive committee. The recommendations must provide sufficient and accurate information for the right decisions to be taken. Detailed technical analyses will not necessarily be understood by all members of the group, but it is important that the control concept being reported and the associated risks should always be clearly stated.

The chief internal auditor should consider the content of the annual report in terms of:

1. Expressed or otherwise known views of each of the recipients on each subject.
2. The depth of knowledge each of the recipients has on each subject.
3. The level of technical comprehension of each of the recipients.
4. Each recipient's degree of understanding of the control concepts being reported on.

These questions are not always easy to answer when writing a report to a collective group and often require some detailed preliminary research work before the annual report can be written. If the subjects being discussed arise from audit findings, this detailed work should already have been completed by the audit process. The writing of the annual report can therefore provide a useful check on the quality of the audit process.

Computer-assisted audit management

Perry (1984) writes:

the degree of automation of the audit function is only limited by the imagination of the auditors.

Although internal auditors have used computers to assist in their audit work for many years, it has been the advances in personal and distributed microcomputers which have encouraged a greater use of the computer. Most internal auditors now either have personal or microcomputers in their offices or have access to these facilities and they will use them to improve performance and often to reduce costs. Perry's statement therefore needs to be addressed by all chief internal auditors seeking productivity gains in the managing process.

Perry identifies three areas which might benefit from automation:

large volumes of work
routine functions
complex logic

Possible computer applications for audit management are set out below.

Audit planning

History of audits	1. Expert system providing risk analyses and future audit plan.
Results	
Frequency of audits	
Risks	2. Record system for audits with budgets, costs, reports issued and follow-up.

Audit process

Assignments	1. Record system of assignments with budget and costs detail, time management.
Reports	
	2. Correspondence system generating automatic letters to progress the audit process.
	3. Customise audit forms and check lists.
	4. Word processing system for reports and letters.
	5. Develop graphic methods to communicate audit results.
	6. Messaging systems for communication throughout organisation network.

Training

Training plans	1. Record system for training needs and results for all staff.
Training results	
	2. Programmed learning using own developed systems or those bought in.

Quality assurance

The chief internal auditor should establish and maintain a quality assurance programme to evaluate the operations of the internal auditing department.

(IIA–UK Specific Standard 560)

A quality assurance programme should undertake the following elements:

1. Supervision;
2. Internal reviews;
3. External reviews.

Supervision of the work of the internal auditors should be carried out continually to assure conformance with internal auditing standards, departmental polices and audit programmes.

(IIA–UK Guideline 560.02)

Internal reviews should be performed periodically by members of the internal auditing staff to appraise the quality of the audit work performed. These reviews should be performed in the same manner as any other internal audit.

(IIA–UK Guideline 560.03)

External reviews of the internal auditing department should be performed to appraise the quality of the department's operations. These reviews should be performed by qualified persons who are independent of the organisation and who do not have either a real or an apparent conflict of interest. Such reviews should be conducted at least once every three years. On completion of the review, a formal, written report should be issued. The report should express an opinion as to the department's compliance with the Standards for the Professional Practice of Internal Auditing and, as appropriate, should include recommendations for improvement.

(IIA–UK Guideline 560.04)

These standards and guidelines establish responsibility for quality assurance on supervision and the chief internal auditor, with some form of outside review by a peer. It is, however, the clear responsibility of all internal audit staff to aim for continuous quality improvement. The first step in encouraging quality is to have:

a quality commitment by management to its people and product – stretching over a period of decades and lived with persistence and passion!

(Peters and Austin, 1985)

The next step is to create a working environment that encourages quality to be measured continuously by the people in the process. It is the process which must be right and which should add sufficient value to the input to achieve the level of quality output demanded by the customers.

Quality needs always to be measured at three stages:

input (supplier)
process
output (customer)

Applying this concept to the activities in the audit process is not always easy, but it should be attempted. Each of the twelve key control elements in the audit process referred to previously under 'Controlling audit activities' is capable of analysis to identify the input, the process, and finally the output product or service.

At each of the three stages it is possible to establish quality control which can be kept under review continuously by all internal audit staff. It is this continuous quality review by everyone that promotes the search for excellence recommended by Peters and Austin (1985).

Quality assurance of the managing process for internal auditing must also include a continuous review of the following:

1. Development of overall audit objectives as established by the charter and standards.
2. Achievement of the audit plan.
3. Implementation of accepted recommendations.
4. Benefits achieved through internal audit activity.
5. Contribution to the development of people in the auditee organisation.
6. Maintenance of the control environment of the auditee organisation.

The most common type of external review of an internal audit function is where this is carried out by another internal audit group in the same auditee organisation.

Most external auditing firms will form an opinion on the quality of internal audit work so far as it relates to their own auditing responsibilities. For this purpose they are likely to use the APC Auditing Guidelines – *Reliance on Internal Audit*, published by the CCAB governing bodies. These guidelines recommend that external auditors should make an assessment of the internal audit function in terms of the following criteria:

(a) degree of independence;
(b) scope and objectives;
(c) due professional care;
(d) technical competence;
(e) internal audit reports;
(f) level of resources available.

If an outside group is asked to evaluate the internal audit function it should use the IIA Standards and Guidelines for the Professional Practice of Internal Auditing as the criteria for its conclusions. An external review conducted on this basis is a sound independent method of judging whether the internal audit department is performing in accordance with the most widely accepted standards and best practice. The outside group may be the organisation's external auditors or other consultants with internal auditing expertise. The Institute of Internal Auditors Inc. has developed a quality assurance review service which is now available outside the United States.

3 Managing the internal audit assignment

Planning, controlling, and recording

Introduction

The auditor should adequately plan, control and record his work.

(APC, The auditor's operational standard)

The internal auditor is responsible for planning and conducting the audit assignment subject to supervisory review and approval.

(IIA–UK Guideline 400.01)

Planning and control are key elements of efficient management. They are interdependent aspects of the same concept which is as applicable to the management of an internal audit assignment as it is to any operational activity. Planning involves the assessment of resources and effort needed to fulfil a defined objective efficiently. Control depends upon disciplined procedures being applied to ensure the objective is achieved in accordance with the plan.

The internal auditor seeks information on which to form an opinion which will be useful to the management of the auditee organisation. To achieve this, the audit assignment must be efficiently planned against a defined objective and conducted in a methodical and effective manner. This means using accepted audit techniques supported by adequate documentation of the evidence which is logically organised so as to be readily available for reference if necessary.

Planning

The objectives of planning should be as follows:

1. Establish the intended means of achieving the audit objective.
2. Assist the direction and control of the work.
3. Ensure that attention is devoted to critical aspects of the audit.
4. Ensure that the work is completed expeditiously.

Planning is a continuous process, not to be considered merely as a necessary overture to an audit assignment. During the audit it may be necessary to react to new or changing circumstances, so that plans for that audit may need to be modified.

At the conclusion of the audit the foundation for planning the next audit should be laid, and throughout the year the auditor should be alert to changes that may have a bearing on future audit planning.

Preliminary planning

1. Ascertain the objectives of the auditee organisation and whether these are set out in a formal statement, are understood by all employees, and are realistic.

2. Establish audit objectives identifying areas of priority. The scope of the audit has to be determined by reference to the defined objectives for the internal audit function in the context

of the scale of risk and the degree of assurance expected. The objectives should be discussed with the management of the auditee organisation and also with the audit team, making clear the standard of accomplishment expected of the audit staff.

3. To plan properly, an understanding of the structure, methods of operation and financial affairs of the auditee organisation is essential.

   For new or changed organisations, fact-finding work will need to be undertaken; for organisations previously audited, the best source of information should be the audit permanent file and previous audit working papers.

4. Establish and maintain good relationships with key officials of the auditee organisation. It will also often be beneficial to develop good rapport with the external auditors.

5. Collect, summarise and schedule latest key management control information and ascertain whether there have been any significant events and developments since the last audit visit.

6. Obtain any necessary approval of the audit plan.

Field work planning
1. Establish the audit approach, that is, the manner by which the audit objectives are to be achieved.

2. Review matters raised in previous audits; where they are of continuing importance, note areas requiring special attention this time.

3. Discuss with the management of the auditee organisation, changes, audit objectives and approach and any special enquiries. Request staff to be available for audit enquiries and records for examination and agree audit timing.

4. Consider changes to the working of the organisation since the last visit by reviewing minutes of management meetings, in-house publications, press cuttings, etc.

5. Review latest management information and extract key ratios, comparing with budget and with previous year and noting variances.

6. Conduct analytical reviews by considering external performance indicators such as results of similar organisations and industry indices. Consider the impact on the business of the auditee organisation of macro-economic factors such as seasonal variations, price trends, inflation, industrial disputes, government influence, etc.

7. Evaluate changes in the internal procedures of the auditee organisation due to changes in organisation, systems, legislation, the business environment and other causes.

8. Assess the risks to which the auditee organisation is exposed and rank them for priority in the context of the audit objective.

9. Assess the numbers and quality of audit staff required to provide an audit team with the skills and experience appropriate to fulfil the audit objective.

10. Brief the audit team and instruct it on time allocation, to concentrate the audit resources in key areas and to achieve completion in an efficient and timely manner.

11. Agree plans for co-ordinating effort with external auditors including reciprocal arrangements for viewing audit working papers files if possible.

12. Open working papers file and prepare outline schedules to include:

    (a) summary of previous audit findings and responses;
    (b) financial and other statistics obtained;
    (c) other review notes;
    (d) location and contact points;

(e) draft audit programme;

(f) audit instructions;

(g) standard check lists.

Audit programme

The audit programme is the work plan prepared for each audit as it is arranged. It comprises written instructions for the basic tests necessary to complete the audit examination work. It should state the time allocated for each area to be examined with some allowance for contingencies, including the necessary investigation of new facts emerging in the course of the audit. The work specified should be regarded as minimum, allowing the auditor to examine further until satisfied.

The audit programme should define the responsibilities of individual members of the audit team and the degree of coverage recommended for each area to be examined. It needs to be constructed so as to encourage the audit staff to exercise judgement in applying their individual skills and experience. Individual auditors may be assisted in their judgement of the extent of detailed examination necessary by the use of standard lists of topics for each area of coverage to prompt constructive thought about potential opportunities and risks.

Audit planning check lists

It can prove helpful to have a comprehensive schedule of all necessary steps to be taken to achieve satisfactory completion of every audit. This schedule would be used as a check list at the audit planning stage, but not in such a way as to override the auditor's considered judgement or in any way to discourage auditors from applying their individual skills and experience. Its primary purpose would be as a means of ensuring that nothing had been overlooked. The check list should be tailored to suit the auditee organisation, size of the audit department and the types of audit to be undertaken.

Controlling

Control procedures

Controlling an audit assignment, involves the following steps:

1. Allocate the work to take account of the experience and technical ability of each individual auditor.
2. Ensure that the audit staff have a clear understanding of the audit objective, of their individual responsibilities and of specific instructions.
3. Promote good working relationships within the audit team and with the staff of the auditee organisation.
4. Specify outline requirements for working papers to ensure that they provide adequate evidence of the systems examined, the tests applied, and the results of those tests.
5. Establish clear review procedures and practice.
6. Establish a discipline for clearing queries during the course of the audit and a monitoring procedure to ensure that it is followed.
7. Maintain a time record and monitor time taken against audit plan.

Review process

Review of audit work done is a key element in the control of an audit assignment. The review is primarily conducted by an examination of working papers. The reviewer should be a member of the audit team who is senior to the person who prepared the working paper.

The reviewer should ensure, firstly, that each working paper is complete and records sufficient evidence to support the conclusions reached, and secondly, that the audit work has been carried out to an acceptable standard. Review is best carried out on site to enable any questions raised by the reviewer to be cleared with the relevant staff of the auditee organisation.

The reviewer should confirm by initialling each working paper reviewed.

Audit control check list

A check list can be a useful aid in the management of an audit assignment. It would be based on the audit plan, giving due emphasis to the most critical areas to be examined. For each area, it should monitor completion of the key stages of audit work, including examination, clearing queries, review, and discussing conclusions with officials of the auditee organisation at appropriate levels. The check list should help to ensure that all basic and routine matters are expeditiously handled and that matters of interest to management are not overlooked.

Recording

Recording audit work means generating meaningful working papers.

Audit working papers may be in the form of paper, tapes, disks, diskettes, films or other media.

(IIA–UK Guideline 420.02.5)

Audit working papers should always be sufficiently complete and detailed to enable an experienced auditor with no previous connection with the audit subsequently to ascertain from them what work was performed and to support the conclusions reached.

(APC Auditing Guidelines – operational)

Working papers should cover the audit from launching the assignment through field work to writing the final report. They should provide the primary record of all audit examination work done, the resultant findings, and the conclusions reached.

Purpose of working papers
1. To record audit work undertaken and information obtained, identifying and documenting deficiencies.
2. To provide a basis on which to form an opinion and to record evidence supporting the audit report. This is necessary if conclusions are challenged.
3. To encourage a methodical approach to the audit and so to facilitate completion of audit tasks and the drafting of the audit report.
4. To provide the basis for supervisory review of progress of the audit work and of the standard of accomplishment. The standard of working papers may also be used as a guide for appraising the quality of individual auditors' work.
5. To assist discussion of audit findings with both management and staff of the auditee organisation.
6. To provide a basis for reference and for continuity on subsequent audit visits.

Preparation of working papers
Working papers are likely to be most effective in fulfilling their purpose if they are neat, uniform and complete. Neatness facilitates legibility; overcrowded pages may be difficult to read. Using one side only of the sheet avoids the risk of material on the reverse being overlooked. Uniformity assists subsequent reference and review. Completeness means leaving no question unanswered and noting all cross-references.

There needs to be sufficient detail to allow subsequent review without the need for oral explanation. There should be no conclusions which are not supported by evidence recorded in the working papers.

Adopting a standard system of indexing will assist control as the audit assignment proceeds; it will also facilitate subsequent reference to the work done and the conclusions drawn. Good referencing will simplify supervisory reviews, it will aid report writing and will help to locate important points quickly at a meeting. It also helps the next auditor.

Whenever practical, working papers should follow a standard format established with the approval of the chief internal auditor. Ideally, the format should be consistent from year to year. This practice will allow audit time which would otherwise need to be spent on format design to be devoted to content. The standard format might include: standard indices for permanent and current files, standard working paper headings on preprinted stationery, standard questionnaires, and certain standard audit programme sections.

Standard information for audit working papers might include some or all of the following:

name of auditee organisation
accounting reference date
initials of auditor
date of preparation
heading: a clear and succinct title
reference number (and cross-references if appropriate)
source of information
reviewer's initials and review date
key to audit marks

objective
work done
findings
conclusions

The audit working papers should include a record of all meetings with management or senior officials of the auditee organisation written up from notes taken at the time. This record should show the date and place of the meeting, the names of those present, the issues discussed and the conclusions reached including a note of any significant contrary views expressed.

Summary working papers may be prepared as the audit progresses. These can provide useful support by helping the auditor to focus on what is relevant and significant and distilling the matters to be dealt with in the audit report.

Audit files

In practice it is wise to maintian two separate files for all recurrent audits. Information which is of continuing significance should be recorded in an audit permanent file to be available for reference on successive audit assignments. Information which is relevant to the current audit assignment only should be recorded in the current audit working papers file.

The permanent file should be subject to review at an early stage of each audit assignment to ensure that it is complete and up to date. Changes to this file should be dated and initialled.

The permanent file should place on record:

1. Basic information about the auditee organisation for which a clear understanding is fundamental to the completion of an effective internal audit assignment. This would include a synopsis of the objectives of the organisation and its main activities, supported by details of the organisation identifying the principal executives and their authority and accountability. It is also useful to maintain a schedule of locations and key contacts at each.
2. A reference schedule of the key features of all the main control systems. It is normally not appropriate to maintain copies of system manuals

on the permanent file since, in a changing environment, the systems are likely to be modified from one year to another. In these circumstances, successive audit assignments will be concerned with evaluating and testing the systems and the proper control of modifications so that the detailed record of this work should be on the current audit working papers file.

3. A progressive record of significant issues raised at successive audit visits, and the management responses to them. Trends revealed by this record should be taken into consideration as an indication of where to place emphasis in subsequent audit programmes.
4. Memorandum and articles of association or other instrument of constitution if the auditee organisation is separately incorporated or constituted.
5. A copy of each audit report issued and each response.

The current audit working papers file is the repository for all working papers accumulated during the course of the audit. It should contain the complete evidence supporting all conclusions and issues raised in the audit report.

It is advisable to plan the format of the working papers file for each audit assignment before the work starts. This should lead to an orderly file which will fulfil its purpose as a key reference and control document throughout the audit work and subsequently.

Current audit working papers files will vary considerably from one audit assignment to another and are likely to contain some or all of the following:

1. Completed internal control questionnaires (ICQs) or internal control evaluation questionnaires (ICEQs) as appropriate.
2. System notes and flow charts.
3. Schedules of the details of transaction tests.
4. Schedules of questions and answers from interviews with staff of the auditee organisation.
5. Notes of meetings with management or senior executives of the auditee organisation.
6. Rationale for all conclusions reached.

Systems evaluation and testing

The scope of the internal audit should encompass the examination and evaluation of the adequacy and effectiveness of the organisation's system of internal control and the quality of performance in carrying out assigned responsibilities.

(IIA–UK General Standard 300)

Systems evaluation

Systems evaluation work involves assessing how effective management control systems are in fulfilling organisational objectives including evaluation of the risks and opportunities open to the auditee organisation.

It may also involve making judgements about the degree of competence of the staff, and possibly also the management, of the auditee organisation; consequently, it can only be undertaken by skilled, experienced internal auditors.

It is advisable to review the system before any detailed audit work is undertaken. This review should be carried out in the context of a thorough understanding of the objectives of the auditee organisation and the environment in which it operates. The review should seek to identify the purpose and objectives of the system and the methods adopted to achieve them. The objectives should be assessed in terms of risks and opportunities with defined parameters and the methods described in terms of outline flow charts.

The review should enable judgements to be made about risks and opportunities so that they can be ranked in order of priority and the critical control points identified. This should facilitate the preparation of a programme of system examination work concentrating on the most vulnerable features of the system.

The detailed evaluation work should be designed to examine the system and to judge its adequacy to fulfil its objectives from four critical aspects:

system logic
management organisation
staffing
internal checks

System logic

Evaluation of the system logic should start from an analysis of the operational needs of the auditee organisation. Ideally there should always be an official system manual which describes the sequence of processes supported by system diagrams and detailed flow charts. When these do not exist the internal auditor will need to construct a description and charts from discussion with the management and staff involved.

Absence of a formal manual is in itself a weakness which the auditor should report on since it could allow drift to occur in control procedures and the rationale for the procedures may be lost as staff changes occur.

The auditor's task in evaluating system logic is to establish that the sequence of procedures will, if properly applied, lead to achieving the objectives of the system by the most efficient route and without undue risk of losing control on the way. If this cannot be established, the auditor should recommend modifications to the procedures, additional security measures, or possibly both.

Management organisation

The objectives of a control system will not be achieved unless operations through the system are effectively directed. Examination of the management organisation is therefore critical. This part of the system evaluation involves identifying the management responsibility for all activity which is affected by the system.

For this it is necessary to refer to an organisation chart which should be considered in the context of the overall allocation of authority and accountability for the auditee organisation as a whole. It is necessary to establish that the objectives of the system are not only compatible with the objectives of the whole organisation but also contribute fully towards their achievement. It means that those responsible for directing the system must have clear delegated authority to do so; they have to be competent to exercise this authority and must be held accountable for achieving the objectives of the system.

Again, if the auditor is unable to confirm that all

these conditions are satisfied, he must offer a positive recommendation as to how the weakness should be resolved.

By way of example: the executive responsible for production from a factory using a computerised production planning and control system needs to be fully responsible for the effective operation of that system. It could not be considered satisfactory if the system were directed by, say, a data processing executive with separate authority from top management.

It would, however, be quite satisfactory for the data processing executive to process information in accordance with the system as a service to the production executive. In this case, responsibility for applying the procedures for processing data should be distinguished from those for collecting data and distributing the resultant management information.

Similarly, responsibility for system modifications and maintenance may be correspondingly divided. There should nevertheless be an overriding priority in favour of the operational requirement in the event of a conflict of objectives.

The internal auditor should verify that the management structure provides appropriate arrangements for supervision of operational staff with an adequate network of internal checks.

Staffing

Evaluation of staffing requirements for a system involves assessing numbers and skills. If the system is running smoothly, it is prima-facie evidence that the staffing complement is right. However, recommendations put forward for improving the effectiveness, efficiency or security of the system may involve simplified methods or additional disciplines and are quite likely to affect staffing needs.

In circumstances where the system is not running smoothly, an extra workload falls on the staff and it is not feasible to judge from superficial observation whether or not the staffing complement is adequate either in numbers or in skills. This is because additional time has to be spent identifying and rectifying errors often requiring skills or knowledge beyond those necessary to complete the routine work.

Prolonged exposure to an additional workload of this kind is frustrating, which may be demotivating as well as exhausting. This in turn leads to reduced working efficiency in individuals and in the team. System failure through inadequate staffing is self-fulfilling.

It is then necessary to analyse the content of the work to be done by the staff who operate the system. It must first be acknowledged that the system is an operational tool and in general those who operate it are members of an operational team who depend upon the system in their pursuit of operational objectives. They do nevertheless need to have the necessary skill and knowledge to make the system work and they must be able to devote an appropriate portion of their working time to this end.

Techniques for work measurement and evaluation have been well established for many years and usually take account of the time and skill necessary for activating control systems.

To ensure that operatives have the necessary knowledge and skill to activate the control system correctly is of course very important. Adequate plans have to be made for the necessary tuition and training on a continuing basis. Retraining or refresher courses may be necessary whenever modifications are made to the system. It is equally important to ensure that there is adequate staff cover for those most critically involved with operating the system, especially in cases where only selected staff have been fully trained for the work.

The internal auditor should examine the basis on which the staffing complement has been established, confirm that the required skills have been correctly identified and verify that adequate provision has been made for training. It is also necessary to check whether or not the appropriate staff have already been properly trained and have the necessary skills.

Internal checks

Internal audit examination of the monitoring and internal control features of systems is best carried out as part of the process of system design and development and before implementation. It is rarely feasible to modify a system in order to correct design weaknesses after completion of the development. The same principle applies to system modifications necessary to deal with changed operational requirements: provision should be made for audit examination of the modifications before they are implemented.

It is a key requirement of every control system that at each stage the procedures incorporate a checking discipline to prove that it has been completed correctly before proceeding to the next stage.

A further basic feature of every control system should be a network of internal checks. These checks should be designed as integrated procedures to operate continuously. Their purpose is to ensure that the work of each member of staff is proved independently by, or is complementary to, the work of another.

Monitoring involves measuring the progress of the operations which are subject to the control system. Measurement may be made at regular intervals, e.g. monthly, daily, hourly, every second, etc.: the snapshot principle. Measurement may also be continuous, to be displayed and used continuously or recorded for subsequent analysis and use: real time systems. It is important to establish that the monitoring methods and devices are appropriate to the objectives of the control system.

A means of monitoring operational progress and correcting deviations from the planned course should be a critical feature of every control system. For some operations the performance criteria are not subject to change. In these cases an adherence system is appropriate and the procedures for correcting processing deviations can be built into the system as automatic process control features.

For other operations it may be necessary to review and adjust the target performance when processing deviations occur. These are likely to be cases where the deviation may have been caused by circumstances outside the area controlled by the system. In these cases an adaptive system is appropriate and it is advisable for the deviation to be reported for management intervention in the control process. This enables operational targets to be

amended to take account of changes in external influences.

Systems testing

The objective of testing a system is primarily to establish that it is being properly applied for the purposes for which it was designed and that the disciplines of the system are being correctly observed. This is compliance testing.

It may also be advisable to carry out substantive tests: these are tests which seek to provide audit evidence as to the completeness, accuracy and validity of information generated by the system.

Transaction testing through the system can often be planned to satisfy both requirements from examination of the same sample. These tests may be arranged on a random sampling basis, or a selected transaction basis having due regard to known areas of risk or vulnerability.

Full details of all transaction tests should be recorded on schedules in the audit working papers. All lapses in procedure uncovered by the audit tests should be discussed with the supervisor and staff concerned. Judgement then has to be exercised to decide whether there is a recurring pattern to the lapses uncovered. If so, can it be attributed to drift in following the procedures, inadequate care or supervision, lack of understanding or training or intentional irregularity?

Consideration must also be given to the question of whether the effect of the lapses is significant. What constitutes a significant lapse will vary from one system to another. In general, insignificant errors or lapses which are not considered to be recurring should be scheduled for the staff concerned to rectify and a note made in the audit file for subsequent follow up. Errors and lapses which are judged to be significant or recurring should be specifically referred to in the audit report.

The internal auditor who has completed the system evaluation and testing will have formed clear opinions as to whether the system provides an adequate basis for effective control in the area where it has been installed and whether or not the procedures are being applied as intended. In some audit assignments the system examined will be found to be sound and working well. In others there will be critical weaknesses in the system design or significant lapses in applying the procedures. In either case the internal audit report should state the auditor's opinion on both the adequacy of the system and the quality of compliance.

A positive assurance to the accountable management that the system is working well is no less important than the identification of weaknesses when they exist.

Audit reporting

The internal auditor's duty to report

Reporting is an essential element of auditing.

Internal auditors should report the results of their audit work.
(IIA–UK Specific Standard 430)

A signed written report should be issued after the audit examination is completed. Interim reports may be written or oral and may be transmitted formally or informally.

The internal auditor should discuss conclusions and recommendations at appropriate levels of management before issuing final written reports.

Reports should be objective, clear, concise, constructive and timely.

Reports should present the purpose, scope and results of the audit; and where appropriate, reports should contain an expression of the auditor's opinion.

Reports may include recommendations for potential improvements and acknowledge satisfactory performance and corrective action.

The auditee's views about audit conclusions or recommendations may be included in the audit report.

The chief internal auditor or an audit manager designated by him should review and approve the final audit report before issuance and should decide to whom the report will be distributed.
(IIA–UK Guidelines 430.01–.07)

Internal auditors should follow-up to ascertain that appropriate action is taken on specific findings.
(IIA–UK Specific Standard 440)

Internal auditing is a service to management and its function is to observe and make recommendations, with no authority to change anything within the area

subject to audit. The recommendations must reflect impartial judgement based upon evidence observed from an independent viewpoint. This service will serve no purpose at all unless the views formed by the auditor are effectively communicated to the accountable management who can act on them.

A written audit report is an essential feature of every internal audit assignment.

1. It constitutes the authentic and permanent record of what the auditor examined, the findings obtained and recommendations made.
2. It confirms the issues discussed with the accountable manager at the end of the audit.
3. It serves as a check list for action that has been agreed.
4. It provides a record for the next auditor to follow up.
5. It informs other interested executives.

Forms of reporting

Reporting may be verbal or written or a combination of both. Both forms have advantages and disadvantages.

Verbal reporting

1. It is immediate two-way communication.
2. Its communicating power can be amplified by body language and visual aids.
3. The speaker is able to test the listener's understanding of the message.
4. The listener's reaction allows the speaker to correct any misinterpretation.
5. Speaker and listener may attribute different meanings to the words because they perceive the context from different viewpoints. The flexibility of language allows scope for ambiguity: many words have more than one meaning and most ideas can be conveyed by a range of different words.
6. Any action agreed upon verbally depends upon remembering what was said or heard: memories can be fugitive, subsequent events may colour recollections and there may be scope for deliberate misinterpretation of what was agreed.
7. It is difficult to monitor progress against a verbal plan.

Written report
1. It creates a permanent record of the message being communicated: once issued it remains available for reference by any interested party.
2. Committing a message to writing facilitates extending the communication to a wider selection of recipients and even to publishing if appropriate.
3. The process of preparing a written report provides opportunities to avoid ambiguity through editorial review of the author's draft and through preview by the principal recipient.
4. These processes take time to complete and consequently although the written report must be issued promptly after the audit, it cannot match the immediacy of verbal presentation of the audit findings.
5. A formal written audit report should be complemented by a formal written response. These two documents then record a firm plan of action against which progress can be monitored.

Reporting practice
It is a common practice for internal audit reporting to be in two stages:

1. A verbal report to the accountable manager of the unit audited at the end of the audit visit: the exit meeting. The audit findings are presented at this meeting and a programme of remedial action may be agreed if appropriate.

   Frequently, audit findings of minor importance may need to be brought to the attention of the accountable manager and can be discussed and fully dealt with on the spot. Such issues would be inappropriately referred to in a formal written report if likely to distract attention from the impact of important recommendations.
2. A formal written report should be completed and issued promptly after the audit visit. It should be addressed to the accountable manager who has direct authority to act on the recommendations. The circulation will normally include other senior executives who have an interest and some authority to influence the action which needs to be taken.

This formal report may incorporate views expressed by the management in the meeting at which the audit findings were presented verbally.

The formal written report should not be the sole vehicle of communication between the internal auditor and the accountable manager.

The substance of the content of the written report should be no different from the issues discussed at the exit meeting. However, individual interpretations of the spoken word from different viewpoints can result in different emphasis of meaning.

As a general rule, unless the audit has uncovered evidence of irregular activity involving him, audit findings should be fully discussed with the accountable manager before the formal report is issued. Failure to observe this courtesy is probably the most effective way to destroy audit credibility. The effectiveness of an internal auditing service is dependent upon a degree of mutual respect and trust between the auditor and the manager accountable for the operation being audited.

Standard format
Organisations usually adopt a standard format for their internal audit reports to suit their own specific requirements. The general nature of the content of every internal audit should however be similar.

1. It should list the areas of coverage for the audit assignment.
2. It should give a brief statement of professional opinion or expert advice arising from the audit examination of each area of coverage.
3. The opinions formed and advice offered should be supported by statements of factual evidence discovered in the course of the audit examination.
4. There should be clear recommendations for courses of action arising from the findings.

All audit reports contain confidential information about the unit audited which the auditor has been privileged to obtain. They should always be distributed under private and confidential cover and the distribution list should be agreed by the account-able manager of the unit concerned.

No audit assignment can be considered complete until all recommendations made by the auditor have either been fully implemented or consciously set aside by the management concerned.

The formal management response to the audit report will assist the auditor in completing this follow-up duty.

4 Practices and techniques of internal auditing

Section 1. Risk assessment

The nature of risk

Risk is an inevitable ingredient in all operational activity and there is an element of it in almost every management decision. Risk is the possibility of incurring misfortune or loss: these will be incurred (that is, planned results will not be achieved) whenever circumstances turn out to be less favourable than those foreseen at the time the decision to act was taken. Similarly every management decision will give rise to opportunities for gain from circumstances turning out better than those foreseen. Management decisions are almost invariably based upon judgement because not all the factors likely to influence the outcome will be known at the time the action is needed. The greatest opportunities for successful performance are likely to flow from management judgements in areas of greatest uncertainty; these also carry the greatest risks.

It is a fundamental responsibility of management to identify the risks and to protect the organisation against their impact. The internal auditing objective must be to assist management in the effective discharge of this responsibility.

The objective of internal auditing is to assist members of the organisation in the effective discharge of their responsibilities. To this end internal auditing furnishes them with analyses, appraisals, recommendations, counsel and information concerning the activities reviewed. The audit object-ive includes promoting effective control at reasonable cost. (Extract from IIA–UK Statement of Responsibilities of Internal Auditing)

This statement of the objectives and scope of internal auditing clearly identifies these objectives with those of the management of the auditee organisation. Achieving management objectives means taking decisions and acting on them, and this involves risk.

The top management of every organisation has to determine a corporate strategy and to establish key policies which will lead to the accomplishment of defined strategic objectives. The risks to which the organisation may be exposed in pursuit of such primary objectives can be very significant indeed. They have to be clearly identified and ranked in order of magnitude so that provision can be made to protect the organisation from serious damage, disaster or catastrophe. Internal auditing is one of the methods of protection available and when it is to be applied in these identified high risk areas, this specific requirement should be written into the internal audit charter.

The contribution of internal auditing is made in terms of independent identification and evaluation of risks and in recommending procedures through which risk exposure may be avoided, eliminated, limited or reduced without unduly restricting or compromising opportunities for gain.

28

Risk management

Taking risks is very much an essential part of the practice of management. Sound management practice aims to take maximum advantage from every opportunity for gain and to minimise the exposure to risk through a risk management strategy.

Key elements of a risk management strategy

1. Well designed information systems which will allow close monitoring and control and trustworthy forecasting.
2. Clearly defined delegation of authority for committing the resources of the organisation with appropriate effective control.
3. Consensus judgement and collective responsibility for decision making on major issues involving significant uncertainty.
4. Appropriate insurance cover when feasible for unpredictable hazards which could damage the organisation and especially for those where the potential damage could be disastrous.
5. Specialist advisory and training functions for fire prevention and protection, safety of employees and security of assets and information.
6. Appropriate back-up for all critical resources related to the degree of dependence and vulnerability, including standby equipment or facilities and emergency services.
7. Clearly defined corporate policies for commercial relationships with the purpose of avoiding restrictive reliance on other parties for critical supplies, services, technology, access to markets or outlets.
8. Internal audit support which should concentrate its attention on areas of greatest risk.

Internal auditing is a critical component in the practice of risk management and has particular significance in the context of securing maximum advantage from opportunities for gain and for minimising risk.

It is of course most important that the internal auditor acknowledges that the key management responsibility to optimise the advantages from favourable opportunities inevitably involves an element of risk taking; consequently, reducing risk exposure will usually entail curtailing or even eliminating benefit.

The internal auditor also often examines with the advantage of hindsight in which the perspective of opportunities and of risks may have changed as uncertainties have been superseded by established facts. Managers will often be fully aware of the impact of such judgemental gaps and internal audit confirmation would not then be perceived as either helpful or constructive.

Audit planning and risk

The chief internal auditor should establish plans to carry out the responsibilities of the internal auditing department.

These plans should be consistent with the internal auditing department's charter and with the goals of the organisation.

(IIA–UK Specific Standard 520 and Guideline 520.01)

Internal auditing is a management service with the objective of assisting management in the effective discharge of its responsibilities. Such a service must be seen to contribute more than it costs, and this principle determines the scale of resources which can be justified in providing it. It is necessary to prepare a budget of resources and an audit plan for their allocation.

Internal audit planning is normally undertaken in two stages: strategic planning, which is likely to extend over a time span of several years; and operational planning, which sets the work programme for one year ahead.

The strategic audit plan has to take account of corporate strategy. All corporate strategic objectives are likely to involve major opportunities for gain and major risks which may have to be subjected to internal audit review.

The chief internal auditor has to decide the quantity and quality of audit knowledge and experience needed to examine the major risk areas in sufficient depth to make meaningful audit judgements which will contribute to the achievement of corporate objectives. These decisions have to take account of the degree of risk in each area allowing for the quality of internal control and risk management.

The internal auditing requirements may be expressed in the strategic audit plan in terms of parameters for the scope and frequency of audit examination for each major risk area. This plan can then define the scale and composition of the resources to be provided.

The annual audit plan of work allocates the resource provided to the operational areas to be examined. It should take account of known operational variations in the spread of risk and also of particular management requirements for audit assistance in the effective discharge of their responsibilities. Emphasis should be placed on the examination of those areas of the organisation which offer the greatest potential for the internal audit service to contribute to the goals of the organisation. For this it is necessary to develop a means of evaluating the service provided in terms of its potential and achieved contribution. The contribution will depend on the magnitude of risk exposure and the extent to which its impact could be reduced by the adoption of well researched audit recommendations. Risk analysis and evaluation thus provide key criteria for determining the scale of internal audit service to be allocated to each specific area of operational activity.

The allocation of internal auditing resources to each separate operational activity should take account of:

1. Contribution to corporate goals – financial contribution, key functions.
2. Risk assessment and ranking – likelihood of occurrence and potential damage.
3. Risk management measures – insurance cover, emergency services, back-up facilities.
4. Standards of internal control – known strengths and weaknesses.

Identification, evaluation and ranking of risk exposure are critical factors in the preparation both of the strategic plan for internal auditing to determine the resource needed and of the annual work programme to determine where and when to apply it.

Identifying risk

Since risk assessment is critical to effective internal auditing the chief internal auditor must be able to place confidence in a reliable means for identifying every significant risk to which the organisation may be exposed.

Certain specific risks will be unique to a particular organisation. However, most of the risks to which organisations may be exposed can be classified into a relatively small number of categories. Each organisation will be exposed to a unique range of risk categories although most of the categories in that range are likely to be common to many other organisations.

The chief internal auditor's means of identifying all risks should include:

1. Regular consultation with the chief executive and top management in order to be fully informed of the views they take of the risks to which the organisation is exposed both from the strategies being pursued and from external influences.
2. Liaison with all executives who have an involvement in risk management within the auditee organisation, for example those responsible for insurance; specialist advisors for particular risk areas such as safety and fire protection; and those responsible for development of control systems.
3. Extensive understanding of the auditee organisation. This should include a wide range of information about markets, products, technology, resources, organisation, management, staff, customers, suppliers, proprietors, competitors, etc. It should be increased by aggregating the knowledge and experience of all members of the audit staff. There should be arrangements for formally recording all significant risks encountered.
4. Maintaining an analysis of all risks identified in formal internal audit reports issued in each successive year. This analysis should be summarised so as to show trends in the different categories of weakness or risk and to isolate specific and exceptional risks.
5. Maintaining an up-to-date schedule of all known common risk categories. This should be compiled from the accumulated knowledge and experience of the audit staff, from published research, from textbooks and papers and from contact with other practitioners in internal auditing. Every member of the audit staff should acknowledge a

responsibility towards keeping this schedule up to date. It should be readily available at all times for reference by all audit staff, to be used not as a check list but rather to prompt constructive thought and enquiry about the categories of risk which may apply in the specific circumstances of every audit undertaken.

Common categories of risk

1. **Size**   The size of a unit will normally determine the magnitude of potential losses but small units may have restricted scope for internal check.
2. **Complexity**   Information and control systems become more complex with increasing operational complexity. This can increase both the probability of error and the effort required to monitor the system.
3. **Management competence**   Although difficult to measure objectively, the competence of the unit's management influences the degree of confidence that can be placed in the effectiveness of internal control.
4. **Management integrity**   Even more difficult to assess or measure, the integrity of management bears an obvious relationship to the probability of losses through overriding the control system.
5. **Rapid growth**   Rapid growth puts strain both on staff and on control systems.
6. **Unsatisfactory performance**   The risk of control breakdown may be increased because of pressure on management for improved results. Control may be compromised in the pursuit of short-term economy.
7. **Liquidity of assets**   Liquid assets are active, mobile resources which can be attractive targets for theft and misappropriation.
8. **Quality of internal control**   The design and past performance of an internal control system are important in judging the probability of lapses in control occurring.
9. **Centralised computer processing**   This creates a hub through which much essential management information passes and could be a potential source of mistrust and erosion of control.
10. **System changes**   A change in system can inval-idate past performance as a control measurement and may increase the probability of errors whilst running in.
11. **Staff changes**   Control systems depend upon competent judgements by key staff. A break in continuity may impair effectiveness.
12. **Low morale**   Low employee morale may be a symptom of a conflict of objectives between management and staff. There may then be a lack of commitment which can lead to reduced performance and lapses in procedures resulting in loss of control and other hazards.
13. **Governmental constraint**   The organisation may be subject to external influences which may put strain on control systems or introduce additional risks.
14. **Audit overdue**   Regular audit visits tend to encourage proper observance of control disciplines. The probability that lapses will occur may increase when the interval between audit visits is extended.

(Source: Patton, Evans and Lewis, 1986)

Specific risk areas

1. Marketing

The fortunes of every commercial organisation are utterly dependent upon the marketing judgements, and particularly the assessments of market size and share and the prices they will bear and, when appropriate, product design preferences. These are all high-risk areas. It is not part of the auditor's role to second-guess the marketing experts, but the judgements have to be seen to be responsibly made and rationally applied.

Other risks in this area may include:

(a) reliance on restricted distribution channels;
(b) customer credit risks and foreign exchange risks;
(c) liability for damage caused by products and product failure.

2. Production

Weaknesses in the production planning and control systems may result in production shortages or excesses or excess waste and can give rise to rectification costs and possibly failures in customer service.

These weaknesses can arise from:

(a) ineffective communication between departments;
(b) inadequate disciplines for data collection;
(c) incomplete or inadequate monitoring or quality control procedures;
(d) ineffective measuring procedures.

3. **Material management**

(a) unlimited commitments on unpriced or open-ended purchase contracts;
(b) unprotected currency risks;
(c) breach by supplier of purchase contract terms for quality or delivery;
(d) failure of a critical supplier;
(e) misdirection of goods;
(f) unsatisfactory evidence of consideration;
(g) evidence of bribery or corruption involving staff or intermediary;
(h) weakness in the system for matching despatches with billing;
(i) stock security;
(j) stock obsolescence;
(k) unreliable inventory records putting at risk: customer service, stock management and financial control.

4. **Employment**

(a) health and safety at work and industrial injury risks;
(b) potential loss or damage through industrial action;
(c) payroll security risks;
(d) lapses in authorisation disciplines for recruitment and terms of employment;
(e) correlation of recruitment, training and development activity with corporate objectives;
(f) damage resulting from misconduct or breach of trust by an employee;
(g) risks to staff of wrongful accusation for loss sustained through system weakness.

Inefficiency may occur throughout the organisation because of weaknesses in the supervisory and management structure where skills may not have been properly matched with tasks or accountability with delegated authority.

5. **Capital development**

Capital development usually involves a relatively small number of major projects likely to influence the performance of the organisation for a number of years ahead. It may include asset renewal and provision for growth and changing shape through capital expenditure, acquisition, merger or divestment or any combination of these. Each major project will probably be a directly identifiable element of corporate strategy. This is likely to be an area of very significant risk. The risks relate to the viability of the strategy and the effectiveness of the management of each project.

If the strategy has not been thought through, or its implementation is misdirected or is disrupted by unforeseen external circumstances, the damage to the organisation could be great in terms of cost incurred and opportunities lost.

Project management is equally critical. It requires disciplined procedures to ensure adequate preliminary research, sound planning, effective direction and reliable monitoring and control. Weakness or failure in any of these areas could result in serious losses.

6. **Information management**

(a) computer failure due to breakdown, explosion, fire, flood or other hazard: consequential loss may be extensive;
(b) corruption or loss of data by accident or wilful damage;
(c) inability to maintain or service ageing or obsolete technology;
(d) dependence upon highly specialised technical staff who's loyalty to the technology may be stronger than that to the organisation;
(e) insufficient flexibility in major control systems to accommodate change in a fast-growing organisation;
(f) inadequate management commitment in systems development;

(g) inadequate provision for testing and evaluating internal check routines at an early stage in systems design;

(h) computer fraud.

7. Financial control

(a) security risks for cash and liquid assets;

(b) investment and borrowings risks in treasury management;

(c) foreign currency exposure;

(d) weak internal check disciplines or lapses in applying them;

(e) accounting inaccuracy, damage caused by reliance on misleading management accounts;

(f) weaknesses in stewardship records and asset security risks;

(g) financial fraud.

Risk assessment and ranking

The allocation of internal auditing resources among the operational areas of the auditee organisation should reflect the risk exposure in each area. Ranking risk exposures in order of priority means assessing the relative importance of the risks involved.

Since the essential characteristic of risk is uncertainty, assessment is a matter of judgement rather than measurement. In many cases it has to be subjective judgement because there is no accumulated record of relevant experience to project as the basis for forecasting events.

Risk has two dimensions, value and time. It is usually feasible to establish a value of maximum exposure with some certainty although consequential loss may be difficult to assess. Timing however is almost always the uncertain factor so that the risk assessment is dependent upon its time probability.

Advanced statistical methods may be adopted to assist in assessing this probability. There are also other less sophisticated techniques which may be used as a guide in making this subjective judgement. It is questionable whether the application of statistical methods is appropriate in many cases because there are often practical considerations which militate against the allocation of internal auditing resources with such a degree of refinement. Allocating re-

sources, like risk evaluation is seldom an exact science.

Statistical methods are very much more suitable in assessing risks underwritten by insurance companies. For this the insurance industry has extensive records of claims experience to draw on and the underwriter has a specified exposure limit and covers only identifiable risks as defined in the policy.

For the purposes of this manual on the practice of internal auditing we will consider just one example of a simple method of assessing risks as a basis for ranking them in relative importance.

Example: 4.1

Risks involving financial loss

This method of assessment ranks the risks on a scale of 1 to 16. The assessment is calculated as the product of two rating factors: maximum loss and probability, each with a graduated scale of 1 to 4.

The maximum loss scale can be related to turnover of the organisation as shown for example, in an organisation with a turnover of £100m:

Maximum loss	Relation to turnover	Rating
More than £100m	Exceeding annual turnover	4
£1m to £100m	Exceeding 1% of turnover	3
£0.1m to £1m	Exceeding 0.1% of turnover	2
Less than £0.1m	Less than 0.01% of turnover	1

The probability scale is based upon the chief internal auditor's judgement as to whether the risk is likely or unlikely to materialise.

Each of these options is then qualified according to whether there is evidence to support the judgement or it is simply based on experience. For example:

Probability judgement	Evidence qualification	Rating
Likely to occur	Supported by evidence	4
Likely to occur	No evidence available	3
Unlikely to occur	No evidence available	2
Unlikely to occur	Supported by evidence	1

This model represents the simplest form of risk assessment as a guide for ranking risks in order of

Table 4.1   Ranking of risks involving financial loss

Maximum potential loss	Probability of occurrence			
	There is evidence it is LIKELY to occur	Experience suggests it is LIKELY to occur	Experience suggests it is UNLIKELY to occur	There is evidence it is UNLIKELY to occur
More than £100,000,000	16	12	8	4
£1,000,000 to £100,000,000	12	9	6	3
£100,000 to £1,000,000	8	6	4	2
Less than £100,000	4	3	2	1

relative importance. Often this is all that is necessary. In other cases it may be feasible and also meaningful to make a more sensitive classification of the probability of occurrence. If so it can quite easily be accommodated by extending this kind of model.

This type of risk assessment model (see Table 4.1) is designed for risks which involve potential financial losses. Some risks may not readily lend themselves to financial evaluation. They are generally those risks which relate to injury suffered by individuals. It should not be difficult to give such risks an appropriate rating so that they can be ranked in relative importance along with the financial loss risks.

Section 2. Statistical sampling

The nature of sampling

When you can measure what you are talking about and express it in numbers then you know something about it; but when you cannot express it in numbers, your knowledge is of a meagre and unsatisfactory kind.

Lord Kelvin

In general it is neither practicable nor necessary for internal auditors to examine every transaction in order to judge whether the system under review provides a sound basis for effective control or whether the procedures are being properly followed.

In some cases the internal auditor uses his experience to determine just which transactions and how many to examine. They may be cases where a qualitative rather than a quantitative audit judgement is needed or where the conclusions follow logically and are quite clear and indisputable. Such cases will often be self-evident so that there is unlikely to be great difficulty in persuading management to accept that the action recommended is necessary.

There will be other occasions however where the evidence collected is inconclusive, or where there could be a number of different interpretations of the evidence uncovered in the sample of transactions examined. Then the internal auditor will be unable to form firm conclusions and consequently unable to reassure management or to convince it that any corrective action is necessary. Further sample testing may or may not resolve the uncertainty. For such cases the internal auditor's judgement needs the reinforcement of a scientific basis from which to project the sample evidence available.

More specifically perhaps, the internal auditor has to evaluate the impact on the organisation of audit findings and to judge whether evidence from a few transactions represents opportunities or risks which are material. It is necessary, then, to have a reliable means of assessing the true extent, including the frequency and materiality of particular circumstances or occurrences uncovered by internal audit examination.

Statistical sampling is a scientific technique for evaluating the whole based on analysis of a part. It is concerned with selecting a sample for analysis which will fairly represent the whole within specified tolerances. The statistical sampling method is thus a useful tool for the practice of internal auditing. It defines a basis for selecting a fair representative sample of transactions for scrutiny. The internal auditor is then able to quantify findings and opinion and express them numerically. This provides a sound basis for confidence in the audit conclusions and a firm case to support the audit recommendations.

The use of this technique does not lessen the need for the internal auditor to exercise sound judgement. Indeed, skill, experience and judgement are the crucial factors in setting reliability levels and risk parameters for statistical sampling. The internal auditor must determine these factors in relation to the audit objectives and the circumstances of the particular audit assignment, having due regard to possible reactions of management to the findings, conclusions and recommendations.

Definitions

Statistical sampling The random selection of a mathematically calculated sample which is capable of analysis and projection so that conclusions can be drawn which are relevant to the entire number of items from which the sample has been drawn.

Population/universe/field The entire number of items under review. The number of items in a population is represented by the symbol n, and the data values by the symbol x.

Sample A specific number of items forming part of and selected from the population, which is considered to be representative of the population as a whole.

Confidence level The degree of certainty that the sample is truly representative of the whole population. For example, a 95% confidence level means that in 95 cases out of 100 we can be certain that the sample value will apply to the population as a whole.

Precision error level/precision tolerance level/sampling error level/sampling tolerance level A range within which we can be certain that a value lies

which fairly represents the population. It is normally expressed as a percentage applicable to the sample value by addition or subtraction. For example: a precision level of plus or minus 2 per cent, where the sample value is 50, indicates that the definitive value for the population lies between 49 and 51.

Attribute A characteristic of the population under review in which we are interested. For example, a coding entry on an invoice.

Variable A characteristic of a unit of the population, which may change. For example, the height of a person in a group.

Error rate A rate, normally expressed as a percentage, which defines the degree of error in a population. This concept is usually related to what is considered to be an acceptable error rate. For example: the proportion of first-time entry errors on keying in data which cause rejection and re-input should not exceed 5 per cent.

Mean The arithmetical average of two or more values in a population. This is calculated as the total of the values of the items divided by the total number of items. It may be used for quantitative data where values are evenly distributed among the population. The symbol used to represent the mean of the population is μ the Greek letter **mu**; and the symbol used to represent the mean of the sample is $\overline{x}$, referred to as 'bar x'.

Median The value which is halfway among the items of the population; or, in another way of looking at it, half the data are less than this value. This may be used for quantitative data where values are not evenly distributed among the population.

Mode The most frequently occurring value of the items in the population. This may be used with qualitative data.

Standard deviation A statistical measure which describes the spread of the values of items about the mean. A large standard deviation indicates a wide spread of values. The symbol used for this is σ, the Greek letter **sigma**.

Other symbols   Other symbols used include Σ, the Greek capital letter **sigma** to represent 'the sum of'; and 'f' to represent frequency.

Sampling procedures

The application of statistical sampling techniques in the practice of internal auditing involves the following progression of logical steps:

1. Define the test objectives.
2. Research the population to be sampled:
   (a) set the sampling risk parameters;
   (b) choose an appropriate sampling plan.
3. Choose an appropriate selection technique.
4. Select the sample.
5. Test and analyse the sample.
6. Evaluate the sample results.
7. Are the results statistically meaningful?
   (a) if not, repeat the process from stage 2;
   (b) if yes, proceed to stage 8.
8. Derive an audit opinion

Sampling plans

Statistical sampling plans should follow a logical sequence; as shown here:

1. Take a representative sample.
2. Find the precision level for the sample, e.g. error or value.
3. Project the sample experience by reference to the number of units in the population.
4. Calculate an estimated total value with a specified precision range and a known confidence level for the population.

The complexity occurs in determining an adequate sample size and a suitable degree of tolerance around the projected estimate. This is where mathematical theory is applied involving standard deviation calculations and other statistical processes.

Fortunately, the application of mathematical theory can be facilitated with the use of statistical tables or 'user friendly' computer software. There are a number of sampling plan software packages available for auditors. It is possible to examine all the transactions in a system by using a computer. Auditors may use the power of the computer not only for statistical sampling but also to interrogate the total population of computerised records. The software packages which are used for this purpose give full instructions on their use.

Sampling techniques

All sampling plans depend on a suitable selection technique for extracting a representative sample. There are a number of plans and techniques to choose from. For example:

Plans

Attribute sampling
This is the most widely used sampling plan and is designed to answer the question – 'how many?'. In other words, it is used to estimate the probable frequency of a specified occurrence. (The occurrence or attribute may be a certain type of error within a population.) It is exceptionally useful when the items examined can be described with an explicit right or wrong number.

The attribute sampling tables enable the internal auditor to define the sample size required on the basis of predetermined criteria:

   expected (or acceptable) error rate
   confidence level
   precision level
   approximate population size

Further tables can be used to restate the precision level when the error rate is found to be higher than expected. The expected error rate may be determined by:

   previous audit tests
   discussion with operating staff
   a small pilot test
   information from other auditors

Example 4.2
The internal auditor may be seeking to establish

whether documents are properly coded for account allocation. Thus the attribute sought is coding error.

Assume a population of 120,000 documents. The error rate is expected not to exceed 2 per cent and a confidence level of 95 per cent is required with a precision level of plus or minus 2 per cent.

Reference to tables of 'Sample size for attribute sampling' gives a sample size of 187. If the error rate is found to exceed 2 per cent, the sample size may be too small. An expected error rate of 3 per cent gives a sample size of 278, so a further 91 units should be examined. (See Tables 4.2(a) and 4.2(b))

Stop-or-go sampling

This form of sampling sets out to achieve the same objectives as attribute sampling but it prevents over-sampling by allowing the auditor to evaluate the test findings progressively.

Stop-or-go sampling tables are available (see below) to show the probable maximum error rate in a population when the actual errors have been quantified from a sample tested. If assurances about findings are not convincing for the auditor, the sample can be progressively added to and the situation reappraised by further reference to the tables.

Stop-or-go sampling has advantages over attribute sampling:

1. It caters for reduced sampling.
2. The auditor does not have to estimate in advance the probable error rate.
3. The auditor does not need to predetermine the precision level, since this is automatically built into the answer shown in the tables.
4. It allows the auditor to extend an existing sample quite easily in order to reappraise the situation.

There is a limitation compared with attribute sampling in that it does not enable the auditor to project the error rate in the population within prescribed limits. It merely gives the upper limit or maximum error rate at various confidence levels.

Population sizes covered by the tables range from 200 to 2,000. For populations falling between the steps in the tables, the next larger size should be used. Populations exceeding 2,000 are treated as infinity and the 2,000 table should be used.

Stop-or-go sampling should not normally be continued after the sample has been increased to three times its initial size. At this stage the auditor should extend the sample to that required for attribute sampling.

Example 4.3

The internal auditor may wish to determine whether the records for 50,000 members of an organisation accurately reflect date of entry.

Assuming the auditor is willing to accept an error rate of not more than 3 per cent, a sample of 120 items is examined and found to contain two errors. With these criteria the tables for 'Sample sizes for stop-or-go sampling' show a certainty of 70.16 per cent that there is less than 3 per cent error in the population. (See Table 4.3.)

If this is not good enough, a further 30 items may be sampled and, provided no further errors are found, the degree of certainty rises to 83.07 per cent. Yet another 30 items tested with no further errors would give 90.86 per cent certainty that errors represent less than 3 per cent of the population.

Discovery sampling

This form of sampling is also known as exploratory sampling. Discovery sampling is appropriate for those occasions when the internal auditor is seeking evidence of certain happenings which are known or are suspected. It is a technique which facilitates assessing the probability of discovering that a suspected happening has occurred. It is based upon using a random sample of a specific size.

When using this sampling technique the auditor is not trying to express an opinion concerning the population as a whole, but merely making a test designed to detect something. The tables quantify the chances that a defined sample contains at least one item with the specified characteristic.

Example 4.4

The auditor may wish to establish whether there is a significant number of items in stock which have not been called for within one year.

Given that there are some 25,000 stock items, the auditor considers that 50 items or less of the population in the 'no call for one year' category would not be significant and seeks to identify one such item.

Discovery sampling tables show the percentage probability of finding one item with the specified characteristics, from a range of totals for such items in the population, for a predetermined sample size. For example:

	Sample	Population	Probability
Total number of items	1,600	25,000	
Identifiable items (or errors)	1	50	96.3%
Identifiable items (or errors)	1	75	94.4%
Identifiable items (or errors)	1	100	91.5%

Thus a random sample of 1,600 items will satisfy the criteria with a 96.3 per cent probability of success. If no more than one of the uncalled stock items is present in this sample, it can be said that there is a 96 per cent probability that there are no more than 50 items in stock which have remained uncalled for one year. (See Table 4.4.)

Variables sampling

This plan is also known as survey or estimation sampling for variables. Variables sampling is suitable for any variable item within the population such as weight, shoe size or blood group in a group of people; or quantity, price or stock code in a batch of purchase orders.

The auditor can use this sampling technique to make quantitative tests. It is first necessary to predetermine statistical parameters. It then facilitates a calculation from the sample experience of how much is involved in total.

The basic concept is to seek to determine the average value for an item from within the population by examining a random sample. The true value for the population is then projected, within the defined parameters. For example, average value per sample multiplied by number in the population gives total value.

There is nothing complicated about the principle of projection as used here: the complexity is in arriving at the correct sample size. A manageable sample size is required which will enable the average value of an item within the population to be calculated. Variable sampling tables assist this part of the procedure. Given a required level of confidence, the sample size may be selected taking account of predetermined parameters for the degree of sampling error and the standard deviation of the population. The latter may be estimated from a preliminary sample of 50 items.

The sampling error and an estimate of the standard deviation should be ascertained and expressed as a decimal ratio which can then be used with the 'Variables sampling' look-up tables to find the appropriate sample size. It is then necessary merely to select additional items to make up the preliminary sample used for estimating standard deviation to the number of items shown by the tables.

Occasionally, adjustment is necessary if an estimate of standard deviation based upon the sample actually used is found to differ materially from the pre-estimate. It could require additional sampling, or the sampling error to be adjusted for projection.

Techniques

Interval sampling

There are many cases in audit work where difficulties could arise through attempting to use random numbers, for example: unnumbered documents; scattered numbers; and significant breaks in the sequence of reference numbers. In these circumstances, interval sampling may provide an unbiased sample.

Three essential conditions must be satisfied for interval sampling to be meaningful:

1. The population must be homogeneous.
2. There must be no items missing from the population.
3. There must be no bias or cyclical arrangement of items in the population.

The selector must first ascertain the total population to be sampled and determine the sample size required. The interval to be used for sample selection can then be determined by dividing the sample size into the population size. The selector then makes a start by randomly selecting an item occurring before the first interval and then continuing to select the items at regular intervals as calculated, from that start point.

Example 4.5
Population size 5,000; sample size 500; interval 10.
Start at any item from No.1 to No.9 and then examine every tenth item from that start point.

For example: 4   14   24   34   44   54 . . . 4,994

Although a homogeneous population is a prerequisite of interval sampling, the technique may be applied to a population which includes some non-relevant items, provided the total number of relevant items is known. The sampling interval is calculated for the total population and sample selection proceeds as described until the process picks a non-relevant item. Then the next relevant item is selected, but interval counting is continued from the rejected non-relevant item. This adaptation does not guarantee that the range of distribution is covered by the sample selected.

When the population has a definite cyclical bias, a reasonable attempt to overcome the bias may be achieved by multiple interval sampling. This merely means that the sample size will consist of a number of subsamples, selected on an interval basis, each with its own random start.

Stratified sampling
All sampling techniques aim to obtain a sample of appropriate size that is exemplary in every feature of the population. If the structure of the population is known and it shows wide variability, then stratification can be used to obtain a higher degree of precision from any given sample size.

For the stratified sampling technique the population is divided into strata or levels. For example, it could be divided into (1) extremely high values and (2) the rest. All the extreme values would then be examined, as well as a small sample of the rest. Because the population is then in two strata, any statistical enlargement can only be applied independently to each. The separate results from each may be combined provided the sampling proportions are known. Each stratum would be given its propor-tionate weighting in the final sample size. Alternatively, each stratum can form a separate population for sampling on its own. For instance, proportionate stratified sampling of a store catalogue will produce a sample which fairly represents the entire catalogue in terms of quantity and value.

Cluster sampling
This technique involves extracting groups of items located within reasonable proximity of each other, such as a file of sales invoices, a week's time sheets, or one month's purchase orders.

It is often termed the poor relation of sample selection techniques. It has nevertheless proved to be invaluable when selection conditions are difficult. Under some circumstances, other selection techniques may be very difficult to apply because of the filing arrangements for documents. Formal techniques may also prove to be expensive where a large sample is required. Cluster sampling may be appropriate in these circumstances.

Since the selection is not completely random the selector must ensure that there is no obvious bias. For example, where a batch of selected invoices relates to a single cost centre, when the total population involves three cost centres, it is a biased sample. To avoid this possibility, as large a sample as possible should be selected in around 20 clusters. This is made feasible by saving time in extracting the sample with this simple technique.

The suitability of cluster sampling for audit testing will depend upon the purpose of the audit test and, in general, whether it is primarily a quantitative or a qualitative test. For evaluating the effective materiality of transactions with a specific characteristic, a more scientific technique of sample selection may be essential. This technique could well be adequate to demonstrate that there is a significant degree of noncompliance.

Random number sampling
Random selection basically means that each and every item in a population has an equal chance of selection when picking a sample. The simplest and most effective way of selecting articles without bias is to put them in a container, mix them thoroughly

Table 4.2(a)   Sample sizes for attributes sampling

EXPECTED ERROR RATE NOT OVER 2%
CONFIDENCE LEVEL 95%

Population size	Sample size for precision percentage of plus or minus						
	0.50	0.75	1.00	1.25	1.50	1.75	2.00
9500	2286	1173	697	458	323	239	184
10000	2314	1180	700	459	323	239	184
11000	2364	1193	704	461	324	240	185
12000	2407	1204	708	463	325	240	185
13000	2445	1213	711	464	326	241	185
14000	2478	1221	714	465	326	241	185
15000	2508	1228	716	466	327	241	185
16000	2534	1235	719	467	327	242	186
17000	2558	1240	721	468	328	242	186
18000	2580	1245	722	469	328	242	186
19000	2599	1250	724	469	328	242	186
20000	2617	1254	725	470	329	242	186
22500	2656	1263	728	471	329	243	186
25000	2687	1270	730	472	330	243	186
27500	2714	1276	732	473	330	243	186
30000	2737	1281	734	474	330	243	187
32500	2756	1285	735	474	331	244	187
35000	2773	1289	737	475	331	244	187
37500	2787	1292	738	475	331	244	187
40000	2800	1295	739	476	331	244	187
42500	2812	1297	739	476	332	244	187
45000	2822	1299	740	476	332	244	187
47500	2832	1301	741	477	332	244	187
50000	2840	1303	741	477	332	244	187
55000	2855	1306	742	477	332	244	187
60000	2867	1309	743	478	332	244	187
65000	2878	1311	744	478	332	244	187
70000	2887	1313	744	478	333	245	187
75000	2895	1315	745	478	333	245	187
80000	2902	1316	745	479	333	245	187
85000	2908	1317	746	479	333	245	187
90000	2914	1318	746	479	333	245	187
95000	2919	1319	747	479	333	245	187
100000	2923	1320	747	479	333	245	187
110000	2931	1322	747	479	333	245	187
120000	2938	1323	748	479	333	245	187
130000	2943	1324	748	480	333	245	187
140000	2948	1325	748	480	333	245	187
150000	2952	1326	749	480	333	245	188
160000	2956	1327	749	480	333	245	188

Source: Lockheed-Georgia Company, Maths Analysis Group.

Table 4.2(b)   Sample sizes for attributes sampling

EXPECTED ERROR RATE NOT OVER 3%
CONFIDENCE LEVEL 95%

Population size	Sample size for precision percentage of plus or minus						
	0.50	1.00	1.50	2.00	2.50	2.75	3.00
9500	3040	1000	472	271	175	145	122
10000	3089	1005	473	271	175	145	122
11000	3179	1014	475	272	176	145	122
12000	3257	1022	477	273	176	146	122
13000	3327	1029	478	273	176	146	123
14000	3389	1035	479	274	176	146	123
15000	3444	1040	480	274	176	146	123
16000	3494	1044	481	274	176	146	123
17000	3540	1048	482	274	177	146	123
18000	3581	1052	483	275	177	146	123
19000	3619	1055	484	275	177	146	123
20000	3654	1058	484	275	177	146	123
22500	3730	1064	486	276	177	146	123
25000	3793	1070	487	276	177	146	123
27500	3846	1074	488	276	177	147	123
30000	3891	1077	488	276	177	147	123
32500	3930	1080	489	277	177	147	123
35000	3965	1083	489	277	177	147	123
37500	3995	1085	490	277	178	147	123
40000	4022	1087	490	277	178	147	123
42500	4045	1089	491	277	178	147	123
45000	4067	1090	491	277	178	147	123
47500	4086	1092	491	277	178	147	123
50000	4104	1093	491	277	178	147	123
55000	4135	1095	492	278	178	147	123
60000	4161	1097	492	278	178	147	123
65000	4183	1099	493	278	178	147	123
70000	4203	1100	493	278	178	147	123
75000	4220	1101	493	278	178	147	124
80000	4234	1102	493	278	178	147	124
85000	4248	1103	493	278	178	147	124
90000	4259	1104	494	278	178	147	124
95000	4270	1104	494	278	178	147	124
100000	4280	1105	494	278	178	147	124
110000	4296	1106	494	278	178	147	124
120000	4310	1107	494	278	178	147	124
130000	4322	1108	494	278	178	147	124
140000	4333	1109	495	278	178	147	124
150000	4342	1109	495	278	178	147	124
160000	4350	1110	495	278	178	147	124

Source: Lockheed-Georgia Company, Maths Analysis Group.

Table 4.3 Sample sizes for stop-or-go sampling

PROBABILITY OF ERROR RATE IN UNIVERSE SIZE OF 2,000

Size of sample examined	No. of errors found	Probability that error rate is less than:									
		1%	2%	3%	4%	5%	6%	7%	8%	9%	10%
50	0	39.50	63.58	78.19	87.01	92.31	95.47	97.34	98.45	99.10	99.49
	1				59.95	72.06	81.00	87.35	91.73	94.68	96.62
	2						58.38	68.92	77.40	83.95	88.83
	3								57.47	66.97	74.97
	4										56.88
70	0	50.52	75.69	88.14	94.26	97.24	98.69	99.38	99.71	99.86	99.94
	1			62.47	77.51	87.03	92.81	96.10	97.93	98.92	99.45
	2				53.44	68.63	79.87	87.59	92.60	95.72	97.58
	3						61.15	73.07	82.10	88.53	92.88
	4							54.77	66.80	76.61	84.12
	5									61.06	71.28
	6										55.82
100	0	63.40	86.74	95.25	98.31	99.41	99.80	99.93	99.98	99.99	100.00
	1		59.67	80.54	91.28	96.29	98.48	99.40	99.77	99.91	99.97
	2			58.02	76.79	88.17	94.34	97.42	98.87	99.52	99.81
	3				57.05	74.22	85.70	92.56	96.33	98.27	99.22
	4					56.40	72.32	83.68	90.97	95.26	97.63
	5						55.93	70.86	82.01	89.55	94.24
	6							55.57	69.68	80.60	88.28
	7								55.29	68.72	79.40
	8									55.06	67.91
	9										54.87
120	0	70.06	91.15	97.41	99.25	99.79	99.94	99.98	100.00	100.00	100.00
	1		69.46	87.82	95.53	98.45	99.48	99.83	99.95	99.98	100.00
	2			70.16	86.28	94.25	97.75	99.17	99.71	99.90	99.97
	3				71.13	85.56	93.40	97.19	98.87	99.60	99.84
	4				52.67	72.18	85.27	92.83	96.75	98.61	99.44
	5					55.85	73.23	85.23	92.47	96.42	98.40
	6						58.50	74.26	85.35	92.26	96.18
	7							60.81	75.25	85.57	92.16
	8								62.85	76.21	85.86
	9									64.70	77.14
	10									52.06	66.39
	11										54.45

Table 4.3 (cont'd)   Sample sizes for stop-or-go sampling

PROBABILITY OF ERROR RATE IN UNIVERSE SIZE OF 2,000

Size of sample examined	No. of errors found	Probability that error rate is less than:									
		1%	2%	3%	4%	5%	6%	7%	8%	9%	10%
150	0	77.86	95.17	98.96	99.78	99.95	99.99	100.00	100.00	100.00	100.00
	1		80.39	94.15	98.41	99.60	99.90	99.98	100.00	100.00	100.00
	2		57.91	83.07	94.16	98.19	99.48	99.86	99.96	99.99	100.00
	3			66.16	85.42	94.52	98.14	99.42	99.83	99.95	99.99
	4				72.04	87.44	95.01	98.20	99.40	99.81	99.95
	5				55.76	76.56	89.17	95.52	98.31	99.41	99.81
	6					62.71	80.16	90.66	96.03	98.45	99.44
	7						68.34	83.12	91.94	96.50	98.60
	8						54.84	72.98	85.58	93.04	96.93
	9							60.93	76.85	87.65	94.00
	10								66.16	80.13	89.40
	11								54.32	70.66	82.91
	12									59.82	74.55
	13										64.70
	14										53.98
180	0	83.62	97.37	99.59	99.94	99.99	100.00	100.00	100.00	100.00	100.00
	1	53.84	87.69	97.27	99.45	99.90	99.98	100.00	100.00	100.00	100.00
	2		70.01	90.86	97.65	99.46	99.89	99.98	100.00	100.00	100.00
	3			79.10	93.20	98.10	99.52	99.89	99.98	100.00	100.00
	4			63.01	84.99	94.93	98.50	99.60	99.90	99.98	100.00
	5				72.95	89.05	96.21	98.84	99.68	99.92	99.98
	6				58.32	80.02	91.93	97.16	99.11	99.75	99.93
	7					68.21	85.15	94.03	97.88	99.32	99.80
	8					54.77	75.79	88.92	95.57	98.42	99.49
	9						64.37	81.58	91.72	96.70	98.82
	10						51.90	72.13	86.00	93.81	97.55
	11							61.13	78.32	89.38	95.37
	12								68.91	83.21	91.96
	13								58.33	75.33	87.06
	14									66.03	80.57
	15									55.86	72.59
	16										63.44
	17										53.63

Source: Adapted from 'Tables of probabilities for use in stop or go sampling' with the permission of the US Department of the Air Force, Auditor General.

Table 4.4   Sample sizes for discovery sampling

PROBABILITY IN % OF FINDING ONE ERROR IF TOTAL NUMBER OF ERRORS IN UNIVERSE IS AS INDICATED

Sample size	Population of 10,000 Number of errors				Population of 15,000 Number of errors			
	50	75	100	200	50	75	100	200
125				92.1				
150				95.3				
200				98.3				93.3
250			92.1	99.4				96.6
300			95.3	99.8				98.3
350		93.2	97.2	99.9			90.6	99.1
400		95.4	98.3				93.4	99.6
450	90.1	96.9	99.0				95.3	99.8
500	92.4	97.9	99.4			92.2	96.7	99.9
550	94.1	98.6	99.7			94.0	97.6	99.9
600	95.5	99.1	99.8			95.4	98.3	
700	97.4	99.6	99.9		90.9	97.2	99.2	
800	98.5	99.8			93.6	98.4	99.6	
900	99.1	99.9			95.5	99.0	99.8	
1000	99.5				96.8	99.4	99.9	

Sample size	Population of 20,000 Number of errors				Population of 25,000 Number of errors			
	50	75	100	200	50	75	100	200
250				92.0				
300				95.2				91.1
350				97.1				94.1
400				98.3				96.1
450				99.0				97.4
500			92.1	99.4				98.3
600			95.3	99.8			91.2	99.2
700		93.1	97.2	99.9			94.2	99.7
800		95.3	98.3			91.3	96.2	99.9
900	90.0	96.9	99.0			93.6	97.5	99.9
1000	92.3	97.9	99.4			95.3	98.3	
1200	95.5	99.0	99.8		91.5	97.5	99.3	
1400	97.4	99.6	99.9		94.4	98.7	99.7	
1600	98.5	99.8			96.3	99.3	99.9	
1800	99.1	99.9			97.6	99.6	99.9	

Source: Adapted from 'Table of probabilities for use in exploratory sampling' with the permission of the US Department of the Air Force, Auditor General.

Table 4.5   Table of random numbers

	(1)	(2)	(3)	(4)	(5)	(6)	(7)	(8)	(9)
1	28421	19536	53416	54372	73856	28615	20700	16252	68585
2	54911	59323	50557	77755	84369	23111	58515	02165	14715
3	63100	53705	15932	99669	71654	16630	03003	18553	09789
4	46541	86218	40032	61434	29290	42725	48725	58421	39937
5	99458	03617	19903	98882	02453	96452	49989	00259	53730
6	79818	37331	31337	09522	32702	00410	01708	33560	32859
7	22275	00966	99204	04547	18495	03670	34143	10387	82045
8	40310	01425	56131	48921	53050	10564	77063	28178	54979
9	52480	74786	40199	11627	52012	73161	06900	63501	31758
10	62126	37642	08387	81002	98160	54599	62161	23456	30140
11	01330	16874	77593	19334	78293	14846	03300	22287	49084
12	57530	28608	05350	61101	67890	50261	59590	24436	25044
13	01849	84858	92705	89919	83278	11730	89591	40686	45319
14	30094	24828	36689	22976	93136	43401	29661	11442	65458
15	51692	40936	78378	84085	64331	23446	06276	01123	15499
16	27217	58636	76792	78431	87139	63739	91618	36888	51753
17	09737	46502	52303	71797	44822	19431	70412	67275	76229
18	47588	11067	91785	61811	03594	85004	12867	87941	34642
19	81332	27116	27504	33280	69446	28807	71697	08570	59169
20	50795	29431	26400	62834	96415	88036	87683	03073	81166
21	29071	13194	10054	02895	92934	03798	51933	59254	86074
22	44823	42245	31176	24518	23321	68006	51107	07477	26966
23	82269	74761	14787	93349	04880	75140	21922	78412	75183
24	77567	26333	12764	00444	54485	78876	14654	43704	98771
25	14057	28319	94858	94322	72854	56482	68676	02650	11886
26	55738	73524	84238	92630	63579	94545	73428	44497	25812
27	35047	25559	95459	93113	59825	55122	64030	55484	84212
28	83696	06300	83331	52563	16380	11814	43953	49950	65497
29	42026	62153	90812	40326	05076	93758	28305	21579	60650
30	80765	28101	39409	48668	56882	50403	73678	35544	72214
31	83897	95241	71783	05835	75423	66995	54650	35000	99083
32	23445	89672	29754	08566	47533	44710	41672	16418	63491
33	90366	55498	44019	64446	20472	72420	86011	93552	46393
34	93738	32930	97381	58921	73671	95789	70337	51494	10055
35	76371	08824	98489	41679	26965	93940	82349	21024	43312
36	21437	63280	31121	34506	97683	85287	15322	13587	20410
37	12282	88691	52602	62957	88013	99810	45860	80799	13590
38	11696	25139	59072	36320	70634	70601	19876	43628	31642
39	61159	08093	55810	09316	08048	74463	11360	22835	15340
40	74688	38618	03844	11178	03287	07514	35976	93450	80974
41	55120	94773	33677	14312	78798	56745	82835	46357	90662
42	46315	22908	17095	27126	89408	07869	52375	07274	42432
43	37878	00120	33822	65398	10433	32544	30387	07931	92211
44	33146	08854	76918	55383	87203	60556	54556	22112	94550
45	65045	35530	61016	23356	10178	52087	79336	23674	17293

Source: Lockheed-Georgia Company, Math Analysis Group

and then pick unseen at random. For practical reasons, this procedure is not suitable for all articles and documents so alternative methods have to be adopted.

The computer may be programmed to select at random from a schedule of numbers and to print out those selected. The numbers so selected may then be matched with corresponding documents or articles, provided these each have identifying numbers which are the same as those listed for the computer selection.

This is the basic principle of random number sampling, and the tables used are produced in this way by a computer. When applying random number tables to sequentially numbered documents, the first step in the process is to ascertain the range of the numbered documents and the number of digits in the highest number.

Example 4.6

To select a random number sample from a batch of documents numbered from 60,001 to 70,000, we have to consult the tables which cater for five-digit numbers (see Table 4.5).

The selected list for this batch of documents may begin to look like this:

63100   62126   61159   65045 . . .

Where any range is broken into blocks leaving gaps in the sequence, those numbers not relevant to the ranges chosen must be discarded.

When numbers have prefix or suffix letters or dates, such additional characteristics should be converted into numerical characters. Often the best way to achieve this is to make two selections: one for each part of the compound number, merging them together to form the selected final numbers. Again, irrelevant numbers will have to be discarded.

Section 3. Flow charting

The nature of flow charts

A flow chart is a diagram which depicts, by means of symbols, the movement and control of documents, or the passing of information, through a system. Its purpose is to present patterns of complex relationships in a graphic format where they can be quickly perceived and readily understood.

Flow charts are used as alternatives to full narrative description. Thus they simplify and clarify, through visual impact, ideas that would otherwise require lengthy and tedious explanation in words.

Basic principles

The interaction between key activities may be represented by a simple block diagram using rectangular blocks or frames containing words, to represent the functions involved and linked by flow lines to represent the flow of information, documents or product, as in Figure 4.1.

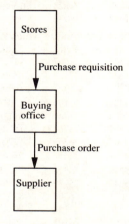

Figure 4.1

When the objective is to analyse or explain the logic of the system, it is necessary to distinguish clearly between decisions and action. This distinction is made in a logic chart by using labelled block symbols to represent action only and diamond symbols to represent query or decision points. (See Figure 4.2)

A technique for internal auditing

An audit flow chart is one prepared by an auditor as part of the process of obtaining an understanding of a system. It uses standardised symbols to show the documents, record books, operations and controls which comprise the system. Its purpose is to record the auditor's understanding of the system for sub-

Figure 4.2

sequent reference in (a) appraising the system; (b) designing audit tests; and (c) interpreting audit evidence.

Flow charting is a technique which offers a range of advantages, as well as disadvantages, to internal auditors.

Advantages

1. A complex pattern of organised activities is normally easier to comprehend from graphic representation in a flow chart than from narrative description.
2. A flow chart enables weaknesses in a system to be readily perceived, for example:
   (a) lack of internal check because of inadequate segregation of duties;
   (b) weak internal control because of an absence of proper authorisation;
   (c) inefficient use of resources because of un-necessary duplication or excessive control procedures.
3. The use of flow charts may enable the internal auditor to survey the system more compre-hensively and probably in greater depth than would be feasible by reliance on written notes.
4. In order to complete the flow-charting process, every aspect of the system under review must be analysed. Its logic has to be resolved and brought to a recognised conclusion.
5. The audit flow charts provide a ready means of communication and comprehension of the system requirements:

(a) when discussing points with the auditee;
(b) when referring to the operation of the system in the audit report;
(c) when preparing the audit programme for subsequent audit visits.

6. The audit flow chart from the previous internal audit examination of the system should be the start point for the system review on the next occasion. This will reveal whether changes have been made in the system either in response to audit recommendations or to reflect changed circumstances. It will also reveal if there has been drift in applying the system procedures. If the original flow chart was carefully prepared, it should be relatively simple to prepare a new edition incorporating the changes, unless a totally new system has been introduced. By concentrating on the system changes, the internal auditor is able to give due emphasis to audit tests which relate to those changes.

Disadvantages

1. Flow charts can be time consuming to draw.
2. Unless flow charts are constructed with care and a degree of skill, they may confuse or possibly mislead rather than clarify.
3. There is always a danger that constructing a comprehensive and presentable flow chart is perceived as an end in itself, as a work of art rather than as an audit tool.
4. Whilst the benefits from using the flow chart technique increase as the complexity of the system increases, the time and effort involved will also be considerable.
5. The technique may have little to offer for simple systems provided there are no significant internal control issues.
6. In many cases the organisation is constantly changing, or the systems are subject to rapid and extensive change in order to keep abreast of market developments or new technology. Flow charts prepared to assist audit appraisal will serve little purpose as a permanent record in such cases.

Conventions

Two standard conventions for flow charting have been developed for use by auditors: one by Skinner and Anderson (1966), the other by Rutteman (1976). The Skinner and Anderson convention uses an extensive range of standardised symbols. The Rutteman convention has fewer symbols with a simpler drafting logic, and uses structured word forms to add further clarification to the symbols.

The Rutteman convention of flow charting is probably the one most widely used by both external auditors and internal auditors in the United Kingdom: for this reason it is the convention presented here. It is quoted and adapted from *Flowcharting for Auditors* by kind permission of The Institute of Chartered Accountants in England and Wales, from whom this publication is available and in whom the copyright rests.

Symbols

The symbols are usually drawn using a template. There are two categories: basic symbols and computer symbols. Basic symbols are used for all systems. Computer symbols are used to supplement the basic symbols in systems which rely on computerised processing.

Basic symbols

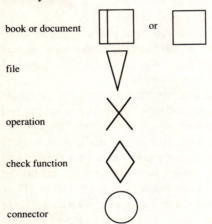

book or document

or

file

operation

check function

connector

Book or document

This symbol is used to denote an accounting document or book of account. A book of account is distinguished by a vertical margin. Each document or book should be clearly labelled.

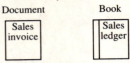

When the separate parts of a multipart document serve different purposes in the system, they should be separately identified.

When documents are serially prenumbered this should be denoted by the code 'N' in the top left-hand corner. For example:

Prenumbered multipart document

Files

Documents which have been processed will normally be found on files which may be permanent or temporary. Temporary files are for documents awaiting a further stage of processing or awaiting further instructions or information to complete the transaction to which they relate.

The symbol for each temporary file should identify it as such with the code 'T'. Codes 'A' for alphabetical; 'N' for numerical; and 'D' for date order may be used to denote the filing sequence used. For example:

	Permanent files	Temporary files
Alphabetical sequence	A	TA
Numerical sequence	N	TN
Date order	D	TD

Operation

A single symbol is used to denote every operation except a check function. Each operation is then described by a narrative alongside the symbol. For example:

(a) Simple operation

Smith totals invoice

(b) Preparing one document from another

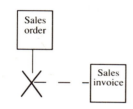

Jones prepares invoice
from order

(c) Operation using a document and a book

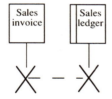

Brown posts sales
invoices to sales ledger
weekly

Check functions

Check functions represent the control points in the system. They need to be identified separately from other operations, so they are highlighted by using a different symbol. For example:

(a) A check involving a single document

Smith totals invoice

Brown checks totals

(b) A check involving two documents

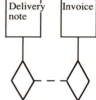

Jones checks that all
goods despatched have
been invoiced

Connectors

A connector symbol is used to denote the movement of documents from one chart to the next. For example:

(a) At the foot of chart A

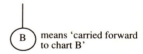

means 'carried forward to chart B'

(b) At the top of chart B

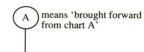

means 'brought forward from chart A'

Drafting conventions

Document flow

The chart starts at the top and follows the sequence of operations and processes down the page joining the symbols by a vertical line. The document flow is then from top to bottom of the page. A separate vertical flow line is required for each copy of a document which is processed differently from the original. For example:

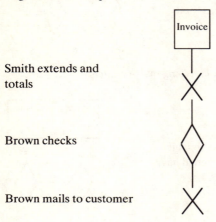

Smith extends and totals

Brown checks

Brown mails to customer

Information flow

Frequently, information is transferred from one document to another, as when posting a ledger. Information flow is shown by a broken horizontal line, as in Figure 4.3.

Division of duties

The flow chart should show clearly how duties and responsibilities are allocated among staff or departments. This is achieved by dividing the flow chart into vertical columns, each headed with the name of the person or department with the responsibility for the operations depicted in that column.

Two further columns should be provided: one for

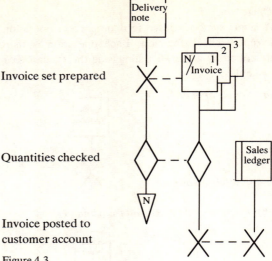

Invoice set prepared

Quantities checked

Invoice posted to customer account

Figure 4.3

a narrative description alongside each operation and the other for the operation reference number. Operations should be numbered in a single sequence throughout the whole chart, as shown in Figure 4.4.

Alternative processing

Most systems contain particular areas where the continued processing of documents depends on certain criteria being met. When these criteria are not met an alternative processing route must be taken; for example, export invoices may have to be priced in currency and posted to a separate export ledger. In cases where a document can be processed in more than one way depending on some predetermined criteria, the flow chart should depict the appropriate choices. For example:

(a) by narrative

For export orders the invoice is passed to bankers for payment.

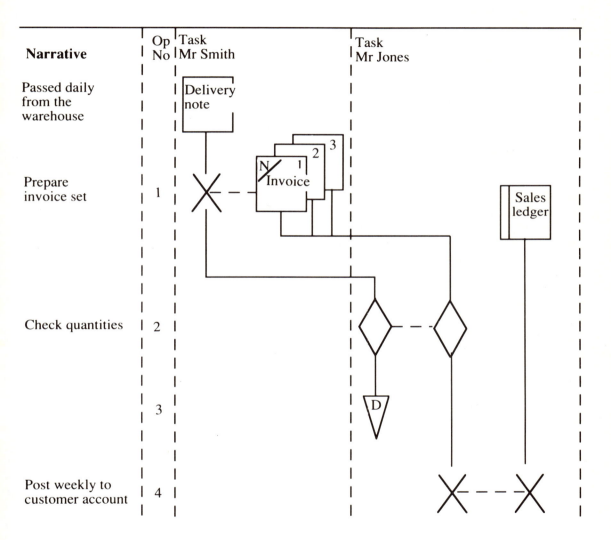

Figure 4.4

(b) on the same chart

Home trade invoices
priced in sterling

Export invoices priced
in local currency

(c) on different charts

Home trade invoices
priced in sterling

Separate procedure for
export invoices

Ghosting
The name of each document is normally written
onto the symbol. Restatement of a document is not
usually necessary. However, when multipart documents are used, the separate parts may be subjected
to different sequences of operations. Then restatement of each part may be the clearest way to depict
these operations. Similarly, a sequence of operations
representing a subroutine may be depicted for
clarity on a separate flow chart. In such cases
ghosting is used for restating the initial document.
This means the symbol is drawn with broken lines.
For example:

(brought forward from
chart A)

Copy 2 of sales invoice
sent to warehouse

Computerised systems
A computer system flow chart is one depicting the
configuration of a computerised system and the flow
of information through it. Its purpose is to explain
the system for the benefit of users, auditors, analysts
and any others who may be interested.

It uses a glossary of standardised symbols to
represent each hardware feature including peripheral equipment and other symbols for each
different process type. It shows the interrelationship
of input, files, processing, controls and output.

Computer flow-chart symbols:

(a) paper tape

(b) punched card

(c) visual display

(d) magnetic tape

(e) disk storage

(f) tabulation

(g) computer process

Computer systems designers and technicians may use a more extensive range of symbols to depict computer hardware and functions in greater detail. However, the computer symbols shown here cover the principal input, data storage and output devices, each with specific characteristics which are significant to the systems in which they are used. These distinctions have to be recognised in the flow charts prepared to assist the practice of internal auditing. The flow chart for a computerised system should incorporate the computer symbols in cunjunction with the basic symbols:

Linking the symbols

Inputs and outputs to process functions are shown by solid lines rather than broken lines for information flow (see Figure 4.5).

Constructing the flow chart

Sources of information

The information required for constructing flow charts will come from a number of sources, such as the following:

    system manuals
    procedure manuals
    interviews with users of the system
    internal audit permanent file
    internal control questionnaires
    observation of system in operation

Stages of preparation

Preparing a flow chart should follow a clearly defined series of steps, such as the ones suggested here:

1. It is usual to sketch out a series of free-hand flow diagrams to facilitate the process of information gathering.
2. The sketches then form the basis for constructing a comprehensive chart, normally using A3 paper.
3. Check through to ensure that there are no incomplete trails. Every copy of every document shown must be accounted for as:

    (a) permanently filed;
    (b) having left the system; or
    (c) destroyed.

4. Check the accuracy of the flow chart by a walk-through test for a selection of representative documents.
5. Examine the completed and verified flow chart to identify areas of the system where internal control is shown to be weak, or where there may be waste of resources. These areas should be noted for detailed audit examination and to be referred to in the audit report.
6. When the chart has uncovered weakness or inefficiency it will be helpful to draw a second flow chart showing proposed improvements to the system. The relevant stages should be highlighted in 'before' and 'after' charts.
7. Internal control questionnaires should be considered in conjunction with the flow charts, noting amendments related to flow chart changes.
8. Computer software packages are available to assist auditors in constructing flow charts. The packages normally incorporate a self-training program to enable the user to develop the necessary skill.

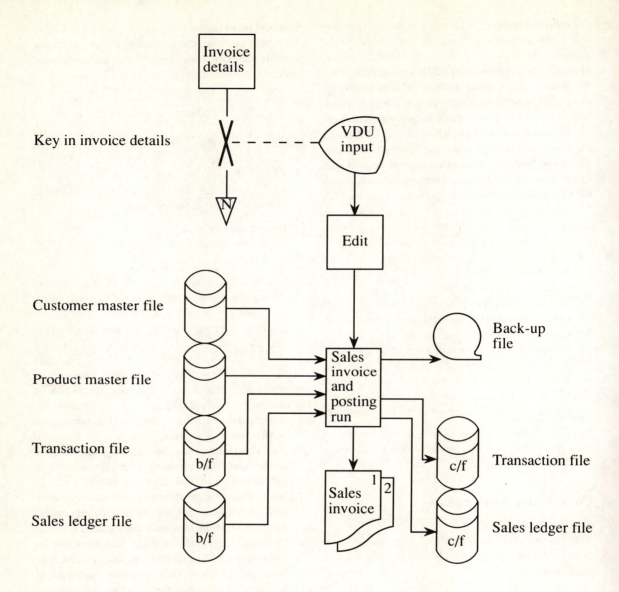

Figure 4.5

Construction rules

Format

1. Each flow chart must be given a title which should clearly identify the system or the area of activity to be described. If the title is not self-explanatory, a brief explanatory phrase should be added next to the heading.
2. The chart should state the date when it was drawn and the name of the person who drew it.
3. A key to interpretation of the symbols and any abbreviations used should always be given.
4. The page should be ruled into columns with titles. Reading from left to right, the columns should be headed 'Narrative', 'Operation No.', and up to five 'Task' columns. A chart with any more than five 'Task' columns is almost certain to prove unmanageable.
5. The flow chart should start at the top of the left hand 'Task' column describing the initial document followed by the first operation.
6. Subsequent operations should then flow down the page in sequence. Whenever an operation also constitutes a check, the check symbol should be used in preference. The flow down the page follows the progress of the document with the lapse of time.
7. When a document moves to another area, or information is transmitted to another department or area of responsibility, the flow should be carried to the next 'Task' column on the right.
8. As each 'Task' column is used to record documents or operations, it must be headed up by identifying the person or section responsible.

Flow lines:

9. The general direction of document flow in a chart should always be downwards. The flow lines may be carried horizontally to the right to continue downwards in the adjacent column. Carrying the lines back to a column on the left is best avoided if at all possible. It is likely to confuse and make the flow chart difficult to read. Flow lines should never lead upwards.
10. Diagonal lines must be avoided. They cause confusion because they conflict with the fundamental concept that vertical flow lines represent movement of documents with the passage of time whilst horizontal lines represent transfer of information and documents from one function to another.
11. Intersecting flow lines tend to make a flow chart difficult to read and every endeavour is necessary to keep them to a minimum. This means careful consideration of the logical placing of each symbol in terms of its relationship with the rest of the chart. Where crossing lines are unavoidable they should be bridged. For example:

12. Connector symbols should always be used when a document is transferred from one chart to the next.

Interpretation:

13. Each operation depicted in the chart should be allocated a sequential reference number in the 'Operation No.' column.
14. A succinct description of each operation and check operation should be noted alongside it in the 'Narrative' column. It should quote timing and frequency when these are critical. The person performing the operation or check should also be identified in the narrative if this is necessary to amplify the 'Task' column heading.
15. Excessive detail can defeat the purpose of a flow chart which is simply to provide an understanding of the controls operating in a system. This objective must be kept clearly in mind and operations which are not relevant to it have to be firmly excluded.
16. Additional notes should be recorded in the 'Narrative' column to describe occurrences which are relevant to, but outside, the system covered by the chart – for example, to explain from whence the initial document comes, or the

criteria for alternative courses when there is a choice.

17. Documents should be clearly labelled in the flow chart with familiar names so that it is immediately apparent what the document is. The use of initials or other abbreviation when referring to commonly used documents may confuse or mislead. It may be wise to show the full title the first time a document normally referred to by initials appears on the chart.

Structure:

18. The system should be divided up into logical sections and a separate flow chart constructed for each. For example, the sales system could perhaps be divided into:

> order processing
> invoicing
> sales ledger recording
> cash collection

Process charts

This is a technique used in work study to describe operational processes with graphic representation. It uses just five symbols as recommended by the American Society of Mechanical Engineers, each to represent a basic function. Internal auditors may find this technique useful to augment flow charting, particularly in the practice of operational auditing. Process charting can be used to describe a wide range of operational activities because it uses narrative description to amplify the meanings represented by symbols.

The technique is fully described in Currie (1981). The examples given here are based upon that source.

Function	Predominant result	Symbol
Operation	Procedures, accomplishes, furthers the process	◯
Transport	Travels	⇨
Storage	Holds, keeps or retains	▽
Delay	Interferes or delays	D
Inspection	Verifies quantity and/or quality	☐

Example 4.7   Flow process chart
Receiving goods in the warehouse, unloading and moving them into stores on the first floor.

Goods into warehouse by container

Await unloading

Unload container to fork-lift truck

By fork-lift truck to goods lift

Await arrival of lift

Unload fork-lift truck into goods lift

By goods lift to floor 1

Await unloading from goods lift

Unload from goods lift to fork-lift truck

By fork-lift truck to store

Await stacking in store

Unload fork-lift truck into store

In store

The technique can be applied to a range of circumstances by varying the amount of detail shown. In the case of outline and flow process charts, the symbols are used to represent steps in the procedure or manufacturing process. In two-handed process charts they represent the elements of the work cycle.

The table which follows lists the most generally used forms, by means of which every normal type of activity should be capable of being recorded in the appropriate degree of detail as required.

Charts	Activities depicted
Outline process chart	Principal operations and inspections
Flow process chart	Activities of men, material or equipment
Two-handed process chart	Activities of a worker's two hands
Multiple activity chart	Activites of men and/or machines on a common time scale
Simultaneous motion cycle chart	Activities of a worker's hands, legs, and other body movements on a common time scale

Section 4. Internal control questionnaires

The nature of internal control

The internal control questionnaire is a device used by auditors to assist in evaluating internal control. In order to evaluate internal control it is necessary to have a clear understanding of what it is and how the practice of internal auditing relates to it.

A control is any action taken by management to enhance the likelihood that established objectives and goals will be achieved.

Controls may be preventative (to deter undesirable events from occurring), detective (to detect and correct undesirable events which have occurred) or directive (to cause or encourage a desirable event to occur).

The primary objectives of internal control are to ensure:

(a) reliability and integrity of information;
(b) compliance with policies, plans, procedures, laws and regulations;
(c) safeguarding of assets;
(d) economical and efficient use of resources;
(e) accomplishment of established objectives and goals for operations or programmes.

Internal audit evaluation should encompass establishing whether reasonable assurance exists that:

(a) objectives and goals have been established;
(b) authorising, monitoring and periodic comparison activities have been planned, performed and documented as necessary to attain objectives and goals; and
(c) planned results have been achieved (objectives and goals have been accomplished).
(Extracts from IIA–UK Guidelines 300.06 and .08)

Features of internal control

There are four key criteria for assessing the effectiveness of an internal control system:

1. **Objectives** The objectives of each control system should be readily recognisable as contributing to the objectives of the organisation as a whole.
2. **Effectiveness** The system should be seen to be accomplishing the management intentions for which it was designed and implemented.
3. **Efficiency** The resources used in the process of operating the system should be applied efficiently in pursuit of the objectives.
4. **Security** The arrangements for operating the system should ensure the quality and accuracy of the work done and the security of assets, information and other resources.

These four criteria need to be kept foremost in mind when formulating the questions listed in all internal control questionnaires. It is often convenient to phrase all the questions to require 'yes' or 'no' answers so that a 'no' answer would signal possible weakness in the system.

Control objectives

Arthur Anderson and Co. cite four pervasive control objectives:

1. **Authorisation** Ensure that only authorised events and transactions can occur.
2. **Substantiation** Ensure that policies and procedures defined by management are adhered to.
3. **Classification** Ensure reliable and accurate recording of accounting and other critical information.

4. **Safeguards** Ensure that assets and information are guarded against loss, damage or improper use.

The internal auditor should consider the operational aim of pursuing economy, efficiency and effectiveness in the context of these control objectives. It is thus necessary to evaluate the control parameters of the system in terms of whether they secure strategic objectives as well as expected standards of quality, quantity, time and cost.

Control effectiveness

The effectiveness of control depends on the quality of the control information: it must be valid, reliable, complete, accurate and timely. Since this is a fundamental requirement, the internal auditor has to consider the impact of each control in terms of monitoring and reporting:

1. **Transaction authority**
   Objective: Authorisation
   Control types: Preventive; detective; corrective.
   (a) Are all transactions authorised by staff with properly delegated authority?
   (b) Does the system ensure that any transaction not so authorised is rejected and that rejected transactions are subject to examination?
2. **Segregation of duties**
   Objective: Authorisation
   Control type: Preventive
   (a) Is there segregation between custodial and recording functions? Does the system ensure that no one who has access to assets in any form is in a position to initiate entries in the accounting records or produce documentation which will result in entries?
3. **Validity of records**
   Objective: Substantiation
   Control type: Detective
   (a) Does the information to be recorded in the records relate to a proper transaction?
   (b) Have the details been independently test checked for accuracy?
4. **Reliability of information**
   Objective: Classification
   Control type: Preventive

(a) Has the source of information been properly processed into and through the records?

Control weakness

Weakness in control procedures may be classified into four categories according to the impact upon the system:
1. **Negligible effect** When the effect on ultimate performance is likely to be negligible, the weakness will not normally be a cause for concern.
2. **Loop-holes** The internal auditor should assess and report the possible consequences of the weakness and recommend protective measures.
3. **Definite weakness** The internal auditor should report the weakness and recommend a means of rectification.
4. **No effective control** Urgent action by the accountable management is required: the internal auditor should evaluate the risk and endeavour to focus management attention on it.

The system should be considered as a whole and the internal auditor must exercise judgement to assess whether the effect of a weak control is compensated by other controls within the system.

The need for evaluation

Evaluating an internal control system means judging its purpose and effectiveness and highlighting its strengths and weaknesses. Audit testing, both substantive and compliance, contributes a necessary element in judging the effectiveness of the system.

The internal auditor has to make judgements about the effectiveness of control and the scale of risk at certain critical stages in each audit assignment:

1. When deciding which activities to examine in detail.
2. When deciding which aspects of each activity selected for examination should be recorded by flow chart or otherwise.
3. When evaluating the controls after recording the system.
4. When reassessing the system in the light of the results of compliance tests.

Progressive evaluation is crucial in deciding what further audit work to do. The internal auditor must react positively and constructively to the circumstances uncovered as the audit assignment progresses. Audit tests, whether compliance or substantive, need to be carefully designed with due recognition of the control procedures and the known and potential weaknesses of the system. The audit working papers should record the evaluations made at each stage.

The ICQ technique

An internal control questionnaire (ICQ) is a series of questions related to a specific system of internal control and designed to assist an auditor to evaluate it. The purpose when using the ICQ is thus to evaluate the system rather than to describe it.

All ICQs comprise a list of questions set against theoretical standards for ideal control, based upon the auditor's concept of sound control objectives. They should be adaptable to many different systems and they should be easy to use.

The questionnaire can be most effective when all questions require 'yes' or 'no' answers, and a 'no' indicates weakness.

For example:

'Are purchase invoices checked to goods received notes before being passed for payment?' . . . yes / no

A 'no' clearly indicates a weakness in the payment procedure.

The questions in the ICQ should cover the entire system. For large and complex systems, review and redraft may be undertaken by sections every two or three years.

The ICQ is used in two ways:

1. To enable the auditor to design or amend the programme of audit tests so that the most effective use is made of audit time, given the constraints of any weakness uncovered.
2. To inform the auditee, both informally and in the audit report, of material weaknesses in the system.

The advantages and disadvantages of using ICQs are listed below.

Advantages

1. The use of ICQs encourages a disciplined approach to the audit assignment.
2. The technique provides a useful supervisory check on audit coverage.
3. The completed ICQ provides a record of the effectiveness of controls.
4. It provides a record of audit enquiry which should prove useful at subsequent audit visits.
5. The technique should simplify and speed up the process of appraising the system.
6. The task of completing the ICQ should be adopted as an effective training medium for audit staff by focusing attention on issues which are critical to effective control.
7. The technique provides the basis for continuity in the tasks which comprise the audit assignment by linking system documentation and assessment with substantive and compliance testing.
8. It is a versatile technique which can be tailored to suit most systems.

Disadvantages

1. The technique is not applicable to small units or sections where the degree of internal control is very limited because of a lack of segregation of duties.
2. The work of compiling an ICQ for very simple situations or non-repetitive audit assignments may not be justified: a more intuitive approach to evaluation may be more relevant.

Designing the ICQ

ICQs should normally have three sections,

general information
control objectives
detailed control questions

General information
The questions in this part should be designed to collect the information needed to build a broad but

comprehensive understanding of the scale of operations and how they are recorded. Examples are listed below:

annual value of receipts
annual volume and value of cash sales
annual value of payments
annual production volumes
details of stock holdings
details of bank accounts
details of cash holdings
details of suspense accounts
key features of the accounting system and methods.
key features of the production control system
key features of the stock control system

Control objectives

Questions in this part should be framed to establish and record the control objectives of the system and to identify the main areas of audit concern. An example from the purchasing area follows.

Main control area: purchasing

1. Control should be established over the ordering procedures to ensure that goods ordered and supplied:

    (a) represent quantities required by the department and are of suitable quality and specification;

    (b) are purchased at the most appropriate prices and terms agreed with the supplier before commitment;

    (c) have been duly authorised in accord with delegated budgetary accountability;

    (d) have been contracted for by formal written order; and

    (e) have been purchased from suppliers selected on the basis of fair competition determined by objective analysis of quality, service and price offered.

2. Control should be established over goods and services received:

    (a) to substantiate suppliers' invoices and to enable liability for unprocessed invoices to be determined;

    (b) as a basis for entries in the inventory records;

    (c) to ensure that only goods and services matching the contracted specification in quantity, quality and time of delivery are accepted.

3. Control should be established over returns and claims:

    (a) to ensure due credit is received;

    (b) as a basis for entries in the inventory records.

4. Control should be established over receipt, acceptance and payment of suppliers' invoices:

    (a) to ensure all invoices received are recorded promptly and processing is monitored;

    (b) to ensure the goods or services have been received and accepted as being in accord with contracted terms;

    (c) to ensure each contracted liability is passed for payment once only with due deduction for any outstanding claims, allowances or returns.

Detailed control questions

This part should consist of a sequence of detailed questions which progressively analyse the system procedures for achieving each objective in turn against standards for ideal control. An example from the stock management area follows.

Main control area: stock management

1. Are there adequate procedures for receiving and checking all intake?

    (a) Is suitable equipment provided for weighing and measuring goods received and is it regularly checked for accuracy?

    (b) Is there a satisfactory alternative discipline for times when the weighing equipment is out of service?

    (c) Have procedures been established for checking the quality of goods received before acceptance into stock?

    (d) Are there adequate procedures for ensuring all goods received are correctly recorded and the stock records are correctly and promptly updated?

2. Are there adequate procedures for authorising and accounting for all issues from stock?

   (a) Is access to the stores restricted to warehouse staff?

   (b) Are there suitable arrangements for ensuring goods may only leave the warehouse via controlled issue points?

   (c) Does the procedure and documentation ensure issues can only be made against properly authorised warrants which then lead to prompt entry in the inventory records?

   (d) Is there an emergency discipline to satisfy urgent requirements when the normal procedure or documentation is not available, and if so does it provide adequate control?

   (e) Are returns to stock properly controlled and accounted for?

3. Do the arrangements for custody of the stock provide an adequate basis for control?

   (a) Is the warehouse adequately equipped to provide protection against fire, flood, weather, vandalism, theft and similar hazards and are potentially hazardous items in stock adequately safeguarded?

   (b) Is the warehouse suitably equipped for marshalling and storing the goods held efficiently and enabling them to be readily identified and withdrawn when required?

   (c) Is the management of the warehouse suitably organised and supported by suitable staff and equipment for handling the goods, recording all movements of stock and accounting for it? Is the executive with delegated authority to manage the stock charged with accountability for the stock investment?

   (d) Are there adequate procedures for counting the stock continuously or periodically and for adjusting the records when necessary and investigating discrepancies? Are there adequate procedures for checking the financial record of stock with the warehouse record?

   (e) Are there adequate procedures for identifying and accounting for obsolete stock and stock which has deteriorated or been damaged, and for properly controlled realisation and disposal of such stock?

Completing the ICQ

The auditor should think of the detailed questions in an ICQ as the questions which have to be answered rather than questions which have to be asked.

It is useful to give guidance notes for inexperienced audit staff so that they understand each control point, why it is necessary as a control, and what might be the consequences of non-control.

Format

1. Questions should be sequentially numbered and prefixed to refer to each specified control objective for easy reference.
2. References to operations recorded on a flow chart should be identified as: F/C Ref.
3. It is necessary to ensure that all identified controls are subject to some compliance testing. References to audit programme tests should be identified as: AP Ref.
4. When the level of control is considered excessive in relation to the scale of risks involved, or when control is duplicated in the system, the excess control should be recorded. References to the record of control excesses should be identified as: RCE Ref.
5. Whenever the main control is found to be deficient, but other factors in the system have a control effect which reduces the risk, the situation is known as compensation control: it should be recorded. References to compensation control should be identified as: CC. Ref.
6. All weaknesses which are not compensated for should be listed by the auditor on a separate document for discussion with management. This document is known as the record of control weaknesses. It should record the discussions with management, judgement of significance of weakness, substantive tests, how the matter is reported, and when management rectifies the weakness. References to the record of control weakness should be referred to as: RCW. Ref.

Section 5. Interviewing

The nature of interviewing

'Their little interview was like a picnic on a coral strand.'
(Henry James, *The Ambassador*)

The internal auditor collects much of the information which forms the basis of audit evidence by listening to and talking with the auditee. Interviewing is thus an essential part of the internal audit process.

Conducting an internal audit interview is a practice which requires skill, but the necessary training to develop this skill tends to be overlooked. Many internal auditors, and indeed many auditees, learn it in the often painful school of experience. There are, however, some basic guidelines which can assist the development of interviewing skills.

The primary purpose of an internal audit interview is to enable the auditor to gather factual information about the work which is subject to audit review; it also enables the auditee to impart information to the auditor.

The internal auditor normally seeks information from the auditee by means of question and answer at routine meetings arranged during the course of an internal audit assignment. By careful questioning the auditor helps the auditee to recall and to give freely the facts pertaining to the subject under discussion.

Where fraud or irregularity are suspected, facts may not be given so freely. The interview in these circumstances also has to be conducted within the constraints of the law as prescribed in sections 68 to 82 of the Police and Criminal Evidence Act 1984. Because of the importance of directing such an interview with precision it should always be conducted by an experienced member of the audit staff with well developed interviewing skills. Such interviews are dealt with more fully in Chapter 8.

Preparation

In interviewing as in most other activities, the key to success is in good preparation. Preparation is concerned with information, knowledge and fact finding, as distinct from the practical administrative arrangements for the interview which may be described as scheduling. Preparation involves the 'why', 'what', 'how' and 'who' questions. Questions of 'where' and 'when' are appropriate to scheduling.

Effective interview preparation means defining just what is expected from the interview and how best to achieve it. This process involves addressing a logical sequence of questions such as those listed here:

The question:	Identifies:
1. Why do you want to interview?	The aim.
2. What do you want to know?	The facts required.
3. Who has this information?	The persons to be interviewed.
4. How are you going to get the facts?	The questions to be asked.
5. What do you want to say?	The information to be imparted.
6. Who has to receive this information?	The person needing the information.
7. How are you going to give this information?	The techniques for presentation.

There are some key issues to be considered when preparing for an interview, such as the following:

1. The terms of reference for the audit assignment.
2. Specific objectives for this part of the audit.
3. Information known on this work area:
   (a) internal audit permanent file;
   (b) previous audit working papers;
   (c) ICQs/ ICEQs/ KCQs;
   (d) pre-audit preparation;
   (e) system reports;
   (f) procedure manual;
   (g) other current reports.

4. Information known about the auditee:

   (a) work background, experience, track record, objectives;
   (b) personal background, education, interests, family.

This information can assist in establishing a good working relationship with the auditee and the development of a participative audit style which has been found to be successful.

Prepare a framework of questions, or check list, for the interview. With a check list you will be better able to control the interview.

In some cases where routine information is required a questionnaire could be sent for completion before the interview, to be confirmed at the interview.

Advise the auditee of any records, documents or books required for examination at the interview and request that they be made available.

Prepare a framework for presenting your information and have sample material to hand.

Scheduling

Aspects of interview preparation also influence scheduling decisions, such as whether to conduct the interview alone, or with another colleague in support or for taking notes. If the area of work under discussion is complex, note taking can be difficult without help.

Key issues to be considered when scheduling an interview are:

1. Where? It is most usual for the interview to take place at the auditee's place of work. The necessary records, documentation and books are most likely to be to hand and the auditee is likely to be more relaxed here than elsewhere.

   There may, however, be advantages in using the auditor's own office if you wish to have more control over the interview and to eliminate interruptions or if privacy is a critical requirement.
2. When? Normally mid-morning or mid-afternoon, Tuesday to Thursday are best: the beginning and end of the day or week are usually busy periods. Find out if there are particular times to avoid when the auditee is unduly busy and avoid these.
3. How long? Allow the auditee the courtesy of being able to plan his day, as you expect to

plan yours, by setting a time limit on the interview. For the first visit an hour may be long enough. Subsequent interviews can then be arranged.
4. Who will attend? Obviously, the internal auditor and the specific auditee. If audit support is required, another auditor may attend. Similarly, the auditee may wish to have a colleague available or bring one in as appropriate to answer specialist questions.

Give as much notice to the auditee as possible. This can help you to avoid making arrangements with the wrong person, and also the danger that the records, documents and books you wish to consult may not be available at the interview.

If your organisation uses an internal audit introductory leaflet setting out the aims and objectives of the function, it is appropriate to pass a copy to the auditee when confirming the interview arrangements.

Conducting the interview

General points

1. First impressions count, and the opening ritual between auditor and auditee is important.
2. Having planned and scheduled the interview you will arrive on time to find the auditee expecting you.
3. Introduce yourself; shake hands, sit down when invited; if not invited, request to sit. Do not invade the auditee's personal space; do not 'take over' the auditee's desk. Put your case on the floor.
4. Avoid the risk of provoking any unhelpful reaction through extremes of dress for working clothes.
5. If you are a smoker, do not smoke unless invited or after requesting and receiving the auditee's permission and ensure that an ashtray is available.
6. Be polite, be natural, be friendly: bring to the auditee the reality of someone coming to provide a helpful service.
7. Put the auditee at ease by reference to some

non-controversial aspect of work or personal interests.

8. Confirm, and explain further if necessary, the aims and objectives of the interview.
9. Try to establish a rapport and to let the auditee feel involved in a successful outcome of the meeting. Stress the value and importance of his or her contribution.
10. Look at the auditee whilst he or she is speaking. Maintain eye contact, but do not stare.
11. Be aware of the importance of non-verbal communication and try to read the auditee's body language in relation to the replies given. Watch for signs of boredom, impatience, aggressiveness or discomfort.
12. Respond to the auditee by demonstrating continuing interest, understanding and encouragement throughout the interview.
13. Confirm your perception of the information you are seeking, and your understanding of the information the auditee gives you, by regular feedback. Summarising the issues in your own words serves to clarify your own understanding, and gives the auditee the opportunity to correct any misconception. For example: 'You mean that . . .', or 'I understand you to say that . . . .'.
14. Be aware of your own body language.

The questions

Ask questions which are appropriate in terms of the topic and ask the right type of question.

1. **Open-ended questions** These are questions which seek opinions, views, descriptions, and allow for a wide variety of responses. For example: How effective do you think the current advertising campaign will be?

    This kind of question is also particularly useful in putting an inhibited auditee at ease. For example: What do you think about the social activities provided by the organisation?
2. **Closed questions** These are questions which seek specific facts and answers which are straightforward and require no interpretation by the auditee. For example: how many times in a week do you check the weighing scales?

3. **Leading and loaded questions** Questions in this category should be avoided. The question should be phrased differently so as to obtain the information sought without giving offence. For example: 'Do you reject all unmatched items?' may be better expressed as 'How do you deal with unmatched items?'
4. **Technical language and jargon** Unless familiar and appropriate to the auditee, the use of technical language or jargon should be avoided.
5. **Operational audit questions** These questions should be framed to reflect the context of the management structure for the operation under review. They will then take account of the objectives of the operation and the control procedures appropriate for achieving them.
6. **Financial audit questions** These questions need to be framed to reflect the context of the financial control structure and the accounting procedures.
7. **Reserving judgement** Do not agree or disagree with any views expressed by the auditee: at this stage it is unlikely that you know all the facts.

Closing the interview

1. Once you feel the end of the interview is nearing, you should summarise all the information you have gathered. This gives the auditee another opportunity to confirm, or correct, your record.
2. If you cannot get all the information you want in the time allocated to the interview, you have to offer the auditee the option of carrying on or continuing another time. If you carry on without asking you may alienate the auditee, particularly if this disrupts the planned day.
3. Finally, thank the auditee for giving the time and information you sought.

Note taking

The information gathered during the interview process must be recorded for use as the audit assignment progresses and for subsequent reference. It is best recorded and confirmed as it is collected during each interview.

1. Be open about making notes during the interview and use them to summarise and obtain feedback from the auditee.
2. In complex discussions, where a separate note taker is used, confirm with the auditee the record made.
3. The split page technique is useful: questions down the left side of the page, answers on the right of the page.
4. Interview notes should be reviewed and finalised promptly.
5. A standard format is helpful:

   assignment title and number
   date
   individuals interviewed
   purpose of interview
   reference to previous work papers
   summary of major issues arising: 1, 2, 3 . . .
   interview issues to be followed up: 1, 2, 3 . . .
   interview notes: 1, 2, 3 . . .

Analysing the interview

1. List all major issues, problems and opportunities.
2. Organise the list according to topic and write a detailed analysis of each.
3. Identify the principal issues using key words.
4. If some topics are covered by more than one interviewee, tabulate the results of each interview.
5. Cross-reference the notes to other audit working papers as necessary.
6. Ensure your notes are legible, permanent and filed where you can easily recover them.

Section 6.   Testing

The nature of audit testing

The aims of internal audit testing are twofold:

1. To evaluate how effectively the implementation of management policy is controlled, and how efficiently operations are controlled.
2. To check compliance with management policy and directives as exercised through the system of internal control.

First, however, the internal auditor has to understand and record the system using flow charts, narrative, organisation documentation, or any combination of these.

Perceptions of the system can differ from reality: it is important that the internal auditor records the system actually in use. This can then be compared with the originally intended version as prescribed in formal system documentation and with the assumed version as perceived by the line manager.

Meaningful testing can be considered once there is an understanding and a record of the system in use. The fundamental concepts of testing can be clearly defined in the context of internal auditing practice and these have to be understood. The testing has to be designed to fulfil a number of separately identifiable purposes.

The internal auditor examines the system documentation and assesses the contribution of each prescribed procedure towards the achievement of the management objectives as defined for the system. This may involve designing a number of walk-through tests in order to confirm the auditor's understanding of the system. The next stage is compliance testing and this may lead to a programme of substantive tests designed for evaluating an identified system weakness in terms of transaction values at risk.

Walk-through testing

The internal auditor selects typical transactions and follows the audit trail through the system. The purpose is to confirm the auditor's understanding of the system.

Walk-through tests should be designed to check that the system is as the internal auditor has described it. These tests should identify separately each stage in the system. For a straightforward system a sample of perhaps six representative transactions may be appropriate, each to be followed through the system, checking each entry in the appropriate record and the application of each control in the sequence recorded. If the system has subroutines the sample should include items from each of the subsystems.

Compliance testing

The internal auditor tests performance in each part of the system against the prescribed procedures. The primary purpose is to verify that the system procedures are being properly applied. Compliance testing may also provide statistical data as the basis for evaluating the effect of system weaknesses.

Compliance testing is probably the most important test activity in the practice of internal auditing. It may influence the determination of further audit work and the degree of substantive testing.

Compliance testing should be focused primarily on the key controls in the system, which should be identifiable from the record which the internal auditor has made of the system and confirmed by walk-through testing.

The compliance tests should be designed to establish whether each of the identified key controls within the system is functioning properly, with a view to providing reasonable assurance that control is effective.

Control effectiveness can be expressed initially as a proportion of errors in the sample tested. However, it is important to consider the significance of this measure, both in terms of the scale of implied risk and of its materiality in the context of the system objectives. As a result, it may be necessary to carry out further testing which could be substantive or compliance or both.

Sample sizes for compliance testing need to be sufficient to enable reasonable conclusions to be drawn from the results. Sound conclusions are crucial to effective internal audit recommendations. This is, therefore, a matter for critical judgement by the internal auditor. It is essentially a question of the degree of 'confidence' needed. The greater the population, the bigger the sample needs to be, though not proportionately so. You may get as much 'confidence' about the reliability of a sample of 100 from 1,000 items as from 120 from 5,000 or 125 from 500,000. This is because a randomly selected sample will mirror the population from which it is selected.

Confidence, in turn, depends upon the scale of risk. The greater the risk exposure, the bigger the sample needed to provide an appropriate level of confidence. Earlier in this chapter we discussed risk assessment.

In the context of compliance testing, the internal auditor has to take account of the overall pattern of controls. Risk exposure from control failure in one area is sometimes mitigated by the effect of other controls, either within the same system or outside it: this is always a possibility which has to be explored.

In some cases, statistical sampling techniques can be used to help quantify the options to be considered both in deciding the sample size and in selecting the sample. These techniques have been discussed earlier in this chapter.

Here we are concerned with the criteria which the internal auditor should consider when exercising judgement:

1. **Importance** All testing absorbs time and effort which has to be weighed against the potential for identifying risks and opportunities where management attention could be focused with advantage. This means allocating priorities in the application of internal audit resources to where they are expected to make the greatest contribution.

2. **Complexity** Compliance testing is much simpler for some systems than for others. The degree of difficulty in getting access to the appropriate data or in performing compliance tests on it will affect the amount of resource these tests will absorb. This factor and the reasons for it have to be recognised in an endeavour to ensure that all risks and opportunities of equivalent ranking receive comparable internal audit attention.

3. **Expectations** Previous knowledge or experience may lead to certain expectations about how the system is functioning. There may be accumulating evidence of failure or success in particular areas, such as high incidence of sales credits. There may be known critical circumstances such as a shortage of fully trained staff. There may be a track record from previous audit tests.

   When a high level of errors can be expected more testing has to be done. Confirmation of an acceptable low error rate may demonstrate that further testing is not necessary.

Compliance tests may take a number of different forms. Some of these are listed below.

1. **Re-performance** For example: reworking a bank reconciliation or recalculating extensions and totals on invoices.
2. **Inspection** For example: examination of documents to confirm correct authorisation.
3. **Observation** For example: watching receipts into the warehouse to see the established procedures are complied with for checking quantity and quality of goods taken into stock; watching delivery of cash to bank to see prescribed security procedures observed.

Other testing techniques

Substantive testing
Substantive tests establish the value of errors found, so enabling an assessment to be made as to whether the impact is material. When compliance tests reveal errors in key control areas, detailed substantive tests will be necessary. For such substantive tests, statistical sampling techniques would normally be used.

Dual-purpose testing
Tests can sometimes be designed which combine the objectives of both compliance and substantive testing. This practice should be adopted whenever it is feasible since it facilitates efficient use of the available internal audit resources.

Analytical testing
In essence this is substantive testing which leads to further 'in-depth' examination and analysis. The internal auditor selects a sample of transactions for testing specific features of processing through the system. The sample is chosen as representative of transaction value or volume for the purpose of comparing information and ratios or relationships.

By this technique, management information may also be compared on a periodic basis to identify trends and to highlight abnormal activity. Variations from normal are then investigated by substantive testing to confirm the interpretation of the analysis.

The analytical testing technique is sometimes described as analytical review and it may well be used for a specific investigation such as a possible acquisition or a divestment.

Vouching and verification
Vouching and verification is a technique of internal audit testing concerned with the authenticity and validity of individual transactions.

Vouching is the process of checking recorded transaction details by reference to source documentation or independent documents.

Verification is the purpose of vouching. It means substantiating that the transaction has been properly authorised, has actually occurred, and has been correctly recorded.

The effectiveness of vouching depends to a large extent on the internal auditor's alertness, auditing experience and knowledge of the organisation. In essence, the aim is to establish that the accounting record of each transaction correctly accords with the prime document. Any unusual transactions, such as the ones listed here, may be noted for the verification process:

> same product at different prices in the same period
> original invoice without a VAT reference
> invoice and statement both shown as paid
> despatch to other than normal delivery point
> incorrect authorisation

Vouching establishes whether there is a need to investigate further. Then verification techniques are applied to establish the authenticity, validity and correctness of the recorded transaction in accordance with the independent evidence of the voucher. Whenever there is a discrepancy, corroborative evidence will be sought for confirmation.

Vouching and verification techniques may be particularly appropriate where there is a high level of local transactions or reliance on telephone orders or where transactions are generated by a large number of staff operating in the field.

Direct testing
Where the internal auditor has reason to believe there is something wrong in a specific area, the most

effective use of available resources may be achieved by concentrating the audit testing in that area. This will be a matter for the internal auditor to judge. Vouching and verification techniques are likely to be appropriate for establishing the validity of transactions in such a case.

Systems-based testing

The systems-based audit approach is a generic term applying to all forms of internal audit testing which have been structured to take account of the logic of a particular control system. It is applicable to all stages of development and application. For example:

System stage	Testing involvement
1. Planning the audit	Analytical review
2. Ascertaining and recording the system	Walk-through tests
3. Assessing controls	None
4. Testing controls	Compliance tests of key controls Substantive tests of weak controls
5. Evaluation of test results	Additional compliance and substantive tests as required

The principle underlying all systems-based audit tests is a recognition that control systems are intended to provide the means of effective management control. Thus, operations managed through the system are effectively controlled through procedural disciplines and an integrated network of system checks which often apply automatically. These features of the system are collectively referred to as controls.

For the systems-based audit approach, tests are specifically designed, first to assess the strength of the system controls and then to sample-test transaction processing, placing appropriate reliance on the controls built into the system.

For large or complex systems there is no effective alternative: the systems-based audit approach is the only efficient way to conduct the internal audit assignment. However, in certain cases some supplementary testing techniques may be added to the basic systems audit techniques to give emphasis to particular internal audit objectives. For example: in the public sector, where proper custody and efficient use of public funds is paramount, it is not unusual for systems testing to be augmented by a significant element of extra vouching and verification.

Classification of audit tests

Audit testing techniques may now be classified according to application and purpose. For example:

Type of test	Application	Purpose
Walk through	Systems	To confirm the auditor's understanding
Compliance	Systems	To evaluate the effectiveness of the system's internal control
Substantive	Systems	To evaluate the effect of compliance weakness
Dual purpose	Systems	To combine compliance and substantive tests
Analytical	Systems and investigations	To compare trends in management performance as a basis for further investigation
Vouching and verification	Investigations and non-systems	To examine propriety and accuracy of records, to confirm the truth and validity of the record and the existence of assets.
Directed testing	Investigations and non-systems	To confirm a suspicion or to resolve doubt

Recording audit tests

It is most important to record meticulously all work related to audit tests:

(a) for subsequent reference when reporting and following up;

(b) to avoid all risk of false interpretation resulting from omissions;

(c) to demonstrate to the auditee that the audit work has been performed to high professional standards;

(d) to provide the basis of audit assurance or to highlight deficiencies;

(e) to provide a basis for audit recommendations;

(f) to provide evidence of professionalism to demonstrate the standard of internal audit work as a basis for external audit reliance.

The internal auditor should record in the working papers:

(a) the area of the organisation under examination;

(b) the evaluation of controls and the tests undertaken, with details of results;

(c) the potential consequences of errors or weaknesses determined by the tests.

Section 7. Evaluation

The nature of evaluation

A degree of evaluation is involved at each stage of every internal audit assignment. It is necessary to evaluate documentary evidence, knowledge gained from interviews and the results of internal audit tests in order to draw conclusions, to form a view and to report on the audit assignment.

Evaluation stages

Pre-audit review

1. Assessing the initial fact finding.
2. Evaluating previous audit evidence.

The recorded system

1. Evaluating the results of walk-through testing.
2. Evaluating system notes and flow-charts.
3. Evaluating system controls.

Initial testing

Evaluating the results of compliance testing.

Weakness testing

1. Evaluating the results of substantive testing.
2. Evaluating the results of follow up compliance testing.

Forming an audit opinion

1. Drawing conclusions from the combined results of all testing and forming an audit opinion.
2. Judging the most suitable course of action and formulating recommendations.
3. Determining future audit needs.

Evaluating the audit output

1. Communicating audit results to management.
2. Evaluating follow-up action.

Pre-audit review

Previous audit evidence

Before commencing the field work a pre-audit review is necessary to examine and evaluate previous internal audit evidence. The permanent file and the working papers from the previous internal audit assignment will be the source for such evidence. However, working papers more than a year or two old are unlikely to be a reliable source of information in a changing environment.

It is wise to assume that all systems will have been changed significantly over a period of three years, whilst over a five-year period significant changes in personnel and working practices can be expected. The pace of change is likely to be more rapid in fast-growing organisations and in those involved in developing markets or new technology.

In order to evaluate past audit evidence, reference should be made to relevant audit notes and reports including the last audit risk analysis of the area to be reviewed. Questions to ask at this stage include:

1. What was the strength of control last time?
2. What was the result of any follow-up?
3. What systems and permanent information do we have?
4. What was the quality of internal audit performance last time?
5. Is there a current risk rating for this area based on audit risk analysis?
6. What specific risks have been previously identified in this area?

Initial fact finding

Armed with whatever source material can be found, the internal auditor will conduct a series of initial interviews with senior staff to establish the scope of required audit work. The next step is to get copies of current relevant information such as organisation charts, system specifications, procedure manuals, written instructions, etc.

Having gathered this combination of written and oral information, a preliminary evaluation has to be made. However it is assessed, this evaluation is a critical requirement. No internal audit assignment should proceed to the field work stage without a reasonable idea of the depth of work needed and the necessary time scale based on considered judgement of the relevant facts. The preliminary evaluation enables the audit manager to determine the skills needed and to allocate appropriate resources.

Evaluation involves judgement which depends upon good internal audit experience and a rational and systematic approach to the assessment of risk. The experience and knowledge of others can be used to help develop each individual's evaluation skills.

The recorded system

The internal auditor needs to evaluate the control system in order to determine the appropriate form and scale of audit testing. This is so whether the information gathered on the system has been recorded by the auditor or by management. Recorded system information is likely to be a combination of narrative notes, organisation charts and flow-charts.

Walk-through testing

Walk-through testing is a technique which primarily enables the internal auditor to confirm information gathered about the system and consequently to form an opinion about the reliability of the sources of this information. Secondly, it evaluates the internal auditor's understanding of the system and effectiveness in gathering systems information. The general nature of this technique is discussed in Section 6 of this chapter.

The internal auditor normally gains a better understanding of how the system works in the process of walk-through testing than from written descriptions or interviews. Consequently particular importance should be attached to interpreting the results of walk-through testing.

Walk-through testing is, however, a necessary element along with consideration of the written record and oral explanations in the process of assessing the effectiveness of a system. This evaluation is then used to determine a testing strategy.

System notes and flow charts

After walk-through testing the internal auditor is in a position to evaluate the system from the information that has been gathered.

Effective evaluation must be focused on the objectives of the system and the key controls. It is important to give priority to the initial evaluation of these key controls. There is little point in evaluating any secondary or minor controls within a system until it has been established that the major controls are sound. Detailed internal audit examination of every control within a system is seldom necessary even if the time and effort could be justified. Consequently, a judgement has to be made as to what can be covered. As far as possible, this judgement should ensure that all key controls do get covered, and then as many secondary controls as time will permit.

Control absorbs resources; it must be adequate to achieve the management objective. Control objectives can often be achieved by more than one means and controls are often interrelated. The internal auditor must keep an open mind in judging the effectiveness of control for the system as a whole.

First, then, the internal auditor must identify as key controls in the system those which are necessary to achieve the management objective; and also those without which the system would either cease to function or would be seriously compromised. The following table gives examples of such controls.

Accounts payable system:

Objectives	Controls
1. To pay the right people	(a) Segregation of duties between recording of invoice and authorisation for payment.
	(b) Check payment details against invoice before releasing payment.
2. To pay the right amount	(a) Check extensions and totals of invoices
	(b) Certification needed that goods or services have been received before payment is released.
3. To pay promptly when due	(a) Date of receipt of invoice to be promptly recorded and monitored for ageing to ensure invoices are cleared for payment in time.
	(b) Regular payment scheduling and checks to ensure that advantage can be taken of any discounts for prompt payment.

Internal control evaluation (ICE)

In order to evaluate control at the systems review stage it is necessary to identify the system objectives and then to relate these to the controls identified when recording the system and confirmed by walk-through testing. This process can be facilitated by adopting conventional internal control evaluation techniques using questionnaire forms. Internal control evaluation forms help the internal auditor to arrive at rational judgements in a systematic way: they are reasonably easy to create.

From examining actual controls found as against ideal control expectations, the internal auditor should determine whether any key controls are missing or only partly effective. His findings will have a direct influence on the nature and scale of the audit tests.

It is important to quantify the risk associated with

absence of control. There is little point in compliance testing for a non-existent control; but substantive testing may be appropriate to establish whether material errors have occurred:

1. What could really go wrong?
2. Is it critical?
3. Are there any compensating controls elsewhere in the system?

Using an ICE form to set out this information systematically, it is then possible to evaluate the overall strength of the system. Compliance tests can then be used to confirm this initial evaluation of strengths and weaknesses.

The internal auditor will have formed opinions about the system using appropriate internal control evaluation techniques. It may well be that fundamental weakness has been uncovered and management is receptive and keen to strengthen the system. Then there would be little point in undertaking detailed testing. However, when the system controls have been judged to be generally sound, a programme of testing is likely to be necessary to evaluate the weaker control areas. It will provide the evidence required to support the initial assessment of control strengths and weaknesses, particularly where the management expects convincing evidence of internal audit judgements.

Initial testing

At this stage we are concerned with evaluating the results of compliance testing. There are likely to be occasions when the initial testing will be the only testing, or when the auditor will go straight to substantive assessment of materiality rather than check compliance.

Testing techniques are dealt with in Section 6 of this chapter. Compliance tests should be designed to answer the questions: (a) does this control work? and (b) what is the quality of control? For example, how many times are invoices correctly certified and how many times do they fail to certify? Evaluation in this context is the process of examining the results of compliance tests and determining what message they bear about the strength of control.

There is no magic formula that will reveal whether a control is effective or not. But well-directed testing will tell the internal auditor the relative effectiveness of each control within a specific system.

The internal auditor has to judge whether the standard of control is acceptable. It is a judgement to be made in the light of the results of testing. These results may be measured statistically and expressed as a percentage error within a certain precision at a given level of confidence; or they may be expressed more simply, for example: we examined 53 invoices and found 12 had been paid without authorisation.

Acceptable levels of non-compliance are influenced by the degree of dependence on the control and the extent it is covered by other controls; they must also be related to the potential loss or damage which a breach of procedure could cause. Different organisations hold differing views about acceptable levels of non-compliance. In some cases the internal audit unit has developed guidance for acceptable levels of compliance. An example follows.

Control need	Materiality or sensitivity	Acceptable error rate	
critical	critical	none	
	high	very low	up to 1%
	medium	low	1% to 3%
	low	medium	3% to 5%
high	high	low	1% to 3%
	medium	medium	3% to 5%
	low	medium	3% to 5%
medium	medium	medium	3% to 5%
	low	higher	5% to 8%
low	low	high	8% to 12%*

Notes:
1. Once error rates exceed acceptable levels, the control can be said to be not effective.
2. All these values assume error rates calculated from a statistically acceptable random sample of at least 50 items.
* If the control value is low and the materiality or sensitivity is low it is questionable whether there is value in examining that control during testing at all.

Weakness testing

Substantive testing is the technique used for evaluating system weaknesses. It is described in Section 6 of this chapter.

The results of substantive tests can be evaluated in a similar way to compliance tests except that the evaluation is concerned solely with materiality.

Where no control exists, substantive tests may be carried out to establish if there has been material error or loss as a result of the absent control. Thus, provided the sample size selected is adequate, the error or loss can be quantified. If nothing has gone wrong, the point about absent control is still valid, although it may be more difficult to convince management that control should be strengthened.

Where controls do exist, substantive tests are usually limited to two purposes: either to establish the effect of weakness where failures in compliance have been found during the compliance testing, or to confirm that where compliance tests have shown acceptable or no errors there are no obvious incidents leading to material loss. In either case, evaluation of the effect of possible weakness by substantive testing involves relating the errors discovered to the value of throughput, and relating that to the organisation as a whole.

Example 4.8
Substantive testing could show that failure to certify invoices has led to two uncertified and incorrect invoices being paid to the same supplier. The net result of the two errors could be nil, although there would still be a valid point about compliance error. However, a net result in favour or against the organisation is equally significant for differing reasons. Say the net error came to £5,000. Would you consider this significant in your evaluation? The answer is that you cannot tell – unless you know the projected likely error value in relation to the whole population under review, and the effect of this value on your organisation's business. Thus, if your turnover in this area is £500 million and the projected likely loss over the whole population is £50,000, you may decide the total risk of loss is too insignificant to get excited about. However, the same projection on a population value of £500,000 becomes materially significant.

Evaluation is not just concerned with monetary effect however. The materiality of an issue is also affected by its political significance to the organisation. A few compliance errors which turn out to be substantively low in monetary value can still be significant if they can embarrass the organisation. The internal auditor's evaluation requires not just seeing the facts, but also judging their likely impact on the well-being of the organisation.

The audit opinion

Conclusions from all testing

The first stage in forming an opinion is the process of evaluating all the tests undertaken as against expected or acceptable criteria. The internal auditor will already have some preliminary conclusions from evaluating the actual system controls against those expected in such a system. From the compliance and any substantive tests it will now be known whether there are any significant compliance failures and whether these are likely to cause material error or loss.

The internal auditor must take special care to avoid getting overexcited about finding compliance errors which turn out to have no substantive test impact. It is important to resist any tendency for the excitement of the chase to cloud sound judgement. It is necessary to sit back calmly and evaluate the findings from the organisation's perspective, not the auditor's.

Have you really found large-scale compliance errors, or simply the work of an incompetent clerk who has already left the organisation? Is the substantive error really material, or just an annoying irritation to the organisation?

Equally, where an important audit principle is at stake, should you dig your heels in and argue for management to take action? The answer in this case is invariably 'yes', but you should not be unmindful of the cost of change which might be prohibitive or might put your organisation in difficulties.

Forming an audit opinion

The results of the internal auditor's systems evaluation are intended to help the organisation have adequate systems of internal control, and to help prevent future error or fraud. All evaluation has to be seen as part of the process of constructive appraisal: that is the essence of the internal auditor's role.

Whether the audit opinion is expressed orally or in writing, formally or informally, the internal auditor will have failed if senior or local management is not convinced by the evaluation of the evidence, or if the evidence proves to be unsound or insufficient to back up his conclusions.

Some form of overall evaluation of the strengths and weaknesses of the system must be given to the accountable management, both in relation to the ideal system and in relation to the quality of control elsewhere in the organisation.

Future audit need

Expressing an opinion on control is the most important part of evaluation, but it is also necessary to determine where the system just audited fits into future audit needs and planning. In some organisations this is done using a computer model which recalculates the risk in the area just audited by keying in the relevant data.

Without such facilities the internal auditor should address such questions as the following:

1. How long can this system be left before it needs another visit?
2. What is the current throughput of the system in terms of materiality?
3. How complex is the system to audit?
4. What resources does this system consume?
5. How politically embarrassing could errors in this system be?
6. How sensitive is this system to the organisation?
7. How much of the organisation's assets are at risk in this system?
8. How dependent is the system on complex technology?

The answers to these questions, based on a simple rating of, say, 1 to 5 for each item, and drawing up a weighting to suit the views of your organisation, will facilitate preparing the audit risk analysis or audit needs assessment. Without such a process, the internal auditor has failed to complete the evaluation of the system.

Evaluating the audit output

Communicating results

Most managers, however scientific the internal audit process may have been, will simply want to know whether you are going to give them a clean bill of health. If not, they will want to know what is wrong and what it will cost to put it right. Therefore the audit evaluation has to be expressed clearly and succinctly, and to the right people at the right time to ensure effective management action. For example:

Recipients	Method	Purpose
System operatives Local management	Informal oral communication	Small compliance errors and errors with low substantive effect
Local management	Audit note or memorandum	Significant compliance and substantive errors as discovered
Local management Audit manager	Draft audit report	Overall audit opinion to confirm factual accuracy of audit findings
As draft plus Cheif executive Audit committee External auditors	Final report	Formal statement of audit opinion, agreed facts and recommendations, and ideally management response and intended action

In every case certain fundamental questions must be addressed in order to express the evaluation effectively. For example:

1. What did you find?
2. What were the weaknesses?
3. What is the material effect of these weaknesses?
4. Are they worth putting right?
5. How can they be put right?
6. What is your opinion of the strength of control?
7. What is your evaluation of the audit risk?

8. What follow-up work will be needed?
9. When should the follow-up work be done?

Follow-up

The evaluation processes are not complete until the internal audit examination has been effectively followed up. Any preliminary judgement about future audit need or about strength of control needs to be reassessed when the follow-up audit work is done. Generally, follow-up should be arranged between six months and a year after the audit examination unless it is an annual task.

Effective follow-up work has to enable the internal auditor to answer certain basic questions:

1. Has the system changed significantly from the one previously audited?
2. If so, is this a result of the audit, or unrelated?
3. If unrelated, is a new audit assessment needed of the risks in this system and of the audit requirements?
4. Have management implemented accepted audit recommendations?
5. If so, are they working effectively?
6. If not, why not – and when will implementation take place?
7. Have management implemented any recommendations rejected at the time; conversely, have management since rejected any accepted recommendations; and if so why?
8. In conclusion, how strong is control now, compared with that at the time of the internal audit examination?

The results of follow-up should be primarily reported to senior management, but may also be communicated to local management in the same way as during the original audit process. Normally, follow-up work either allows the audit files to be closed or triggers off a further round of communication between internal audit and management.

Finally, the evaluation process may be rounded off by seeking the views of auditee management about the effectiveness of the audit and about their relationships with the internal audit staff. This is sometimes done formally, by means of a brief and simple questionnaire.

Section 8.   Reporting

The nature of internal audit reporting

Internal auditors should report the results of their audit work.

(IIA–UK Specific Standard 430)

The Oxford English Dictionary defines a report as 'an account brought by one person to another especially of some matter specially investigated', and this succinctly sums up the nature and purpose of an internal audit report.

Oral reporting

It should be normal practice for the internal auditor to meet with the accountable management during the course of each internal audit assignment to discuss progress. Such meetings are necessary to clarify any matters of uncertainty or confusion, to discuss problems identified, and to explore possible solutions. Matters of significance can be promptly brought to light and considered, and when necessary appropriate management action can be urged and may then be implemented without delay.

The frequency of oral reporting during the assignment must be determined by the circumstances of each situation. Meetings may be initiated by the internal auditor or by the accountable manager or a nominated deputy. The internal auditor must however ensure that there is a meeting before starting the audit examination and another at the end of the visit. Both meetings are necessary in terms of due courtesy. However, both meetings serve important purposes in the internal audit process. The first meeting is necessary to arrange introductions and communication with staff, to confirm the plan of work and to consider any special requirements. The meeting at the end of the visit is necessary to discuss the audit findings and recommended action to enable these to be considered by management in advance of receiving the written audit report.

The internal auditor should discuss conclusions and recommendations at appropriate levels of management before issuing final written reports.

(IIA–UK Guideline 430.02)

Matters of importance may sometimes be best dealt with by an interim report in writing.

Interim reports may be used to communicate information which requires immediate attention, to communicate a change in audit scope for the activity under review, or to keep management informed of audit progress when audits extend over a long period. The use of interim reports does not diminish or eliminate the need for a final report.

(IIA–UK Guideline 430.01.1)

The auditor must give the same care and attention to planning and scheduling the report meetings as when interviewing staff as discussed in Section 5 of this chapter. This makes for effective use of both the auditee's and the auditor's time.

Oral reporting should cover all the ground that will be dealt with in the written report. The auditee will then have the opportunity to correct any factual errors or misplaced emphasis, to amplify the background to any findings, and to express a view on any matter which is to be raised in the written report. It may then be appropriate to incorporate the management comments in the formal written report.

Written reporting

A signed written report should be issued after the audit examination is completed. Interim reports may be written or oral and may be transmitted formally or informally

(IIA–UK Guideline 430.01)

The formal written report is one of the most important features of internal auditing. Management's perception and evaluation of the service will be dependent upon the quality of presentation of the results. A good internal audit report has the power to persuade and to influence action. To this end the internal auditor must rank the production of effective reports as a major objective.

Nothing in the written report should come as a surprise or as a shock to the accountable management.

Objectives of the written report

1. To state the internal auditor's findings, conclusions and recommendations arising from the internal audit examination.
2. To persuade the accountable management as to the validity of the internal audit conclusions and the need for the recommended action:

   (a) by providing assurance where controls are judged to be sound and effective;

(b) by evaluating the impact and materiality of any control weaknesses identified and offering feasible recommendations for appropriate strengthening; and

(c) by evaluating opportunities identified for improving operational economy, efficiency or effectiveness and offering feasible recommendations for exploiting them.

3. To stimulate action by the accountable management to implement the internal audit recommendations.

4. To inform others entitled to know of the result of the internal audit examination.

5. To provide a formal record of each completed internal audit assignment.

Effectiveness

A successful report is one which not only informs recipients of the results of an internal audit examination, but also persuades them of the validity and value of the work done. But most important, it influences the addressee to act in accordance with the recommendations offered.

To achieve successful reporting in these terms, it is necessary to understand that all internal audit findings have five fundamental attributes. These have been defined by IIA in an internal auditing guideline. The internal auditor must keep them firmly in mind throughout the audit examination and especially when drafting the report.

Criteria
The standards, measures, or expectations used in making an evaluation and/or verification (what should exist).

Condition
The factual evidence which the internal auditor found in the course of the examination (what does exist).
If there is a difference between the expected and actual conditions, then:

Cause
The reason for the difference between the expected and actual conditions (why the difference exists).

Effect
The risk or exposure the auditee organisation and/or others encounter because the condition is not the same as the criteria (the impact of the difference).

Action
The reported finding may also include recommendations, auditee accomplishments and supportive information if not included elsewhere.

(Extract from IIA–UK Guideline 430.04.6)

Distribution

The effectiveness of internal auditing depends upon the establishment of mutual respect and good rapport between the internal auditor and the accountable manager. For this reason the internal audit report must be readily recognisable as a personal communication between them. The accountable manager, as the person with authority and responsibility to act on the audit recommendations, is the person to whom it should be addressed.

The accountable manager may also nominate subordinates, to whom he has delegated authority and responsibility for action, to receive a copy of the internal audit report.

In every organisation there will be other persons who, by virtue of their position in the organisation, have authority to influence the action taken on internal audit reports or have a right to know. These are senior managers, the heads of specialist functions, and members of the audit committee.

The pattern for internal audit report distribution should be formally established and made known to all concerned in the organisation. It should define the principles for determining to whom copies of reports should be sent subject to the chief internal auditor's discretion in special circumstances.

Limited distribution may be appropriate when irregularity is suspected.

Internal audit reports are normally copied to the external auditor.

Every internal audit report should disclose its distribution list in full.

Report format

Each organisation adopts a format, style and tone of report appropriate to its own culture. The form may be adapted to match different management tasks within the organisation. For example: a report on treasury operations is likely to take a different perspective from a report on design and development activities.

Reports should present the purpose, scope and results of the audit; and, where appropriate, reports should contain an expression of the auditor's opinion.

(IIA–UK Guideline 430.04)

To incorporate these basic requirements the report is likely to have sections for objectives, findings, conclusions and recommendations and there may also be other features. There follows a detailed list of basic requirements.

Title page

1. The use of a well-designed preprinted cover sheet for the title page helps to support the professional competence of the audit work done.
2. The title page should first show prominently that the document is confidential.
3. It should be clearly laid out with the briefest statement of information necessary to identify the document readily. For example:

   (a) a bold title: 'Internal Audit Report';
   (b) the name of the unit being reported on;
   (c) the date or year of the internal audit examination.

Contents page

1. This page should repeat that the document is confidential.
2. A contents page needs to be clearly laid out to show what is in the document.
3. It should first amplify the information on the title page and then list the key sections of the report and identify them with page numbers.
4. Amplification of title details would include:

   (a) the name of the addressee (the accountable manager);
   (b) the names of all other recipients;
   (c) the name of the unit examined;
   (d) the name of the internal auditor who has done the work;
   (e) the date of the audit visit;
   (f) the date of the report.

5. The list of contents should cover:

   (a) the areas examined (audit coverage);

(b) the detailed findings;
(c) the internal auditor's opinions (audit conclusions);
(d) the recommendations;
(e) management comments received;
(f) a summary or synopsis of the results of the audit;
(g) appendices or exhibits.

Careful thought needs to be given to the sequence in which the contents of the report are presented. Items (a) to (f) shown here are in the logical sequence of the audit process: it is not necessarily the best sequence for reporting them. Indeed, the internal auditor's opinion is often the element of greatest interest to most of the recipients. There is therefore a case for starting with the conclusions page. Alternatively, if a comprehensive but succinct synopsis is presented with each internal audit report, this may well be the page to start with.

The text

The internal audit report is a personal communication from the internal auditor who has examined certain areas of activity to the manager who is accountable for them. It is important that it is recognised as such, and this is probably the most powerful argument for starting the report with the conclusions. When this format is adopted:

1. The first page would be addressed to the accountable manager by name.
2. The internal auditor should then:

   (a) state briefly the purpose of the internal audit assignment;
   (b) list what has been examined;
   (c) state the opinion he or she has formed on each item. Each of these conclusions should be expressed in a single sentence wherever possible and the most important should be stated first.

3. When this form of report is used, the remainder of the report takes the form of supporting schedules. Reference should then be made to the detailed findings and recommendations scheduled in subsequent pages.

4. Reference should be made to the standards of internal auditing practice adopted leading to the conclusions drawn.

5. It is usual to acknowledge the assistance given by auditee staff in the course of the internal audit examination; indeed it would be discourteous not to do so.

6. If further work is believed to be necessary and is feasible as part of the internal audit service this may be offered.

7. Finally, the report should request a formal response.

8. This part of the report should be dated and signed personally by the internal auditor who has done the work or headed the audit team.

Detailed findings

1. The factual evidence on which the internal auditor has based each conclusion reported should be stated in the findings section of the report.

2. Findings should be reported in detail under a heading for each area of audit coverage in the same sequence as they are listed in the first page of the report, described in precisely the same terms and using the same reference numbers.

3. Findings must be factual and must be seen to be reported by the internal auditor as facts. Any tendency to write a judgemental interpretation into a schedule described as 'findings', will not only confuse it will risk destroying the credibility of the entire report: it must be rigorously avoided.

4. Findings should state clearly the situation as found and in sufficient detail to substantiate the conclusions stated. The internal auditor must be able to substantiate all findings reported as facts and should have the relevant evidence readily available in the working papers.

5. Areas found to be well controlled should be fully reported as a basis for reassurance.

6. Reporting on areas with inadequate control should highlight significant deficiencies or weaknesses uncovered and seek to identify the cause.

7. When weakness has been uncovered and brought to the attention of the accountable manager who has acted promptly to eliminate it, the internal audit report should acknowledge the action taken.

8. Wherever appropriate, the findings should be quantified and the sources of evidence identified. For example:

   (a) in a sample of 56 purchase invoices, five, with a total value of £12,560, had been passed for payment without an appropriate authorising signature;

   (b) your bankers paid cheque No.100805 drawn for £500 on 20 December in favour of Smith & Co. notwithstanding that it had not been signed in accordance with your mandate to the bank.

Recommendations

1. As with findings, recommendations should be grouped under audit coverage headings with the same descriptions, sequence and references as appear on the first page of the report.

2. The recommendations should follow logically from the conclusions expressed in the first section of the report.

3. Recommendations must be feasible courses of action. Wherever possible the internal auditor should discuss with the management the realistic options open to it. This involves assessment of risks, both with and without the recommended course of action, and evaluation of the advantages and costs it would entail.

4. The internal auditor should be prepared to demonstrate the justification for all recommendations made. For example:

   (a) showing what can be done;

   (b) showing why it should be done;

   (c) explaining what is needed to implement the recommendation.

The audit report has to convince the accountable manager that the person putting forward the recommendations has seriously considered and genuinely understood the practicalities of the course of action recommended. Even the best researched recommendations can fail to gain acceptance through poor communication. Here again, the internal auditor should remember that an internal audit report is a personal communication to an accountable manager from someone who has been privileged to examine the circumstances closely. The report should reflect this. In presenting recommendations, the use of active language by stating specifically 'who has to do what' is more likely to stimulate the recipient's enthusiasm than the usual passive form of stating what 'should be done'. Using active language also helps to identify the internal auditor more closely with the management objectives.

Management comments

1. Management comments usually relate to the internal audit recommendations and it is reasonable to report them together in the same part of the report if possible. The comments may confirm acceptance of the recommendation and indicate when implementation is to start. In other cases the recommendation may be rejected and the reason given, or an alternative course may be implemented to deal with the problem identified in the findings.

2. Prompt reporting is a fundamental requirement for effective internal auditing and this requirement must not be compromised by waiting for management comments. Every endeavour should be made to finalise these comments in time for inclusion in the report, but if they are unavoidably delayed it is better to issue the report without them.

3. The internal auditor may sometimes be able to present a clear set of recommendations at the exit meeting and the accountable manager may be able to respond in positive terms. The formal report can then record the recommendations as presented at the meeting and the manager's responses as 'Management comment'. This report can then be used as the basis for a committed plan of action, against which progress can be monitored.

4. In other cases, the internal auditor's views may change as a result of additional evidence emerging from discussion at the meeting, or there may be sound reasons for a shift of emphasis. Further, the accountable manager may wish to do some research before giving a firm response to the audit proposals. Such circumstances introduce an element of delay. Even so it is often still feasible to clarify the uncertainties in time to enable the management comments to be incorporated in the final report without delaying it.

Appendices and exhibits

1. Tables of relevant information too extensive to be incorporated in the text should be dealt with as appendices at the end of the report with suitable cross-referencing with the text.

2. Other documents such as photographs, drawings and plans necessary to the report should be listed and suitably cross-referenced as exhibits. Exhibits should be enclosed in a folder which should be securely attached at the end of the report. An index of exhibits should be incorporated as an appendix.

Synopsis

Certain of the recipients of internal audit reports are not ordinarily concerned with the detailed audit findings. This applies particularly to senior management and to members of the audit committee. Their view will be that internal audit findings and recommendations are the proper concern of the accountable operational managers. However, the views formed by internal auditors about the effectiveness of control in operational units may be of considerable importance to senior management and the audit committee.

It is to satisfy this interest that, in some organisations, a summary or synopsis is issued with every internal audit report. It may be a summary of conclusions and recommendations or it may be a synopsis of the conclusions only. Brevity and conciseness are the principal characteristics of a synopsis, which might state the following:

1. Assignment reference number.
2. Unit reported on.

3. Audit date.
4. Internal auditor.
5. Information for each area of coverage:

    (a) the area examined;
    (b) each conclusion in a one-line sentence;
    (c) each recommendation in a one-line sentence;
    (d) abbreviated management comments.

For example:

Coverage:
Purchasing
Conclusions:
Purchasing of goods is well controlled.
Authorisation for procurement of services is inadequate.
You could be paying twice due to lapses in invoice approval.
Recommendations:
Extend goods purchasing procedures to cover services.
Impose an additional supervisory check in invoice approval.
Management comment:
All recommendations accepted.

Report style

Reports should be objective, clear, concise, constructive, and timely.

1. Objective reports are factual, unbiased, and free from distortion. Findings, conclusions and recommendations should be included without prejudice.
2. Clear reports are easily understood and logical. Clarity can be improved by avoiding unnecessary technical language and providing sufficient supportive information.
3. Concise reports are to the point and avoid unnecessary detail. They express thoughts completely in the fewest possible words.
4. Constructive reports are those which, as a result of their content and tone, help the auditee and the organisation and lead to improvements where needed.
5. Timely reports are those which are issued without undue delay and enable prompt effective action.
(IIA–UK Guideline 430.03)

Objectivity

Objectivity is achieved through an unbiased professional attitude on the part of the internal auditor: it is reflected in the writing of the report by dealing with the audited activity and not with the auditor's activity.

Each topic should be dealt with using the auditee's terminology rather than that of internal auditing. The report should be impersonal: it should concentrate on operations and controls and avoid personalities. Above all it should avoid any projection of the internal auditor's personal feelings. The facts must speak for themselves.

The internal auditor should write with authority, but not as an authoritarian. The report should state the objectives and scope of the internal audit assignment in clear and simple terms, to be followed with a straight factual report of the findings, and with interpretation and evaluation of the consequences. Finally, recommendations must be reasonable, practicable and cost effective.

The internal auditor's role is to provide a service to management. To do this effectively requires empathy with the auditee and this needs to be reflected in the report. For example:

1. Present the results of the internal audit examination in a proper perspective related to the total activity of the unit.
2. Avoid exaggeration or overstatement of deficiencies.
3. Report positively on activities found to be adequately controlled and well managed.
4. Acknowledge significant auditee achievements related to the areas subject to audit.
5. Acknowledge circumstances beyond the control of the auditee which have significantly influenced the matters being reported.

Clarity

When an internal audit report is clear and unambiguous, the reader finds it easy to read and can readily grasp its meaning. Every statement must be capable of one interpretation only, the one the internal auditor intended.

It is achieved by coherent paragraphs, logical and

grammatical sentences and the use of the correct words.

Choose words with precise meaning. Words generally used to describe a wide range of circumstances often have meanings which are imprecise or vague. Other words have more than one meaning: this can lead to uncertainty or misunderstanding. Give preference to short, simple words.

Use words correctly. Nouns, adjectives, verbs, adverbs and prepositions all have specific roles in sentence construction; when a familiar word is assigned a different role it confuses the reader. The practice of using nouns or adjectives as verbs and nouns or verbs as adjectives and so on is common in much technical jargon. The internal auditor may not assume that all recipients of the report are familiar with any particular body of jargon and must avoid using it.

Keep sentences short, preferably not more than one idea per sentence. Take care to ensure that all sentences are of sound grammatical construction. In particular the subject and the verb should be immediately identifiable. Special care is necessary to arrange the words and phrases in the most appropriate sequence in the sentence. The purpose of this is twofold: firstly to make the meaning clear and secondly to avoid awkward sentence constructions. Meaning often starts to become obscure when adjectival or adverbial phrases get separated from the words they are intended to qualify.

Arrange the sentences in a logical sequence, each leading on to the next with no missing links hand grouped into paragraphs. Each paragraph should deal with a single topic. It is helpful to use paragraph headings in internal audit reports: they enable the reader to find particular subject matter quickly. Such headings serve as signposts: they should be as short as possible; a single well-chosen word is usually adequate. *The Complete Plain Words* (1986 edn) is a helpful guide to the use of English for civil servants. It contains much that is also relevant to producing clear internal audit reports.

Conciseness

Conciseness is achieved by concentrating on the subject and avoiding irrelevant discussion. It is also necessary to avoid repetition. If detailed expositions are necessary to substantiate the conclusions drawn they should be assigned to the appendices and exhibits at the end of the report.

Tone

Internal audit reports should reflect the role of internal auditing as a specialist service to management. The internal auditor is allowed access to interview the staff and examine the records and operations of the auditee organisation. He or she is expected to apply both general and specialist skills in interpreting the evidence uncovered. The accountable manager is entitled to expect something of value to result from this. It may be in the form of assurance that control is effective in some areas, or of identified weakness which can then be addressed, or in the form of discovered opportunities or risks not previously known about.

To communicate these possibilities most effectively, the internal audit report has to be recognised by the accountable manager as an expert document. That is to say, it has to be perceived as the product of a competent professional who has clearly understood the auditee organisation and has identified with its objectives. This can be achieved in three ways:

1. By reporting findings factually and with due emphasis to reflect their significance to the objectives of the organisation.
2. By presenting conclusions boldly and with appropriate authority for those areas where the internal auditor is expected to be an expert.
3. By offering recommendations which are both sensible and feasible and which have been fully discussed with the auditee management or staff as appropriate.

Findings, conclusions and recommendations should be impersonal and unemotional. The internal auditor's job is to evaluate operations, processes, controls and results objectively. The facts should speak for themselves.

The internal audit report is nevertheless a personal communication from the internal auditor to the accountable manager. It should be signed personally by the internal auditor and addressed to the accountable manager by name. It will also be likely to achieve more impact by using active language whilst at the same time retaining the necessary formality, rather than using passive language forms.

Timeliness

Effective internal auditing depends upon management accepting and acting upon internal audit recommendations. Some management action may result from discussion with the internal auditor in the course of the field work. In most cases, however, the action is the result of implementing the recommendations offered in the formal internal audit report.

There, is therefore, an element of delay between establishing the facts at the time of the internal audit examination and applying the corrective action after receiving the formal report. When the pace of change is escalating rapidly, it becomes increasingly important to keep the interval between fact finding and action to a minimum.

There is a further reason for issuing the written record as soon as is feasible after the internal audit field work. Without the written record, memories tend to fade and recollections become influenced by subsequent events. An internal audit report issued with unreasonable delay forfeits both usefulness and credibility.

The process of preparing and distributing internal audit reports should have a time scale which is both reasonable and practicable. At a maximum this may be within two or three weeks after the end of the field work.

Good internal audit working papers help to ensure the speedy drafting and final distribution of the report. Ideally, the working papers should be so designed as to summarise the results of each section of the work in the form required for the report.

It may then be feasible to have the draft report available for discussion at the exit meeting. In any event the draft report should be in the hands of the accountable manager within one week after the exit meeting.

Management must be allowed reasonable time in which to consider the draft report. It is wise to set a date in a covering memorandum by which time approval should be given. A period of one week is probably reasonable in most cases. Unless the draft report has already been cleared by management, the internal auditor must start pressing for clearance to issue the final report, as soon as the time allowed has expired.

Follow-up

No internal audit assignment can be regarded as complete until all the recommendations offered to the accountable management have either been accepted and fully implemented or carefully considered and consciously set aside.

The internal auditor who issued the report should maintain the follow-up procedure which should be designed to ensure this requirement is fulfilled. In many organisations every operational unit is subject to an annual internal audit visit and a key task in each internal audit assignment is to follow up action and progress in implementing the recommendations from the previous year's internal audit visit. The key elements of an effective follow-up procedure would be:

1. The internal audit charter as approved by top management and notified to all operational managers should make clear that accountable managers who receive an internal audit report are expected to respond formally, stating whether they intend to implement each recommendation or, having assessed the risk, intend not to implement any.

2. Every internal audit report issued should include a request to the accountable manager for a formal response, and a reasonable time interval should be specified for responding.

3. The internal auditor who issued each report should monitor management responses and send reminders where these are slow in coming forth.

4. Management responses to internal audit reports should be distributed to all recipients of the original report.

5. A follow-up visit should be made by an internal auditor within a reasonable time to examine progress in implementing the accepted recom-

mendations. If this visit coincides with the next annual internal audit visit, it is most likely that all accepted recommendations will be fully operational and it will be possible to evaluate the impact.

The report should remain 'open' until all audit points have been resolved by either: effective action on recommendations, or a clear statement by the appropriate level of management of the acceptance of the risk of non-implementation of audit recommendations.

Errors in internal audit reports

If an audit report has been issued and is subsequently found to contain an error of fact, the chief internal auditor should issue an 'amended audit report' highlighting the information being corrected. This should be distributed to all individuals who received the original report.

It must be established how the error occurred and appropriate steps taken to prevent any recurrence.

5 Computer audit

Introduction

Change is a characteristic of the environment we live in. The changes are fundamental, vast and rapid. The development of information technology is crucial in this environment both in stimulating or facilitating other developments and in providing a basis for control.

Management in a changing environment is one of the most exciting and yet most daunting of tasks, because change involves unprecedented opportunities and enormous risks. Sophisticated computer systems provide an indispensable management tool for addressing this challenge.

There is nothing more difficult to plan, more doubtful of success, nor more dangerous to manage than the creation of a new system.

(Niccolo Machiavelli, *The Prince*)

Although Machiavelli expressed this view with respect to statecraft, it is a comment that is particularly apposite when considering computer systems. Computerisation has brought with it a whole series of interlocking new systems which are all built around a technology that is new and unfamiliar to most. There is the computer itself; there is a new environment for processing data; the application systems are all new; the systems for developing new systems are new; the work patterns of all involved with computers are changed, often beyond recognition; and there are new management control systems.

Internal auditors have a key role in assisting management to meet the challenge both by giving assurance where the control is sound and by recommending improvement where it is needed. Computer auditing is therefore a very important and indeed onerous area of responsibility.

A framework for auditing computer systems relating the principal control objectives to the relevant sections in this chapter is given here. The final section deals with using computer technology as an audit tool.

Computer auditing framework

1. **D P management** Ensures that data processing is carried out effectively, efficiently and economically to meet the needs of the business and to comply with the law.

   Section 1: Internal controls in computer systems.
   Section 2: Legal issues.

2. **The D P environment** Ensures that the data processing environment is well controlled, available, secure and has integrity.

   Section 3: Security of computer systems, contingency planning and recovery.
   Section 4: Networks and on-line processing.
   Section 5: Operating systems and systems software.
   Section 6: Database systems.
   Section 7: Microcomputers.

3. **Application systems** Ensure that there is security,

integrity and availability of application systems.

Section 8: System development.
Section 9: Auditing application systems.

4. Auditing techniques Use computer technology as an audit tool.
Section 10: Computer-assisted audit techniques.

Section 1.   Internal controls

Control systems

A control system is a set of procedures designed to facilitate achievement of a management objective:

1. It enables control to be established with predetermined accuracy and frequency.
2. It enables actual performance to be monitored against standard.
3. It enables exceptions to be reported.
4. It enables corrective action to be taken.

The key elements of every effective control system are represented in the table below.

Control systems	Objectives
Setting the standards	Should be predetermined, indicating precision levels and reporting frequency
Recording of actual	Should be routine action in a format that enables comparison with standards
Periodic comparison of actual with standards	Essential if control system is to have meaning. Noncomparison negates the purpose of setting standards
Report exceptions	To report and explain discrepancies between actual and standards
Corrective action	Intervention to restore activity to predetermined standards or Revision of standards for future use in light of current information

Types of corrective action

1. Eliminate the source of error and then report the operation correctly.
2. Take action to ensure that in future things go to plan, but accept that it is not possible to alter what has already happened.
3. Whilst accepting that it is not possible to alter what has already happened, the near future requirements are adjusted so that over a longer period the standards will be achieved.

Internal control techniques

Internal controls are systems established by management:

1. To achieve compliance with management policies.
2. To promote operational efficiency.
3. To safeguard assets.
4. To secure accuracy of records.

Although computerisation has brought with it a change in control techniques, the underlying principles have not changed. Control is achieved through supervision and segregation of duties.

Supervision means that the work of every individual is checked or reviewed by another. Such control is represented by the vertical lines on the organisation chart. With the introduction of computers there is often an upward shift in the lowest level of supervisory control. This may influence the effectiveness of control.

Segregation means that functions are divided up and allocated to departments and duties are allocated among individuals. Such control is represented on an organisation chart by the horizontal lines between departments on the same level.

The principle of segregation should be applied to:

custody of assets
initiation of transactions
authorisation
recording of financial entries
control accounts and reconciliations
sensitive information (need to know basis)
job functions and duties

If satisfactory control can not be achieved by one means of segregation, then another must be considered. Failing this, increased supervision must be applied either personally or through controls programmed into computer systems.

Some forms of segregation are less satisfactory than others. Some have negative side effects such as a reduction of job interest or satisfaction. With the introduction of computers more departments become involved where there was formerly only one user department; for example: data preparation; data control; and computer operations. Consequently there is a need for additional horizontal controls.

It follows that controls which were considered adequate for manual systems often do not provide adequate control when computerised. The effectiveness of supervisory controls may be reduced so that less reliance can be placed upon them. The emphasis on segregation controls such as control totals or validation checks is then increased.

Computerisation often causes a shift in emphasis from supervisory to segregation controls and it brings two additional control benefits:

1. It enables extensive integrity checking to be performed on input data thus improving the quality of the data entering the system, for example: check digit verification; valid transaction type, etc.
2. It introduces new technical controls such as parity bit checking (also called redundancy checking) to ensure the integrity of the magnetic data. Parity bit checking has been incorporated into computers to ensure that data is not distorted during a process. Each Magnetic data representation consists of a number of 0 and 1 bits (binary digits) plus one extra bit known as the parity bit. The purpose of the parity bit is to maintain an even or odd (depending on the computer) number of bits. In the event of bit corruption, deletion or addition, the parity check will detect that the even or odd ratio is no longer present.

   In addition to parity bit checking (also known as vertical redundancy checking) most computers would also utilise longitudinal redundancy checking, diagonal redundancy checking and block and message check sums. Such controls are just not feasible in manual systems.

Classification of controls

Controls can be further classified into preventive, detective or corrective controls.

Preventive controls are those which reduce the frequency with which causes of exposure occur. They are a guide to how things should happen and as such are often passive, with no direct physical activity. Some examples follow.

standards and procedures
employment of high-calibre personnel
segregation of duties
rotation of duties
restriction of sensitive information (need to know)
authorisation
logical access controls (user identity, passwords, keys)
physical access controls (restricted entry, keys)
prenumbered input documents
turnaround input documents
dual custody of keys (physical, logical)
write protect (hardware, software)
preventive hardware maintenance

Detective controls are those which detect an exposure after it has happened. Some examples follow.

supervision
reviews (independent management, audit)
eyeball verification
keystroke verification
validation checks (reasonableness, check digit, duplicates, missing documents, completeness, sequence)
batch control and reconciliation
control totals (including run to run)
exception reporting
redundancy checks (parity bit, longitudinal redundancy)
detectors (fire, smoke, water, temperature, humidity)

Corrective controls are the reaction to the registering of an occurrence. The initial reaction is either to terminate processing or to register the occurrence for subsequent action. Where data is subject to corrective controls it is axiomatic that such data is resubjected to the same preventive and detective controls, or even more stringent controls because of the higher risks associated with such data. The lack of a reaction to a detective control trigger or ineffective or non-existent corrective control is often the Achilles' heel of computer systems and may result in erroneous data never being corrected for re-input or being input incorrectly again. Examples of corrective controls follow.

standards and procedures
error reports
error source statistics
recovery procedures
fire extinguishers
dismiss incompetent personnel
uninterruptible power supply

Cost of controls

Controls cost money and have an impact upon work patterns. It is necessary to set the level of controls commensurate with the level of risk involved and the cost of such controls. It is possible to be overcontrolled as well as undercontrolled and audit should be reporting upon both aspects.

Controls generally cost less, and are usually more effective, if they are designed into systems *ab initio* and not bolted on later as an afterthought. Generally speaking, preventive controls cost the least and corrective controls the most. However, in designing optimum control systems, preventive controls are seldom adequate on their own, so there must be a cost/benefit balance between the preventive, detective and corrective controls.

Computers and control systems

The introduction of computers can enhance the effectiveness of control systems compared with those found in manual systems, provided proper consideration is given to designing such control systems. However, if the control system is poor, a computer system can be a very bad risk.

In considering controls for new computer systems one cannot rely upon what happened, and what was regarded as adequate in earlier systems, whether manual or computer, because there are bound to be differences between the systems.

Consideration also needs to be given to the boring nature of computer control work. In well controlled systems the clerks will spend their time checking data which is usually correct and, as a result, it is difficult to keep high levels of interest and discipline. Consequently, when something goes wrong it may be undetected.

Control should be seen as an overall process within a system, shared between management, the clerical parts of the system and the computer processes. Computer programs and routines may act as a check on data and clerical work, whilst clerks can check computer processes in total. Strengths in either clerical or computer routines may act as a counterbalance to weakness in the other.

However, one of the often overlooked dangers in reviewing computer control systems is that there is a tendency to look at the controls in the computer system in isolation and to ignore the strengths and weaknesses of the controls, or lack of controls, in the wider environment.

The specific impact of computers on control systems includes the following points:

1. Computer systems may produce exactly the same reports and information as their manual predecessors but the controls will be different.
2. Manual systems controls may not be defined or identified as controls and are then overlooked upon computerisation.
3. Systems are sometimes designed by computer specialists with little or no understanding of business and business control systems.
4. End user computing often brings with it a breakdown in controls over the system development process.
5. There is often a loss of audit trail in that there may not be a direct correlation between input and output, e.g. a number of orders may be received from a customer in quantity terms but the invoice will be in financial and quantity terms for what was delivered in a given period.

6. The number of clerical staff involved in handling data tends to be reduced, and often this makes the segregation of duties much more difficult.
7. The automatic nature of computers is sometimes overlooked. Consequently, once information has entered the system there may be inadequate checking thereafter.
8. Although computer processing is consistent, a combination of circumstances may occur which causes inconsistent or inaccurate output.
9. The computer department often processes all aspects of a transaction, e.g. from ordering through invoicing through ledgers to cash payment or receipt.
10. In integrated systems the sheer volume of data processed can be so large that human approximate checking does not occur.

Section 2.   Legal issues

Computer evidence in civil cases

When an organisation is engaged in civil litigation it needs to prove its case using evidence that is legally admissible. The opposing lawyers may ask the judge to exclude any piece of evidence they can argue is not admissible and, if successful, the disputed evidence has to be ignored by the court in coming to its decision.

Section 5 of the Civil Evidence Act 1968 states that computer printouts are admissible as evidence in civil cases providing that certain conditions are satisfied:

1. The printout presented as evidence must have been produced by the computer during a period when it was in regular use to store or to process information for the purposes of any activity regularly carried out over that period.
2. Over the period concerned there should have been regularly supplied to the computer in the ordinary course of the organisation's activities, information of the kind contained in the said printout or of the kind from which the information so contained is derived.
3. Throughout the material part of that period, the computer must have been operating properly.

4. The information contained in the said printout must reproduce or be derived from the information supplied to the computer in the ordinary course of those activities.

Alistair Kelman, a lawyer specialising in computer issues, has suggested that these conditions might present difficulties to contemporary computer users in that they were drafted for use with computers which worked in batch mode and reflect that technology rather than that subsequently developed for on-line systems. He also makes the point that since that legislation, computer programs have become more complex and information may be placed in printouts which is generated automatically by the computer itself.

Despite these limitations in the scope of the legislation, it ought to be possible to provide a statement to the courts confirming that for all practical purposes any printout presented as evidence was produced in accordance with the four requirements stated in the 1968 Act.

Computer evidence in criminal cases

The admissibility of computer evidence in criminal cases is determined by Section 69 of the Police and Criminal Evidence Act 1984. This provides that a statement in a document produced by a computer shall not be admissible as evidence of any fact stated in the document unless it can be shown that:

1. There are no reasonable grounds for believing that the statement is inaccurate because of the improper use of the computer.
2. At all material times the computer was operating properly, or if not, it was not such as to affect the production of the document or the accuracy of its contents.
3. That any relevant conditions specified in Rules of Court are satisfied.

Part II of Schedule 3 to the Act states the rules for presenting computer evidence. This requires the production in court of a certificate:

(a) identifying the document containing the statement and describing the manner in which it was produced;

(b) giving such particulars of any device involved in the production of that document as may be appropriate for the purpose of showing that the document was produced by a computer;

(c) dealing with any of the matters mentioned in sub-section (1) of section 69; and

(d) purporting to be signed by a person occupying a responsible position in relation to the operation of the computer.

The expression 'occupying a responsible position in relation to the operation of the computer' in subparagraph (d) above suggests that the certificate should not be provided by the internal auditor even if he is providing other evidence. In a large organisation with a mainframe system, a senior data processing official should provide the information. In the case of a microcomputer system the 'best' person to provide the certificate might be the user who manages the system.

The same criteria would apply for selecting the appropriate person to produce evidence regarding the proper operation of the computer for civil cases.

It is sufficient for any statement in this context to be made in the best of the knowledge and belief of the person making it. Such a certificate is acceptable evidence but the court may also require additional oral evidence which would involve cross-examination of the provider of the certificate.

Anyone making a statement in a certificate which he knows to be false or does not believe to be true is guilty of an offence punishable by imprisonment or a fine of up to £2,000 or both.

The weight to be attached to evidence from a computer is also covered by Schedule 3. Greater weight is to be given to information recorded on a computer at the time of the event than to data entered later. This is consistent with the court's attitude to witnesses who may refresh their memories by referring to notes made contemporaneously but not to those made later.

Also, less weight would be given to computer evidence where the person supplying that information to the computer or concerned with its operation had any incentive to conceal or misrepresent the facts.

The Data Protection Act 1984

Principal objectives

The Data Protection Act introduced completely new requirements for computer users in the United Kingdom. Its principal provisions are:

1. It is concerned with the protection of personal data and requires all personal data to be processed in accordance with principles defined in the Act.
2. Organisations processing personal data need to register that fact with a Data Protection Registry and may then only process the registered data in accordance with the terms of registration.
3. Any individual may inspect the register, find out whether an organisation holds personal data on him or her and, subject to certain exceptions, request to see the data held. If the data held is inaccurate, the data subject may take steps to have it corrected or erased.

Key definitions

A data user is a person who 'holds' data. This may be an individual or bodies such as partnerships or companies. For data to be 'held':

1. The data should be held for processing by the data user 'by equipment operating automatically in response to instructions given for that purpose'. This can cover printed material to be read by optical character readers and microfilm processed under the control of a microprocessor in addition to data processed by a computer.
2. The data user has control of the contents and the use of the data concerned.
3. The data is in the form in which it has been or is to be processed.

Processing personal data covers amending, deleting or rearranging the data and extracting the information contained in the data by reference to the data subject. It excludes straightforward text processing using word processors.

Personal data is data on a living individual who can be identified from the data itself or other information held. It may include expressions of opinion but it does not include intentions.

Main provisions

Here is a brief summary of the main sections of the Act. Readers should refer to the specified sections of the Act for specific details.

The Data Protection Act 1984 requires a data user who holds and processes personal data to register that fact with a data protection registry. There are, however, exemptions, some of which apply only if the personal data is of limited types or used in limited ways, so it is important to refer to the specific wording of the Act. Exemptions from registration may include:

1. Personal data which is exempt for the purposes of safeguarding national security (section 27).
2. Personal data held for payroll purposes only (section 32).
3. Accounting data (section 32).
4. Personal data which is already public information (section 34).
5. Other exemptions include personal data held by an individual concerned with his personal, family or household affairs or only held for recreational purposes; personal data held by an incorporated club relating to members of the club; and personal data held for distribution purposes.

   In each case, the data subjects should have been asked and should have not objected to the holding of the data.
6. Data which is processed only outside the United Kingdom and not used or intended to be used within the United Kingdom.

Data protection principles

The data protection principles which are consistent with those defined by the European Convention are specified in paragraphs 1 and 2 of the Schedule to the Act as follows:

1. The information to be contained in personal data must be obtained and the personal data processed fairly and lawfully.
2. Personal data shall be held only for one or more specified and lawful purposes.
3. Personal data held for any purpose or purposes shall not be used or disclosed in any manner incompatible with that purpose or those purposes.
4. Personal data held for any purpose or purposes shall be adequate, relevant and not excessive in relation to that purpose or those purposes.
5. Personal data shall be accurate and, where necessary, kept up to date.
6. Personal data held for any purpose or purposes shall not be kept for longer than is necessary for that purpose or those purposes.
7. An individual shall be entitled:

   (a) at reasonable intervals, and without undue delay or expense, to be informed by any data user whether he holds personal data of which that individual is the subject and to be allowed access to any such data held by a data user; and

   (b) where appropriate, to have such data corrected or erased.
8. Appropriate security measures shall be taken against unauthorised access to, or alteration, disclosure, or destruction of, personal data and against accidental loss or destruction of personal data.

Control of personal data

Information contained in personal data must be obtained and processed fairly and lawfully. There must be no deception as to its purpose. (Principles 1 and 2)

Registered personal data may only be used for the lawful purpose for which it has been registered. It must not be disclosed or used in any way which is incompatible with that purpose. (Principle 3)

This constraint may not prevent disclosure in certain cases:

1. Disclosure to the data subject or to a person acting on his behalf, or where permission has been given by the data subject (section 34(b)).
2. Disclosure to the servant or agent of the data subject (section 34(b)).
3. Disclosure for the purpose of safeguarding national security (section 27).
4. Where nondisclosure might prejudice the prevention or detection of crime, apprehension or prosecution of offenders, assessment or collection of any tax or duty (section 28(3)).

5. Disclosure for the purpose of preventing injury or other damage to a person's health (section 34(8)).
6. Cases where the law or a court order requires disclosure (section 34(5)).
7. Certain exemptions relating to payroll and accounting data (section 32).
8. Disclosure of anonymous statistical data (section 33(b)).

Personal data can only be held for registered purposes and it must be adequate and relevant and not excessive for that purpose. This information must be accurate and where necessary kept up to date, and it must not be held any longer than is necessary for the purpose for which it is held. (Principles 4, 5 and 6)

Right of access

The data subject can find out from the register the data registered by data users and request within 40 days a copy of any data held on him or her. Such requests must be in writing and be accompanied by the relevant fee. (Principle 7)

Exemptions from this right of subject access include:

1. Data exempt from the Act.
2. Data held to safeguard national security; for prevention or detection of crime; for apprehension or prosecution of offenders; or for assessment or collection of tax or duty (section 27).
3. Data which might prejudice the regulation of financial services (section 30).
4. Data accessible under other legislation; for example: Consumer Credit Act.
5. Back-up data (section 34(4)).

Security

The data holder must adopt appropriate security measures to protect the personal data held, against unauthorised or accidental access or corruption. (Principle 8)

When determining what are 'appropriate security measures' the data user should consider:

1. The nature of the data.

2. The risks of harm from unauthorised access, etc.
3. The level of physical and logical access controls.
4. The measures taken for ensuring the reliability of staff having access to the data.

A data subject can require rectification or erasure of erroneous data.

Registration procedures

The Data Protection Registrar maintains a public register of data users holding personal data and computer bureaux providing services involving the processing of personal data. The Act applies to England, Wales, Scotland and Northern Ireland and requires registration from data users who process personal data within the United Kingdom. (Section 4)

The particulars required to be registered using the forms provided are:

1. The name and address of the data user.
2. A description of the personal data to be held by him and of the purpose or purposes for which the data are to be held or used.
3. A description of the sources of the data.
4. A description of persons to whom the data will be disclosed.
5. The names or a description of any countries or territories outside the United Kingdom to which the data may be transferred.
6. The addresses for the receipt of requests from data subjects for access to the data.

The Registrar can refuse registrations where he considers that insufficient information has been provided or that the applicant is likely to contravene any of the principles.

Data protection audit

The audit of compliance with the data protection principles and the legislation has the following objectives:

1. To confirm that the current registered particulars cover all personal data held and that an effective system is in place to ensure that registration is amended as systems change.

2. To confirm that the person responsible for Data Protection has taken steps to make all members of staff aware of their obligations under the Act.

3. To confirm that the organisation has set up adequate procedures to comply with the requirements for dealing with subject access requests, including procedures:

(a) to verify the identity of the requester;
(b) to deal with requests or instructions for the rectification or erasure of data.

4. To review data held and the applications which process it in order to ensure that it is obtained, held and processed in accordance with the data protection principles. This aspect may be taken into account when conducting application audits or in the case of Principle 8 (security) as part of a security review.

Section 3.   Security

Computer security risks

Evaluating security risks is extremely difficult, both in terms of assessing the likelihood of occurrence and quantifying the potential impact of financial loss, loss of control, fraud, additional costs, etc.

The three key elements in any data processing system are availability, security and integrity. Most managers seem to be concerned as to the integrity of data processed, but are often unaware of the importance of the other two elements. Perhaps this emphasis can be explained by a familiarity with the double entry balancing controls of manual systems and early batch control systems where it was relatively easy to reconcile inputs and outputs.

Security is a corporate concern: it requires positive support and action by top management. A lack of awareness at board level of the risks and threats to the organisation due to increasing reliance upon data processing could have far-reaching dire consequences. Even so, there is often a lack of management awareness of the scale of the risks attributable to lax security. This has led to a situation where the security protection provided for many computer installations is totally inadequate or ineffective.

In Peat Marwick McLintock's *Access Control Software Survey*, only one in four of the organisations responding had a security policy and only one-third of these were supported at board level.

In an EEC-funded study into *The Security of Network Systems in Europe*, Coopers and Lybrand found controls over telecommunications to be, on average, below acceptable levels. Controls over the administration of security, microcomputers and contingency planning were also found to be inadequate. Most of the other categories reviewed were considered borderline.

Yet, in most cases, management had confidence in the level of computer security provided. This low level of awareness of computer risks amongst general managers tends to permeate through to all aspects of information technology within organisations. The lack of awareness is apparent not only among individual managers using computers as a management tool, but also at corporate level.

These and other studies confirm that management is not sufficiently aware of the risks of increasing dependence, and seemingly unaware of the importance of availability of data processing systems. Management's reluctance to allocate a budget for computer security which is commensurate with the threats to the organisation demonstrates its lack of full recognition of the risks involved.

This ominous state of affairs reflects a rapid escalation in the scale of risk attributable to reliance on computer systems due to increasing computerisation, compounded by progress in on-line transaction processing. It also reflects misplaced confidence in outgrown protective measures.

There may well be a belief among management that it will only happen to someone else. There is also a lack of reliable information available on the losses attributable to computer incidents: we have only guesstimates extrapolated from small survey samples.

Probably the greatest challenge to be addressed by internal auditors is a need to focus management attention on the scale of threats to the organisation from computer security risks. Management's lack of recognition of the significance of these threats may be partly due to communication problems associated with the explosive growth rate of information technology. It is a practical science which has become a powerful tool of management. The experts in this practical science have some responsibility to educate the users so as to enable them to appreciate both the benefits and the risks, and to be in a position to assess the impact of both.

Those in the vanguard of this particular development have had to create a sophisticated language for communicating complex ideas among themselves: this is the language of computer jargon. There is a clear need to explain these ideas to practical managers so that they can be put to practical use. Such explanations will usually be long and laborious because they must involve detailed translation into everyday language, of concepts which are often complex but which the expert can readily recall through a single word or phrase of jargon.

Often the potential benefits perceived from computerisation generate pressure for progress at a speed which does not allow time for full comprehension of the technology. When such pressure is given way to, the inherent risks can remain obscured in a fog of ignorance and misconceptions.

Security is a people problem. People cause breakdowns in security that should concern us; but more important, lack of management awareness leads to lax or non-existent security: weak security is also a people problem.

Security control areas

Security policy

1. Is there a formal documented security policy?
2. Are the responsibilities for security clearly defined?
3. Is there a security awareness programme?
4. Does security enjoy the full support of senior management, with its own budget?
5. Is compliance with the policy monitored?
6. Does non-compliance with the policy lead to possible disciplinary action?
7. Is the security policy regularly reviewed?

Physical security

Location

1. Is the site free from natural hazards or is there adequate protection against them?
2. Is there protection from vandalism etc.?
3. Are windows eliminated or protected?
4. Are doors protected?
5. Are services protected?
6. Are there security guards?
7. Is surveillance equipment provided?

Building

1. Is it structurally sound?

Power

1. Is there a reliable, clean supply?
2. Is there protection from voltage changes, power surges, etc.?
3. Has the power supplier been informed that there is a computer on the line?
4. Is there an emergency power supply available?

Air conditioning

1. Is the air conditioning exclusive to the computer area?
2. Are the temperature and humidity recorded and monitored?
3. Does the environmental control pertain for 24 hours?
4. Is there an alarm system for exceeding operational parameters?
5. Is the equipment regularly serviced?
6. Is standby air conditioning equipment installed? Is it adequate? Is it regularly tested?
7. Are the air intakes protected?

Other services

1. Is there a telephone line independent of the main switchboard?
2. Is the computer suite kept clean and tidy?
3. Is there a ban on food and drink and if so is it effective?

Fire

1. Is there a fire prevention programme?
2. Are fire resistant materials used for furnishings and fitments?
3. Do the fire walls extend to true ceiling and true floor?
4. Are the fire doors to correct rating?
5. Are fire officers appointed and trained?
6. Are fire drills held regularly? Do they comply with legislation?
7. Is fire protection provided to BS6266?
8. Has a fire detection system been installed with smoke and heat detectors?
9. Which fire quenching system has been installed: Halon, CO2 or water? Is it set to automatic? (except CO2). Does it require two-knock activation?
10. Are portable fire extinguishers of the correct type provided? Have staff been trained in their use?
11. Are fire alarms linked to security? fire brigade? third party? Is there 24-hour protection? Are the alarms regularly tested?
12. Are the power supply and air conditioning automatically closed down on fire alarm activation?
13. Is smoking prohibited?

Water

1. Is the building below ground level?
2. Are water detectors installed? Are they regularly tested? Are they linked to alarms? Is there 24-hour protection?
3. Are flood control pumps installed?
4. Is there provision for drainage of floor voids?
5. Is there a water-resistant sealed ceiling or roof?
6. Are the doors and windows watertight?
7. Are there any water pipes in the computer room?
8. Is the computer room protected from leaking water pipes and tanks elsewhere in building?

Physical access control

1. Is the organisation a target for vandals or extremists?

2. Is there a 24-hour guard?
3. Are only authorised personnel permitted access?
4. Is access controlled by badge, key, biometric, password?
5. Are employees trained to challenge strangers?
6. Are intruder devices fitted, e.g. alarms, detectors, CCTV? Is there 24-hour protection? Are alarms linked to security? police? third party?
7. Are passwords changed frequently?
8. Is there adequate control over badges, keys, etc.?
9. Are visitors restricted? logged? escorted?
10. Are engineers and cleaners controlled and supervised?
11. Are ex-employees prohibited access?

Network security

Terminals

1. Is access to terminals and networked personal computers restricted to authorised employees?
2. Is access controlled by hardware (cards, badges, keys etc.) or by software (passwords)?
3. Are the actions permitted at each terminal defined and controlled by computer?
4. Is all terminal activity logged and reviewed by management?

Communications

1. Are alternative communications facilities available in the event of line failure?
2. Is confidential and high security data encrypted for transmission?

Logical access control

1. Is a valid identifier and password required before on-line access is permitted?
2. Are passwords: unique to individuals; nondisplayed; minimum length (6–8 characters); forced expiration (30 days, but dependent on system); one way encrypted; user changed; flip-flopping prohibited; removed immediately for leavers?
3. Are users prohibited from using favourite passwords? Are users instructed on the requirement

for sensible passwords? Are password tables securely protected?

4. Are users restricted in what they can access and the type of access (read, write, update, delete)? Are the restrictions regularly reviewed?
5. What is the policy relating to security and confidentiality of passwords and are users aware of it?
6. Are all log-on violations logged; monitored; and reviewed?
7. Are all default and demonstration passwords removed?
8. Is the use of powerful passwords monitored?

Data security

1. Are regular back-up copies taken of data files, programs and systems software?
2. Are back-up copies moved off site quickly?

Contingency planning

At the start of this section we identified availability, security and integrity as the three key elements in any data processing system. We have considered security, which relates to management's actions to reduce the likelihood of a disaster happening. Disaster may mean anything from the loss of a computer file to the total destruction of an organisation's data processing facility.

We now consider availability of data processing, which relates to the ability of an organisation to continue all or part of its data processing activity irrespective of any incident or disaster.

A 1988 UK survey found that 84 per cent of the organisations had no budget for contingency planning, 56 per cent had no disaster recovery plan, and 62 per cent had no back-up facility. Despite the high dependence of most organisations on their computer systems, contingency planning continues to be the Cinderella of computer security. Where action is taken, it all too often only extends as far as signing a contract with a back-up facility. There is no underlying disaster recovery plan to support it and most organisations fail even to take up the free testing at the back-up facility.

The first step in the disaster recovery planning process is for senior management to realise that disaster recovery planning is not a data processing technical problem of wheeling in another black box. It is a corporate problem which needs the full commitment of all management to achieve success.

The next step is to conduct a business impact review in order to assess the likely impact upon the organisation of different types of disaster. Having identified those systems that are critical to the well-being of the organisation, a disaster recovery strategy can be formulated. Then the disaster recovery plan should be developed and documented. The plan should be tested and refined and procedures established to maintain it.

Business impact review

This is designed to assess the impact on an organisation of various disaster scenarios which reduce or curtail the data processing activities over various time-scales. It should identify those areas of the business which rely heavily upon data processing, and would, therefore, be seriously affected by a disaster. It thus provides information on the level of disaster recovery planning required. This review should cover:

1. Critical applications: those that are critical to the well-being of the organisation, e.g. cash flow.
2. Disruption time scales: ascertain impact over various time scales (say, day, week, two weeks, one month).
3. Probability of disaster: identify the probabilities of disaster occurring (say, very likely to extremely unlikely).

Types of impact

1. Lost sales: unable to process and/or ship product.
2. Reduced manufacturing capability: unable to manufacture product and, in the longer term, unable to design new product lines.
3. Impaired cash flow and profitability: reduced revenue with increased costs.

4. Increased overtime, expenses, temporary staff costs: to cope with extra work required.
5. Increased inventory levels: 'just in time' systems.
6. Interest payments: incurred on bank loans or overdrafts.
7. Increased debt levels: inability to recover debts, credit check, etc.
8. Impaired credit status: inability to pay bills, possible refusal of vendors to continue supplying.
9. Increased risk of fraud: loss of control of computer systems leaves them vulnerable to fraud.
10. Invocation of penalty clauses: for nondelivery of goods or services.
11. Customer dissatisfaction: potential loss of market share.
12. Loss of information: reduced ability to make business decisions.
13. Devaluation of company image, falling share price.
14. Increased market vulnerability: possible take-over target.
15. Legal implications: Companies Act, Data Protection Act, Financial Services Act, VAT, etc.

Disaster recovery strategy

From the business impact review, the minimum data processing requirements in terms of hardware, software and telecommunications can be ascertained for the critical applications.

The disaster recovery strategy can now be formulated which encompasses both the short- and long-term requirements of the organisation. There are a number of alternative strategies that can be adopted, either on their own or combined. An organisation may choose to use a hot site for immediate back-up followed by use of a cold site a week later, when it has been set up. Not unexpectedly, the hotter the back-up site, the quicker data processing can recommence and the more expensive it is.

Reciprocal agreement

This is an agreement with another site which has compatible equipment. Whilst this may, at first sight, appear to be an inexpensive alternative, it seldom works in practice. In order for them to work, both sites must maintain full compatibility of hardware and software and must have sufficient spare capacity available to accommodate all or the critical part of the other's processing. Testing may also prove to be difficult to achieve.

Cold start standby

Cold start can range from having an empty shell, or a shell which has services such as power and telecommunications installed, to Portacabin units. When a disaster occurs, the equipment suppliers are contacted to obtain replacement hardware. The setting up of such a facility could take from one week to a month, depending on the vendors. Testing will also prove to be difficult to achieve.

Warm start standby

Using a bureau or a mobile facility (fully equipped caravan computer centre) can have the advantages of immediate availability (within 24 hours for mobile) and the economy of only having to pay for the time used. However, long-term processing at a bureau is very expensive and may not be available at short notice.

Hot start standby

Hot start means a fully equipped facility on continuous standby. This may be provided in-house or through a company specialising in the provision of such facilities. This can be a very expensive option.

Disaster recovery plan

The disaster recovery plan must set out clearly to those responsible for the recovery process:

what to do
how, when and where to do it
what resources are available
where those resources are located

Format for a disaster recovery plan

Introduction

1. The purpose and scope of the recovery plan.
2. Recovery policy.
3. Schedule of critical applications.
4. Responsibility schedules.

Plan activation

1. Detection of the disaster.
2. Notification to management.
3. Damage assessment.
4. Activation of recovery procedures.
5. Invocation of alternative processing facilities.

Recovery Team

1. Membership.
2. Objectives.
3. Action checklists.
4. Critical resources and vital records lists.

Testing

1. Testing summary: It is essential to test that the plan actually works. The time to find this out is not at the time of the disaster. Testing may be conducted by the 'big bang' approach or through module testing.

    The important point is that all aspects of the plan are tested over a reasonable time scale and that a post-mortem of every test is conducted and the plan amended accordingly.

Maintenance

1. Responsibility
2. Procedures

The plan should be regularly reviewed to take into account changes within the organisation relating to data processing and disaster recovery.

Vital records for invocation

1. Alternative site location(s).
2. Off site data storage location(s).
3. Staff contact lists.
4. User contact lists.
5. Critical resources checklists.
6. Supplier contact lists for: hardware; software; communications; consumables; services; local authorities; insurance; and emergency services.

Section 4.   On-line processing and networks

The nature of on-line systems and networks

On-line systems

On-line systems may have one or more of the following features:

1. On-line enquiry system permitting the operator of an on-line terminal to access stored data.
2. On-line data entry permitting the operator to enter individual transactions for transmission to the central computer for editing, validation and update on an overnight basis.
3. On-line data entry with real-time update permitting the operator to enter individual transactions for editing, validation and immediate update of master files.

Computer networks

Networked systems are comprised of communications software with associated hardware and circuitry.

Communications software includes the main networking software which drives the communication system and handles the data traffic. It also maintains protocols which are sets of standards to ensure that data moves efficiently within the network. Message distribution software which sends messages to users, logging software which provides management information on the performance of the network, back-up and restart procedures, and validation routines are all elements of communications software.

Communications hardware includes devices such as visual display units, printer terminals, electronic point-of-sale tills (EPOs) and automated teller machines (ATMs). Some systems also use a front-end processor to control the network. It then carries out activities such as message scheduling, receipt of messages from the mainframe and directing messages to the appropriate terminals.

Networked systems may be centralised or distributed. Centralised networks involve a number of remote terminals which are connected through the network to a single computer. All terminals then use the same applications. Alternatively, distributed networks provide facilities for linking several remote computers together: each of these may have terminals connected to them. Terminals in a distributed network may have access to all the computers within the network.

Network controls

The key control issues of interest to the auditor are:

1. Control over messages including:

   (a) authorisation;
   (b) validation;
   (c) security of data leading to successful message delivery; This control objective also includes accountability, which means ensuring the accepted message reaches its appointed destination at the intended time without loss or corruption.
   (d) provision of an audit trail.

2. Adequate back-up and recovery facilities.
3. Effective provision for security of the network.

Auditing networked systems

When auditing a computer network the control objectives should be as follows:

1. To ensure that the security, integrity and availability of the network is safeguarded.
2. To ensure that the design of the network is effective, efficient and economic.
3. To ensure that the network is operated effectively and efficiently.

The first of these objectives is a fundamental audit issue and the approach to the audit should be:

1. Obtain a detailed understanding of the network by identifying its hardware, software and circuitry so understanding the nature and purpose of its component parts.
2. Establish the purposes for which the network is used to identify the key business objectives of the network and the degree of risk which exists especially in relation to the types of data transmitted and held within the network.
3. Carry out a systems review to examine the level of control over messages, back-up and recovery

and security of the network. Such a review should also consider the duties and responsibilities of the network controller.

4. Carry out tests, where appropriate, to confirm whether the controls established are operating efficiently and effectively.
5. Report on the results of the review.

To meet the control objective relating to the effectiveness, efficiency and economy of the network design, stages 1 and 2 would be followed by a review of the performance data relating to the network.

Control over messages

1. Control over message authorisation includes:

   (a) Controls to ensure that the message has been initiated at an authorised terminal. These include physical and logical means, polling terminals included in a table of authorised terminals or automatic redialling by the computer to the terminal to confirm that it is known and acceptable to the system.

      The controls may also include those to ensure that only certain authorised activities are carried out at specific terminals.

   (b) Controls to ensure that the operator is authorised to transmit the message. These include physical controls such as locating terminals in lockable rooms and the use of terminal locks, badges or tokens to gain access.

2. Logical controls will be largely based on passwords. Access control is normally achieved by the operating system, specialist systems software or within application systems. Logical controls should consist of means to identify the operator and the access rights given to him or her. Thus, a user may be granted permission: to read data only; to update data; or to delete data; and the system may need to grant different access rights for different types of data.

When the system rejects a terminal or a user, it

may: merely reject; reject and report; or disable the connection and report. All activity should be logged, both valid and invalid.

Password controls

1. Passwords should be a minimum of 4 characters, and preferably 6–8 characters: the longer the password, the more difficult it will be to guess it.
2. Passwords should not be easily guessable and the practice of alternating between two passwords should be avoided.
3. Passwords should be changed periodically, the frequency depending on the risks. Password attempts should be restricted so that after a defined number of unsuccessful attempts to 'sign on', the terminal should automatically shut down.
4. There should be a defined control procedure for dealing with users who forget their passwords.

Message validation

Validation checks should confirm that the correct message has been received, that it is valid and comes from a valid address. The system should preferably acknowledge the receipt and validation of the message to the originator.

Security of data

Successful message delivery depends upon security of data controls. The purpose of these controls is to ensure that:

1. All messages are delivered and accounted for.
2. Messages have not been fraudulently altered, duplicated, accelerated or delayed.
3. The origin and destination of the message are valid points for the type of message.

Various means may be used to achieve these control objectives. They include: encryption; sequence number allocation; and checking and control totals. Multiple copies of messages need to be stored to ensure accountability if a device fails.

Audit trail

The auditor should undertake tests to ensure that there is an adequate audit trail which identifies:

1. The source of each transaction or message.
2. The operator involved.
3. The date and time of input.
4. The sequence number involved.
5. The message; any errors recorded; and whether the message is original or a duplicate.

Back-up and recovery

Adequate back-up and recovery procedures are necessary to minimise downtime whenever there is a failure of all or part of a communications system.

Back-up diciplines

The auditor should consider three key areas:

1. Messages in transit. The software should be capable of identifying which messages were in the system and the status of all transmissions.
2. Historical logs. Retrieval files and message logs should be protected from corruption or destruction.
3. Line monitoring. Network control should monitor and record: the status of all communication lines and terminals; any short term re-routing to other terminals; and error statistics relating to line failures.

Recovery procedures

Recovery procedures should be fully documented and should cover: terminal devices; other hardware; software; and line failures. Checkpoint disciplines and restart procedures should also be fully documented.

Security of the network

The reviews of control over messages and back-up and recovery will have addressed many of the issues relating to the security of the network.

To complete the security review, the auditor should consider the threats, the level of risk, and the control measures in place for protection against:

1. Line tapping (for example: test keys and encryption).
2. Line break-in (for example: encryption).

3. Monitoring radio frequency radiation (for example: shielding to 'tempest' standards).

Section 5.   Systems software

The nature of systems software

Operating systems

An operating system is the software which in advanced systems performs key processing management functions such as: resource allocation; job scheduling; multiprogramming; controlling access; and recording activity on the system.

An operating system normally consists of a principal control module which is resident in the core storage and subsidiary program modules which are called in to an area of core storage as required. Operating systems also interface with other specialist systems software such as data communications software, database management software, and access control software.

Systems programmers

Modern operating systems need to be customised or configured to the specific computer installation in which they run. The highly technical nature of this work has led to the creation of specialist groups of technical support staff, often known as systems programmers. Their duties include:

1. Initial installation of the operating system.
2. Subsequent maintenance or update.
3. Monitoring and fixing operating systems software problems.
4. Developing additional software routines to deal with certain conditions which arise, such as writing 'user exit' routines where faults occur.
5. Monitoring and optimising the performance of the software.

Implementation and maintenance of operating systems software involves significant risks. Systems programmers use powerful tools and have special capabilities. They may need to have access to all application systems and the ability to by-pass normal installation controls. If their work is ineffective, insecure or inefficient serious damage is likely to result. It is therefore important that additional controls are exercised over this work and this is of special concern to auditors.

Auditing systems software

The audit approach should be based on a review of the operating systems facilities: the way in which they have been customised, and an evaluation of the extent to which they meet the key control objectives:

1. The operating system should provide adequate security for the programs and data processed and stored by the computer.
2. The integrity of the operating system as specified by the vendor should be maintained.
3. The security, reliability and availability of the operating system should be safeguarded.
4. Maintenance of the operating system should be controlled, meaning that changes may only be made under proper control.
5. There must be adequate controls over the development and amendment of all systems software including the operating system.
6. There must exist adequate controls over the use of systems software.

Auditing system programming activity

This is a high-risk area. Systems programmers have the ability to carry out tasks prohibited to other programmers and to by-pass some security systems. The audit review of systems programmer activities should include an evaluation of the controls exercised over them. There should be firm supervisory controls; for example:

1. Management control over work plans, including segregation of duties to restrict knowledge or sphere of operation.
2. Involvement of two people in sensitive activities, supervisory checks, spot checks and peer review.
3. Insistence that the manufacturer's standard system support utilities must be used whenever carrying out any changes to operating systems.
4. Standards of documentation which ensure the creation of a complete audit trail of work undertaken.
5. Controls to detect and prevent any unauthorised

use of utilities programs which can modify data, programs or systems software without leaving an audit trail.

6. Systems which will ensure that file reconciliations or program testing are performed, whenever 'fixes' have been applied to data and programs, in order to confirm their effectiveness and propriety.

7. Restrictions on access to data files and systems on a 'need to know' basis.

Section 6.   Database systems

The nature of database systems

Definitions

A database system is one in which data is held as a central resource and independently of a number of applications which share the data. Such data is then available to all authorised users of these applications. This feature distinguishes database systems from other computer systems in which each application has its own discrete data files.

A database management system is an essential feature of every database system. It is a sophisticated software system which handles the data transfer requirements. It also controls access to the data and updating allowing access to one or more authorised users at the same time.

A schema is the structure of a database as defined by the database management system. The view of the database from each application program is known as a subschema.

Advantages of a database system

1. Data is held once only, so redundancy is avoided.
2. Updating of data is facilitated – there is only one version of the data to be updated. Inconsistency is eliminated and accuracy is more readily achieved.
3. Access control is facilitated through restricting access by schema or subschema to fields of data. Different types of access can be accommodated, for example: 'read only' or 'write'.
4. Use of a data dictionary in conjunction with a database should improve documentation and control over the structure of the database.
5. Program maintenance time and effort should be reduced since there is no need to amend all application programs which deal with the data.
6. Data storage requirements are reduced.
7. Recovery facilities are improved because, when processing errors are detected, the system can restore the database to its last intact state.

Disadvantages of a database system

1. It is costly to acquire the software package and to recruit trained and experienced staff.
2. The vulnerability of the organisation is increased due to a high degree of dependence on database management software and the database administration.
3. Processing may be more time consuming than with conventional file structures and therefore less efficient.

Key features of a database

Database management software

The database management software, together with the operating system and other systems software, provides the interface between the computer application and the data. Its functions are as follows:

1. To create and maintain the database.
2. To store and retrieve data in response to requests from application programs.
3. To provide recovery procedures, and security and privacy over the data held.

Database management software should have certain key components:

1. A data description language describing the schema (physical description of the database) and sub-schema (representation of data items for use by application programs).
2. A data manipulation language used by application programs to access the database.
3. A query language.
4. Recovery and reorganisation procedures and integrity routines.
5. Data lock-out facilities to prevent two applications accessing data simultaneously.
6. A data dictionary of data items.

Data dictionary

The data dictionary holds details of data items such as the following:

1. Field names and synonyms.
2. Field size, format and how held, for example: clear form; encrypted; compacted.
3. Field description.
4. Relationships between data field and other data items.
5. Data sources.
6. Names of programs or persons able to read data; amend data; delete data; validate data.
7. Validation rules for the field of data.
8. Owner of the data.

The data dictionary system will probably include a suite of programs to update, maintain and control the data dictionary although these operations could be manually based.

Database administrator

The database approach, with its view of data as an independent resource, necessitates a co-ordinating and controlling role. This may be dealt with by an individual or a small team responsible for the integrity of the database. The responsibilities of the database administrator (or team) should be clearly defined, as follows:

1. Define the ownership of data and decide who shall have access rights, and for what purpose.
2. Mediate between users and resolve conflicts regarding formats, access, privileges.
3. Control the design and maintenance of schema and subschema.
4. Apply integrity controls over the database.
5. Set standards for back-up and recovery
6. Set database documentation standards and monitor compliance.
7. Implement security controls and monitor access violations.
8. Monitor the effect of program changes and consider their effects on data held.

This gives wide powers to the database administrator and increases risks associated with dependence on one person with wide ranging opportunities for fraud or abuse. There must therefore be:

(a) effective supervision of his or her activities;
(b) limitations on his or her activities to ensure they include no authority or responsibility for any transaction processing.

Data integrity

Within a database system, all application programs which use the data place great reliance on the completeness and accuracy of data held. Validation or verification of data is crucial. Proper authorisation of transactions, and the availability of an audit trail, are essential.

Procedures should be in place to ensure that once data is in the database it is not lost or corrupted. Most database management software systems incorporate integrity checking routines. These are, however, likely to be costly on time resources, so judgement needs to be made on the frequency of running them. Run-to-run controls as used on nondatabase systems are not suitable.

Certain disciplines are necessary to ensure completeness and accuracy:

1. Dump data to tape on a regular basis for back-up and recovery purposes.
2. Send periodical printouts of portions of the database to users for verification.
3. Log all transactions to the database and record 'before' and 'after' images of the record so that in the event of a malfunction, the database can be restored to its previous balanced state.
4. Maintain counts of data segments on the database and compare them with totals maintained by application programs.

Auditing database systems

The stages in auditing database systems may be similar to those for auditing other systems. There are, however, some key elements which should be noted, for example:

1. A review of the procurement procedure to confirm the reasonableness and cost justification of the decision.

2. A review of data integrity to confirm the adequacy of the controls over the creation and maintenance of the database and the completeness and accuracy of data.
3. A review of data access controls to test the reasonableness of data access privileges granted.
4. A review of the controls over the database administrator.

In carrying out audits of database systems, auditors should find the data dictionary valuable in obtaining an understanding of the data held and its validation rules.

The use of standard audit interrogation packages may not be possible in all cases, although such facilities have been developed for leading database management systems.

The auditor may be unable to use standard audit software to interrogate the database directly: there are then alternative means at his disposal:

1. To convert the database to a conventional file and interrogate it in the normal way: this may be impractical, inefficient, or costly.
2. To use the database report generator: this is likely to be a powerful tool, but it may not necessarily be user friendly.

Section 7. Microcomputers

The nature of microcomputers

A microcomputer is a small desktop computer configuration typically comprising a processing unit with integral hard or floppy disk drives, a visual display screen, a keyboard for input and a printing device for output.

Microcomputers may be used as stand alone units or as part of a network; they may also be used as intelligent terminals or as the control centre of a network system.

Microcomputers linked in a local area network may participate in shared data storage, as provided by a disk and file service and shared printing, as provided by a print and print spool service.

Where microcomputers are linked to mainframe computers, they may share in the use of peripheral equipment such as high-capacity disks or high-speed printers. Data may be transmitted from mainframe to microcomputer or vice versa for further processing.

Microcomputer applications often use package software such as:

word processing, e.g. 'Wordstar'
spreadsheet, e.g. 'Lotus 1–2–3'
graphics, e.g. 'Paintbrush'

Advantages of microcomputers

1. Low cost.
2. User may have total responsibility for own system.
3. Simplicity in use encourages computer literacy, initiative and innovation.
4. Capability to provide speedy solutions to business problems by use of standard software packages.
5. Capability to improve efficiency and cost effectiveness through computer-assisted clerical and administrative tasks.

Disadvantages of microcomputers

1. Control weakness due to:

   (a) a lack of the sort of development and operational disciplines normally adopted in mainframe applications;
   (b) an absence of any segregation of duties in systems developed, operated and controlled by the same person;
   (c) a risk that information prepared for critical management purposes by an inexperienced user could be wrong.

2. Security weakness due to probable lack of the sort of disciplines normally adopted in mainframe applications for:

   (a) providing audit trails;
   (b) providing systems documentation;
   (c) making back-up copies of data files and programs;
   (d) making provision for physical and logical security.

3. Unless procurement and application of micro-

computer hardware and software are properly co-ordinated and firmly controlled, incompatible systems will give rise to organisational inefficiency.

Control issues

There is a need for management control of microcomputers within an organisation in the following areas:

1. Control of procurement of hardware and software.
2. Control of custody of the hardware and software.
3. Control of the environment in which microcomputers are used.
4. Control of systems development.
5. Control of files and programs.
6. Control procedures to ensure back-up and recovery.

Procurement

There should be a corporate strategy for the development of microcomputer facilities incorporating the definition of criteria to be considered before acquiring microcomputer hardware or software. By adopting a co-ordinated approach, maximum advantage can be taken of the available range of compatible package software and the technical support offered by suppliers of hardware and software.

Hardware procurement should take account of:

1. The reliability of the equipment.
2. Vendor support in spares, components, maintenance, training.
3. Availability of compatible peripheral equipment such as printers or communications facilities such as modems.
4. The technical and commercial reputation and the financial viability of the supplier.
5. The experience of other users.

Software procurement should take account of:

1. How well the software matches the business requirements.
2. How easily the software can be customised or amended.

3. The availability of systems documentation, training manuals and support.
4. The technical and commercial reputation and the financial viability of the supplier.
5. The experience of other users.

Custody

Control should be maintained over the hardware and peripheral equipment by means of:

1. Labelling for identification.
2. Registration by serial number and location.
3. Regular inspection and verification.
4. Appropriate physical means such as clamping equipment to fixed locations.

There should be a policy concerning movement of equipment, defining in particular the circumstances in which equipment could be taken out of the office.

Environment

Microcomputers do not need the same controlled environment conditions as those applicable to mainframe computers. Nevertheless, some precautions should be taken including:

1. The protection of keyboards, screens or other equipment by plastic covers.
2. Easy access to a Halon fire extinguisher.
3. The use of lockable library containers for diskettes.
4. Instructions for the careful handling of data media should be provided and enforced.

Systems development

Controls should cover the following:

1. An acquisition procedure for software (see above).
2. Development standards including a clear definition of the problem to be solved, documentation of the software, written operating instructions.
3. Registration of data protection information, where necessary.
4. Appropriate user controls or programmed application controls to cover the authorisation, completeness, accuracy, and timeliness of all data processed and the provision of an audit trail.
5. Proper listing facilities.

Files and programs

The purpose of controls over data files and programs is to prevent data and programs being accidentally or deliberately erased, stolen or used for improper purposes. Methods to be considered include:

1. Physical security at the microcomputer location.
2. Storing data on removable diskettes and locking them away after use.
3. The use of software which provides password control.
4. The use of encryption for sensitive information.
5. The use of access control software on a network system to control access to mainframe data.

Backup and recovery

Systems should be set up to ensure that users take back-up copies of files at appropriate intervals and store back-up files securely. Basic housekeeping procedures should be set up to ensure that file retention periods are defined and that dead files are pruned when the retention period has expired.

The procedures should also include steps to ensure the security of back-up copies of computer software.

Auditing microcomputer systems

It is first necessary to conduct an audit review of the control environment by considering the issues as outlined above. A review of a microcomputer application should then cover the same elements as a review of a mainframe application. For example:

1. Review the input controls to ensure all input is authorised, complete, accurate, timely and not previously processed.
2. Review the processing controls to ensure that all data is processed and accounted for.
3. Review the output controls to ensure the completeness and accuracy of computer output.
4. Confirm the existence of adequate audit trails.

Section 8.   Systems development

The nature of systems development

Internal or external development

Computer systems are required to fulfil business needs. Many of these needs are concerned with basic accounting and record keeping and are common to many organisations, for example payroll, and purchase ledger.

Computer manufacturers and software houses have developed software packages for many of the common applications. These packages are offered for sale and may be purchased to be installed for use without modification, or they may be adapted by the business or software house to meet the special requirements of the purchaser; they are then said to be 'customised'. It may be less costly to buy such a package instead of developing one's own software and the implementation time scale will be shorter.

An alternative approach is to commission a software house to develop an in-house solution instead of using the organisation's own development staff. The software house would assign its own analysts and programmers to provide the technical expertise, with user expertise provided by the organisation.

A third option is to develop systems in-house using the organisation's own team of systems analysts and programmers. This process is described later under 'Systems development cycle'. Where an independent software house provides the computer development staff, the process will be similar.

System design risks

Mair, Wood and Davies (1978) provide a list of things which could go wrong when systems are not developed soundly or documented correctly:

1. Systems design staff acting without proper control or supervision may introduce unauthentic accounting policies or give effect to unauthorised changes in existing policies. Both of these actions may lead to false record keeping and misleading information.
2. Design inadequacies might lead to interruptions to the business; for example, consider the likely

effect on bank customers of a cash dispenser network which was regularly out of action. Would they not tend to move their accounts to a more reliable network?

3. Design inadequacies might lead to bad management decisions due to reliance on inaccurate or incomplete information.
4. Systems may violate mandatory statutes or regulations, leading to legal sanctions.
5. Badly designed systems may operate with excessive costs.
6. An inflexible design might make subsequent amendments difficult to incorporate within reasonable time scales leading to failure to meet legal or financial requirements or to respond to competitive pressures.
7. Facilities for fraudulent practices may be built into systems during the development phase.

Standards

The need for standards

Operational management, data processing management and auditors all benefit when computer systems are developed in a controlled manner.

Unless the development process is directed in accordance with defined standards, there is unlikely to be:

efficient systems development
effective control over the development process, or
a high-quality product

The methods to be adopted and the documentation to be maintained should be defined, specified in writing and followed. There should be management and supervisory controls to confirm that the standard procedures are being used.

The standards should cover all the key elements of systems development:

procedures
performance
documentation
control
supervision
authorisation

Standard procedures are often established with three levels of authority: they may be mandatory, preferred or advisory. The mandatory standard procedures are those which must be strictly adhered to by all, whilst preferred and advisory standards are optional. Increasingly, use is being made of proprietary structured development methods which incorporate their own standards.

There are clear advantages in adopting standard practices for the process of systems development, for example:

1. Standards provide a sound basis for effective control and supervision.
2. Properly documented systems will aid the amendment process subsequently.
3. Standardisation facilitates communication with other members of the development team and with system users. Explanation of the process and progress reporting are greatly simplified when all involved already have an understanding of the standard methods.
4. Standardisation aids continuity. Experienced systems designers should be able to take over another person's work, understand what is happening and continue with the development work.
5. Since work methods and documentation requirements are specified for those involved in the development process, they do not need to spend time developing and defining their own methodology.
6. The auditor's task is simplified when the intended methodology and documentation have been defined by standards.

Content of standards

Systems development standards should cover control procedures and documentation for each phase of development, for example:

1. Procedural requirements including the organisational structure of the data processing function, the allocation of responsibility, supervisory controls, authorities, delegation, financial responsibilities.
2. Project control and accounting arrangements for new systems and modifications to existing systems.

Each development project should have defined checkpoints for monitoring progress. Each checkpoint should precede a significant phase of the project or a critical expenditure commitment. Checkpoints are, in essence, management decision points. The decision made at each checkpoint confirms whether the project is to continue.

3. Documentation standards for each phase, including conventions for flow charting and standards for the production of decision tables, narrative descriptions and reports. The standards should ensure that documentation produced will be understandable to those who need to read it, whether systems development staff, users, management or auditors.

4. Control requirements, including standard requirements for: data security and integrity; data protection; suitability for audit; backup and recovery; and determining checkpoints.

There should be specific standards for programming, as for example:

1. The approach to be adopted for the design of computer programs, including:
   (a) segmentation or modular concepts to be incorporated;
   (b) flow charting or coding conventions;
   (c) compilation and testing requirements.

2. Documentation requirements, including the types of information to be retained for each program, as for example:

   (a) a written specification describing the function of the program and its relationship to other parts of the program suite or system;
   (b) lists of inputs, files, and outputs used or created;
   (c) a specification of the processing performed using narrative, flow charts or decision tables;
   (d) recovery and restart requirements;
   (e) program listings;
   (f) test plans, schedules, data and results;
   (g) details of standard data or tables used by the program for example: prices file, discounts file;
   (h) subroutines or macros used by the program;
   (i) job control instructions;
   (j) data dictionaries or directories used in conjunction with the program;
   (k) some form of project control documentation containing evidence of the checking carried out by supervisors.

Other standards may be set for file conversion, implementation and post-implementation reviews.

Systems development cycle

The stages in the process of systems development will generally follow a sequence such as the one described here:

1. Initiate project and establish management.
2. Feasibility study.
3. Outline design.
4. Detailed design.
5. Program development and testing.
6. Implementation planning.
7. Implementation.
8. Post-implementation review.

A summary of the activities, participants and documentary outputs relevant to each phase is set out on pages 108–9.

Each phase of this cycle represents a management review point. At each stage the documentary output should be checked for quality and the objectives, costs and benefits should be reviewed as the basis for taking a decision to proceed further. The allocation of resources for future plans should be reviewed and revised where necessary at the end of each phase. The internal auditor may be involved in any or all of the phases.

Auditing systems development

At the outset, it is necessary to consider why the internal auditor should want to get involved in systems development.

Phase	Activities	Participants	Output
1. Initiate project and establish management.	1. Determine and rank projects to be considered. 2. Set terms of reference for each project. 3. Allocate initial resources to each project.	High-level management, probably in some form of steering committee involving user and DP management.	Project terms of reference. Initial project plan.
2. Feasibility study.	1. Identify scope and objectives of system. 2. Consider possible alternative approaches and economics of each. 3. Prepare feasibility report.	Users and systems analysts.	Feasibility report.
3. Outline design.	1. Define user requirements. 2. Design system to meet these in high-level terms. 3. Consider technical feasibility, likely costs, time scale and resources. 4. Produce outline specification with revised cost/benefit analysis.	Users, systems analysts and programmers (for technical consultation only).	Outline systems proposal.
4. Detailed design.	1. Define systems requirements in detail with provision for exceptions, variations and user procedures. 2. Prepare detailed systems specification.	Systems analysts in consultation with users and programmers.	Detailed systems specification.
5. Program development and testing.	1. Convert systems specification into a series of programs by: (a) flow charting; (b) designing files and outputs; (c) coding instructions. 2. Document the system. 3. Test the system by: (a) desk checking; (b) modular checking; (c) suite testing. 4. Further testing by analysts and users.	Programmers. Programmers. Systems analysts and users.	Program documentation. Testing plans and results. Testing plans and results.

Phase	Activities	Participants	Output
6. Implementation planning.	1. Decide and plan method of implementation: (a) parallel running; (b) pilot scheme; (c) phased conversion.	Users, analysts and programmers.	Implementation plan.
	2. Plan creation or conversion of computer files.		File conversion instructions.
	3. Prepare procedural instructions for users and operations staff.		User and operations manuals.
	4. Plan and carry out training.	Training specialist.	Training plans and materials.
7. Implementation	1. Implement the plan.	Probably under control of an implementation committee consisting of users, IT management and staff.	Initial processing results.
	2. Carry out any required parallel running checks or monitor results in pilot phases before proceeding to full implementation.		
8. Post-implementation review	1. Review the system 3–6 months after implementation to measure how far it meets the original objectives, costs and benefits.	Users and representatives of systems analysts and programmers.	Post-implementation review report.

Audit objectives

The internal auditor has two objectives to bear in mind:

1. To determine whether or not the total system, incorporating user manual controls and programmed procedures, will provide adequate internal control and meet user requirements efficiently.
2. To establish that there is a controlled process of systems development which proceeds in accordance with established standards. This process should ensure that at all phases adequate information is presented for management decisions and that management authorisation is obtained before the project moves on to the next phase.

There are, then, two distinct audit aspects. The first is that it is necessary to confirm that adequate internal control is built into the system which is being developed and that this system matches user requirements. For this there must be audit involvement before implementation.

The second aspect is audit of the process of systems development. Here, the internal auditor is concerned to ensure that there is adequate internal control over the development process. This involves a review of the standard procedures used to develop systems for which there will be subsidiary objectives:

1. To determine that standards exist.
2. To evaluate the standards in order to confirm:

   (a) that they are reasonable;
   (b) that they will ensure well-documented systems;
   (c) that they provide a sound basis for project management and effective control.

3. To confirm compliance with the standards.
4. To report on any weakness in the standards and on any non-compliance.

Audit approach

As a practical consideration it is often not feasible to commit internal audit resources to be fully involved in every systems development project which is in progress. It is therefore a matter for internal audit management to assess each new systems development proposal, to judge priorities and to determine the degree of audit involvement.

In order to make more effective use of internal audit resources, there may be an advantage in separating the two aspects of audit involvement in systems development. Thus, the review of the process of systems development which is concerned with standards and compliance with them, would be dealt with as a separate audit assignment. This would probably be undertaken every two years or whenever changes were made in standards.

If the results of this audit work confirm that systems are being developed with good management control and in compliance with standards which are both sound and clearly defined, the auditor may consider that the amount of audit work required on individual applications could be reduced.

Auditing the development process

This type of audit involves the review of a number of projects already completed by examining project files and systems and programming documentation produced together with any procedural instructions. The purpose is to determine the extent to which they provide evidence that the process of systems development is completed in accordance with installation standards and in a controlled manner. Essentially, the audit is in four main stages:

1. Determine whether standards exist.
2. Determine from the standards the critical controls on systems development and evaluate them for strengths and weaknesses. Assess the reasonableness of the standards in providing a controlled basis for systems development.

3. Confirm that the standards are documented and are made available to those who need them. They should also be updated when required.
4. Review the sample projects and consider the extent to which the project files and documentation confirm that they have been developed in a controlled manner and in accordance with the installation standards. The checking of documentation should be supplemented by interviewing staff to confirm their understanding of the required standard procedures and the extent of compliance with them, particularly in those areas where confirmation cannot be found purely by examination of documentation.

If the initial review revealed a lack of standards there is unlikely to be a consistent approach to systems development. If standards exist but, in the view of the internal auditor, there are aspects which require reconsideration, the audit report should contain recommendations for change.

The audit report on the process will also highlight any areas where there is noncompliance with the standards as laid down. The identification of noncompliance might highlight weaknesses in the quality checking procedures by data processing management or instances where there is nonacceptance by data processing supervisors and staff of the standard requirements.

At each phase of this audit the following key issues will have to be considered:

1. **Initiation of project and establishment of management:**

   (a) Review the system of management to confirm that it results in due consideration being given initially to the identification of priorities and the allocation of appropriate resources to projects for development.
   (b) Confirm that all project management groups, whatever their level, are provided with suitable and reliable information for monitoring the progress of project developments in terms of both time and cost.
   (c) Confirm that the development of each system selected for review bears evidence of

having been soundly planned and effectively controlled.

2. Feasibility study, outline design, and detailed design:

(a) Confirm that responsibilities have been allocated to staff with appropriate skills to perform the work at each stage.

(b) Confirm that adequate resources have been allocated with effective project control at each stage.

(c) Confirm that costs and benefits were soundly assessed at the feasibility stage and have been updated at the outline design and detailed design stages to enable management approval to be given for continuation of the project.

(d) Confirm that at each stage appropriate documentation has been produced in compliance with the defined standards and that it provides an adequate record of the development.

(e) Confirm that there is user agreement to the proposed system; and management authority to proceed to the next stage.

3. Programming:

The review should confirm that detailed documentation prepared in accordance with the standards exists for computer programs.

The existence of such documentation will be critical when it is necessary to make subsequent changes to programs to reflect changed requirements or to correct errors. This is especially important when the programming staff originally involved on the projects have left the organisation.

The review should also confirm that all backup copies of program documentation are updated to reflect the current state.

4. Testing:

Confirm that the standards define an appropriate approach to testing and require it to be properly planned and controlled, and to involve programmers, analysts and users.

The results obtained from all tests should be compared with anticipated results prepared for the purpose.

The review of the testing should confirm that it has been performed to a sufficient depth to cover all likely situations. This should include testing with exceptional situations, errors and normal working volumes of data.

When formal acceptance testing is involved, the documentation authorising the programs to be transferred to the production libraries should be examined to confirm that the necessary signed authorisation was given.

5. Pre-implementation:

Confirm, by examining documentation and discussion with data processing staff and users, that due attention was paid in the projects selected to pre-implementation planning in terms of:

(a) implementation method;
(b) conversion procedures;
(c) user training;
(d) procedural instructions.

6. Implementation:

Confirm that the systems went live without serious problems. Confirm also that all appropriate documentation was completed and filed in compliance with the standards for systems file preparation and retention. Critical documentation should also be filed on a remote site for contingency planning purposes.

7. Post-implementation review:

Confirm that a post-implementation review was carried out within the prescribed time and that appropriate action has been taken on matters reported in the review.

Other development options

Software packages

For many common applications it is possible to choose proprietary software packages instead of in-house development. It may then be necessary to arrange that corporate procedures conform to the package requirements. Alternatively, it may be possible to customise the package to meet the organisation's needs.

It is most advisable to make a full and detailed evaluation, of both the package and the software house providing it, to confirm that it is suitable and that there is assurance that it will be adequately maintained in the future.

When the software package route is chosen, the development cycle takes a different form. For example:

1. Identification of requirements.
2. Evaluation of the package's ability to meet these requirements.
3. Acceptance testing of the package.

The implementation stages of the cycle should then be similar to those for in-house development.

At the earliest opportunity the internal auditor should assess the package against user requirements, evaluate the systems of control within it and confirm that the package was fully tested before implementation.

End-user developments

In many organisations, first stages in computing have resulted in the creation of corporate data files and databases. This situation led to the demand by users for report generators or retrieval programs to facilitate the preparation of management information. In other cases data processing has been extended through the use of desk top micro-computers and intelligent terminals with personal computing facilities. These solutions can be cost-effective. They increase the ability of the user to harness computing power and free the development team to concentrate on fundamental development projects.

Proper control of end-user developments is nevertheless necessary a..d it has to be exercised firmly in order to ensure that:

1. They are cost-justified.
2. They do not lead to unnecessary duplication of facilities.
3. They are properly documented.
4. Adequate provision is made for back-up.

5. They are not totally dependent on one member of staff.

The internal audit review of the development process should cover procedures for the development of end-user systems.

Fourth-generation languages

Fourth-generation languages have been developed for generating application systems on the computer by providing information, often in yes or no responses, to simple questions on screen displays. Prototyping enables a prototype of the system to be developed quickly, shown to the user, and then amended quickly. This process can greatly reduce the systems development time.

Prior to the development of fourth generation languages, programming languages used for development were procedural languages in which the program had to be written line by line, in the same sequence as the computer would execute it.

Fourth-generation languages are nonprocedural and may be used by a computer user with or without the assistance of a systems analyst.

In this environment, there are obviously limitations on the extent to which the internal auditor can be involved in the systems development cycle. The audit review of the process should concentrate first on the steps taken to ensure effective user agreement and adequate documentation of the system. Then special care must be taken to ensure that acceptance testing and operational testing stages are comprehensive and thorough.

Section 9.   Auditing application systems

The nature of systems auditing

Audit objective

The objective when auditing an application system is to confirm that it incorporates adequate internal controls:

1. **Input** controls should ensure that it is properly authorised, complete, accurate, timely; and processed once only.

2. **Processing** controls should ensure that the right data is used, the right files are used and the work is processed completely.
3. **Output** controls should ensure that it is complete, reasonable, timely and then disclosed only to those authorised.
4. **Audit trail** should exist and it should be adequate.

The review thus seeks to confirm that the controls within the application ensure that the information it produces is authentic and reliable.

System controls

The controls to be reviewed are in two categories. There are those within the computer installation and those which form part of each application system.

Application system controls may be programmed into the system or they may be dependent on clerical or supervisory disciplines to be applied by the user. It is feasible to review both types, either during the systems development process or following implementation.

The basic review method for both pre-installation and post-installation audit will be the same, but the time span will differ. For a system under development, the complete review could extend over many months; for a live application it is likely to be completed in days or weeks.

The need for audit

Organisations place great reliance on the satisfactory performance of their information processing systems. Audit assurance is therefore most important to confirm that key functions are being performed properly and that critical operations are adequately controlled. Audit examination will focus on the following two areas:

1. Application systems service the information needs of many key business functions. Review of each of these systems to confirm that it achieves its purpose efficiently could be critical to the health of the business. Examples of such key functions include:

   (a) sales order processing;
   (b) production planning and control;
   (c) stock control;
   (d) payroll;
   (e) maintenance of accounting records;
   (f) credit control;
   (g) accounts payable.

2. Many application systems serve as management tools in areas which are crucial to the organisation's success or failure. In such cases the risk of a control failure in the system is too onerous to be ignored. Audit examination to confirm that controls are adequate and effective is then of the utmost importance. Examples of crucial activities which place great reliance on effective system controls include:

   (a) automated teller systems in banking;
   (b) customer service which depends upon efficient stock management;
   (c) billing and collection in a mail order business;
   (d) airline flight reservations;
   (e) computer typesetting in publishing.

Audit approach

Systems under development

Early involvement of the internal auditor has a number of benefits, including the following:

1. Weaknesses in control can be identified and recommendations for change made before systems implementation or, with very early involvement, before completion of the programming phase. Delayed changes can be very costly or quite often just not feasible.
2. The knowledge of the strengths and weaknesses within the system which the auditor accumulates as a result of involvement during development is invaluable when planning subsequent audits.
3. An auditor who is involved during the development of a system is in a position to consider whether special audit modules or embedded audit facilities should be incorporated in the development.

There can also be problems relating to the early

involvement of an internal auditor in systems development, for example:

1. Involvement can be time-consuming if attendance at development meetings is requested.
2. There may be concern about jeopardising audit independence. However:

> The internal auditor's objectivity is not adversely affected when the auditor recommends standards of control for systems or reviews procedures before they are implemented. Designing, installing and operating systems are not audit functions. Also, the drafting of procedures for systems is not an audit function. Performing such activities is presumed to impair audit objectivity.
>
> (IIA–UK Guideline 120.03)

The internal auditor should make arrangements to be kept informed of all systems development projects which are proposed, in progress, completed or abandoned. Plans can then be considered and agreed for the extent of audit involvement, if any, and at which stages, in the development programme for each project.

Systems in operation

The step-by-step systems audit approach should be:

1. Obtain an overview of the system.
2. Define the business control objectives of the system.
3. Define the audit objective and scope.
4. Obtain a detailed understanding of the system.
5. Identify and evaluate the controls within the system.
6. Design audit procedures and test the system.
7. Undertake a final control evaluation.
8. Discuss findings.
9. Issue a formal report.
10. Arrange any necessary follow-up.

The notes which follow provide further information on certain of these steps.

Step 3: Audit objectives

Control objectives might cover:

1. Achievement of business objectives.
2. Safeguarding assets.
3. Compliance with regulations.
4. Reliability of information.
5. Processing efficiency and effectiveness.

Any condition which limits the audit objective and scope must be identified.

Step 4: Understanding the system

The level of understanding required depends on the audit objectives. The type of information required will include:

1. The function of the system.
2. The principal outputs of the system.
3. The inputs to the system, how they are originated and authorised.
4. The processing cycle.
5. The interface of the system with other systems.
6. The controls within the system and an identification of their purpose; the reliance placed on programmed controls; the key clerical controls; and error routines and correction procedures.

This information should be obtained from systems documentation, and from discussion with development staff and users. Questionnaires or checklists may be used to gather the information.

Step 5: Identifying the controls

The auditor should identify the controls over each aspect of the system: which will be detective, preventative or corrective. They may be:

(a) organisational, for example division of duties;
(b) clerical, for example authorisation of input;
(c) programmed procedures, for example check digit checking.

It is useful to identify each individual control objective and then establish how this control objective is achieved.

Important control methods which should always be considered are:

(a) segregation of duties;
(b) the system of internal checks;
(c) random or regular supervisory checks.

The check lists which follow state the principal control objectives and give examples of the means to achieve control (the lists are not exhaustive).

Input controls – check list

1. Data properly authorised:

   (a) initials, signatures (batch input);
   (b) password controls, supervisor key use (on-line input).

2. Data complete:

   (a) computer check for missing transaction, sequence, or batch numbers;
   (b) computer check for presence of all required fields;
   (c) clerical checks of control total or record counts.

3. Data accurate:

   (a) control totals;
   (b) format, range, compatibility checks;
   (c) check digits on account numbers.

4. Data not already processed:

   (a) discipline for cancellation of documents;
   (b) programmed tests for duplicates.

5. Data timely:

   (a) clerical review;
   (b) programmed data checks.

Processing controls – check list

1. Correct data processed:

   (a) file header label checking;
   (b) coding checks;
   (c) clerical control procedure.

2. Correct file used:

   (a) file header label checking;
   (b) media library file control systems.

3. Correct account updated:

   (a) matching account numbers.

4. Data processed securely:

   (a) supervisory and access controls.

5. All data accounted for:

   (a) control total or hash total checks on batch input;
   (b) comparison of manual control accounts;
   (c) comparison of record counts.

6. Data conforms to standards:

   (a) input validity checking.

7. Error reports actioned:

   (a) reports signed, dated and filed.

8. Controlled stationery protected:

   (a) reconciliation of stock to records of work processed.

Output controls – check list

1. All output produced:

   (a) media librarian control procedures over disk and tape files;
   (b) schedules of printed output required checked.

2. Output complete:

   (a) control totalling or record count checks;
   (b) sheet numbering;
   (c) printing 'end' at end of last report.

3. Output useful:

   (a) reviews required by users.

4. Output timely:

   (a) detailed timetable prepared and monitored.

5. Confidentiality maintained:

   (a) secured printing;
   (b) reports delivered to named persons;
   (c) receipts obtained;
   (d) access controls in on-line systems.

6. Reasonableness of output:

   (a) check of volumes;
   (b) quality control checking of output reports;
   (c) 'Cusum' technique (cumulative sum).

7. Audit trail provided:

   (a) a system to ensure that a complete and accessible audit trail is available.

Having identified the controls, the next step is to assess their expected strength. The stronger controls will provide the basis of the control structure which the auditor would expect to test later. Weak controls should be assessed in terms of adequacy and cost effectiveness. Any unnecessary or duplicated controls which do not appear to fulfil a control objective should also be identified.

Step 6: Designing audit procedures

Having understood the system and evaluated the controls, tests should be designed to establish how effectively the controls are working. Controls to be tested may be:

1. Manual controls by users such as endorsement of documents.
2. Manual controls by computer operations staff such as checking file controls.
3. Operating software controls such as access controls.
4. Programmed control within the application systems such as validation checks.

When evaluating those controls achieved through application software or operating software, consideration must be given to the overall standard of controls within the computer installation. Thus, for example, if tests have previously confirmed that input validity checking within an application program is effective, reliance must then be placed on controls which ensure that all amendments to the software have been properly authorised and have been applied correctly and tested.

The strengths and weaknesses of general controls in the installation will therefore influence the degree of application testing necessary. If compliance testing uncovers control weakness, the auditor will need to consider whether substantive tests are required.

Step 9: Reporting

The auditor should analyse the system control evaluation including the test results and then determine what must be reported. In computer application audits, reports may need to be made to technical staff as well as to users.

The report should be prepared in draft form, and discussed with those who will be responsible for correcting any weaknesses before a final version is issued. The incorporation of agreed action or management response in the final report is preferable. Every report should explicitly request a formal response.

Step 10: Follow-up

The report should be followed up after an appropriate interval to confirm that action has been taken. It is then appropriate to assess the time scale for outstanding amendments.

It is also necessary to establish whether there are any areas where a decision has been taken not to implement the audit recommendations. When there are, unless the auditor considers the reasons for rejecting the recommendation are valid, it is necessary to consider whether to refer the matter to a higher level of authority.

System modifications

Change is a fundamental ingredient of progress. The organisation must adapt to a changing environment in order to remain competitive. This may result in changed information needs or changed procedures. Methods must respond to advances in technology in order to avoid obsolescence and inefficiency. It may then be necessary to change procedures to adopt new practices. All systems design involves judgement of future uncertainties in some areas so that adjustment becomes necessary to match subsequent experience.

There are, then, a number of reasons why changes may be required to operational programs:

1. Changed requirements, for example business requirements or legal requirements.
2. Enhancements.
3. Correction of errors.

A degree of flexibility should be incorporated in

the design of all systems to accommodate foresee-able variations in circumstances or requirements. It is nevertheless inevitable that changed requirements which necessitate program amendment will continue to occur.

Program changes

A controlled procedure for program amendment is an essential requirement to ensure operational programs remain protected from unauthorised changes. There has to be a sound basis for confidence that changes can only be made to operational programs with proper authority and with formal documentation.

The auditor may place reliance on controls which have been programmed into a computer system, and will not need to carry out regular tests on those program procedures.

Those operational staff who are responsible for the operational program library should observe strict disciplines for maintaining the library. No new programs should be added unless they are supported by formal documentation which must confirm that the system has been accepted and they must be properly signed in compliance with standard procedures.

Control procedures for program changes may be similar to those devised for the systems development cycle. For major changes a feasibility report, an outline design proposal, and a detailed design specification may be necessary and then the procedures for each of those phases would be appropriate.

There are some additional key aspects to consider:

1. There should be a formal method of requesting and authorising changes; the reasons for the change should be fully documented.
2. All amendments should be properly documented and the systems and programming documentation brought up to date.
3. There should be an independent check and scrutiny of program amendments to ensure that only the changes authorised have been made.
4. Amendments should be tested by programmers and analysts, and in the case of major changes by the users. The testing should not only confirm

that the changes work but also that they do not have an adverse effect on other parts of the program or other related systems.
5. A record of program amendment requests should be maintained for project control purposes; there should be management supervision to ensure that all valid requests for change are accounted for and properly effected within required time scales. Control over program amendments might be exercised by using serially numbered documentation to record amendments or by use of a register of changes.

Special problems

1. **Urgent changes** There is a need for flexibility to undertake changes in emergency situations where the personnel who are normally required for authorisation are not available, for example overnight, or on those occasions when deadlines need to be met. These 'fixes' should be properly authorised, checked and approved retrospectively by responsible officials. Systems and programming documentation should be amended to reflect the changes.
2. **Real-time systems** With a real-time, or on-line system, there is a need to control the timing of changes closely. When the system is not available for a full 24 hours, the changes should be made after the scheduled daily close-down. With 24-hour operation a temporary close-down of the system may be necessary. The modified program might be placed in a 'pseudo production' library until the end of a specified quarantine period to allow for reversion to the original program in the event of difficulty. In practice, the impact on the organisation of a program failure in a real-time system can be significant. It is important, then, that before an amended version of the program is implemented, it is adequately tested. It may be wise to make changes one at a time if this is feasible.
3. **Program libraries** A controlled procedure for amendments to the operational library is essential to reduce the risk of error or fraud through unauthorised amendments to operational

programs. Access to the production library should be restricted by using appropriate access control and password restrictions. When an authority is raised for an amendment of an operational program, a copy of the program should be transferred to a separate testing library. All amendments to the program should be made within the testing library, to which access should also be controlled to avoid unauthorised amendments to programs within that library. The amended program should be transferred to the operational library only when it has been fully tested and proper authority obtained for its transfer. The original program must then be withdrawn.

Auditing the changes

The internal auditor should review the program amendment procedure to confirm that changes are conducted in a controlled way. For example:

1. All changes should be properly documented.
2. All changes should be subject to formal project control.
3. All amended programs transferred to the operational program library should be supported by formal documentation confirming the approval of interested parties and that the changes have been adequately tested.

Section 10.   Computer-assisted audit techniques (CAAT)

The nature of CAAT

CAAT are computer applications designed specifically for use by auditors. They enable internal auditors to test data processing activities independently of both the computer department and the user department. They can be used to review systems controls or to review data.

Organisations are becoming increasingly sophisticated in their use of computers. Internal auditors have to address this challenge and also to consider every opportunity offered by computers for improving efficiency in their own work.

The internal auditor's role is to provide independent assurance, or otherwise, as to the reliability and effectiveness of the management control system. This depends upon the auditor's evaluation of the control strengths or weaknesses of each processing system; and the accuracy, relevance and integrity of the management information produced.

CAAT are tools to be used by internal auditors in pursuit of their responsibilities and must not be perceived as techniques looking for problems to solve. Their use can contribute to an effective and more efficient internal audit service. The prime objective in using CAAT should be to assist in performing audit tasks in the most effective and efficient manner.

Techniques for reviewing system controls look at the systems rather than the data processed through them. The internal auditor is concerned to establish whether or not controls exist and are functioning. However, the results from applying these techniques may lead the auditor to question the accuracy and integrity of the information produced by the system.

Techniques for reviewing data are all based upon the examination and extraction of operational data and manipulating it through audit programs. Such data is usually extracted from application systems but can also be extracted from system software and from logs such as the computer log or teleprocessing log.

As in all internal audit assignments, the auditor must first identify the audit objectives and then adopt the best method available for achieving them. In deciding upon which technique to use, the internal auditor should consider:

1. The importance of the system to the organisation.
2. The level of audit assurance required.
3. The extent to which there are recurrent conditions in successive audit assignments.
4. The time and cost needed to set up the technique.
5. The time and cost needed to maintain the technique.

Interrogation software

This is a term which covers techniques alternatively known as:

(a) programming languages
(b) generalised audit software (GAS)
(c) retrieval software
(d) report generators
(e) special audit programs

Interrogation software is the generic term for programs written for auditors to retrieve and manipulate data held on magnetic storage media. These programs enable auditors to make use of the power of the computer and they allow auditors independent access to data. They are by far the most popular of the CAAT and they may also be used in some of the other CAAT, for example, embedded data collection and parallel simulation.

(a) Programming languages
Examples:

    Assembler
    Fortran
    RPG
    PL/1
    Basic
    Cobol

Interrogations may be written directly in one of the programming languages. Whereas the high-level languages are general in application and tend to be supported by most manufacturers, the low-level languages tend to be specific to individual computer manufacturers, but they do allow more efficient manipulation of data.

Advantages

1. There are practically no restrictions on program logic, the types of file that may be accessed, or the output.
2. These techniques are efficient in terms of computer processing.
3. There is no acquisition cost for the audit function.

Disadvantages

1. These techniques require a high level of programming skill and technical knowledge.
2. Development takes longer than with packages and amendment is more difficult.
3. They are more suitable for regular reviews than isolated studies.

(b) Generalised audit software
Examples:

Accounting firms:

Coopers and Lybrand	Auditpak II
Peat Marwick Mitchell	System 2190

Software houses:

LA Computing	CARS
Pansophic	Panaudit
Cullinane	EDP auditor

The external audit firms were early pioneers in the field of interrogation packages. They had a need for packages which ran on the wide range of computers that their clients used, and so they commissioned software houses to write packages that were machine-portable. As a result, these packages tend to be parameter-driven program generators. Over the years, the audit firms have made their packages available to clients' internal audit departments.

Software houses, seeing the market potential, produced packages for computer auditors. Some were barely concealed variations of their interrogation packages, whilst others were specifically designed for auditors, for example, Panaudit.

The prime difference between generalised audit software (GAS) and retrieval software is that the GAS packages have been specifically developed for auditors and have most of the commonly used audit routines pre-programmed.

Advantages

1. The techniques are relatively easy to learn.
2. Limited technical knowledge is required.
3. The software is easy to amend.
4. The packages are relatively inexpensive to acquire and use.
5. The systems contain many precoded routines.

Disadvantages

1. These techniques may be less efficient than a programming language.
2. They may be restrictive on program logic, on the types of file that may be accessed, or on the output.

(c) Retrieval packages (commercial)
Examples:

Software houses:

Pansophic	Easytrieve
NCC	Filetab

Manufacturers:

IBM	Query
ICL	Find

These packages were designed for data processing departments. In many respects, they are similar to generalised audit software, except that they do not include specific audit routines. Nevertheless, there is no reason why internal auditors should not use them, especially where the data processing department has already acquired them.

Advantages

1. The techniques are relatively easy to learn.
2. Limited technical knowledge is required.
3. The software is easy to amend.
4. The packages are relatively inexpensive to acquire and use.
5. These systems incorporate many precoded routines.

Disadvantages

1. These techniques may be less efficient than a programming language.
2. They may be restrictive on program logic, the types of file that may be accessed or the output.

(d) Retrieval packages (in-house)
Examples:

British Leyland	BLIP
Grindlays Bank	PROBE
Rolls-Royce	CODAR
Dorset County Council	DEKE

Before commercial packages were generally available, some organisations wrote their own. Some, like those produced for external audit firms, became commercially available. Others were developed for specific hardware or software within an organisation. Indeed, such developments continue to occur, either because the commercial packages are too restrictive, or there is no package available for the computer in question.

Advantages

1. They are designed specifically for one organisation.
2. They may be more efficiently coded than commercial packages.

Disadvantages

1. They are designed for specific hardware. Upgrade or replacement of the hardware may require a major rewrite.
2. They are likely to be expensive to develop.

Interrogation features

The most important feature of all interrogation software is the ability to select and retrieve data and then to manipulate it. Packages contain a number of subroutines to enhance their capability to do this, some of which are listed here.

Integrity routines

These enable the auditor to test the integrity of data and files. They include tests such as duplicate testing; validity of data testing; missing records testing; alpha or numeric sequence testing; file or data comparisons.

Data and time routines

These enable the auditor to convert formats of data and time and to calculate elapsed time and ageing of data.

Statistical routines

These enable auditors to use scientific or empirical bases for the selection of audit samples.

Test generator routines

These enable auditors to generate test files and test data, good and bad, to assist in testing systems.

Encryption routines

These provide additional security for data being processed by auditors.

Interrogation elements

File

This element defines the file or files to be used in the interrogation. It is essential that the auditor identifies the correct file and the correct point in the processing cycle.

For example: in an interrogation of a sales system, the auditor may wish to look at delivered sales net of returns in order to check the commission payable to a salesman. He must first decide precisely what information is to be tested. He must then define the requirement in specific detail and identify which of the files in the sales cycle is to be interrogated and at what point in the cycle. It may be that the information required is created in a temporary file during the sales cycle but not 'permanently' recorded on file. The auditor would then need to interrogate the temporary file and would have to ensure that this file is retained by the operators and not overwritten. He would also need to be certain of obtaining the correct version where a number of generations of a file exist.

Field

Having identified the correct file, the auditor will need to determine which field or fields are of interest. It may be that the field of interest does not exist. For example, the auditor may be interested in the sales value of an invoice but the system records only quantity and unit price, so that he has to calculate the gross sales value and take into account discounts, VAT, etc.

The auditor should be wary of the file layouts in the systems documentation. They may be out of date and thus be inaccurate: it is often the case where indicators are used. For example, the file layout may specify that only indicators 401, 402 or 403 are permitted, whereas 404 may also be permitted. It is therefore prudent for the auditor to print out the first (say) 100 records of a file to confirm the file layout. It is also sensible to put print limits on invalid data. For example: an instruction to print out all records where the indicator is not 401, 402 or 403 could in the example above result in a large printout for indicator 404 unless a print limit of (say) 100 occurrences is specified.

Selection criteria

Having identified file and field, the auditor must decide how data are to be selected, for example: every record; every 'n'th record; every record in excess of $£x$; or every record which exceeds a specified record by more than $x\%$. Statistical methods may also be used as the basis for sample selection.

Calculations

This element is optional. The auditor may be interested in a straight extraction only and therefore have no need of calculation. When the purpose is to check calculations in an operational suite of programs, it is essential that the same criteria are used. For example, if the operational program codes arrears over one month as over 28 days, then the auditor must use 28 days for checking the reported arrears. Alternatively, the auditor's purpose may be to evaluate the distortion caused by the 28-day convention adopted in the operational program when a calendar month would be the appropriate calculation factor.

Output

This is, in many respects, the most important stage in writing an interrogation. It is important to think through the purpose for which the output is required. For example: the selection criteria for an exception report must be set to limit the output to a size that the auditor can use. Too many exceptions would be unusable.

It is usually a good idea to limit an exception

report printout to (say) 100 items to avoid excessive printing. In such circumstances, accumulating a count of occurrences enables the auditor to know how many there were in a particular file.

The output should be structured in the best order to facilitate subsequent audit use. When the purpose of the program is to extract a sample for subsequent audit checking, the checking requirements must be considered at the design stage. For example, if sales invoices are filed in invoice number sequence, it would be useless to print out a sample in account number sequence or customer name sequence. Blank columns should be printed on the output report to facilitate recording the results of subsequent audit tests on the same document when appropriate.

Interrogation functions

Whilst the number of different interrogations that can be processed against computer files, be they data files, programs, or computer logs, is limited only by the auditor's imagination, they do tend to fall into six main types:

1. File extractions

This is the most common type of interrogation. Master files or transaction files are interrogated to extract a sample to provide the basis for subsequent audit examination. The sample may be selected as: every 'n'th item; at random; by statistical methods; proportional to size; or, indeed, any method favoured by the auditor. Examples are:

1. Sales ledger accounts with balances in excess of credit limit.
2. Responses to a circularisation of debtors.
3. Sales ledger or purchase ledger balances in excess of £x.
4. A listing of stock for a specific location.
5. Sales ledger or purchase ledger names or addresses;
6. A random sample of employees' pay details.

2. Exception reports

In this type of interrogation, the auditor is looking for oddities and exceptions in master files or transaction files, as the basis of audit investigation. Examples are:

Range checks

1. Employees over retirement age.
2. Salary increases in excess of £x.
3. Overtime in excess of x hours.
4. Discount over x%.
5. Credit notes in excess of £x.
6. Nominal ledger account balances with increase in excess of x% over previous year.

Testing for duplicates

1. Employee names or numbers.
2. National insurance numbers.
3. Bank account numbers.
4. Supplier reference numbers.
5. Customer reference numbers.
6. Invoice numbers.
7. Identical cash payments.
8. Bank account numbers in payroll compared with those in purchase ledger.

Testing for missing fields

1. No national insurance number or category code.
2. No employee number or name.
3. No credit limit.

Testing field validity

1. Alpha characters in numeric field and vice versa.
2. National Insurance number or category code not valid.
3. Employee over retirement age and national insurance category code C.

Testing for irregular account activity

1. Sales accounts with high rate of returned goods.
2. Sales accounts with high rate of cancelled invoices.
3. Sales accounts with abnormal change in turnover this year compared with last year.
4. Sales accounts with round sum payments.

3. Analyses and patterns

Master files and transaction files are analysed seeking for patterns or areas of concern for specific investigation. Examples are:

1. Frequency analysis of cash receipts or payments by amount, account or department.
2. Distribution analysis of sales by sales period or sales area.
3. Distribution analysis of credit notes by salesman or customer.
4. Analysis of cash versus credit sales by sales period or sales area.
5. Analysis of purchase ledger activity this year compared with last year.

4. Control totals

In these interrogations, the auditor prepares totals of specific fields to prove those reported by the application system and also to check file totals against those reported on file headers. These check totals would also be used for confirming that the correct version of the master file was being processed in the audit interrogation.

5. Process logic

These interrogations check the processing logic and algorithms in an application system. Examples are:

1. Check the updating of stock fields on processing stock movement.
2. Check National Insurance calculations.
3. Check tax calculations in payroll.
4. Check sales invoice calculations.

6. File and program integrity

In this case, files are interrogated to check on their integrity. Examples are:

1. Comparison of operational program with audit copy to check for differences.
2. Comparison of operational files with the back-up copy to check for differences.
3. Comparison of two generations of a file for subsequent verification of the differences.

Verdict on interrogation

Advantages

1. Interrogation software and techniques give the internal auditor a considerable measure of independence from the data processing department and from users.
2. Using these techniques enables the auditor to concentrate upon auditing rather than on extracting data for auditing, so making more effective use of audit time.
3. Using interrogation software and techniques leads to more effective internal auditing by enabling the auditor:

   (a) to review the integrity of data files by interrogating for oddities and exceptions;
   (b) to extract audit samples and produce computer prepared working papers;
   (c) to check file totals;
   (d) to check processing logic;
   (e) to extract information not otherwise readily available;
   (f) to perform more comprehensive checking through the use of test data;
   (g) to compensate for loss of audit trail in some cases;
   (h) to assess the accuracy, consistency, flexibility, and speed of data processing.

4. Interrogation techniques are relatively easy to learn and can be used by relatively nontechnical auditors.
5. Interrogation techniques are relatively inexpensive to set up compared with other computer assisted audit techniques and cheap to use.
6. Interrogation software offers considerable flexibility through selection of suitable parameters.

Disadvantages

1. Interrogation software is expensive to purchase.
2. It can be expensive to train staff in the use of computer-assisted audit techniques.
3. Inexperienced users of interrogation software may produce false or distorted results which lead to the wrong audit conclusions.

4. Interrogation software deals with real data but does not review system controls, although the results may indirectly imply control strengths and weaknesses.

Embedded data collection

This term covers techniques which are alternatively known as:

(a) tagging
(b) cusum (cumulative sum)
(c) resident audit monitor (RAM)
(d) integrated audit monitor
(e) system control audit review file (SCARF)
(f) sample audit review file (SARF)

Basically, these are variations of interrogation software where the program is embedded within an application either as part of the application software or the systems software. The embedded program may operate continuously or in response to specific parameters, for example, a specific transaction or an audit signal. It is suitable for real-time systems as it enables continuous monitoring of transactions being processed.

Those transactions of interest to the auditor may be reported in a number of ways:

1. Hard copy report.
2. Output to an audit file on magnetic media for subsequent audit checking. This technique is sometimes referred to as SCARF (system control audit review file) or SARF (sample audit review file).
3. The transaction may be tagged or flagged for subsequent audit checking, but it remains as a transaction of the application files.

The method may be used to achieve three audit objectives:

1. To extract a sample of transactions for subsequent audit checking.
2. To report transactions of special audit interest, for example: all transactions initiated by a specific cashier; or to report exceptional or unusual transactions, for example withdrawals in excess of £100,000.

3. To check periodically the integrity of the files being processed.

(a) Tagging

This is a variation of an embedded program where transactions contain an additional field which may be activated or tagged in response to a specific event, for example:

1. A transaction selected as a result of an audit sample.
2. A transaction of specific audit interest as, for example, one initiated by a specific cashier.
3. An exceptional or unusual transaction such as withdrawals in excess of £100,000.

The tagged transactions may be output to a specific audit file or stay with the rest of the application transactions, in which case the auditor will subsequently interrogate the application files searching for them.

A disadvantage of tagging is that, in providing a method of identifying specific transactions and processing them differently from the norm, it could also be used to compromise the system.

(b) Cusum

Cusum is a diminution of cumulative sum. In this technique the embedded program accumulates a total or a moving average for all occasions when the specified conditions occur during processing. It then reports upon significant variances from the norm.

Cusum can be used to identify:

1. The number of validity errors on input.
2. Posting errors for transaction data against permanent data.
3. The incidence of specific conditions such as exceeding the credit limit.
4. The nature of output, such as the average number of lines per document or the average numbers of document per run.

Advantages

1. This technique facilitates concurrent auditing.
2. It permits continuous monitoring of transactions.
3. It allows immediate follow-up to control problems.

4. It reduces the need for separate audit runs.
5. It is particularly useful for very large files.
6. It enables unusual transactions to be extracted for subsequent audit checking.

Disadvantages

1. It must be incorporated at system specification time.
2. It normally has to be programmed by DP staff and this involves loss of auditor independence.
3. It involves high set-up and maintenance costs.
4. Program maintenance is difficult.
5. Processing overheads may be high.
6. To be effective, an auditor must be assigned to follow-up.
7. Continuous review may not be seen as an audit function but as a line function.
8. Program access controls and change control will need to be reviewed regularly to ensure the integrity of the monitor.
9. Knowledge of the testing criteria may lead to circumvention.

Parallel simulation

This technique is also known as 'Normative simulation' In this technique, auditors recreate all or part of a system by writing programs and then process data through this parallel system to compare with output from the original system.

This method is often used to recreate only the critical functions or controls. Comparison of output may be a manual task or may be achieved with a comparison program on the computer. All differences should be reported for further audit investigation. The simulation may usually be written using interrogation software.

This technique tests the correct operation of specific programs with live data, whereas the test data method uses the auditor's data and the organisation's program.

Advantages

1. The cost for this technique is usually no greater than interrogations packages.

2. It offers simple positive verification of specific programs and programmed controls.
3. It offers simple positive verification of data integrity.
4. It uses live data files but does not corrupt them.
5. The tests are repeatable.
6. It can check all or part of a system.

Disadvantages

1. It may require considerable programming skills if the simulation is of a complex system.
2. Detailed knowledge of the target system is required.
3. It may be expensive to set up and maintain.
4. Discrepancy between the live result and that simulated can be caused by error in the live system or in the simulation.
5. Changes to the live system and the parallel simulation must be synchronised.

Test data

This term covers techniques which are alternatively known as:

(a) base case
(b) test decks
(c) test packs
(d) integrated test facility
(e) mini company

Test data is a technique in which the auditor submits data to be processed by the operational programs. Such data may be submitted in computer readable format or by the submission of input documents. In the latter case, the manual pre-input controls may also be tested. This technique uses fictitious data and in this respect differs from parallel simulation in which the auditor tests the processing of live data through the operational programs. The technique enables auditors to evaluate system controls and procedures including the algorithms used.

Test data can be used for many purposes such as the following:

1. To test control procedures for input and output. The data can be submitted on normal input

documents following normal routines for the purpose of checking the effectiveness of those procedures. The auditor can also check whether all the expected output from the system has been received.

2. To test controls over data input. Normal and abnormal data, including nonsense data, can be submitted in order to test the data validation and update procedures.
3. To test processing logic in order to confirm that the master files contain validly processed data.
4. To test algorithms within programs to check their accuracy and consistency.

There are a number of different methods of using the test data technique, depending upon the audit objective: these are variations in live and dead processing.

(a) Live data – live processing
This method involves identifying live operational data which conforms to test specifications, following it through the system and checking the output against predetermined results.

Advantages

1. This technique saves preparing own test data.
2. It tests real data in live processing.

Disadvantages

1. It is difficult and time-consuming to sift through the mass of input data searching for the specific audit conditions for the test.
2. Live data does not usually include abnormal or nonsensical data.
3. Cyclical variations of input data could be overlooked.
4. Errors could be overlooked where the results are not predetermined.

(b) Dummy data – dummy processing
This variation attempts to overcome the disadvantage that live data seldom includes the conditions that the auditor wishes to test, especially abnormal or nonsensical data. To remedy this, the auditor creates fictitious test data. The submission of dummy data would corrupt the control totals in a live application system, so the auditor uses copies of the application system programs and master files in a special audit run.

This approach offers the benefits of more exhaustive and effective testing, but it is not live processing and the auditor will have to perform further tests to confirm that the copies of files and programs used were true copies of the correct operational versions and that normal operational procedures were followed.

Advantages

1. This technique does not interfere with live processing.
2. It enables the auditor to carry out more exhaustive testing.

Disadvantages

1. Computer staff assistance will probably be needed to set the test up, thus losing audit independence.
2. Additional computer time will be needed.
3. There is no assurance that the test followed normal processing procedures.

(c) Dummy data – live processing
In this variation dummy data is submitted into live processing. This is to overcome any lack of assurance about dummy processing; but it does create additional problems. Live data files and control totals are corrupted by the dummy data and steps must then be taken to negate the corruption:

(a) by manual adjustment of the computer output reports, but this is messy and time-consuming;
(b) by journal voucher adjustment, but it may not be feasible to correct all corrupted files this way;
(c) by reversing the dummy data entries, for example, returning sales goods, but this is not always feasible;
(d) by programming, but this is expensive and it introduces a way of intercepting audit data.

Advantages

1. Programs are tested under normal live operating conditions, thus giving better assurance that current versions of programs are being used.
2. No special arrangements have to be made for computer processing and thus it can take place without the knowledge of operations staff.
3. Less detailed technical knowledge is necessary when using the normal live system.
4. No special 'dummy' files need to be created, thereby reducing initial costs and making reruns in subsequent years easier.

Disadvantages

1. Submitting dummy data corrupts live files.
2. User and computer staff approval must be obtained to update live files.
3. There will be a loss of auditor credibility when corruption occurs.

(d) Integrated test facility (ITF)

This is a refinement of the dummy data – live processing approach. The ITF is integrated into the live system, often by creating a fictitious division or company for all the dummy data. It is then feasible to program out the effects of the dummy data. Such programming may not be necessary where the operational system is processing data for discrete divisions and there is no consolidation of control totals.

The ITF approach enables the auditor to monitor a system continuously. It is a method which must normally be programmed in during system development. However, where there are discrete nonconsolidating divisions, ITF can be introduced with minimal effect upon the operational system. Because this is a continuous test, it does give auditors assurance over the integrity of the processing of the live systems. It also enables auditors to perform comprehensive testing of the system:

(a) by testing controls over input data;
(b) by testing data validation procedures;
(c) by testing processing logic and controls in order to obtain assurance on the integrity of master files;

(d) by testing algorithms within programs;
(e) by testing manual procedures and controls relating to the computer system.

Advantages

1. It offers continuous comprehensive testing.
2. It does not require additional computer resources.
3. It uses normal live programs and files.
4. Once set up, it does not involve users and DP staff.
5. An error condition can be reconstructed without affecting live processing.

Disadvantages

1. High cost of set up and maintenance.
2. Audit data has to be identified to avoid causing corruption and is therefore open to being processed differently from live data.
3. The approval of users and computer staff has to be obtained to update live files.
4. Computer staff assistance will probably be needed to set up the ITF.

Verdict on test data

Advantages

1. It provides positive assurance of the integrity of program controls.
2. It requires little technical expertise.
3. It is not expensive to set up or to run from year to year.
4. It provides a repeatable test which can be applied year after year subject to program changes.
5. Tests may be extended or amended easily.
6. It can be portable.
7. Audit independence can be sustained.
8. It is capable of focusing attention on one or on many facets of a computer system as for example, input, process, output, user department controls, etc.

Disadvantages

1. Considerable set up time may be required.
2. Findings may lack audit significance because

the audit data is unique compared with user data.

3. It introduces control risks by processing against live files.
4. Amendment may be necessary when program changes occur.
5. It may need to be designed in at the development stage.
6. It is often extremely difficult to anticipate every logic combination.
7. There may be a tendency to test anticipated rather than unexpected conditions.

Checking programs

Set out below are techniques for checking the integrity of programs.

Desk checking

In this technique the program code is reviewed:

(a) to verify processing controls;
(b) to check adherence to programming standards;
(c) to check the accuracy of algorithms.

Desk checking would usually be carried out on 'source code' rather than 'object code' because of the considerable difficulty of reviewing the latter. This is not checking the operational program, however, but the purported source of it. Consequently the auditor must take steps to ensure that the version of the source code reviewed is the same as that of the operational object code. There must also be strict control over changing an object program.

The auditor may find it advantageous to compile object code from the source code which has been checked and then to use code comparison software to compare it with the operational object code.

Once the auditor has established that the program functions as specified, continuing assurance may be obtained by taking an audit copy of the checked program and using code comparison software to compare it with later versions.

Advantages

1. It gives the auditor a degree of assurance about the integrity and functional performance of the program.

2. It has a psychological effect in deterring programmers from making unauthorised amendments.
3. It facilitates checking of adherence to programming standards.

Disadvantages

1. A high level of programming knowledge is necessary.
2. It is extremely time-consuming and costly.
3. The tedious nature of the technique may result in it becoming ineffective.
4. It is normally very difficult to confirm that the program being checked is the latest version and that the source code examined is the equivalent of the object code.

Code comparison

Code comparison programs are used to compare two versions of a program, identifying all differences for subsequent verification. The comparison may be executed on the source code or object code versions. The auditor must balance the comparative ease of reviewing source code against the increased assurance from reviewing object code.

Advantages

1. It provides a means of evaluating program changes and also the change control procedures.
2. Having once established that a program has integrity, the auditor need only review the changes.
3. Code comparison programs are easy to use and they are not expensive to run.
4. Knowledge that the auditor holds control copies of programs may deter programmers from making unauthorised amendments.

Disadvantages

1. A high level of programming knowledge is required.
2. There is no guarantee that object programs correspond with the source programs checked by this technique.
3. Two versions of a file may agree at a point in

time; but this is no guarantee that the operational copy has not been amended to agree and subsequently had the amendment reversed.

4. Some software does not realign records once a mismatch has occurred.

Code analysis techniques

Techniques used by programmers to debug programs can be used by auditors. Snapshot, mapping, and tracing, are techniques which analyse code during the execution of a program.

(a) Snapshot

This technique checks at specific points in the program. The routines have to be embedded into the application program at predetermined points. They are triggered by specific attributes of the data being processed, for example: an asterisk in column 80, a specific name, or a defined value.

The auditor may predetermine the criteria and the points in the process at which the status of the data is to be checked, together with the status of switches, accumulators, storage areas, computer code and any other relevant information that is available in the computer memory.

Advantages

1. The technique enables auditors to look at the contents of memory during processing.
2. It enables processing logic to be verified.
3. It monitors how data is altered during processing.

Disadvantages

1. A high level of technical expertise is required.
2. Additional coding is embedded into an application program.

(b) Mapping

This is a technique for monitoring the frequency of execution of instructions and thus identifying unused coding. It will identify a list of source state-ments executed, how many times and the duration of execution. This technique is used as a tool to improve the efficiency of coding. It enables statements that were not used to be identified, usually due to inefficiency or error. But it could be due to a 'time bomb'; for example, coding to erase the program that is only triggered when a specific programmer's name no longer appears on the payroll. The time bomb situation may be described alternatively as a 'Trojan horse'.

Advantages

1. This technique enables unused codes to be identified.
2. It enables program efficiency to be evaluated.

Disadvantages

1. A high level of technical expertise is required.
2. The software is costly to acquire.

(c) Tracing

This technique traces the logic path followed by specific transactions wherever there is a break in instructions. If all instructions run sequentially there will be nothing to trace, but if a split, a go to, or a loop occurs in the logic path it will be traced. Tracing can be applied to a complete program or part of a program or for specific data as for example, Customer X. It can be used on the source or object versions; it would be compiled and embedded in the object version.

Advantage

This technique shows the logic path taken during processing of a transaction.

Disadvantages

1. A high level of expertise is required.
2. It involves high processing costs.

6 Operational audits

Section 1.   Materials management

The nature of materials management

Materials management is the name applied to that management function which co-ordinates and controls those activities in an organisation responsible for the purchasing of materials, their scheduling from supplier and from internal sources, their handling, storage and movement through the organisation, and their despatch and delivery to customers. To assist in this, the function must also be responsible for the control of inventory, materials handling, engineering and associated work study and layout planning.'

(Institute of Materials Handling, 1965)

Stelzer defines materials management as the total control of costs of goods and services from raw materials to the consumer.

Definitions

Materials management   The requisitioning, purchasing, receiving, holding and delivering of goods as necessary for the successful achievement of the organisation's objectives. It means ensuring that the right quantity of goods of the right quality are in the right place at the right time and at minimum cost.

Purchasing   The process by which an organisation procures the goods and services it requires in specified quantities of defined quality to be delivered at a specific time and place for an agreed price.

Stock control   The arrangements for determining the quantities of goods which need to be held and for maintaining those quantities. This is achieved by planning, directing and monitoring the movement of goods into and out of the storage place, in the course of pursuing the organisation's objectives. The purpose may be servicing material requirements for uninterrupted production or satisfying customer service needs with minimum investment and adequate protection and at minimum cost.

Warehousing   The arrangements for the storage of goods until they are required for use or for sale, so as to protect them against loss, damage or deterioration at minimum cost to the organisation.

Risks

Material handling activities involve significant risks; consequently, effective control procedures form a critical element of the management process. The principal risks are set out below.

1. Inadequate control of purchasing leads to inefficiency. For example:
   (a) failure to seek quotations leads to buying at uncompetitive prices and results in excessive costs;
   (b) contracting to buy without adequate consideration of the supplier's financial status and ability to supply can result in costly failure and consequential loss;

(c) procurement commitments on verbal contracts can be prone to differences of interpretation to the buyer's disadvantage;

(d) unpriced purchase orders are open-ended commitments which can prove very costly;

(e) buying activities often provide opportunities for malpractice and breach of trust which pose risks both to the organisation and to its staff.

2. Ineffective stock control leads to operational inefficiency and inability to manage stock investment. For example:

(a) failure to have the necessary materials available when and where needed may result in production waiting time, customer service breakdown, breach of contract and lost opportunities;

(b) having too much material or the wrong or unsuitable material available results in unnecessary stock investment, excessive handling and storage costs, and deterioration and obsolescence risks;

(c) using material of unsuitable quality in production may result in excessive costs of processing or scrap. Delivering unsuitable material to customers can damage goodwill.

3. Unreliable records for stock and material movements can lead to extensive inefficiency by impairing the effectiveness of controls throughout the organisation. For example:

(a) false purchasing requirements;

(b) inaccurate production planning and control;

(c) unsatisfactory stock control;

(d) inadequate control of despatches and invoicing;

(e) misleading cost information and management accounting;

(f) loss of financial control.

4. Inadequate warehousing arrangements may result in losses due to deterioration or damage to stock or pilferage. Materials may be inflammable, corrosive, toxic, noxious or hazardous to handle due to weight, size, shape or other physical properties. Ineffective packaging, absence of proper handling equipment or storage facilities, untrained or unprotected staff or lack of safety disciplines pose serious threats to the organisation and to its employees.

5. Movement of materials attracts a range of transportation risks. For example:

(a) loss or damage whilst in the custody of others including fire, explosion, impact, flood, contamination, deterioration, theft, confiscation, or distraint;

(b) loss or damage during transit by road, rail, sea or air including traffic accidents, mechanical failure, shipwreck, hijacking, piracy, terrorism and war risks;

(c) damage caused to third parties;

(d) consequential losses.

Care in selecting transportation agents and the terms contracted with them with appropriate insurance coverage may provide a degree of protection against these risks.

Procurement

Objectives

There are four key purchasing objectives:

1. Competitive prices.
2. Consistent quality.
3. Reliable service.
4. Assurance of supply continuity.

Purchasing decisions have to reflect the conflicting requirements of each of the functions affected by the results. For example:

1. Buyers want competitive prices from a range of reliable suppliers and large orders for maximum discounts and minimum administration.

2. Sales managers want large stocks and reliable quality to ensure best service to customers, and design flexibility to match changing market trends.

3. Production managers want reliable quality and service and low prices with long runs to minimise production costs.

4. Stock controllers want predictable demand and regular deliveries for fast turnover and few changes in design or specification to avoid obsolescence.
5. Transport managers want long hauls with good pay loads and the goods to be adequately packaged.
6. Financial controllers want minimum stock investment.

Price

Competitive prices take the following into account:

1. Net prices quoted for supplying. These may be from a published list price for standard product less a negotiable customer loyalty or trade classification discount, an order quantity discount and sometimes a promotional discount. Alternatively, prices may be quoted for unique product to match the buyer's specification with or without specific customer, quantity or promotional discounts.
2. Any price reservations by which the supplier reserves the right to adjust the price charged for any reason; this may be particularly relevant for major contracts and those involving long lead times.
3. Any tooling costs chargeable by the supplier.
4. Delivery charges.
5. Any other charges.
6. Settlement terms including settlement discount and the value of any credit allowed.
7. Any retrospective rebate terms.

In addition to the terms contracted with the supplier there may be further costs incurred in the procurement of materials from some sources. When appropriate, these must be taken into consideration in comparing the net prices of materials from different sources. For example:

8. Collection costs.
9. Importation costs including handling and dock charges, duty, freight and insurance.
10. Foreign exchange conversion costs.
11. Any commission payable to agents acting for the buyer.

Quality

Effective quality control is often attainable only through an integrated programme for the entire organisation. This ensures that the quality standards adopted for materials purchased are compatible with those set to maintain the quality of finished output.

A clear quality specification is a critical element of every purchase order for materials and services. The quality must be adequate for the required purpose. If the quality is below this standard the material may be unusable or, if used, may prove very costly in terms of scrapped or inferior output. Better quality than is necessary adds cost without benefit.

Having defined the quality standards required, quotations may be invited from suppliers only where there is a reasonable basis for confidence that they will match them. The principal factor in this confidence judgement will be experience of the 'track record' of each supplier.

However, buyers should use every endeavour to solicit new suppliers and alternative materials on a trial basis. It is a form of protection against the risks involved in becoming overdependent on any single supplier.

Quality testing is an important feature of the material receiving procedures. Disciplines need to be established for appropriate expert inspection or sample testing promptly on receipt and maintaining a complete formal record of these tests. The testing record should be compared without delay against the specification as defined in the purchase order. Materials matching the specification may then be accepted and taken into stock. Materials failing to match specification should be rejected for return to supplier.

It is most important to notify suppliers about rejected materials at the earliest possible moment. It is necessary to correct the supplier's assumption that the delivered goods have been accepted and will be paid for in due course. But more important, delivery of unsuitable goods has the same effect as overdue delivery and it will be necessary to urge the supplier to deliver suitable goods without further delay.

Service

Service in the context of material procurement is concerned first with meeting the buyer's reasonable delivery requirements.

Delivery promises will be influenced by the nature of the goods or services required.

Standard commodities or products are likely to be stocked by a number of competing suppliers who are thus able to offer delivery within days. In this area, service standards have great competitive importance and suppliers are prepared to invest significantly in distribution facilities to enhance customer service as a marketing tool. Limitations to prompt delivery may be caused by:

1. Location: National suppliers usually establish a network of regional stocking and delivery depots. Local suppliers may become uncompetitive outside their own locality.
2. Uneven demand: The distribution resources provided may be sufficient to meet demand at most times but overloaded at peak periods.
3. Administrative standards: Competitive service standards in distribution demand efficient order processing, effective stock control, good warehouse management and well organised, reliable transport facilities. Weakness in any of these will be reflected in indifferent service to customers.

Purchase contracts for discrete goods or services designed specifically for the buyer may be subject to long lead times. Delivery promises will be influenced not only by the time required to do the work but also by the state of the supplier's order book. Thus, when early delivery is important to the buyer, the supplier who is busy will be at a competitive disadvantage.

The credibility of suppliers' delivery promises is a critical factor. The attraction of early delivery, if uncertain, will usually be outweighed by confidence in a reliable delivery promise for a later date.

A second and equally important feature of supplier service is in technical support made available to buyers. Suppliers of specialist materials or products which involve some element of technology will often have made a significant investment in technological development before bringing their product to the market. They will also be concerned to ensure that their customers are sufficiently well informed to appreciate the full potential of the product offered. Good technical support to customers is an important marketing tool.

Technical support may be provided in various forms:

1. Helpful information and advice on the handling and use of the goods supplied.
2. Consultancy services assisting the buyer to analyse specific problems leading to appropriate technical solutions.
3. Training services for staff.
4. Skilled maintenance services for technically advanced equipment supplied to the buyer.

These services may be charged for at commercial prices or as nominal charges or they may be offered as 'free of charge' – which of course means 'included in the price of the goods supplied'. The buyer must evaluate the quality of technical support offered when comparing competitive quotations.

Continuity

Contracting for the supply of critical materials means placing considerable trust in the suppliers selected. Lack of continuity in supply could seriously damage the prospects of any organisation. Uncertainty about the ability to maintain a product range discourages potential customers. Disruption in material supplies could result in inability to fulfil commitments to customers. They cannot be expected to forgive and forget: they are much more likely to decide to place their trust elsewhere.

Continuity of material supplies will be at risk when too much reliance is placed in a single supplier or when the future of a key supplier is insecure for any reason; for example, withdrawal from the market, financial weakness or a candidate for take-over.

Research to establish the prospects of continuing reliability for every potential supplier of critical materials is an essential element of procurement activity. This research will identify not only vulnerable areas but also opportunities.

Material requirements can be classified according

to their importance to the organisation and related to the supply risk. This will enable supplier strengths and buyer strengths to be compared with the object of matching them.

A clear strategy is therefore needed to determine the most advantageous policy to adopt towards each supplier or group of suppliers. Policies would range from exploitation where there is a buyers' market to protection through diversification in suppliers' markets where the buyer is vulnerable.

Specification

Separating the specification of requirements and due authorisation elements of procurement from the commercial negotiation and order placing elements is an important internal control feature of materials management.

In a manufacturing organisation material requirements will be derived from a production plan prepared by production management to satisfy forecast sales demand. A bill of materials will identify material specifications, quantities, and conditions of delivery.

Some goods may be held in stock, so providing the necessary buffer between the flow required for efficient production and economic buying quantities. There will then be an inventory programme with appropriate maximum and reorder stock levels.

Goods to be delivered as and when required for production have to be scheduled with precise delivery times and arrangements made for alternative supply lines.

Purchasing requirements other than those specified to meet planned production requirements are initiated by departmental managers who should have delegated authority to procure the materials and services needed for effective departmental operation.

Budgetary control is the management tool for controlling departmental performance in terms of measured output and cost. Accountable budget holders normally exercise their purchasing authority by issuing purchase requisitions to the buying department.

Control

Effective control in the procurement of goods and services is dependent upon a sequence of key procedures:

1. Purchasing control procedures must be applicable to all those authorised to request the purchase of goods and services, including all those authorised to change purchase order terms for quantity, quality, delivery or price.
2. There must be a means of identifying all such individuals as having budgetary accountability.
3. There should be a means for controlling what goods and services are to be requisitioned in terms of quality, quantity, time and place of delivery and acceptable price range: this is normally a budgetary control procedure.
4. There may also be authority limits established for each authorised individual, in terms of the quantity, quality and value of materials and services which may be requisitioned at any time and cumulatively.
5. There should be a defined procedure for submitting purchase requisitions.
6. Minimum conditions of purchase should be defined. Desired standard conditions may be set up in printed form to be distributed with and forming part of every invitation to quote and every purchase order. However, since many suppliers also have standard conditions of sale, the agreed conditions are often a matter for negotiation when minimum conditions of purchase will be relevant.
7. Procedures and criteria for selecting and inviting suppliers to quote and for choosing from the offers received need to be clearly defined. This is necessary to avoid possible conflict of interests, unfair or unjustified preference, and to minimise the opportunities for bribery or other forms of corruption. It also serves to provide proper protection for buying staff against wrongful accusation.
8. There should be clearly defined disciplines for agreeing acceptable purchase terms, including price with the supplier, before commitment.
9. The use of serially prenumbered formal pur-

chase order stationery facilitates the exercise of a measure of control over all orders issued and all outstanding commitments.

10. It is necessary to establish firm procedures for ensuring that all goods and services ordered are received in accordance with the contracted terms of purchase, and in particular, quantity, quality and delivery place and time. This means a proper checking and recording procedure for goods received at all receiving points. It also means regular monitoring of the outstanding orders and chasing overdue supplies.

11. There must be an efficient purchase invoice approval procedure which ensures that the goods and services received and accepted are charged for by the supplier contracted with, at the prices contracted.

12. All invoices received should be recorded on receipt so that further action may be monitored. Those which are not related to a formal purchase order should be subjected to approval control procedures covering authority and receipt of goods or services like those applying to purchase orders.

Organisation

In large organisations with dispersed plants, branches or subsidiaries, consideration needs to be given to the degree of corporate involvement in buying activities.

The aggregated material requirements of the whole organisation will usually command considerably more buying power than that which any of the separate units can command operating alone. There are likely to be advantages in price savings for bulk buying and in the favourable terms suppliers are prepared to offer in consideration of the potential for greater volume.

These advantages of aggregation may be secured by establishing either a centralised buying operation, or a corporate function to co-ordinate local buying operations.

When all the local operating units are similar, for example in a retail chain, centralising buying is likely to be suitable and may offer savings in administration costs. The purchasing function must, however,

maintain close links with all the other functions it services. Extending these links for centralised buying sometimes results in communication problems.

Centralised buying is unlikely to be as advantageous in those cases where the operating units differ significantly; for example, in a group of manufacturing plants, each specialising in a different sector of the product range. In these cases the local management, concentrating on its specialist technology, is in a stronger position to secure maximum technical support and service from specialist or local suppliers.

Stock management

Stocks of materials or products are necessary to avoid critical delays in supply. Efficient production and competitive customer service depend upon having the right goods in the right place at the right time and readily available to meet demand as it occurs.

Stocks also serve as reservoirs to match different patterns of demand and supply:

1. Demand may be steady when servicing a continuous production process or a consumer product market. It may also be seasonal or subject to random trends, or subject to external influences.

2. Supply is likely to be conditioned by other considerations. To be competitive, goods must generally be procured either by purchase or by manufacture in economic batch quantities. These are determined by the relationship between 'first off' costs and 'run on' costs.

However, stocks absorb financial resources which could otherwise be working to earn revenue. Stock holding also involves costs of protection, handling, administration and potential loss, damage and obsolescence.

In the light of these benefits and burdens, stock management is an important function in most organisations. Effective stock management depends upon sound stock control and efficient warehousing. It is crucial for activities such as retail distribution, where sales are utterly dependent upon immediate availability. In this environment stock investment often represents substantially the whole of the capital employed.

In manufacturing industry the need for effective stock management is also likely to be critical with emphasis on efficiently servicing the material requirements of a production line. Here, stock investment usually has to compete with other demands on available financial resources such as capital expenditure and customer credit.

Stock investment

Operational efficiency in every organisation depends upon making the most effective use of available financial resources which are always limited and costly. Consequently, it is necessary to evaluate every demand for finance and to measure the cost. This requirement places an important constraint on all material management activity. It is unusual, however, to evaluate the need for stock investment in terms of return on capital other than as an integral part of a capital development project. Total stock investment may be monitored against a financial budget and it is usual to monitor trends in service levels in terms of the rate of stock turnover.

The concept of integrated material management is fundamental to effective financial control of stock investment. It is important to recognise that the investment in materials starts with placing purchase orders and it is not realised until that material is sold and paid for. The investment has to be financed throughout all the intervening processes.

Goods received from suppliers for payment become raw material stock. This is issued for production and becomes work in progress, with added investment in processing costs. At the end of the production line the same material, modified by the production process, becomes manufactured stock. Further warehousing and distribution cost may be added before acceptance and payment by the customer.

There are thus two key factors which influence stock investment:

1. The placing of purchase orders: these establish the commitment to receive and pay for materials.
2. The time interval between the purchase and sale

transactions involving the same material: this is the measure of materials in the 'pipeline'.

Procedures for controlling stock investment must take due account of conditions necessary to achieve the organisation's objectives but should focus control action on these two critical features.

In a merchanting organisation the supply 'pipeline' may be relatively short. The necessary stock investment will be determined by customer service needs and bulk buying benefits and risks.

In the case of a manufacturing organisation there are additional issues to be considered. When the manufacturing operation is complex it will have a long time cycle and there may be a need for intermediate stocks to enable production at different stages to be matched. The most significant part of the stock investment will be the amount necessary to finance work in progress.

Complex manufacturing cycles are common in most spheres of engineering work, from durable consumer goods and cars to heavy machinery and job contracting. Complexity arises when manufacture involves a number of distinct operations or stages which must be performed separately. For example:

1. Component production, which may involve a range of separate processes or operations such as foundry, press shop, machine shop, plating, etc.
2. Assembly, which may involve a number of separate stages of subassembly.
3. Fnishing, with a range of options, each probably involving a sequence of different processes.
4. Testing and packaging.

This example may not be appropriate to process industries such as brewing and much food processing, oil refineries and chemical works. But similar principles may apply.

In process industries, production cycles reflect the nature of each process and its requirements; output will be directly related to input of raw material. However, process industry is often complex too, because most operations involve a number of different processes and a range of options for combining them. This usually means holding intermediate stocks of part-processed product to facilitate matching the different processing demands.

Production efficiency depends upon sound production planning and effective production control. It is likely to be critically influenced by the volume of work in progress held to maintain supply reservoirs between production stages. Material yield is also an important element. It is influenced by product design, quality control of materials used, production methods, supervision and control, and accounting for all waste material.

Stock control

Sound stock control depends upon effective procedures and disciplines for each of the key following tasks involved.

1. Establishing what goods are required, and when and where they are needed to fulfil the organisation's objectives.
2. Directing the appropriate movement of goods.
3. Ensuring that the necessary stocks are maintained.
4. Ensuring that the stock investment is maintained at the minimum amount necessary and within planned parameters.
5. Ensuring that reliable, concurrent records are maintained.

Accurate and timely detailed information on all movements of goods and on the stocks held is the key to effective stock control.

Control has to be exercised in terms of both quantity and value. Consequently, the recording system must capture both features of every transaction. However, whereas quantity information is meaningless unless it relates to each separate stock line, the significance of value is primarily in the total.

In view of this distinction, the separate data on value and quantity are often captured separately and usually processed by separate routes. Quantity data are recorded by goods received notes, stores issue warrants, delivery notes, stock bin cards and detailed stores ledgers. Value data are recorded from purchase invoices, and evaluated summaries of

stores issues, transfers of production into stock, cost of sales and sales invoices.

Documents recording stock movements usually serve other purposes additional to updating the stock records:

1. Goods received notes serve for:

   (a) clearing the purchase order;
   (b) evidence for invoice approval;
   (c) adding to the stock record.

2. Stores issue warrants serve for:

   (a) reducing the stock record;
   (b) adding to work in progress record;
   (c) evaluation in summary for reducing the stock value record.

These are examples of documents raised within an organisation for the purpose of recording operational activity as it occurs and generating control data. There are a number of principles to be considered:

1. Documents should be designed in a format which ensures all the information needed is recorded.
2. Separate unit documentation for each separate transaction is appropriate whenever subsequent use or processing is likely to be in a different sequence from that in which the documentation is generated. For example, goods received notes are generated in the sequence in which goods arrive from suppliers; they may then be sorted:

   (a) into stock location sequence for checking the movement of goods into stock;
   (b) into stock account sequence for up-dating the stock records;
   (c) into supplier account sequence for matching with purchase orders and purchase invoices.

3. When documents are required for several different purposes it is usual to use multipart stationery so that each function concerned receives its own copy to act on and to file for subsequent reference if necessary and for audit trail.
4. Whenever multipart unit documents are used, it is important to establish a means of control which

enables each of the functions which use them to verify that all documents have been received and acted upon. This is achieved by use of preprinted serial numbers which appear on all copies. It is then necessary to maintain a record of the serial numbers of the blank forms used and documents generated and to ensure that the stationery is used in strict numerical sequence.

5. Transaction information is most reliably recorded by the operation itself, if this is feasible, in preference to clerical intervention. Common examples are in time recording devices, tachographs and printing weighing machines. Devices for automatic process control are often also capable of recording. The record may be hard copy or it may be electronic data for computer input.

6. When a computer terminal with a visual display unit is used for data entry, it can offer validation checks before accepting the record entered. Thus it may refuse acceptance if any sector of data has been omitted or is outside predetermined parameters, or if the new data is incompatible with information already on file; for example, the purchase order.

In some cases of on-line systems with distributed networking, where data is on computer files, it is possible to dispense with hard copy for certain traditional documents. Computer sorting is generally faster and more flexible than the clerical process. The system must incorporate essential checking controls and exception reporting for continuity checks.

Stock records

Here are the essential features for reliable quantity recording:

1. Accurate recording of all goods received at the point and time of receipt. For example:

   (a) purchased goods received and accepted from suppliers;
   (b) part manufactured goods, manufactured components and subassemblies taken into stock;
   (c) part manufactured or finished goods received and accepted from subcontractors;
   (d) returned goods from issues for production taken back into stock;
   (e) manufactured products taken into stock as finished goods;
   (f) returned goods accepted from customers and taken back into stock as finished goods.

2. Accurate recording of all goods delivered from stock at the point and time of delivery. For example:

   (a) materials, components and subassemblies issued for production;
   (b) materials supplied from stock to subcontractors for production;
   (c) materials issued for consumption;
   (d) previously accepted materials returned to suppliers;
   (e) materials identified as surplus to requirements, withdrawn from stock and sold;
   (f) materials identified as obsolete, damaged or perished, withdrawn from stock and disposed of;
   (g) goods withdrawn from stock for sale to customers;
   (h) goods withdrawn from stock for samples to customers.

3. A stock ledger for maintaining an up-to-date continuous record of the quantity of stock held for each stock line by recording all receipts and deliveries.

   It may record other information needed for stock management such as storage location, anticipated future receipts, reservations for specified future issues, maximum stock level, reorder level, price or standard cost.

Stock counting

A procedure is required for checking the stock records by physical counting. It may be achieved by periodical full stock counts. However, this is often disruptive, particularly as it is usually necessary to suspend operations temporarily in order to establish a clean cut-off of all movements.

It is more usual to have a programme of continuous cyclical stock counting planned to ensure that every stock line is counted once in each prescribed period. This is not likely to be disruptive, but special care is necessary to establish the precise status of all movements recorded in relation to the time the count is made.

Stock counting is a control function to be performed independently by staff reporting to someone other than the warehouse manager. The cyclical count programme should also be independently determined. The stock counting function is sometimes described as 'stock audit', so emphasising the significance of an independent role.

In some cases the cyclical stock count programme may be augmented by a practice of recording, on each issue document, the balance left in stock whenever a delivery is made. This practice is not always feasible and in any event it should only be relied upon as supplementary confirmation. It is not independent stock counting.

When stock differences are identified by stock counting it is usual to make a confirmatory check and then the quantity record has to be adjusted to the confirmed count. All stock adjustments so made should be scheduled and reported for investigation. The schedule will also have to be evaluated to enable a corresponding adjustment to be made in the record of stock value.

When stock count discrepancies are significant in quantity or value, or if they are persistent, it is important to establish the cause. It may be due to inaccurate recording, delivering inaccurate quantities, delivering the wrong goods, or stock shrinkage through theft or pilferage.

Stock value

It is necessary to have a procedure for confirming the value record of stock by periodical comparison with an evaluation of the quantity record. This task is necessary at least annually to support inventory values in audited accounts. However, to achieve effective control it may be necessary to confirm both value and quantity records at more frequent intervals.

The comparison is achieved by first extending a schedule of in-stock quantities for all stock lines at appropriate prices, normally standard cost for each line. Particular care is necessary to ensure that the two records to be compared have reached the same stage in recording all transactions. Special attention must be given to cut-off disciplines for the recording of all movements. It may be perceived as a formidable task, particularly so when large volumes of transactions and complex patterns of movement are involved.

However, stock control information is frequently generated from integrated systems which may cover elements of purchasing, stock control, production control and sometimes standard costing. Such systems are often computer based and provide the means of extracting the relevant data and performing the necessary calculations with speed and accuracy.

Moreover, the need to confirm the inventory value of the stock records at regular intervals, or even continuously, may well have been provided for in the system specification. It is a possibility to be considered in designing new systems.

Warehousing

Efficient warehousing depends upon effective control procedures and disciplines for the operational activities of handling and custody of stock which include:

1. Receiving, storing and delivering goods as directed.
2. Maintaining all necessary custodial protection for stock.
3. Generating accurate records of these activities.

These activities are concerned with the efficient direction and use of the appropriate resources for moving goods to where they are required at the time they are needed and providing custodial protection meanwhile.

Warehouse management involves planning the layout and organising the resources for efficient operation. It then means directing and supervising the work force.

A responsibility for custodial protection means protecting the safety and security of the goods in custody. This involves ensuring that appropriate equipment is installed and maintained in working order, ensuring that staff are aware of the risks and trained to deal with emergencies, establishing safe working practices and emergency disciplines. Finally, it means ensuring that appropriate and adequate insurance cover is maintained.

Resources

The resources may include the following specifications:

1. Suitable warehouse accommodation in appropriate locations. Many organisations need just one, or perhaps two, warehouses adjoining the production plant for keeping stock of raw materials and finished goods. Large organisations, and particularly those serving consumer markets, often need a network of strategically located regional warehouses as local distribution points in a national or international market-place.

   Servicing a network of warehouses may require a fleet of specially designed vehicles as an additional resource in some of these cases. In other cases it may be considered more economic to subcontract inter-warehouse haulage.

2. Necessary warehouse fittings and equipment. For example:

   (a) racking, shelves, cupboards, safes, cages, bunkers, bins, pallets, tanks, silos, containers, strong rooms, cold stores, etc. as appropriate for the stock held;
   (b) weighing devices and other measuring and testing equipment suitable for receipts into store, deliveries from store and in-store stock checking and testing;
   (c) handling equipment for marshalling receipts and deliveries, breaking bulk and in-store movement: this may include tractors, lifting trucks, trolleys, cranes, lifts, hoists, lifting tackle, conveyers, pumps, etc.;
   (d) security and protection equipment for stock and warehouse staff: this may include smoke and fire detectors and alarms, fire fighting equipment, security locks, door and window bars, intruder alarms, flood control equipment, environmental conditioning equipment, and protective clothing for staff.

3. A staff trained in a range of suitable skills for:

   (a) planning the layout and organisation of the warehouse facilities to fulfil the function expected of it;
   (b) receiving, checking, testing and recording goods received;
   (c) moving and stacking the goods received in store;
   (d) picking goods required for delivery, marshalling and recording them;
   (e) maintaining cleanliness, tidiness, safety and the security of the warehouse.

Receiving goods

Goods should be checked on receipt, and a goods received note raised immediately. It is an important record and care must be taken to ensure that all the necessary information is correctly recorded. In some organisations the system secures this accuracy by having 'pro forma' goods received data prepared in advance as part of the process of preparing purchase orders or even purchase requisitions. The goods received record may serve a number of purposes:

1. It enables progress on each outstanding purchase order to be monitored.
2. It provides evidence of receipt for invoice approval.
3. It may initiate an entry in stock records or production progress records as appropriate.
4. It may be the basis of entries in accounting records for stock control, cost recording or for liabilities for which the invoice is awaited.

Goods should be inspected or tested as required for quality control as early as it is feasible to do so, and the results recorded. If the goods accord with the order specification and any other prescribed quality standards which apply, they may be accepted and should then be moved to the appropriate storage area without delay.

If the goods are not accepted for any reason,

arrangements must be made to inform the supplier promptly. The goods may be returned to the supplier, or it may be appropriate to move them to a temporary place of storage to await inspection or collection by the supplier.

Delivering goods

Delivery can be achieved in different ways depending on the nature of the organisation:

1. In a manufacturing organisation materials may be withdrawn from stock to be used in production and finished goods may be delivered to customers.
2. In a service organisation goods may be withdrawn from stock to be used by the organisation often in the course of providing a service to customers.
3. In a merchanting organisation goods are generally delivered from stock to customers.
4. In a self-service retail organisation customers are given access to the stock of goods to select and withdraw the items they need.

The procedures for recording and control of deliveries in these differing circumstances may vary significantly. There are, however, some basic principles which apply:

1. When there is advance notice of the requirements, documentary authority and instructions for delivery can be raised in advance. The movement of the goods is then effectively controlled and recorded. This is the case for issues to production by stores warrant and deliveries to customers with despatch notes in satisfaction of an established sales contract.

   In these cases it is feasible to take account of delivery commitments in stock planning not only to ensure the goods are available when delivery is due, but also to initiate stock replacement for future demand. Running out of stock is a serious failure because it means disrupted production plans or broken delivery promises to customers.
2. When goods are delivered on demand, a general authority to release the goods must be presumed and the record is created at the point of delivery.

This is the case for service type casual supplies issued from stock and retail selling from stock. There always remains a final sanction to refuse delivery in the absence of an acceptable form of payment.

In these cases, provisioning to meet anticipated demand means careful market research, close observation of short-term trends and replacing stock as it is depleted. Running out of stock means lost opportunities.

Distribution and transport

The objective in distribution is to provide the best service to customers for the least cost to the organisation, adding both value and cost to the product.

Distribution is sometimes organised as a marketing function, as it is a customer interface activity. It is then perceived as a marketing tool contributing positively to the value of the product. However well the product is designed, however persuasively promoted or competitively priced, it is worth nothing unless it is available when and where the customer wants it.

In other cases, the concept of materials management is perceived as an integrated service function covering procurement of goods and services, stock control, warehousing and distribution as an organisational entity. Organising these closely related activities in this way may provide significant opportunities for improving efficiency from synergy.

Transportation may account for 10 per cent of the cost of a product at the point of sale, which is additional to the associated costs of warehousing and stock management.

Planning

Many organisations operate a distribution system which has grown over time and may be less than ideal. The system needs to be flexible to accommodate present conditions and expected future trends. It is important to keep the ideal in view and endeavour to move towards it.

The development of a strategic plan for distribution starts by accumulating marketing data relevant to delivery objectives, such as the data suggested here:

1. Location of customers and potential customers.
2. Projected volumes of deliveries to each customer or each category of customers.
3. Demand patterns, and whether they are seasonal.
4. Frequency of deliveries and lead-times.
5. Projected volumes purchased by customers from competitors.
6. Projected service levels of competitors.
7. Targeted service levels for the product range.

This data may then be summarised to arrive at an assessment of transport capacity which needs to be provided taking account of the most suitable methods of delivery, appropriate types and size of vehicle and the times needed for loading, travelling and unloading.

In seeking the best service to customers at minimum cost it is important to consider the total cost of both warehousing and delivery: the two elements are so closely related that reducing the cost of one often increases the cost of the other.

The simplest form of distribution system may be to have just one central warehouse from which to deliver direct to all customers. The most suitable location for a central warehouse may be established by starting with 'centre-of-gravity' measurement to find the point from where aggregate tonne miles for all collection and delivery would be least.

For some products, a measure other than tonne miles may be appropriate, as for example merchandise of high value in relation to its weight, or products which involve high technology, where the supply of goods is subordinate to the provision of a technical service.

Other factors may then be considered against the added cost attributable to displacement from that point. These would include regional development incentives, site availability and costs, labour availability and costs, accessibility of the motorway and railway systems, etc. It may also be necessary to be located in close proximity to key customers to maintain a competitive delivery service.

All feasible options involving more than one distribution warehouse have also to be considered.

It may be necessary to construct a progression of models synthesising various combinations of warehouses with associated transport, stock and personnel to find the most effective way of meeting customer service demands at the lowest total cost. Transport costs will need to take into account trucking in bulk from supply points and local deliveries to customers.

Freight options

An important factor in achieving an efficient distribution service is the choice of the most appropriate methods of transport. Consideration must be given to all the alternatives: road, rail, air, parcel post, customer collect, inland waterways, etc. In each case, the objective of keeping transport costs to a minimum must be balanced against customer service requirements and storage, handling, packaging and other costs.

Road freight

This is by far the most used method for movement of goods in the UK, accounting for over 90 per cent of all inland freight tonnage. It offers particular advantages:

1. **Through movement** Goods can be moved speedily by road from consignor to consignee without trans-shipment. This avoids double handling and reduces the risk of loss or theft.
2. **Flexibility** Movement by road can be more closely controlled than for other forms of transport: routes and loading routines may be more easily changed.
3. **Fast turn-round** The use of articulated vehicles and demountable bodies give considerable advantages to road freighting. This is important where loading and unloading is lengthy in relation to transit time: trailers are often loaded from the end of production lines.
4. **Industrial action** Whether using own vehicles or a haulage contractor, most consignors believe disruption due to industrial action initiated by third parties is less likely with road transport than with other transport methods.
5. **Overseas** Roll on/roll off (RO/RO) ferry ser-

vices greatly facilitate road transportation into Europe with minimum delays.

Sometimes the economics of operating a delivery vehicle fleet depend upon obtaining a minimum proportion of return pay loads. In other cases the delivery vehicles have to be specially designed for the task and are then unsuitable for general haulage or they must be protected from contamination, for example: refrigerated food transporters and bowsers for bulk transport of specific liquids.

Some organisations entrust part or all of their delivery work to a retained haulage contractor; others contract competitively for each load. These practices are common for industrial materials and products not requiring specially designed vehicles.

They may be more flexible and less costly than maintaining an in-house delivery fleet at varying levels of utilisation through all seasons.

Organisations serving a consumer product market usually maintain their own delivery fleet to add a competitive edge to customer service. The high-sided covered vans often used for this work provide a bonus in the form of highly visible, mobile, outdoor advertising space.

Rail freight

The rail network of Great Britain had already been extensively developed and was dominant when the internal combustion engine was invented. Road transport competed by offering greater flexibility and now carries more than 90 per cent of national freight.

The UK road network now enables any two locations to be connected within a few hours, without transfer. This is a standard of service which leaves the railways unable to compete for a large proportion of freight. In some areas, however, rail is competitive. For example:

1. **Bulk traffic** Useful where large volumes of freight are moved between two points, for example: moving iron ore from dock side to steel works or coal from pithead to power station. Special handling equipment and techniques are used in the coal, steel, cement, petroleum and chemicals industries to optimise the advantages of rail freight.

2. **Container traffic** Freightliners provide a high-speed rail freight service between two terminals relatively far apart on routes where there is high-density traffic. Marshalling yards are unnecessary in this operation.

   Freightliner trains depart at scheduled times for specific destinations. They consist of a number of continuously coupled flat bogies. Loaded containers, of standard sizes, are brought by road to the terminal and loaded onto the train. Door-to-door delivery is completed by road collection from the destination terminal, or by shipment overseas for export consignments.

   The freightliner service is an efficient and economic method for moving full container loads over long distances. It is unlikely to be competitive for consignments which do not fill the standard three-metre container of 14 cubic metres capacity.

3. **Wagon load traffic** A significant amount of mixed rail freight is moved in wagon loads. However, this class of business tends to lose out by being less competitive than road transport and it can take considerably longer through marshalling yards.

4. **Express parcels** This includes the Royal Mail Parcel Force and other parcel services and letter mails such as datapost, British Rail Red Star, National Freight, etc. These services are suitable for express delivery of packages, which may be either handed in at post offices, stations, depots, or collected by road vehicles.

Air freight

Air freighting accounts for only a small but growing proportion of total freighting within the United Kingdom. Although speed is the principal characteristic, significant time savings are not achievable for domestic consignments. Its relevance increases for the longer hauls involved in export business. It can be a viable method of transport for livestock, medical supplies or perishables with a high value-to-weight ratio.

Routing and scheduling

This is the process of detailed planning for making

the most efficient use of the available vehicles to satisfy the total customer delivery requirements each working day. It is a complex process because many variables are involved:

1. The size of each individual customer order.
2. Distances to be travelled: this may be from warehouse to customer's premises, from customer to customer, from customer back to base, according to the scheduling chosen.
3. Average speed of travel for each leg of the route chosen: this will depend upon the type of highway, vehicle restrictions, and traffic conditions; these may vary throughout the day and from season to season.
4. Loading and unloading times, both at the warehouse and at each customer's premises. Delivery vehicles may have to wait to unload at some customers' premises. Unloading time may depend upon the assistance and handling equipment available at customers' premises.

Compounding all the variables and uncertainties would produce an impossibly vast number of options to select from. Computers are often used to assist the scheduling and routing process and there are a number of suitable package programs available for this.

An element of experienced management judgement is necessary to reduce the range of options to a manageable matrix suitable for the particular distribution job to be done. The preselected format may take the form of establishing a number of standard daily or weekly routes to deal with a significant proportion of the deliveries where there is a recurrent pattern.

It is also necessary to build some flexibility into the plan so that when changed circumstances occur at short notice they can be reasonably accommodated.

Motivating drivers

Most transportation of goods takes place by individuals working without supervision and often alone. Moreover, the driver is a key contact between the customer and the supplying organisation. Consequently, motivation and attitude are both very important and need to be cultivated. In directing the transport team, motivation should be focused not only on success in achieving completion of the schedule, but also on the quality of performance in terms of courtesy, helpfulness and attitude to customers.

Internal audit considerations

Material management for many organisations involves control procedures which have far-reaching effects throughout the organisation. For this reason these procedures are likely to be of particular interest to the internal auditor. Purchasing and stock management tend to rank high as potential risk areas because of the large total amounts involved and the complexity of involvement with most other functions. However, the potential risks may well have been fully recognised by management and an appropriate system of control procedures developed.

The task for the internal auditor is to examine all the risks and to evaluate the control systems in place to establish whether they still provide a sound basis for protection and to recommend developments where gaps are found.

Equally important in this area, however, is how well the established control systems are being applied. The effectiveness of a complex network of control procedures is often dependent on all of them working properly. A weakness in the application of one procedure can become the refuge for inefficiency when other procedures combine to impose tight control in all other areas.

In many cases the constituent elements of material management – procurement, stock control, warehousing and distribution – will not be organised as a single integrated function. Nevertheless, operational efficiency will be dependent upon close interaction between all these activities. The internal auditor's perspective is often unique in having a detailed comprehension of the entire fabric of control for this key area. This is a situation which presents both responsibilities and opportunities.

The techniques by which the internal auditor can pursue these objectives have been fully described in Chapters 4 and 5. In particular, risk assessment, and the evaluation of control systems (especially those where computers are used) are critically important to internal auditing of materials management activity. It is an area with considerable potential for objective operational auditing to contribute significantly to the means of achieving organisational objectives.

Section 2.   Financial management

The nature of financial management

In the broadest sense the function of the financial viewpoint is to serve as the point of contact between the uses of funds within an enterprise and its sources of funds.

(Solomon, 1963)

Financial management involves two distinct elements, both of which are essential to the successful performance of any organisation. They are: servicing the need for financial resources (the treasury function) and controlling the use of all resources to secure operational efficiency within the scope of available financial resources (financial control).

Financial planning

Planning is the first stage of all management activity, to be followed by direction, monitoring and control. Without adequate financial planning, intended developments may be frustrated or, worse, commitments may mature when no funds are available to meet them. It is a management failure likely to result in missed opportunities, sub-optimal performance, unduly restricting burdens of financing cost or conditions, or insolvency.

A corporate plan is a projection of the organisation's intended activity into the future. The starting point is the current status of the organisation which incorporates a particular state of available financial resources and established commitments. The projection takes account of intended action to achieve defined strategic objectives in the context of a forecast pattern of assumed environmental conditions.

All such action will affect cash flow: it may create demands for financial resources and it may generate financial resources. The financing plan is therefore an essential component of the corporate plan: it provides the basis for control in servicing the need for resources.

The purpose of the corporate plan is to provide a guide for directing management action and a basis for measuring performance. The key measure of performance for a business enterprise is profitability: it measures in financial terms how efficiently capital is employed. The corporate plan must therefore be evaluated and summarised in financial terms: it then provides the basis for effective financial control.

Since funding needs and financial control criteria are both determined by the view taken of environmental conditions, and the strategic objectives adopted, further consideration needs to be given here to the nature of these elements of corporate planning. Here are some examples of environmental conditions to be forecast and taken into consideration in corporate planning:

1. **Economic factors** National and international economic trend indicators including exchange rates, interest rates, inflation, commodity prices, government policies, etc.
2. **Technical factors** Technical and other developments likely to affect markets, products and processes, transportation, etc.
3. **Commercial factors** Plans of main competitors, main suppliers and main customers and potential customers, etc.

Here are some examples of strategic objectives:

1. Intentions for changing corporate structure, for example:
   (a) integrate subsidiaries into a single entity;
   (b) 'hive off' a particular activity;
   (c) concentrate on core activities;
   (d) change shape by defined acquisitions and divestments.

2. Intentions for strengthening the marketing position, for example:
   (a) maintain or increase market share;
   (b) exploit new markets;
   (c) extend into additional market territories;
   (d) change distribution channels;

(e) improve the competitiveness of customer service;

(f) change customer profile.

3. Intentions for technical development; for example:

(a) change product profile;

(b) develop new products;

(c) develop new processes.

4. Intentions to improve industrial strength, for example:

(a) relocate production facilities or reorganise to concentrate or specialise;

(c) re-equip or refurbish;

(d) extend manufacturing plant.

5. Intentions to improve financial performance, for example:

(a) planned funding to improve debt/equity relationship;

(b) rearrangement of borrowings to reduce the interest burden or achieve more suitable terms and conditions;

(c) sale and lease back of premises;

(d) rationalisation to save costs and reduce working capital;

(e) changes to strengthen management accountability, such as incentives for improved profitability.

Treasury function

The management of funding involves financial planning, raising and allocating funds as required by the organisation in pursuit of its objectives, and cash management.

Having identified funding requirements, the corporate plan should define the parameters of temporary accommodation needed to match total cash flow generated and total funds required.

Preliminary cash flow projections reveal when additional permanent funding would be necessary to finance all the operational intentions. It is then necessary to examine the feasibility and viability of raising the additional capital when needed: this could lead to reconsideration of some of these intentions, particularly in terms of timing.

Ultimately, the planning process enables permanent funding needs to be clearly established well in advance, so providing time for the necessary research and negotiation to secure the funds, when needed, in the most suitable form, from the most appropriate source, on the most favourable terms.

Here are some examples of operational programmes likely to give rise to a need for additional permanent finance:

1. The acquisition of additional business as a going concern.

2. Capital expenditure to increase productive capacity.

3. Increased working capital associated with growth in turnover.

4. Increased stock support needed to improve the competitiveness of customer service.

5. Maturity of existing borrowings.

Detailed cash flow planning is likely to reveal periods when cash surpluses may be available for temporary investment alternating with periods when short-term borrowing may be appropriate. Flexible cash management arrangements can then be established with bankers and others to accommodate such seasonal trends.

Temporary additional finance may be needed to fund:

1. New product development.

2. New product launch.

3. Seasonal trade variations.

4. A rationalisation programme involving terminating activities.

5. Normal operations where revenue is collected once annually, to defray expenses accruing evenly through the year, for example: many public-sector organisations, clubs and associations.

Raising funds

Once a clear need for additional permanent finance has been identified, careful consideration must be given to the form it should take. For private-sector organisations the initial choice is between equity and loan capital. Certain key factors need to be taken into account when making this choice:

1. It is important to maintain the debt/equity relationship within generally acceptable limits. It is one of the criteria by which capital markets may judge a well-managed company.
2. It is necessary to consider the effect that additional equity could have in diluting the interests of existing substantial shareholders. A rights issue to current shareholders may be the way to resolve problems on this count.
3. The alternative burdens of dividends or interest have to be carefully compared.

   Initially, the interest payable for new loan capital may well be more than the dividends payable on the same amount raised as new equity capital. This reflects the relative risks and opportunities associated with these two forms of investment. Loan interest is a contractual commitment, whereas dividends depend on earning profits: loan capital stands in front of equity capital in a liquidation.

   Loan interest is, however, fixed for as long as the loan is outstanding, whereas dividend distribution is likely to increase with profit growth.

There are other intermediate options available for those cases where the choice between equity and loan capital is not a clear one. These include preference shares, which may also be cumulative and participating or redeemable, and convertible loan stock.

Ordinary shares may sometimes be issued with differential rights in either profit or capital distribution or in voting to address particular circumstances.

Loan capital may be issued as unsecured, or it may be secured by a charge on specified assets or a floating charge on the undertaking.

In general, loan capital is repayable, equity capital is not. Loan stocks issued for public subscription usually have defined dates and terms for repayment or redemption. These will be specified in a trust deed which will also appoint a trustee with specific duties to protect the interests of the stockholders.

It is necessary to issue a prospectus for all forms of permanent or long-term finance to be raised by public subscription. For a UK registered company, the requirements as to information and undertakings to be given in a prospectus and the penalties for breach are defined in ss. 56 to 71 of the Companies Act 1985.

If the security is to be traded on the International Stock Exchange of the United Kingdom the organisation must complete a listing agreement undertaking to observe the listing rules. These rules are published in the Stock Exchange 'yellow book', *Admission of Securities to Listing*.

Public issues of capital and loan stock are normally underwritten by an investment house undertaking, in consideration for a fee or commission, to take up any of the stock not subscribed for.

The capital market is a complex one, demanding a high level of skill and experience to avoid mistakes, oversight or errors of judgement which could lead to disastrous consequences. Specialist guidance is essential from merchant bankers, stock brokers, and law firms specialising in this field.

Other forms of long-term and medium-term finance which do not involve public subscription may be appropriate for particular circumstances, for example:

1. **Placed borrowings** Sometimes stocks are placed in the capital market as an alternative to public subscription. This involves making a formal long-term borrowing agreement with a finance house, investment institution or a consortium. Secured borrowings are sometimes raised in this form as mortgage debentures. A private mortgage on real estate is similar.
2. **Finance leasing** The finance company holds title to the leased assets and may claim tax allowances. This is sometimes advantageous to both parties.
3. **Hire purchase** This is a form of funding for specific capital expenditure which enables payment to be made from the earnings generated by the asset.
4. **Revolving credit** This is a form of bank borrowing facility on formal terms which may be regularly renewed; it may be drawn down and repaid by agreement as required.

5. **Acceptance credits**   This is a form of short-term borrowing. The borrowing organisation draws and accepts bills of exchange on itself which it then discounts in the money market. It thus gains the use of the discounted value throughout the term of the bill and must repay to the holder, in due course, the face value at maturity.

6. **Bank overdraft**   This is the most flexible form of bank borrowing. Bankers normally require their lending to be self-liquidating, so that this is not an appropriate form for permanent finance.

Cash management

All organisations need a working fund of cash for settling transactions when due and it is an important part of the treasury function to ensure that the cash resources are used efficiently and are properly controlled.

Efficient cash management involves marshalling all elements of cash flow to ensure that the necessary funds are available as and when needed for all planned spending, whether capital or revenue. It also means ensuring that surpluses of cash that may build up from time to time are suitably invested on temporary terms to earn the best return attainable.

Except for retail selling, transactions are mainly settled through current accounts with bankers. It is, however, also sound practice to bank retail receipts promptly and intact. Leaving cash to accumulate in a current account with a banker is unlikely to be the most efficient use of the resource.

It may be necessary to operate the bank account in overdraft at certain times: indeed, it may be economically advantageous to do so. Whether the bank account is in credit or overdraft, it is necessary to establish operating parameters within which the balance must be controlled.

The lower limit will be fixed by the terms agreed with the bank, whilst the upper limit will be determined by considerations of efficiency in the use of cash resources.

Many large organisations divide their operations for effective management control among a number of self-accounting units. It is usually convenient for each unit to settle its own transactions through its own bank account. There is thus a need to co-ordinate the separate banking arrangements in the interests of efficient use of the total cash resources of the organisation.

This may be achieved through the bankers' MASS service (memorandum account statement system). In effect, this is a single bank account for the whole organisation. Each unit controls its own cash transactions and receives an individual memorandum statement from the bank for them. Each unit's transactions are aggregated in a single monthly entry in the central record of the account to be acknowledged through inter-unit accounting. Each unit is effectively banking with the centre.

Cash has immediate value to anyone possessing it: it is readily movable and in its convertible form virtually untraceable. Consequently, close control is critical for reasons of security as well as efficiency. This is necessary for the proper protection of both the organisation's property and its staff. There are certain essential control principles which need to be strictly observed:

1. A key feature of all cash handling and recording procedures should be an effective network of internal checks to ensure total accuracy.

2. There must be proper segregation of duties; in particular, those responsible for handling cash should not have any part in accounting for it.

3. All disbursements should require consideration by at least two people and both should sign the documentation. For example, both the requester and the cashier should sign petty cash vouchers and all cheques should require two authorised signatories.

4. All petty cash accounts should be maintained on the imprest system and subject to frequent supervisory checks.

5. All cash receipts should be promptly banked intact daily.

6. Bank mandates must be strictly observed, both by the organisation's staff and by the bank.

7. Bank reconciliations should be prepared at regular intervals and subjected to supervisory checking.

8. Special controls are needed for the maintenance

of the master records used for regular payments such as payrolls and purchase ledger.

9. Special care must be exercised in the recruitment and appointment of staff to positions of trust with responsibility for handling or recording cash.

10. Bonding may be considered appropriate for executives entrusted with handling large amounts of cash. As with other forms of insurance, one of the perceived benefits may be in the control disciplines imposed by the underwriter as a condition of cover; it must not, however, be adopted as a substitute for firm management.

Currency management

Financial reporting and control must ultimately be expressed in the language of a single currency; for a UK organisation it is normally sterling. However, it is unlikely that all the transactions of an organisation will be denoted in the same currency. Importing materials or equipment, export selling, overseas investment and currency borrowings may all introduce a mixture of currencies to be accounted for. Movement in exchange rates can then result in translation losses or gains which are outside the organisation's control.

For sound management of financial resources it is necessary to adopt measures to protect the organisation against currency exposure risks.

Pursuit of profits from holding and dealing in currency may be a legitimate objective for money market traders. Others should endeavour to stabilise the monetary value of every transaction denoted in a foreign currency at the time the deal is struck.

A purchase contract denoted in a foreign currency for settlement in the future may be covered by a forward contract with a banker to purchase the necessary currency on the due date for payment. The sterling cost of the imported goods is then fixed by the forward exchange rate agreed.

A sales contract for future settlement denoted in a foreign currency may also be covered by a forward currency sale contract, provided there is reasonable certainty about receiving payment from the foreign customer on the due date. Sometimes this is assured by delivery of goods on cash against documents' terms or by confirmed bill of exchange or banker's credit. In other cases, by the nature and custom of the trade, goods may be supplied on credit, trusting the buyer to settle on the due date. There may then be a degree of uncertainty in the expected date of receipt.

Organisations which have a significant volume of transactions denoted in foreign currencies may be in a position to balance expected receipts and payments in the same currency. Forward currency dealing may then be reduced or may be eliminated. For a large organisation with a number of operating units, the opportunities for 'off-setting' in this way may be greatly increased by arranging the settlement of all currency transactions through a central treasury function.

Multinational organisations are those which operate in more than one country. In some cases a UK organisation establishes overseas branches, but more usually a separate legal entity is established in the overseas country to manage operations there. In either case the overseas operation will represent an investment in assets denoted in a foreign currency. There is then exposure to exchange movement risks. When overseas investment is funded by borrowing, it is wise to borrow in the same currency as the investment. The currency risks associated with both the investment and the borrowing then 'off-set' each other: this principle applies similarly to the income receivable and the interest payable.

Financial control

Financial control is that aspect of general management concerned with the most efficient use of resources as measured in financial terms.

Accounting is the expertise developed for measuring and interpreting all aspects of management concern in financial terms.

Definitions
Financial control
The use of management accounting information, the comparison of planned and actual performance and taking action to correct adverse trends or optimise favourable conditions.'

This is not to be confused with the control of finance, which is the main function of treasurership.'
Accounting
1. The classification and recording of actual transactions in monetary terms, and
2. the presentation and interpretation of the results of those transactions in order to assess performance over a period, and the financial position at a given date, and
3. the projection in monetary terms of future activities arising from alternative courses of action.

(Extracts from *CIMA Official Terminology*, first edition 1982)

Accounting records

Sound financial management is dependent upon properly maintained reliable accounting records. The accounting records should provide an integrated financial data base for all accounting services within the organisation as follows:

1. **Transaction accounting:** recording and classifying transactions of the organisation including; sales, purchases, receipts, payments etc.
2. **Personal accounting:** recording indebtedness and other terms of relationship with suppliers, customers, employees, etc.
3. **Impersonal accounting:** recording, analysing and summarising revenues and expenses, assets and liabilities including detailed inventories of stock and fixed assets, etc.
4. **Management accounting:** including cash flow monitoring, performance monitoring, budgetary control reporting, cost reporting, project progress monitoring, etc.
5. **Stewardship accounting:** including statutory reporting requirements, detailed records of shareholders, lenders, etc.

Throughout the accounting procedures there must be effective internal control through proper supervision, division of duties and internal checking disciplines. Verification of records is a crucial requirement and is achieved by regular reconciliation with independent external documents such as bank statements, creditors' statements and debtors' remittance advices.

The essential qualities of accuracy, completeness and integrity are then achievable through applying the principles of double-entry bookkeeping. In computerised accounting systems the double-entry discipline is often enshrined in the software. For example: the program for processing purchase invoices may require both the expense code and the supplier account to be identified for simultaneous posting.

A balance sheet is an important statement of the financial status of an organisation. But equally important, it testifies to the integrity of the accounting records from which it was produced.

UK companies are required by the Companies Acts to keep accounting records which:

(a) are sufficient to show and explain the company's transactions and to disclose the company's financial position;
(b) enable accounts to be prepared as required by the Act;
(c) contain a day-to-day record of monies received and expended;
(d) contain a record of assets and liabilities;
(e) contain, for a company dealing in goods, statements of year-end stock, of stocktaking and of goods sold and purchased.

Management accounting

Management accounting is the application of accounting techniques to the pursuit of management objectives.

Definition

Management accounting
The provision of information required by management for such purposes as:

1. formulation of policies;
2. planning and controlling the activities of the enterprise;
3. decision taking on alternative courses of action;
4. disclosure to those external to the entity (shareholders and others);
5. disclosure to employees;
6. safeguarding assets.

The above involves participation in management to ensure that there is effective:
(a) formulation of plans to meet objectives (long term planning);
(b) formulation of short term operation plans (budgeting and profit planning);

(c) recording of actual transactions (financial accounting and cost accounting);

(d) corrective action to bring future actual transactions into line (financial control);

(e) obtaining and controlling finance (treasurership); and

(f) reviewing and reporting on systems and operations (internal audit, management audit).

(*CIMA Official Terminology*, first edition, 1982)

This is a comprehensive definition which also emphasises the principal areas where management accounting services contribute to the achievement of management objectives.

The quality of management performance is judged by its effectiveness, that is to say, whether or not it achieves its objectives and how efficiently it does so in terms of the resources used compared with the results achieved. To be able to compare objectives and performance meaningfully, they have to be quantified and ultimately expressed in a common language, in effect in financial terms.

Thus the interpretation of management concerns in financial terms is an essential feature of management accounting. It involves managing information which includes collection, verification, storage, analyses and summarising; and then interpreting it in the context of management objectives.

Effective management activity follows a cyclical pattern: it involves planning – directing – monitoring – control – planning, and so on. Because of the need to measure in financial terms, management accounting is an integral feature of the planning, monitoring and control phases of the management cycle. This involvement for the most common management accounting applications at different management levels is illustrated in Tables 6.1 and 6.2.

Table 6.1   Management accounting applications for corporate management

Application	Planning	Monitoring	Control
Corporate planning	Evaluation of corporate planning.	Presentation of consolidated short-period accounts and financial statements compared with plan.	Interpretation and analyses of trends to identify opportunities and risks for review of strategies and policies.
Cash management	Cash flow forecast and financial plan.	Recording, summarising and reporting cash flow compared with plan.	Analysis of trends and interpretation in terms of revisions to forecast and modifications to the financing plan.
Stewardship accounting	Programming annual accounts with auditors.	Preparation and audit of statutory accounts.	Ensuring all statutory accounting obligations are met.

Table 6.2   Management accounting applications for operational management

Application	Planning	Monitoring	Control
Standard costing Budgetary control	Evaluation of standards. Evaluation of budgets.	Recording and reporting actual performance.	Variance analyses and interpretation for corrective action.
Period accounts	Forecasts of operating results, cash flow and financial status.	Presentation of short-period accounts, cash flow statements and balance sheets.	Interpretation and analyses of trends to highlight opportunities and risks for corrective action.

Table 6.2 (cont'd)   Management accounting applications for operational management

Application	Planning	Monitoring	Control
Project control	Evaluation of development project proposals and plans.	Recording, analysing and reporting progress and results of the project. Post-completion evaluation.	Interpreting variations from plan for corrective action. Interpreting post-completion evaluation.
Decision making	Evaluating and participating in the selection of alternative courses of action.	Recording, analysing and reporting progress and results of the course selected.	Interpreting variations from criteria adopted for selection.
Safeguarding assets	Establishing and maintaining systems of control for recording and safeguarding assets.	Verifying continuous existence, ownership and security of recorded assets.	Participation in specifying procedures for control and security.

Budgetary control

In a large organisation the management task must be devolved through a hierarchy of managers, each with a share of delegated authority. Effective management depends upon the accountability of each individual manager.

Budgetary control is the management tool which gives effect to accountability as the motivator for management action. It also ensures that the objectives being pursued by each member of the management team contribute as an integral part of the corporate objectives. For this to be effective there must be a sound organisational structure with rational delegation of authority and effective reporting lines.

As the planning phase of the management cycle, the budgeting process is a critical activity to be undertaken with great care. It is the phase where opportunities can be identified, evaluated and action planned to take full advantage of them; similarly, risks can be minimised or avoided. The alternative is to react to events as they occur which is often too late to be effective.

It is most important to ensure that the budgetary control process is effectively applied to every part of the entire organisation. If any area is left uncontrolled it may well become the refuge for inefficiency and so defeat the purpose of the control tool.

Definition
Budgetary control
The establishment of budgets relating the responsibilities of executives to the requirements of a policy, and the continuous comparison of actual with budgeted results,
either to secure by individual action the objective of that policy or to provide a basis for its revision.

(*CIMA Official Terminology*, first edition, 1982)

A budget is a management plan prepared by the departmental manager who has to execute it: the accountable manager. It defines the departmental objectives and maps out the intended course of action needed to achieve them in the most efficient way. It must take account of confirmed strategic objectives and corporate policy directives.

Before it can become effective, every departmental budget must be approved by corporate management. The approved budget then becomes the agreed programme of management action and it provides the basis against which each accountable manager monitors his or her own performance.

These management plans have to be phased over the budget period to facilitate effective monitoring of actual performance. This normally means dividing the annual budget into monthly periods to coincide with the accounting cycle. It involves taking due account of trends in the routine activities of the department and identifying 'bench marks' against which to monitor the progress of particular activities or developments.

Departmental budgets have to be mutually compatible and must aggregate to form the corporate plan for the entire organisation. For the purposes of consolidation into a corporate plan, all departmental management plans must be interpreted in a common language and evaluated in the terms used to measure corporate performance.

Thus budgetary control is the management tool for achieving the most efficient use of resources as measured in financial terms. For this, accounting techniques are applied for measuring and interpreting all aspects of management plans and activity in financial terms.

The necessary co-ordination may be achieved by directing the annual planning round from the corporate centre by stages, as follows:

1. Preliminary research at corporate level and requests for information on significant opportunities and risks as foreseen by departmental managers.
2. Determination of corporate strategies and formulation or review of corporate policies.
3. Notification to all accountable departmental managers of the budgeting parameters, for example:

   (a) strategic objectives;
   (b) corporate policy directives;
   (c) budgeting timetable.

4. Departmental budgets to be prepared and submitted to corporate management for approval.
5. Corporate review and approval of departmental budgets. At this stage there may be an element of trimming to match corporate resources.
6. Consolidation of approved departmental budgets to produce the corporate plan.

Monitoring actual performance against the plan is an essential feature of the budgetary control process. There are some key benefits:

1. It enables any deviation from the plan to be identified so that prompt corrective action can be taken when appropriate.
2. It enables new opportunities or new risks to be identified as they arise so that the plan can be modified when appropriate.
3. It reviews the validity of assumptions and projections incorporated in the plan so that they can be refined for subsequent interpretation and for preparing succeeding budgets when appropriate.

Standard costing

Economy, efficiency and effectiveness are control objectives in management. By attributing monetary values to these objectives they can be interpreted in terms of revenue, expenditure, assets and liabilities. The control process depends upon measuring the activity, but the measuring scale must first be calibrated. Budgeting provides one form of calibration; standard costing refines this process.

Standard costing is the technique by which actual activity may be measured against standard values which reflect the levels of performance being sought. Variance analysis then enables control to be exercised by exception.

Definitions

Standard costing
A technique which uses standards for costs and revenues for the purpose of control through variance analysis.
Standard cost
A predetermined calculation of how much cost should be under specified working conditions.
It is built up from an assessment of the value of cost elements and correlates technical specifications and the quantification of materials, labour and other costs to the prices and/or wage rates expected to apply during the period in which the standard cost is intended to be used. Its main purposes are to provide bases for control through variance accounting, for the valuation of stock and work in progress and, in some cases, for fixing selling prices.
(*CIMA Official Terminology,* first edition, 1982)

Standard costing is a comprehensive control tool which is equally applicable to complex production processes and to commercial operations. It is, however, most commonly used in manufacturing industry.

As a control tool it is involved with three stages of the management cycle – planning, monitoring and controlling:

1. **Planning** This is the stage for determining the standards to be used for measuring the activities being planned.

   (a) Standards have to relate to individual units of output, so enabling total activity to be measured as the product of output volume and the standard.

(b) The activity being planned is analysed into its elementary components and standards set for each element. For example: material, labour and processing elements for each manufacturing process involved.

(c) Standards must be derived from technical specifications. However, it is important to incorporate reasonable tolerances, recognising that it is rarely possible to achieve perfection in practice. This provides a degree of positive incentive to perform better than standard.

(d) Standard defined in physical terms become standard values by applying a standard price. For example: the cost price of materials applied to standard quantities, appropriate labour cost rates applied to standard operation time allowances, and the budgeting cost rates applied to standard processing time allowances.

2. **Monitoring**   This phase involves recording activities as they occur and measuring the results in terms of the standards adopted.

(a) It is necessary to establish appropriate systems for capturing data in a degree of detail which matches the elements from which standards have been compiled. This means collecting the data in physical and monetary terms as appropriate.

(b) The data collected must be capable of analysis to relate it directly to specific control segments. For example: information on material prices which can be used to influence buying activity must be separated from usage quantities which may reflect production efficiency or quality control.

(c) Data collection must be accurate and authentic. This is best achieved when the accounting record is derived as a by-product of information generated by the process itself as part of its own control mechanism. For example: recording weighing scales, flow meters, time clocks, and cash tills.

(d) Data collection must be complete and comprehensive. To ensure this requirement, the standard costing records should form a fully integrated component of the organisation's accounting system. Operating budgets will then be evaluated in terms of standard costs: operating financial reports will be built up from summaries of the performance records maintained for standard costing.

3. **Control**   For this phase the results from measuring are analysed and interpreted in terms of adherence to or deviations from planned activity. In this form the information is used to guide action for optimising favourable trends and correcting adverse trends.

(a) Variances need first to be identified with particular spheres of control for reporting to the manager in a position to exercise control. For example: perhaps the sales manager for production volume variances and the production manager for material yield, labour utilisation, and process efficiency variances.

(b) Timing for reporting variances to the relevant manager needs careful consideration in terms of both promptness and frequency. When the operational cycle is short, the environment changes rapidly. Historical information is irrelevant unless it contains lessons which can be applied to future activity. Moreover, such lessons are unlikely to be learned once recollections of the original circumstances begin to fade. Some variance information may need to be reported progressively daily for the previous day, weekly on the first day of the following week and monthly within one week, of month end.

(c) For accounting control all variances are evaluated in monetary terms. However, when reporting variances to be acted upon, they should be interpreted in terms of physical measurement wherever it is appropriate. It is likely to be more meaningful to those closest to the activity and in a position to influence performance.

Project control

The term 'capital project' is generally applied to any major development which will have impact on the future performance of an organisation for more than one year. It may involve capital expenditure, acquisitions, divestments, plant closures, rationalisation, product development, launch of a new product, control system developments, and so on.

Capital projects of this kind have to be undertaken from time to time to maintain corporate effectiveness. They may involve an element of corporate restructuring and there are likely to be a number of alternative courses to choose from. They are usually high-risk undertakings because they involve large sums of money and also because, by extending far into the future, the outcome becomes progressively more and more difficult to project as uncertainties are compounded.

Effective control is essential, but every project undertaken is unique and creates its own control challenge for which there is usually no established control system already functioning. It is necessary to consider all reasonable options and to evaluate the project particularly carefully before taking any decision to proceed.

The critical stages in the control process for all major projects are as follows:

1. **Identifying the need** The need to undertake a special project often emerges in the course of pursuing a particular corporate objective. For example:

   (a) pursuit of market growth, maintaining or increasing market share or improving competitive edge;

   (b) reducing costs, improving efficiency or improving return of capital;

   (c) renewing exhausted assets or replacing obsolete technology.

2. **Feasibility studies** Every reasonable option must be considered and its respective potential benefits and burdens assessed for comparison. The choice may be influenced by strategic considerations, risk content, timing factors and financial expectations. For example:

   (a) the choice for extending a product range could be between long-term investment in product development, a potential acquisition

of a going concern with the appropriate product profile, and a licensed user agreement with another organisation with a suitable patented product;

   (b) a need to renew exhausted plant will usually provide an opportunity to consider developments in processing; the choice may be between proven technology and new ideas which offer greater potential but are untried.

3. **Selecting the best course** This is a strategic decision to be made at corporate management level and preferably by consensus, for example: a Board decision. No authority should be given at this stage to enter commitments. However, when it is necessary to incur expense for proper evaluation of the course selected, this should be specifically authorised, for example: test drillings on a potential construction site.

4. **Evaluation and planning** At this stage it is necessary to develop a detailed plan for the project. A well considered plan will provide a sound basis for evaluating the investment of resources and the benefits expected. It will also become the programme for directing the project and against which it will be possible to monitor progress.

   Evaluation must take full account of the specialist judgements of marketing, commercial, technical, engineering and other experts as appropriate. It must identify major risk areas and the proposed methods of protection. When the project involves major contracts with other parties such as suppliers of capital equipment, firm offers of terms should be secured.

   The evaluation must ultimately be expressed in financial terms compatible with the financial objectives of the organisation. This is usually a continuing return on capital investment. However, for most projects both the investment and the return are likely to occur in an irregular pattern over extended periods of time.

   (a) Discounted cash flow is a useful technique for computing the present value of expenditure and revenue, taking due account of timing.

(b) Sensitivity analysis is another useful technique for evaluating the impact of tolerance factors in key criteria reflecting forecasting uncertainties.

Major projects are often complex and usually involve bringing together a number of separate operations, each with a different time scale. In such cases, a network analysis may be necessary and this should be incorporated in the proposal. The arrangements for project management and the necessary recording and control systems should be defined in the proposal.

5. **Authorisation**   This is the decision to proceed with the project. It is a critical decision for the organisation to be taken objectively by corporate management. Formal procedures are necessary for addressing such decisions:

(a) There must be a clear definition for a major project as being one requiring specific authorisation at corporate management level. This definition should set the parameters in terms of value and time span for both the resources to be used and the impact upon the organisation. The key criteria may also include the scale of risk.

(b) The corporate organisational structure must make clear how authority is delegated within the organisation with defined limits in specific areas such as capital spending and other major projects.

(c) Authorisation decisions should be taken on a consensus basis from a general management viewpoint supported by appropriate specialist technical and financial advice. In some large organisations all major project proposals are considered for approval by a committee of specifically nominated corporate executives. In other cases it may be a matter for the main management board.

(d) The proposal needs to be fully documented in a prescribed standard format to ensure that the principal issues affecting the evaluation of the project have been adequately considered, and also to minimise the possibilities for misinterpretation.

(e) Time must be allowed for the proposal to be fully considered and debated to enable informed objective judgement to be formed by all who contribute to the decision.

(f) Variations in the course of implementing major projects are inevitable. Whenever any significant departure from the plan is unavoidable the alternative course chosen must be identified and its impact on the project evaluated. Limits should be specified for project management discretion on variations.

6. **Controlling implementation**   Once the project has been authorised to proceed, the plan developed for evaluating the proposal becomes the implementation programme.

The control aspects of project management involving major capital contracts are discussed in detail in the contract audit section of Chapter 7. There are, however, some important principles to be applied to all projects at this stage:

(a) It is most important to establish accountability from the start in the appointment of a project manager.

(b) The specified recording systems must be put in place before work starts on the project. This may involve defining responsibilities, briefing and training staff, and introducing special documentation, coding and procedures. It is necessary to capture data required not only for control of the implementation processes but also for subsequent assessment of the impact of the project on completion.

(c) Work can now start and commitments may be entered in accordance with the authorised project plan. The project manager may have to recruit a project management team, specialists and possibly a workforce. It is then necessary to allocate responsibilities and to brief, train and direct those involved.

(d) Whenever significant departure from the authorised plan is unavoidable, the circumstances must be identified to enable the impact on the project to be evaluated.

(e) Regular monitoring and reporting progress against the plan to the project manager is an essential feature of project control. Such reporting should be in terms of stages completed against bench marks and evaluated in financial terms against the project budget with emphasis on significant variances.

7. **Post-implementation review** Assessing the impact of a project after implementation has no control significance for that project. Any measurement of the impact within one year after implementation is likely to be inconclusive. Its purpose is primarily to learn from experience and so to improve the quality of decision making for subsequent projects.

The review should be concerned with the validity of the key assumptions used in the original projections. It is important to distinguish differences attributable to external factors from those attributable to management judgement or controllable internal factors.

The form of post-implementation review may vary depending on the nature of the project. For example, a project to launch a new product may be concerned with how commercial judgements such as pricing and servicing may have influenced the impact. An acquisition project to achieve the same strategic objective could be much more concerned with problems of corporate synergy.

Credit control

Credit is an important element of the terms for which goods and services may be sold introducing a time lapse into the cash flows of both buyer and seller.

It is a marketing judgement whether or not to sell on credit terms, taking account of the following:

1. **Market forces** There may be a firmly established trade custom, customers may refuse to buy other than on credit terms, competitors may be offering attractive credit terms.
2. **Financial constraints** Customer credit adds a financing cost to the sales transaction; the investment in working capital has to compete with other demands on available financial resources.
3. **Credit risks** The buyer has to be judged as being both able to settle when due and trust-

worthy to do so. The ability to withhold delivery is forfeited in a credit sale.

Credit control is concerned with the financial aspects of sales transacted on credit terms. For example:

1. **Funding the policy** When a policy of selling on credit terms is adopted it is necessary to assess the working capital needs and arrange for the funds to be available.
2. **Credit limits** It is necessary to assess the credit worthiness of each credit customer or prospective credit customer and to set individual credit limits. Credit limits are normally determined from the customer's track record, taking account of past peaks in demand and settlement pattern. Alternative sources for new and prospective customers are credit-rating agencies, trade references and evidence provided on request.

Credit limits must be kept under continuous review: the status of customers can change rapidly. Sales force calling should include a discipline for sensing and reporting symptoms of change. Other important sources are trade and national and local press reports.

If credit risks have been insured, credit limits are agreed with the underwriter who is likely to have considerable information on the credit worthiness of most buyers.
3. **Credit approval** All contracts for credit sales should be tested before acceptance against the available headroom of the limit: that is, the amount left after deducting outstanding credit orders accepted including all unpaid invoices. When the business of the organisation involves contracting infrequently with individual customers, the credit testing should take place before issuing a priced quotation offering credit terms. When the business involves a steady flow of orders from regular customers, credit testing should occur before acceptance of each new order. Orders which pass the credit limit test should be accepted and acted upon.

When orders fail the credit limit test, the circumstances should be reviewed by an authorised executive. There may be new evidence to justify extending the credit limit, or a discretionary temporary extension may be considered appropriate. Alternatively, it may be decided to inform the customer that further credit cannot be granted.

4. **Debt collection**   Sales invoices should be issued promptly at the time of sale which usually occurs on completing the delivery of the goods or service. Delayed invoicing results in delayed settlement. Statements listing all invoices outstanding should be sent before payment is due.

   Special care should be taken to ensure that the information on the invoice is correct and clear: if the invoice has to be adjusted or further explained it will delay settlement. Particular attention should be paid to the name and address of the customer, customer's order reference, the quantity, description, price and total value of the goods supplied, and the terms of payment.

   The sales ledger should be kept up to date: invoices and remittances should be posted promptly. For each remittance the invoices being settled should be identified in the account. Invoices should also be identified with due dates for settlement.

   Aged debt schedules should be extracted for monitoring debt collection. These schedules should be reviewed regularly by the relevant marketing and financial executives.

   As soon as any part of a debt becomes overdue, it is necessary to consider appropriate action to secure early settlement. This will differ from one organisation to another depending on the nature of the business undertaken.

   For example: a regular competitive supplier of raw materials to a large manufacturing organisation would act with diplomacy, being concerned not to damage prospects for a continuing profitable trading relationship by ill-considered pressure for payment.

   On the other hand, the publisher of a local newspaper with unpaid accounts for classified advertising in small amounts by numerous private individuals cannot justify the expense of extended courteous correspondence; he would probably instruct collecting agents without further delay.

   Here is an example of a programme for chasing overdue debts by weekly stages:

   (a) reminder offering help to clear up any query;
   (b) second reminder demanding early settlement;
   (c) final demand with time limit before legal action.
   (d) writ issued or debt passed to collection agency.

Stewardship accounting

'Stewardship accounting' is the term used to describe the process by which those entrusted to husband resources report on their stewardship to those who have so entrusted them. Demonstrating that affairs have been conducted efficiently within the authority granted is a key objective and historical accuracy is an essential quality.

Stewardship accounting requirements are often formally specified. This may be by a trust deed, by the rules of a club or society or by statute for companies, building societies, public-sector organisations, etc. In most cases the accounts have to be prepared annually and subjected to independent audit examination and often they are expressly required to present a true and fair view.

Stewardship reporting is a fundamental requirement for corporate entities in general and for the limited liability company in particular.

The fundamental objective of corporate reports is to communicate economic measurements of and information about the resources and performance of the reporting entity useful to those having reasonable rights to such information.

To fulfil this objective . . . corporate reports should be relevant, understandable, reliable, complete, objective, timely and comparable.

(extract from *The Corporate Report*, 1975)

The Companies Act 1989

The prescription for external reporting by UK companies is embodied in the Companies Act 1989 which replaces and extends most of the accounting requirements of the 1985 Act. The obligations are extensive and onerous and the responsibility for meeting them is placed firmly upon the directors. These Acts prescribe the following:

1. Minimum requirements for accounting records and how long they must be retained, with penalties for failure to comply.
2. Rules for determining accounting dates and reporting periods.
3. The duty of the directors to prepare accounts in the form of a profit and loss account and a balance sheet in respect of each reporting period.
4. The options for format of the accounts and the minimum disclosure requirements.
5. An overriding condition that the accounts must present a true and fair view of the profit or loss and of the state of affairs.
6. The accounts must be signed by two directors or the sole director.

The Auditing Practices Committee (APC) of the Consultative Committee of Accountancy Bodies (CCAB) sought counsel's opinion concerning accounting records in 1977. A summary of the points raised and opinions given was published by APC in 'True and fair' Issue No. 6. It included the following response to the question 'what are accounting records?':

Accounting records comprise the orderly collection and identification of the information in question, rather than a mere accumulation of documents. The accounting records need not be in book form, they may take the form of, for example, a loose leaf binder or computer tape. It will even be sufficient if the books of prime entry are in the form of a secure clip of invoices with an add-list attached. The essence of the matter is that the information is organised and labelled so as to be capable of retrieval. A carrier-bag full of invoices will not suffice.

Five basic accounting principles are prescribed to be applied in preparing financial statements:

1. **Going concern** basis to be presumed.
2. **Consistency** in accounting policies from year to year.
3. **Prudence**: only realised profits may be taken and full provision made for all expected liabilities and losses.
4. **Accruals concept**: attributable revenue and expenditure to be taken into account irrespective of date of receipt or payment.
5. **Severally determined component values** for determining aggregate asset and liability amounts.

Companies must appoint auditors whose duties will be as follows:

1. Report to the members on whether or not in their opinion the profit and loss account and the balance sheet give the respective true and fair views of the profit or loss and the state of affairs of the company.
2. Satisfy themselves, or report if they are unable to do so, that proper accounting records have been kept and that the accounts agree with them.
3. Report any case to the members where they have been unable to obtain information or explanations, or where the directors' report is not consistent with the accounts.

The nature and practice of statutory audit is discussed in more detail in Chapter 9 (External Audit).

The directors are required:

1. To send a copy of the accounts, directors' report and auditors' report to every member and every debenture holder.
2. To lay the accounts before the company in general meeting.
3. To deliver a copy of the accounts to the registrar of companies.

The purposes and usefulness of the annual report and accounts are extensive, as shown below:

1. They enable the directors to inform shareholders on the results of their stewardship and the effectiveness of their direction of the enterprise. This is measured in terms of profitability and maintenance of capital.
2. They enable the performance of the management to be evaluated in terms of employment, market presence, products, investment and returns.
3. They enable judgements to be made about the company in terms of economic stability, liquidity, capacity to use resources and future prospects.
4. They enable the economic strength of the company to be evaluated, for making comparisons

with others and for assessing claims against the company.

The report and accounts will interest shareholders, potential shareholders, lenders, employees, creditors, customers, suppliers and anyone else placing an element of trust in the company or contemplating doing so. They will also interest competitors and anyone pursuing a claim against the company or contemplating doing so.

Internal audit considerations

Every organisation is unique and has to develop its own systems of control to match its own circumstances. However, management effectiveness must ultimately be measured in financial terms. Financial security is crucial and the financial control system must be closely linked with all other functions to provide a focus for control.

In financial management, sound control systems and strict disciplines in applying them are essential. This must be an area of primary concern for the internal auditor.

In this section we have discussed the main features of financial management. We have considered the risks and the principles of control to be observed with a number of examples of application. All control systems should be evaluated in terms of these general principles and interpreted in the context of prevailing circumstances.

The internal auditing techniques discussed in Chapters 4 and 5 will all have some relevance in the financial domain: risk assessment, systems evaluation, and compliance testing have special significance. The internal auditor must also be alert to the possibilities for irregular activity: these are fully discussed in Chapter 8.

Whenever control is found to be effective, this fact should be reported to the accountable manager: it is important reassurance.

Whenever weakness is discovered, it is important to evaluate the risk and to report it and to offer practical suggestions for improvement.

An organisation with a well-developed management accounting service will use it as an operational management tool. The operational auditor equipped with the appropriate skills and experience is also able to assist management by looking beyond the financial reports to the operational activity they portray.

Section 3.   Information management

The nature of information management

Sound management is crucial to the successful performance of every organisation. It involves making judgements about the courses of action most likely to achieve the organisation's objectives and directing activity on the chosen courses. This is the cyclical process of planning, directing, monitoring, controlling, planning, and so on.

Experience, confidence, and information are key elements of varying significance in all management judgements. Information in this context means organised detailed factual knowledge which is relevant to the management task. For example:

1. Recorded history of the organisation's performance.
2. Status information on the organisation's resources.
3. Market intelligence and market and other projections.
4. Financial interpretations of history, status and projections.

In large organisations, complexity extends the uncertainty in management decision taking, and the information element then assumes increasing significance. It becomes an indispensable management resource which must be readily available, appropriate and reliable. It is therefore necessary to establish formal procedures for managing this resource. This is information management and it may involve all or any of the following stages:

1. Research and analysis to define information needs.
2. Design and development of systems for servicing the information needs – a management information system (MIS).
3. Specification, procurement and installation of data processing hardware and software.

4. Systems implementation including document-ation and training.
5. Data collection and validation.
6. Data transmission, storage, retrieval and processing.
7. Distributing and presenting processed information appropriate to the management needs.

The MIS concept was originally envisaged as a large integrated computer system complete with facilities for scenario planning and 'what if' analysis and extensive financial modelling capability. Such a system would encompass the full range of the organisation's business functions such as forecasting and business planning, sales order processing, production planning and control, procurement and stock control, sales and distribution, invoicing, payroll, accounting and administration.

Experience has shown that these large all embracing computer systems are too complex to design and implement. Instead, large organisations have adopted a strategy of developing systems for each functional area as separate modules and linking these together to produce integrated management information.

The scope of MIS can vary considerably from one organisation to another. A large organisation may have a number of computer system modules linked to a corporate data base. A smaller organisation may be able to fulfil all its perceived management information requirements with a single system designed essentially for sales order processing, for example.

The term 'MIS' encompasses any system or collection of systems by which information is processed to assist management decisions in pursuit of the organisation's objectives. This includes all manner of existing systems such as sales and purchase ledgers, stock records, order processing and budgeting models, whether computerised or not.

Definitions

Here are some definitions specifically related to computer technology from the Collins English Dictionary (second edition):

management information system: n. an arrangement of equipment and procedures, often computerised, that is designed to provide managers with information.

information technology: n. the technology of the production, storage and communication of information using computers and microelectronics.

data: n. the information operated on by a computer program.

information: n. the meaning given to data by the way in which it is interpreted.

data processing: n. a sequence of operations performed on data, esp. by a computer in order to extract information, reorder files, etc.

MIS structure

The structure of the MIS should match the organisational structure. The management hierarchy may be viewed as a pyramid model. The base of the pyramid then represents operational management requiring timely, current information relating to its areas of responsibility. The information available must therefore be appropriate for the day-to-day management decisions which are mostly taken at this level.

The middle tier of the pyramid represents middle management. It too will require information relating to its defined areas of responsibility, but in summary form with exception reports. This will enable it to monitor the performance of each operational segment of the area.

At this level strategic information such as trend analyses may also be required, to assist in identifying problem areas to be addressed in the short or medium term.

The apex of the pyramid represents the executive board. For this level of management, consolidated information is required for the process of defining strategic goals for the organisation and for monitoring progress towards their achievement. The time horizons for this information will be more distant and it will be required to be presented less frequently.

The pyramid may also be used to depict the communication structure by which authority is delegated from the apex down in terms of contributing to strategic goals with individual accountability and reporting from the base up.

Systems development

Developing an effective management information system is a major undertaking for most organisations. In large organisations, it is likely to be a continuous task because the requirements are constantly changing. Organisations progress through growth and changing shape. They must adapt to changes in the environment in which they operate. To remain competitive they must respond to technological developments both in operational activity and in data processing.

Systems development usually involves a significant investment of resources and the results may have considerable influence on the performance of the organisation for several years ahead. These factors place the systems development work in the major project category, requiring the active involvement of the top management. Control criteria for major projects are discussed in detail in the financial management section of this chapter.

The starting point for systems development work is a need perceived by management for information to assist the management task. From this point it is necessary to consider the feasibility of satisfying the management need. Feasibility studies should evaluate:

1. The management need and potential benefits.
2. The practical feasibility and cost.
3. The technical feasibility and cost.
4. The financial viability of each option considered.

Assuming that feasibility is established and there is a financially viable option, it is likely to lead to a decision to proceed. It is then necessary to nominate the project manager and the project team. An internal auditor should be nominated as a key member of the project development team at the time authorisation is given to proceed.

Steering committee

It is usual to establish a steering committee of executives with particular interest in each systems development project. The role of the committee is to co-ordinate the requirements, steer the planning, and monitor progress in design and implementation.

A major systems development project may affect more than one function of the organisation and the development work may be expected to have a time span of several months or even years. It is therefore important to have top level management involvement on the steering committee. This ensures that appropriate authority can be brought to bear to move 'log jams' if they occur. The views of all those affected need to be represented in the work of the steering committee.

Systems analysis and design

The first stage is analysing the business requirement. It is an important feature of the project management to ensure that the needs and expectations of all the managers who are affected are considered.

Where conflicting requirements occur every effort must be made to resolve the issue rationally, seeking a senior management ruling only as a last resort. The overriding consideration must always be serving the best interests of the organisation and pursuing the organisation's objectives.

The next stage is systems design. At this stage, a balance has to be struck between the ideal system which satisfies every possible requirement and the practical constraints of time, operator effort and cost in both development and operation. It is important to ensure that essential control is not compromised in the process of designing the system within the practical constraints.

Management commitment to the system design concept is crucial to successful operation in practice. Close liaison between system designers and all the managers concerned is a fundamental requirement.

The internal auditing function has an important contribution to make in systems design work. It is infinitely better to have control weakness identified at the design stage, when it can be rectified, than after implementation, when satisfactory rectification may be impossible or exorbitantly expensive.

To fulfil this role adequately, the internal auditor has to establish a rapport with both the operational management and the systems development team. It is important that the internal auditor fully understands the requirements and what is expected from the new system. It is equally important that the systems analysts and designers understand and respect the contribution expected from the internal auditor.

Having established the right relationships, (a) the internal auditor should invest time to gain familiarity with the management requirements; and (b) systems designers should consult the internal auditor as they proceed, allowing time in their planning for audit testing and design modifications if necessary.

Formal acceptance of the final design proposals by the user management is generally advisable before starting the construction phase of the project. There are a number of reasons for this. For example: (a) by confirming acceptance of the design, the user management is also accepting responsibility for making it work; (b) acceptance of the design effectively imposes a design freeze before cost is incurred on construction work.

Computer application

Most major system development projects are likely to be designed for computer processing as the most efficient way of achieving the objectives of the system. This may involve choosing suitable equipment and programming facilities. For example:

1. Hardware options:

   (a) using available capacity on existing in-house mainframe facilities;
   (b) procurement of new hardware with or without specific software;
   (c) renting computer bureau facilities.

2. Software options:

   (a) programs written in-house;
   (b) programs written by a retained software house;
   (c) package software.

Whichever options are adopted for the project, the internal auditor's role is to continue the testing which started at the system design stage and applying the same principles. Here the internal auditor is concerned to establish the effectiveness of the controls written into the programs for each processing function. For example:

> system management (the computer operating system)
> application management (access and operational controls)
> data collection and entry
> data communication
> data storage and retrieval
> computer processing
> output

There are a number of established audit techniques for the task of testing computer systems which are discussed in Chapter 5. It should be noted here that when embedded audit data collection facilities are required, they normally have to be introduced at the time the programs are written.

Implementation

This is the final stage in the process of developing a new system. It involves testing the system, training user staff and controlled introduction or conversion.

Acceptance testing is a critical feature marking the point at which responsibility for running the system is handed over to the user management. The internal auditor should participate in the arrangements for acceptance testing with the objective of giving reassurance to the user managers that adequate controls have been incorporated and that they are working properly.

A new system is likely to involve changed methods of working for the user staff. It may involve using new and sophisticated equipment, changed documentation, or new skills. Training will be necessary and it is primarily a management responsibility. It is important that the staff who have to work with the new system perceive it as a change required by their own management and supervision.

It is important to assess very carefully the change in working practices in terms of a retraining need and this must be planned and adequately provided for. Technical guidance is usually required from the systems development team. Professional training skills are also likely to be necessary through the personnel function.

Controlled introduction means taking care to ensure that the new system is working reliably before reliance is placed in it.

Where the new system is intended to supersede an existing system, the usual control method is parallel running. However, this may be difficult if both systems have to be operated by an already overloaded staff.

The project development team, including the internal auditor, has a particular role to assist the user management through the implementation period. It is important that output is monitored very closely until it has achieved reliability. Until this stage is reached the detailed understanding which the development team accumulated will enable it to diagnose problems quickly and to explain how to rectify them.

For a major project, implementation is often planned in stages so that part of the system may be brought into use whilst construction work is still proceeding on other parts. This serves to spread the workload involved and also the risk. For example:

1. A sales order processing system may be designed to record orders, allocate stock, generate warehouse instructions and despatch documentation, and provide the basic data for sales invoicing. It might be implemented in three phases:

    (a) order recording and stock allocation;
    (b) warehouse instructions and despatch documentation;
    (c) using the data in the sales invoicing system.

2. A retail sales system for a supermarket chain may be designed to respond to bar code reading at the check-out, producing an itemised customer bill and till receipt, whilst updating stock management records generating documentation for stock replenishment. This might be implemented in one branch at a time so that the implementation team would progress from store to store week by week.

Internal audit considerations

When addressing MIS in operation the internal auditor's primary objectives would be to evaluate whether:

(a) the MIS meets the requirements of the organisation efficiently and effectively;
(b) there are adequate controls over the integrity of the data;
(c) data held within the system is afforded a level of security appropriate to its sensitivity.

Audit scope

The scope of internal audit review, which will vary depending on the particular circumstances of the organisation, may encompass:

1. A new system under development.
2. An existing management information system.
3. The use of MIS within a review of a particular function.

It is important that the audit scope and the boundaries of the system under review are clearly defined during audit planning. The internal auditor should identify the following:

1. **Users:** These include those managers who directly receive information from the system under review. The internal auditor should also identify the people who are responsible for managing the system itself.
2. **Inputs:** These may include manual inputs or feeds from other operational or management information systems; they may also include external information, for example: market or competitor analyses.
3. **Outputs:** Management information may include physical reports on screen-based reports. The output may be predetermined or produced on request. The internal auditor should also identify any outputs produced for the purposes of systems and database administration.
4. **Processes:** The internal auditor should determine the main system and manual processing procedures and flows of information.

Audit evaluation

The MIS is unlikely to be tailored to the exact needs of each individual user. The internal auditor must reach a judgement about the adequacy and efficiency of the system in relation to specific criteria, as set out below:

1. **Validity of data:** Since a management information system will provide information to support important management decisions, the system must contain controls to ensure that reports from the system are based on authentic and legitimate data.

   The internal auditor will therefore be interested in controls over the inputs to the system. These will include authorisation checks and access controls to ensure that persons inputting or amending data have the authority to do so. There may be management checks of the data which has entered the system on a periodic or an ad-hoc basis. Management may also check the access record to the system, and analyse usage, frequency and staff, etc.

   The MIS may receive feeds from several other systems dealing with functional areas of the organisation. It is important that the internal auditor recognises the cut-off for the audit tests.

   It is likely that verifying the data within the feeder systems falls within the scope of auditing those systems. The internal auditor will then need to examine the interfaces in the MIS audit assignment. This involves reviewing the procedures for initiating and processing the feed and evaluating the controls. These may include authorisation controls, system version and validation checks and reconciliation or comparison checks to the feeder system.

   It will also be necessary to establish that the feeding systems have recently been, or soon will be, subjected to internal audit review.

   The internal auditor must also identify and evaluate the controls which ensure the integrity of data within the system: that is, controls which prevent or detect unauthorised amendments or corruption through system or program errors.

   The procedures for handling and delivering system outputs should be reviewed to ensure that the management information reports received by managers contain valid information. The extent of control will of course depend on the sensitivity of the information.

2. **Accuracy of data:** The internal auditor must again be satisfied that adequate controls exist around the input and update of data as well as confirming the accuracy of the calculations embodied in the system.

   Controls which are appropriate to the achievement of this objective include:

   (a) separation of duties;
   (b) independent appraisal of system logs and update reports;
   (c) a full audit trail providing documentary evidence of all changes to the data.

   System controls such as validation checks and database integrity checks are also important. The internal auditor should ensure there are adequate procedures for dealing with exception reports where data has failed these checks.

3. **Timeliness of data:** Each user of management information must be assured that the data he receives is sufficiently timely or up to date for the purpose for which he is using it. The precise meaning of 'timely' will vary according to that purpose, and according to the significance of decisions made on the basis of the information.

   As a general rule, operational management will require the most up-to-date and probably the least processed information for day-to-day operational decisions. Senior management will require the same data with some further processing to present summaries and analyses.

   The internal auditor should review the methods and frequency of data updating and production of reports and compare this with users' needs. It is necessary to consider whether users receive data too frequently as well as whether it is sufficiently up to date in order to evaluate the efficiency of the system.

4. **Security of access:** Loss of information constitutes a major threat to every organisation in many ways. Total loss of information due to a disk crash, for example, is likely to lead to very serious consequences, especially if backup procedures are shown to be inadequate.

   The possibility of sensitive information falling

into the hands of a competitor may be particularly damaging since it is likely that the organisation will not be aware that its security has been breached.

Access to data on individual transactions and customers may be of some use to competitors but the potential damage is insignificant in comparison with that which could occur if strategic data got into the wrong hands. The senior management of other organisations could well make effective use of top-level information to gain competitive advantage.

Often, the lowest level of a system security control is very tight, with features such as automatic timeout, automatic password expiry, secured data entry areas, etc., while at the highest level such features are not used because they are not considered necessary, or because they are an annoyance to the manager.

The internal auditor should seek to ensure that the degree of control of access to sensitive information should be commensurate with the scale of risk attributable to any leakage or breach of security. It is necessary to confirm that security awareness exists and is practised by all staff and all management throughout the organisation.

It is important to confirm that managers are aware in particular of the following implications:

(a) leaving terminals logged on while they are away from the office;
(b) selecting obvious passwords such as wives, husbands, children's names which could be guessed by anyone with the briefest knowledge about them;
(c) leaving printed output open and unattended where it may be read, copied or removed from the office.

Every organisation should have a security policy for the protection of information. It needs to be confirmed and promulgated by the top management. It should prescribe specific procedures and guidelines to be adopted throughout the organisation. It is most important to ensure that everyone with access to the information system understands clearly the need for the rules and the risks of failing to observe them.

5. **Availability of data:** Often the least tested areas of a computer system are the arrangements for backup and recovery. Flaws in the backup and recovery procedures will not then be picked up until something goes wrong, and it is necessary to use them in anger. Failure to recover from a major crash can be extremely damaging to an organisation and in the worst case could lead to going out of business.

The internal auditor should ensure that sufficient resources have been channelled into producing, testing and maintaining an effective set of backup and recovery procedures. It is vital that the users of the system are aware of the dangers if the system were to be unavailable for an extended period.

It is important to realise that just as effective MIS may contribute to increasing the efficiency and productivity of an organisation in a very short space of time, so too the loss of such a system may cause dire consequences to the organisation within an even shorter time span. The opportunities and risks associated with computerised services, and the control principles involved, are discussed in detail in Chapter 5.

Section 4.   Personnel management

The nature of personnel management

Personnel management is about people. An organisation is a collection of people enjoined by contractual relationships to pursue a set of common organisational objectives. Achieving these objectives is dependent upon effective planning, direction and control of the endeavours of all involved: that is the role of general management.

Personnel management is that sector of the general management role which concentrates on people. This management task involves building and leading a team of people with appropriate skills and attitudes. Success will reflect the quality of leadership and the application of sound principles in recruitment, training, development and motivation.

The contribution each employee makes to the performance of the organisation depends upon the extent of that employee's commitment to the organisation's objectives. It is a key management task to develop commitment by stimulating employee motivation.

The burden of responsibility which falls upon every line manager when employing staff is formidable. It involves compliance with a substantial body of employment law within a framework of sound personnel policies. There is a clear need for specialist support.

Organising the personnel function

The personnel policy adopted by an organisation in pursuing its objectives will be crucial to successful achievement. Personnel policy is thus a matter to be determined by the top management of the organisation as for example the executive board or board of directors.

Many organisations establish a central personnel function which provides accountable managers with professional advice and assistance in fulfilling employment obligations. It is particularly appropriate for large complex organisations which may comprise many management centres.

When there is a central personnel function, the head of that function should be a member of the top management board or should report directly to the chief executive of the organisation.

Each organisation divides the personnel management tasks between line managers and skilled personnel specialists to suit its own organisational culture. The overriding principle must always be that ultimate responsibility remains with line management. Here, for example, is a typical arrangement.

Function	Line management responsibility	Personnel specialist responsibility
Recruitment	Identify vacancies and describe the job content.	Write and place job advertisements.
		Receive and process applications.
		Select for interview.
		Preliminary interviewing.
		Short-list for second interview.
	Interview short-listed candidates.	
	Select appointee.	Take up references.
		Send formal offer of appointment and contract of employment.
		Open and maintain confidential employee file.
Remuneration	Prepare job descriptions, gradings and evaluation.	Advise and guide on job evaluation.
	Carry out merit reviews.	Survey employment market for current rates of pay.
	Carry out performance appraisals.	Establish pay scales and salary brackets.
		Set parameters for pay review.
	Carry out pay reviews.	Co-ordinate pay review administration including arrangements for senior management authorisation as appropriate.
	Implement authorised changes.	
	Administer payroll and pay wages and salaries when due.	Maintain detailed personnel records for all employees.
	Determine pay and conditions negotiating brief and instruct negotiating team.	Lead negotiating team on pay and conditions with employees' representatives.

Function	Line management responsibility	Personnel specialist responsibility
Training	Specify skills required.	Develop training policy.
	Assess employees' skills and potential.	Advise and assist.
	Indentify training needs.	Establish appropriate training facilities.
	Plan and initiate training programmes.	Organise appropriate training resources.
	Organise on-the-job training.	Supervise all training.
	Budget and control training costs.	
	Monitor and evaluate training.	
Staff development	Conduct annual staff appraisals to review progress and assess potential.	Develop staff development policy.
		Establish procedures for annual staff appraisals.
	Agree development objectives with individual employees.	Establish development training facilities.
	Plan development programmes.	Advise and assist.
	Organise internal development opportunities.	Organise external development opportunities.
	Periodical review of management needs, resources and potential and succession planning.	Advise and assist.
Employee relations	Administer discipline in individual cases.	Develop policies.
		Advise on procedures.
	Determine negotiating brief on procedures and instruct negotiating team.	Lead negotiating teams on procedures with employees' representatives.
	Decisions within advice on individual contracts.	Advise on the application of procedures and legislation.
		Represent the organisation at appeals and tribunals.
	Maintain compliance with the law.	
Health and safety	Cultivate a climate of safety consciousness.	Develop a safety policy.
	Establish local safe working practices.	Advise on legislation.
	Establish arrangements for safety monitoring.	Advise on safe working practices.
	Arrange safety training.	Advise and assist with safety training.
	Provide, maintain and test fire and safety equipment.	
	Organise regular safety and fire drill.	
	Maintain the accident record book.	
	Maintain statutory and other insurance cover.	
	Maintain compliance with the law.	

Personnel policy

There are some necessary conditions for establishing sound corporate personnel policies. For example:

1. Every organisation which employs people should have a definitive personnel policy as the basis for conducting its relationships with employees with consistency and in the common interest of the organisation and its employees.
2. In all large or complex organisations, personnel policies and essential procedures should be defined in detail and expressed in writing to give clear guidance so as to ensure consistency in application by all line managers.
3. Every organisation is unique in terms of its established employment culture, customs and practices. Corporate personnel policies must have due regard to these.
4. Personnel policy should be formulated by experts having skill and experience in this specialist field. Particularly important are a thorough knowledge of employment law and a sound understanding of personnel management practice.
5. The personnel policy proposals formulated by the experts must be submitted to the top board of management for approval and promulgation throughout the organisation.
6. Expert specialist support should be available to all line managers to ensure proper understanding and interpretation of corporate personnel policies and to assist implementation. This may be provided from a central personnel function or by an appropriately qualified specialist as a member of the local management team.
7. Having promulgated a policy, the top management board needs assurance that it is being applied. The head of the central personnel function should have functional authority to monitor and ensure compliance throughout the organisation.

Personnel policy should address the principles and practices applicable to every aspect of relationships between management and employees. For example:

1. Recruitment policy, practice and procedures.
2. Contracts of employment policy and practice.
3. Remuneration scales, review procedures and authorisation.
4. Incentives policy and control.
5. Fringe benefits, policy and control.
6. Training policies, practice and resources.
7. Performance appraisal and communication.
8. Development: assessing potential, planning and resources.
9. Management development and succession policy and practice.
10. Industrial relations policy and practice.
11. Health and safety at work policy, procedures and practice.
12. Social responsibility policy, and practice.
13. Termination of employment procedures and practice.
14. Retirement policy, procedures and practice.

Manpower planning

Manpower planning is a key element of corporate planning. The feasibility of plans for growth, changing shape, market changes, changes in technology and so on, will depend upon the organisation's ability to secure the necessary human resources.

For meaningful manpower planning, three conditions are essential:

1. The organisation must have clearly defined objectives.
2. Manpower planning must be fully integrated with corporate planning.
3. Comprehensive personnel records and statistics must be available.

It is necessary to plan for these requirements in the context of national factors such as demography, legislation and education. For example:

1. **Forecasting demand:** Examine the organisation's objectives and intentions and translate these into people requirements, classified according to skills and taking account of anticipated developments in technology. Evaluate managers' judgements and predicted technological developments, using

statistical methods and work measurement techniques.

2. **Assessing supply:**

   (a) Internal: examine the current labour force and extrapolate numbers of staff leaving and retirements.
   (b) External: examine population figures, particularly school, college and university leavers, married women likely to return to work, any special local factors and possible developments affecting other organisations competing in the same employment market.

3. **Balancing supply and demand:** Determine the necessary actions so that the right numbers of people are available to match the pattern of work demand.

Recruitment

Every post should have a job description agreed between job holder and manager. It should give the operational details of the job in terms of department, location, immediate superior, resources, constraints and a list of duties and responsibilities.

When the post is vacant it is necessary to identify the qualities a person should have to perform the job successfully. This is the person specification. It should list the knowledge, skills and attributes required.

Rodger's seven-point plan provides a commonly used basis for classifying these qualities:

1. Physical make-up.
2. Attainments.
3. General intelligence.
4. Special aptitudes.
5. Interests.
6. Disposition.
7. Circumstances.

Establishing job descriptions and person specifications is an important line management responsibility in the process of properly controlled recruitment. The task can be greatly assisted by professional guidance from the personnel function.

Attracting applicants

The objective in recruitment is to fill every vacancy by appointing the most suitable person available for each job. The suitability of each candidate is a matter of judgement, the evidence for which is inevitably incomplete and inconclusive. Moreover, since employment involves personal relationships, much of the judgement must be subjective.

Misjudgement in this field is likely to be costly for the organisation and traumatic for the individual. A disciplined approach to selection is necessary to avoid the worst of these risks.

The first step in the process of filling a vacancy is to invite applications. The possibility of internal candidates should always be considered. There are usually advantages in appointing an existing employee:

1. More should be known about the suitability of an internal candidate than an outsider.
2. The internal candidate will already be familiar with many of the organisation's disciplines.
3. Encouraging internal career progression helps to build loyalty and morale.

It is usual for large organisations to adopt a policy of advertising all vacancies internally and giving priority to internal candidates.

External candidates may be sought in various ways:

1. Through Department of Employment job centres.
2. Through professional registers.
3. Through school or university careers officers or job fairs.
4. By advertising in the local, national or trade press.
5. Through employment consultants.

Applicants should be asked to complete an application form wherever it is feasible. It then provides a written record of considered answers by the applicant to carefully framed questions from the employer. This will be useful evidence in judging the suitability of all candidates from a common viewpoint.

Selection

Interviewing is the principal method used for assessing the suitability of candidates. Obtaining the maximum relevant information from an interview is a particular skill. All line managers need to cultivate this skill, but it is an essential element of the expertise of the professional in personnel management.

When the position requires a specified skill, technical proficiency or professional expertise, it will be necessary to involve an appropriate expert in the interviewing process.

Selection disciplines should allow for professional assistance, but it is fundamental that the final choice is made by the line manager with the vacancy to fill.

Completed application forms and impressions from professionally conducted interviews provide a basis for judging a candidate's suitability, but they are not infallible. References should be taken up for all positions of trust or responsibility or where a substantial investment in training is contemplated.

Taking up references is an important discipline which rarely produces positive evidence of a candidate's unsuitability. An absence of unqualified support on every aspect of suitability in a reference should alert the prospective employer to make further enquiries. Referees are naturally reluctant to condemn a friend seeking help. In cases of doubt or uncertainty, a verbal exchange is usually more revealing than a formally written reference.

Contract of employment

Once references have been received and considered satisfactory, firm offers of employment can be made to the selected candidates. The written offer should specify in detail the full terms of employment:

job title and to whom responsible
starting date
remuneration, frequency of payment and review
  terms
fringe benefits
notice required to terminate by either party
place of work
hours of work
holiday entitlement
sickness absence entitlement
superannuation terms
secrecy obligations

Acceptance establishes the contract of employment. This initiates a number of administrative procedures for which there should be a well-defined discipline to ensure that every one is completed. For example:

opening a personnel record file
entering on the payroll
PAYE documentation (P45)
pension scheme membership
induction training
fire and safety briefing

Training and development

The performance of an organisation will reflect the teamwork of its people. Success is dependent upon training and motivation. The management task is to ensure that every employee is contributing through having both the competence to fulfil his or her assigned role and a commitment to the objectives of the organisation.

Good leadership is crucial, but it is also necessary to invest in both training and motivation to secure the best contribution from the human resources and to sustain high standards in teamwork.

Training

The essential elements of the training process are:

1. **Identifying the training needs:**

    (a) **Group needs:** Manpower planning projections will contain considered estimates of long-term requirements for new recruits and for possible changes in working methods and technology. These estimates will give an indication whether or not in-house training facilities could be supported as the basis for a training strategy.

    When a change in system, methods or technology is being contemplated it is likely to change the requirements of groups of jobs. The employees affected may need to apply new knowledge, new skills, and to develop proficiency in new methods. Anticipating this kind of need and planning the necessary retraining is therefore a critical feature of implementing the changes.

In mass production operations there are likely to be many repetitive jobs requiring specially developed skills. A steady turnover of employees is not uncommon in this kind of work, creating a continuous flow of new recruits to be trained. This kind of need is sometimes met by establishing a training school with a practice production line close to the actual work place.

(b) **Individual needs:** Regular performance reviews or employee appraisals provide a basis for comparing the knowledge, skills and proficiency of individual employees against those required for efficient performance in the job. Where gaps are identified, it may be appropriate to prescribe specific training from a range of available courses.

2. **Analysing the need:** Careful analysis is necessary to determine the most effective way of resolving the problems caused by gaps between the available knowledge, skills and proficiencies and those required.

It is important to endeavour to separate poor performance caused by these differences from that caused by unsatisfactory job design, inadequate equipment or ineffective management control. A general lack of skill may contribute to poor performance in a department but will be difficult to diagnose, and motivation will also have to be considered.

An important element in the work of constructing training plans is the assessment of the cost to enable the training budget to be evaluated. It is also important to endeavour to assess the benefits expected from each separate training plan and to allocate priorities.

If the budget is subjected to financial limitation, it is necessary to identify the operational effect of postponing or abandoning any of the training proposals.

3. **Designing courses:** All training courses should be designed with specific objectives and should identify the criteria for selecting participants. The training methods and appropriate facilities should be specified and the cost should be assessed.

Functional specialists who have knowledge of the subject area should participate in the design of specialist elements in the training courses.

4. **Implementation:** This stage involves setting up the agreed training facilities and ensuring that they are used as intended. It requires close liaison between line management and the training function in planning the release of candidates for training and the availability of the agreed training facilities.

Training courses may be arranged in-house or purchased from external sources. The choice may be determined by specialism, convenience or value for money. Organisations seeking regular training in particular areas or specific technology often find it advantageous to establish in-house training facilities. In other cases, contracts are made with external training establishments to provide training courses specifically designed for the organisation. External courses of general application may also be used.

5. **Review and evaluation:** The purpose of evaluation is to assess the effectiveness of the training processes in meeting their objectives and to amend plans if necessary.

It is important to ensure that monitoring arrangements are in place to record progress as the training proceeds. This should include cost analyses of the facilities provided and suitable means of appraising the results achieved. It may take the form of assessing individual performances before training and at intervals after training.

In all appropriate cases, participants of training programmes should be required to record their own impressions on completion of the course. These reports should be in a standard format designed to assess:

(a) whether the course addressed its specified objectives;
(b) how well it achieved these objectives;
(c) the quality of instruction;
(d) the standard of administration;
(e) a personal view of benefits gained.

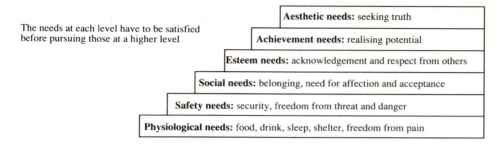

The needs at each level have to be satisfied before pursuing those at a higher level

Aesthetic needs: seeking truth

Achievement needs: realising potential

Esteem needs: acknowledgement and respect from others

Social needs: belonging, need for affection and acceptance

Safety needs: security, freedom from threat and danger

Physiological needs: food, drink, sleep, shelter, freedom from pain

Figure 6.1   Maslow's hierarchy of needs

Development

Encouraging and assisting every employee to achieve his or her full potential will serve the best interests of the organisation.

Motivation

In order to motivate employees, managers need to have an understanding of human behaviour and attitudes. A significant amount of research has been conducted in this field. The American behavioural scientist Abraham Maslow (1943) classified the needs of individuals on an ascending scale, as shown in Figure 6.1.

Maslow's hierarchy of needs has considerable relevance to attitudes to work. In motivational terms, it implies that appealing to the higher level needs is unlikely to be effective if lower needs have not been satisfied.

The needs most likely to concern employers are in the social, esteem and achievement classifications. Employees need to feel part of a team, they need their work to be appreciated with encouragement and praise when it is due. Fulfilling these needs is an important factor in job satisfaction which stimulates a desire to progress and achieve more.

Frederick Herzberg (1974) carried the research further to show that job satisfaction was influenced more by job content than other factors. He classified these influences as either 'motivators' or 'hygiene factors':

Motivators

stimulating work
responsibility
achievement
recognition
advancement

Hygiene factors

pay, status, security and working conditions
supervision and interpersonal relationships
policies and administration

Horngren has identified two further concepts of motivation:

1. **Incentive:** The driving force which stimulates action to achieve goals.
2. **Goal congruence:** A situation where the objectives serve the interests of both the individual and the organisation.

MacGregor (1960) defined the contrasting elements in two extremes of management style:

1. **Theory X:** Assumes that people do not like work and shirk responsibility: they prefer to be told what to do rather than decide for themselves, and work best for high financial reward and under threat of punishment. Characteristics of this management style are autocracy, absence of consultation, strict disciplines, and the perception of pay and punishment as the motivating tools.

2. **Theory Y:** Assumes that people regard work as a natural activity and enjoy responsibility: they can contribute most when directing their own efforts; achievement and success in their work are more satisfying to them than the financial reward. Characteristics of this management style are caring, consultation, participation and delegation of authority with responsibility.

Child and Whiting summarised the findings of many in relating motivation to success and failure. The principal conclusion of this work was that success raises levels of aspiration and failure depresses them, reflecting the individual's confidence in an ability to attain goals.

McClelland (1961) identified striving for achievement and striving for power as separate causes for motivation. He distinguished high achievers as those who enjoyed responsibility and set high standards for their own performance. Recognising these differences between individuals helps to maximise the contribution each can make.

Appraisal

Regular appraisal of individual employees is generally perceived as a key factor in successful personnel management. Its purpose is to assess performance in the current job and to explore the potential of each employee with a view to identifying or creating development opportunities.

Appraisal is a review and planning process in which employee and manager together examine strengths and weaknesses and take stock of progress and prospects within the organisation. It should provide the basis for agreeing a plan of action in training and development. This plan may then be designed not only to overcome weaknesses but also to develop the strengths identified, to the mutual benefit of the individual and the organisation. This is a motivational objective which also has goal congruence.

The appraisal process is normally accomplished as an annual exercise. It is time-consuming and needs to be well planned in advance to secure full advantage. Preparatory thinking by all participants about the issues to be considered is likely to enhance

the outcome. This means reasonable advance notice, with an outline of the areas for discussion.

The essence of the appraisal process is a frank discussion between each individual employee and his or her immediate superior. For jobs in specialist functions it may be appropriate for the relevant functional superior to be present to contribute a functional dimension to the discussion of performance and potential.

The outcome of the appraisal interview needs to be fully recorded. It is also usual for both parties to confirm their commitment to the agreed course of action by signing the record. The record provides the basis for each individual to monitor his or her own progress and the starting point for the following year's appraisal.

Using a standard format for the appraisal record will help to ensure a measure of consistency and comparability for all employees of the organisation. It becomes the agenda for each appraisal interview, serving to prompt proper consideration of all appropriate issues.

Here are a number of key requirements to be listed on a standard appraisal record form:

1. **Personal details:** In addition to name, job title and grading or evaluation with relevant dates this section should make reference to skills and qualifications, whether or not relevant to the current job.
2. **Achievement of objectives:** This section should deal with progress on plans agreed at the previous review for both performance in the job and training and development objectives.
3. **Objectives for the future:** Personal objectives should be agreed for the year ahead, and also longer term if applicable. It may be appropriate to agree bench mark dates for achieving these objectives.
4. **Training and development:** The appraisal interview should explore the employee's latent abilities, aptitude, expectations and potential as well as performance in the current job.

   It is the manager's task to counsel the employee to appreciate the possibilities and how they might be achieved. It is then feasible to consider training and development to equip each individual to achieve full potential.

Training and development could take the form of internal or external courses or a temporary or permanent change of job to gain experience of new techniques, or practices.

5. **Strengths and weaknesses:** The form will normally list groups of qualities to be considered:

   (a) managerial strengths;
   (b) technical or professional strengths;
   (c) interpersonal strengths;
   (d) personal strengths.

6. **Expression of views:** Space should be provided for both participants to comment briefly on the outcome of the interview; these comments should be signed. For example:

   (a) management comments might express a view on performance and potential;
   (b) employees might be asked to record their own views on achievements and aspirations.

Most organisations will take particular care to avoid relating the appraisal process directly to the reward structure of the organisation. This attitude recognises a fundamental distinction between motivational factors, like job satisfaction and responsibility, and remuneration, which is classified as a hygiene factor.

Nevertheless, there are sometimes cases where it is appropriate to grant merit awards on the basis of performance appraisal. In these cases the appraisal process serves a different purpose and is likely to be structured differently.

Internal audit considerations

It is first necessary to define the objective of internal audit examination in the field of personnel management. This must be to evaluate the effectiveness of critical control procedures. In this field it means those procedures designed to ensure the success of activities most critical to the achievement of the organisation's objectives.

In order to establish which are the most critical activities it is necessary to consider the potential areas of failure:

1. Inability to achieve planned growth through inadequate human resources would be a serious failure reflecting on the policies and practices for recruitment, training and remuneration.
2. Significant losses or damage might be suffered as a result of poorly motivated employees, unsafe working practices or untrustworthy employees in positions of trust.

Control procedures designed to provide protection against such hazards include:

1. Sound manpower planning as an element of corporate planning.
2. Properly controlled recruitment including taking references.
3. Rational training plans effectively carried through.
4. Fair pay and conditions strictly applied.
5. The cultivation of positive attitudes to safety at work.

Pre-audit preparation and a preliminary survey are necessary for gathering information and documents from which to gain an understanding of the function and how it achieves its purpose. For example:

1. **Organisation:**

   (a) organisation chart;
   (b) details of staff of the personnel department;
   (c) policies, objectives, work plans, methods and practice;
   (d) committees dealing with personnel topics;
   (e) external audit reports referring to personnel management activities.

2. **Manpower planning:**

   (a) objectives;
   (b) human resource plans and succession planning;
   (c) turnover, recruitment, retirement profiles;
   (d) work plans for specific operational areas.

3. **Staffing functions:**

   (a) recruitment procedures;
   (b) job evaluation procedures;
   (c) appraisal procedures;

(d) personnel records systems;

(e) pay systems;

(f) pay review procedures;

(g) industrial relations status and practice;

(h) superannuation procedures.

4. **Training functions:**

(a) forums for identifying training needs;

(b) training facilities and programmes;

(c) use of training facilities;

(d) training manuals;

(e) assessment of training performance;

(f) training budget and cost.

Section 5. Marketing management

The nature of marketing

Marketing is the management process which identifies, anticipates and supplies customer requirements efficiently and profitably.

(Wilmshurst, 1984)

Business organisations are concerned primarily with profitability and maintaining the asset base and they depend upon success in servicing markets for achieving these objectives. The essence of marketing is endeavouring to match supply capability to demand by the use of a range of functions collectively described as 'the marketing mix': a combination of various policies and activities which are in effect marketing tools.

The marketing mix

Product	Promotion	Price	Place
Quality	Advertising	List price	Distributors
Features	Personal selling	Discounts	Retailers
Name	Sales promotion	Allowances	Locations
Packaging	Public relations	Credit	Inventory
Services			Transport
Guarantees			

Source: Doyle (1984).

Market segmentation

A market is not a homogeneous collection of people but is made up of many types of buyers, all with different perceptions of their needs and how to satisfy them. It is feasible to classify consumers in various groupings according to broad analyses of perceived wants. A market segment is a group of buyers with similar purchasing characteristics.

Differentiated marketing is the practice of tailoring separate product and marketing programmes for different segments of the market. A single marketing mix offered to the whole market is rarely successful because of the wide range of consumer preferences within a market.

Concentrated marketing is the development of the optimum market mix for one particular market segment.

Success is achieved by providing the most suitable product or service promoted by the most effective method, selling at the right price for the market and available through the most convenient outlets for the customer.

The right price for the consumer is related to concepts of value for money and the competing options for spending it; for the supplier it is the price which yields adequate profitability.

Marketing strategy

Target markets

The starting point for the marketing cycle is to determine which market segments the organisation is best equipped to service and what products or services should be supplied.

Target markets are select groupings of actual and potential buyers for the particular products or services to be offered. These market segments have to be defined within limits which best match the organisation's servicing capability, but each segment must be sufficiently large to offer reasonable prospects of profitable exploitation.

The following factors will influence the selection of target markets:

1. **The organisation's strengths:** These may include technology and experience in particular product

types, established contacts and reputation in the market place including brand recognition, the advantages of established production and distribution facilities.

These strengths should take into account:

(a) the cost of maintaining or increasing market share for established products;
(b) the cost of entering the market and sustaining operations until profitability can be achieved;
(c) the lead time necessary to become established in the market and achieve profitability.

2. **Potential customer wants:** Products will not sell unless someone wants to buy them. It is necessary to have confidence that enough people will want to buy at a price which will enable the product to be offered at a profit. It is also necessary to consider the importance of local availability, established distribution channels and transportation. Such confidence must be based upon intelligent interpretation of consumer expectations and trends.

The potential demand believed to exist for the product or service may be extrapolated from national and industry statistics in the light of market research and accumulated knowledge and experience of the market. This may involve questioning customers, potential customers and ultimate consumers or representative samples, and then analysing the answers and the trends revealed in recent experience to arrive at a forecast of demand.

3. **The marketing environment:** A significant factor in this category is the impact of competition. This means assessing the availability of similar products in the market and their potential for competing. But it also means considering the alternative options available to the consumer and how demand may be influenced by the economic climate.

Assessing the potential impact of competition requires a comprehensive analysis of present and potential competitors in the market, market share, financial strength, production facilities, sales outlets, product range, quality, service standards, pricing policy, main customers, development plans, etc. This involves collecting all available information about competitors and in particular making reasoned assumptions as to their plans.

Market shares

Unless there is a monopoly, there are likely to be many suppliers competing to service every market segment, each with a different share of the total demand. The market leader is the supplier whose share is the largest, having a greater volume of sales in the segment than any competitor.

The market leader in every market segment is in a position to secure the greatest profit from supplying that segment. This is because profit margins from high sales volume are likely to be enhanced by production cost benefits from economies of scale. This important principle is the key to marketing strategy. The organisation should aim to become market leader in every market segment it services.

To interpret such a strategy it is first necessary to identify with care those demand characteristics which the organisation intends to service; the preferred market segments will then become clear.

1. **Niche markets:** Often a product with insignificant market share in a large market segment has specialist appeal to a particular group of consumers. The market segment for this product can then be identified separately and its specialist characteristics can be exploited by a specialist supplier as the market leader.
2. **Product life cycle:** Markets are dynamic. Consumer wants change continuously. All products and services which survive in the market place have definite life cycles. Each has a growth phase, a period of maximum performance and a decline phase. Successful products will usually take time to achieve market dominance.
3. **Financing growth:** To increase the market share is costly, it requires concentrated marketing activity, product design, promotion, price competition and distribution. The sales volume growth is also likely to involve increasing investment in production resources and working capital.

The Boston Consulting Group demonstrated the importance of market share by focusing on its impact on cash flow. Their work examines combinations of high and low market shares with high and low market growth. The names adopted to describe how the product performs can be identified with the phases of a product's life cycle:

1. **'Question mark'** (Low market share in a high growth market)
   A product in this category will be at a disadvantage with weak profit margins and pressure to invest in increased volume just to maintain market share. It may represent a recent entry into the market in the growth phase of its product life cycle. Its potential for achieving a high market share, and the necessary investment, need very careful consideration. Progress should then be closely monitored.
2. **'Star'** (High market share in a high growth market)
   Products which have reached this stage should have cost advantages over competitors from economies of scale. This will yield strong profit margins, but investment in volume growth to maintain market share through the growth phase is likely to absorb substantial cash resources. It should become a high cash flow generator when market growth levels out.
3. **'Cash cow'** (High market share in a low growth market)
   At this stage products should still have a cost advantage over competitors which will continue to yield strong profit margins. The investment required to maintain market share in a low growth market will be low. This combination will generate a good cash flow, providing funds to finance growth of 'stars' and selected 'question marks'.
4. **'Dog'** (Low market share in a low growth market)
   Products in this category will be at a disadvantage. Costs are likely to be higher than those of competitors. Profit margins will be weak. Investment to increase market share is unlikely to be an attractive option for the declining phase of the product life cycle; controlled withdrawal from the market may be more appropriate.

Products

A product may take the form of goods, such as cans of beans, microwave ovens or bespoke packaging; or services, such as airline passages, policies of insurance or haulage of goods. The most important feature of a product is the concept of satisfying a customer want.

It is important to recognise the customer's perception of what is required because there may be alternative ways of providing it and the customer is likely to prefer the most convenient way. Ball-point pens and electric shavers are examples of products which achieved success by breaking away from traditional technology to satisfy a traditional need.

All markets are subject to continuous change in terms of consumer needs, and consequently all products have a finite life cycle. It may sometimes be extended so long as the product is capable of being adapted to keep pace with changing needs as new technology is developed. Eventually, however, the consumer's perception of the requirements progresses beyond the scope of traditional products and an entirely new product concept emerges. For example: typewriters progressed from mechanical to electric versions, to be superseded by electronic word processors.

All products eventually reach a point in the life cycle where production is no longer viable because demand has collapsed. Long before this, however, the organisation must have established new products in their markets if it is to continue to prosper. This is because new products generally take time to achieve profitability, and many will not succeed.

A successful business organisation should have a product profile which includes mature products which are generating healthy profit margins and cash flow, as well as a succession of developing products of later vintage and technology with good potential.

Research is concerned with advancing technology, development with the commercial exploitation of new technology. Continuous research and development are necessary to ensure that the organisation maintains a marketable product profile. It is, however, most important to ensure that the natural enthusiasm which all experts have for their technology is directed towards satisfying the requirements of the market. Product designers must work closely with customers to get to know and understand these requirements and the underlying causes.

Product development has to be driven by customer demand for enhancement. It may result in totally new concepts of products or production processes, such as, for example, laser-sensed compact disc recordings; or it may lead to modifying existing concepts by incorporating new technologies, such as quartz controlled clocks and watches, or the incorporation of electronic ignition or antilock braking systems in motor cars.

Product design will be influenced by both functional requirements and aesthetic considerations. The product has to perform up to expectations, but it must also be styled to accord with current fashion. However, whilst technological development is progressive, the fashion element tends to be cyclical. It is therefore necessary to study trends and to anticipate where they may lead.

In some consumer markets aesthetic quality has greater significance than in others. For example, it may be a crucial factor in such industries as wallpaper or textiles, and a necessary feature in motor cars or civil engineering, while not relevant at all in agricultural chemicals or oil refining.

Control

The organisation's survival and progress may well be dependent upon successful direction and control of product development. In such cases, it is appropriate to appoint a senior executive to be held fully accountable to top management for these activities.

The scale of resources necessary for development of the product profile may be related to the expected life cycles of the existing product range. Account should be taken of:

past experience
current performance
intended marketing developments

This will give an indication of the rate at which new products have to be launched to maintain product momentum. Experience will also give an indication of the scale and cost of research and development time and the effort necessary to bring new products to the launching stage.

Having established the scale of resources it is necessary to establish a plan to be approved and adopted as the budget for the work to be done. The work has to be divided into projects for effective control. Projects may be defined to focus on:

identified market needs
potential market developments
specific technological developments with market
    potential

Each project should have a defined objective and specific bench marks at defined intervals, against which progress can be measured. Timing is often critical in product development work. Progress should be monitored and reviewed at regular intervals.

Normal budgetary control procedures should be applied to help accomplish planned programmes of work and to secure effective financial control. In this field it is most important to ensure that control is effective without inhibiting creative flair and endeavour.

The performance of new products should also be regularly assessed from the time of launching as the basis for reviewing the adequacy of resources allocated to product development and how effectively they are being applied.

New products which satisfy customer needs better than other products currently in the market have advantages over those others which should enable them to gain market share rapidly. However, competitors will respond quickly to losing market share. Some may well have their own new product with similar or even more advanced features for satisfying customer needs. Even so, being first in the market usually secures an extremely valuable lead over 'me too' products.

The race to launch before competitors, and the need to protect valuable information from leaking to them, means that time and secrecy are critical features of product development work: to deal with both effectively calls for firm management.

Testing

Pressure to launch at the earliest opportunity is understandable. But creative ideas sometimes refuse to respond to such pressure. There is therefore a risk of launching a new product with unresolved problems, which could prove disastrous. A carefully planned programme of testing is essential for most new products. It must be rigorously followed, the results analysed and performance approved before proceeding to the next stage.

Product testing is most effective when carried out independently from those who have designed and developed the product. Testing techniques and practices will of course vary considerably, depending upon the nature and purpose of the product. Testing should however address three critical aspects:

1. Technical evaluation of the design, construction, recipe, production processes, etc.
2. Technical evaluation of performance against criteria established by market needs including safety and environmental and legal considerations.
3. Market acceptance: this is usually tested by controlled trials in a sample market region.

Security

Information in the field of product development has great strategic importance to the organisation and could be enormously valuable to competitors. Particular attention must be paid to security. Serious loss or damage could result from a leakage of sensitive information which could occur in any of three ways:

1. Carelessness by employees in handling information, such as inadequate control of documents or unguarded talk.
2. Disloyalty by an employee or past employee in passing information to a competitor.
3. Theft of information by or on behalf of a competitor through break-in or industrial espionage.

Some of these offences may seem less serious than others, but all could lead to the same serious consequences so that equal diligence is necessary to ensure they cannot happen. For example:

1. **Staff security:** Thorough vetting of all staff employed on sensitive project work is fundamental. Special care needs to be taken in the recruitment and appointment of these staff to confirm that they are totally trustworthy. Obtaining credible unqualified references for new recruits is particularly important. Employees handling sensitive information should always be required to give secrecy undertakings in their written contracts of employment.
2. **Procedural security:** Strict disciplines need to be imposed for handling all sensitive documents including files, working papers, reports, etc. relating to strategic planning, product planning, research and development. It is necessary to define sensitive information and to emphasise personal responsibility to protect it. The disciplines need to cover secure storage, restrictions on access and control of copying, removal from the office, and destruction.
3. **Environmental security:** Premises where sensitive work is carried out may need to be equipped with intruder alarms and subject to 24-hour security surveillance. All staff need to be alert to the possibility of industrial espionage and to deal promptly with any suspicious happening.

Patent protection

For a newly invented product or process, patent protection may have considerable commercial importance. Patent protection reserves for the proprietor all rights of commercial exploitation in the territory covered by the patent. These are the exclusive rights to make, use and sell products which incorporate the invention for the life of the patent. The maximum life of a patent is usually 20 years but annual renewal is necessary to maintain it in force. The owner can assign these rights to others and can grant licences to other parties to exploit part or all of the rights.

The process of obtaining patent protection starts with the patent application: this means filing in the Patent Office a detailed technical description of the invention with a definition of what is believed to be inventive. An essential qualification for novelty is that the invention has not been publicly disclosed.

In most countries in Europe the application is published 18 months after the application date. A patent application will be examined to ensure it meets legal requirements as to inventiveness and adequacy of disclosure. During pendency marking with 'patent applied for' indicates protection is anticipated. Though the patent cannot be enforced while pending, once granted certain awards are available back to initial publication in regard to infringement.

Securing patent protection may be vitally important to organisations pursuing new technology in the process of developing their product ranges. When this is so, some critical control conditions need to be established:

1. **Inventor's rights:** Title to a patentable idea vests in the inventor unless the inventor is an individual engaged on product development work which is intended to generate patentable ideas for the benefit of the organisation where it vests in the employer. The contracts of employment for all such 'inventive' employees should specify the nature of the duties. All employees should have contracts agreeing to give first rights to the employer for inventions relating to the business. These contracts should contain explicit undertakings by the employee to assist the employer in securing patents.
2. **Secrecy:** Leakage of information about any invention before filing the patent application will almost certainly result in successful contest of the claims for novelty and failure of the application. This emphasises the need for special attention to security in product development work.
3. **Patent management:** Patent law is a complex subject and the price of mistakes could be very high: skilled professional advice and guidance is usually considered essential.
4. **International protection:** Patent laws throughout the world are generally similar but there can be major differences which affect the protectability and enforceability of patents, for example the United States and Japan. Separate patents must be applied for in each territory where protection is required. A priority period of one year is allowed in most countries after filing in the country of origin. This means that during the year nothing disclosed will have an adverse effect.

Very careful consideration needs to be given to the possibilities for foreign exploitation of an invention. The potential benefits should be evaluated, they must include: exporting; overseas manufacture; licensing overseas manufacture for a royalty; or assigning the overseas rights to another party for a capital consideration. Against these possibilities is the cost of securing overseas patent protection. Much specialist work is involved in preparing an application for the requirements of local patent law.

Promotion

John Wilmshurst (1984) describes sales promotion as using one's own media for communicating messages about the product, as distinct from advertising which uses media controlled by others.

Advertising

The objectives of advertising are to:

1. Create brand awareness.
2. Make the public aware of the product.
3. Create a favourable climate for definitive selling.
4. Give post-purchase reassurance.

Any proposed advertising programme agreed with an agency should have agreed financial limits. The programme should identify separately the creative work, alternative types of copy, presentation media, media timings, and estimated itemised costs. The proposal should lead to a firm agreed action plan properly documented and budgeted throughout the period of the programme.

Each advertising campaign should have a defined purpose and this will determine the nature of the advertising copy, the timing and the media used. For example:

1. In a seasonal market where manufacturers' branded products are distributed through independent retailers, the promotional campaign

must start some weeks before the season. It may include a programme of advertising in the trade press, directed at distributors and announcing promotional offers to encourage them to stock up. It would be followed by a programme of brand advertising in the national press and television from the start of the season.

2. Travel agencies generally launch their major advertising campaigns promoting packaged holiday services on national television and in consumer magazines around Christmas time.

Sales promotion

Sales promotion often means a campaign, employing such techniques as temporary price reductions, gifts, competitions and special displays and events. All sales promotion campaigns should be designed as an integral part of the marketing plan. The campaign may be directed at ultimate consumers or at intermediaries in the distribution chain and the techniques adopted will reflect this:

1. Wholesalers may be offered a loyalty bonus or extended credit to stock up with the product in advance of the peak selling season.
2. Retailers may be offered price incentives for a limited period and assistance with presenting the product (merchandising) and with point-of-sale promotional material.
3. Ultimate consumers may be offered extra product for the usual price (premium offers) or gifts, etc.

Dealer support may take the form of advising dealer customers on ordering procedures, care of stock, presentation of sales. It may also include a technical advisory service for the use and maintenance of products.

Customer support is an extension of dealer support to the final consumer. It provides for information regarding the use of the product and the operation of the product or service and satisfaction of any warranty or guarantee, or dealing with customer complaints.

Personal selling is sometimes used as an important element of a promotional campaign. It can be adapted to suit individual negotiations with customers in response to particular needs and may cover the complete selling process from the initial contract with the customer to collecting money for the sale.

Branding

The purpose of branding a product is to convey a promise of quality to potential consumers. The quality of most consumer products has to be taken on trust by the buyer: the proof of the quality will be in consumption or use after purchase.

For some products the consumer is better able to judge quality by inspection before purchase than for others. For example, fresh foods are rarely branded, whereas packaged processed foods are almost invariably branded.

Similarly, the quality of performance of products intended for use such as motor cars, carpets, soap powders or garments made from synthetic fibres must all be taken on trust at the time of purchase. A respected brand name gives the buyer a degree of confidence that the product will perform effectively and be reliable in use.

The essence of successful branding is in establishing a reputation for consistency in the quality of the branded product. The quality must of course match the wants of a sufficient number of consumers to establish a viable market. It is therefore necessary to ensure that quality is maintained consistently.

The brand reputation, once established, has considerable commercial significance. Consumers are prepared to pay for quality assurance, consequently branded goods command a premium price and brand promotion is thus financed by enhanced profit margins.

Many consumer products are branded by the manufacturer to be distributed through independent retail outlets. The manufacturer then promotes the brand down-stream by national advertising to consumers and appropriate support schemes to facilitate availability through the distribution pipelines.

Retailers' own-label products are those manufactured to the retailer's specification with critical quality control standards. For these products the brand promise includes the retailer's reputation for quality, service, value for money and so on.

Brand names need to be protected by registration

to prevent anyone else using them. Vigilance and prompt action against any infringement or 'passing off' are necessary to avoid risks of damage to the reputation of the brand.

Control

Advertising and sales promotion are activities in which innovation and creativity should predominate and it is particularly important to have sound planning and effective control to secure full benefit from them. The budget then provides an effective sheet anchor.

The budget should be based on a definitive marketing plan in which detailed proposals for each promotional campaign are specified with costs and expected benefits. The progress of each campaign can then be closely monitored and controlled throughout the budget period.

Sales force

The primary purpose of the sales force is to maintain direct communication between the organisation and individual customers and potential customers. This communication is a necessary element in the process of fulfilling a number of important objectives:

1. To ensure that customers and potential customers are kept fully aware of the strength of the organisation's range of products and services and the terms on which it is willing to do business.
2. To receive specific information from customers in the form of purchase enquiries and to initiate formal responses in the form of quotations or priced offers to sell.
3. To negotiate sales on mutually acceptable terms.
4. To monitor performance of customer orders including delivery and settlement.
5. To receive and deal with customer complaints as necessary.
6. To glean evidence which may be significant in assessing strengths and weaknesses of customers and potential customers, particularly concerning purchasing potential and credit risks.
7. To gather information on the needs and prospective needs of customers and potential customers which may contribute to the organisation's assessment of market demand as a basis for its own planning.
8. To explore customers' perceptions of the organisation, its product range, quality, service and value for money.
9. To glean information about competitors' activities and plans, product range and terms of business and how they are perceived by customers.

The brief for the sales force of an organisation may include some or all of these objectives. The range of options is extensive and choice could reflect the structure of the market, the nature of the product, the culture and customs of the trade or of individual organisations, and many other factors.

Similar factors will also influence the methods a sales force can adopt for fulfilling the objectives. The ways of deploying a sales force include:

1. Formal meetings by appointment with the buyer.
2. House-to-house peddling.
3. Retail shop service.
4. Freephone telesales service.
5. Cold call telephone selling.
6. Mail order selling by catalogue or mail shot.

In general, the sales force is the organisation's means of direct communication with its customers, relying essentially on verbal communication. Its effectiveness will depend upon the performance of each individual member working alone in the field.

Verbal communication has the advantages of being quicker and easier than writing, its message will be augmented by body language, and correct understanding can be verified at the time. However, memories are often fugitive and recollections can be coloured by subsequent events or by a prejudged interpretation of what was heard. It is necessary to make a record, for subsequent reference, of critical issues discussed with customers. There should be established reporting disciplines for the sales force covering confirmation of orders taken and information received about future needs, competitor activity and complaints.

In order to contribute fully to the achievement of organisational objectives the sales force must be:

1. Properly directed and controlled to ensure it is effectively pursuing the organisation's objectives.

2. Well motivated to inspire each member to perform alone in the organisation's interests.
3. Sufficiently well informed about the organisation, its products and its marketing philosophy to communicate a favourable understanding to customers.
4. Skilled in selling and verbal communication.

Directing and controlling the sales force is the role of sales management. It involves:

1. **Sales planning:** The development and implementation of a plan of action for the sales force aimed at fulfilling organisational objectives through achieving the sales forecast. The sales plan should define the organisational structure of the sales force and set targets for individual sales staff.
2. **Staff management:** The recruitment, training, motivation and briefing of sales staff and monitoring their individual performances.
3. **Training:** This includes both the development of selling and communication skills and product and technical training to the standards needed for the job. Sales conferences provide a forum for new product familiarisation and morale building. Although selling is solitary work, it demands gregarious qualities like enthusiasm, confidence, optimism and a positive outlook.
4. **Motivation:** Challenging work, responsibility and recognition of achievements are important motivational forces for sales staff. Sales conferences also assist through morale building. Individual sales targets provide a basis for individual accountability.
5. **Remuneration:** Sales force remuneration often includes incentives in the form of performance-related elements of bonus or commission. In some cases the remuneration may be wholly commission. Proper control of these variable elements is necessary to ensure that the amounts paid fairly reflect genuine sales for the benefit of the organisation.

Price

The market price of a product reflects the relative strengths of demand and supply:

1. Demand strength is influenced by social, demographic, economic, functional, emotional and economic factors. Consumer wants are also competitive among themselves.
2. Supply strength is influenced by competition and by the relationship between market price and the cost to produce. Cost to produce will depend upon the volume of production which in turn reflects the size of the market and market share.

Price is a critical element of the relationship between buyer and seller. For the buyer it influences the strength of the will to buy; for the seller it determines profitability.

Price setting involves judgement about the strength of market forces. They need to be judged with considerable care and within the framework of a clearly defined pricing policy.

Pricing policy

In view of the impact on profitability, pricing policy should be determined as a key element of corporate strategy. This is because profitability is the ultimate corporate objective of a business enterprise and it is influenced by all of its activities. Whilst the primary objective of these activities will be the pursuit of profitability in meeting identified market needs, the sales pricing structure must also take account of the specific objectives of each activity:

1. **Procurement:** The policies adopted for procurement of goods and services will influence cost of production, reflecting the relative emphasis placed upon price, quality, service and continuity of supply. These considerations may in turn influence make-or-buy decisions, quality control, technological progress, and so on.
2. **Employment:** The policies adopted for recruitment, training, development and remuneration of employees will have an important bearing on the competence of an enterprise to address particular market demands. This will be a key factor in the choice of markets to serve and it will

have an impact on profitability through both market strength and production costs.

3. **Investment:** Profitability is measured in capital markets in terms of return on investment and this sets the parameters for profit objectives which must be reflected in the sales pricing policy. Pursuit of growth requires new investment. In the investment policy adopted, the profit objectives will reflect the relative emphasis given to such options as:

    (a) new product development;
    (b) securing critical resources;
    (c) expansion of production facilities;
    (d) extending distribution facilities;
    (e) increasing market share.

4. **Product profile:** The product profile will reflect product development policy and long-term profitability decisions based upon market judgements. However, the objectives being pursued in product development are unlikely to be achieved unless they are also acknowledged consistently in the sales pricing policy.

5. **Marketing strategy:** The essence of corporate planning is in defining strategic objectives in the pursuit of profitability. It is therefore necessary to adopt marketing policies which will allow the organisation to achieve its strategic objectives. These policies will also identify the criteria for a pricing policy. They constitute the marketing strategy and concern such endeavours as:

    (a) identifying target markets;
    (b) setting targets for market shares;
    (c) defining product profile criteria;
    (d) planning promotional activity;
    (e) defining distribution policy and planning its implementation.

Price setting

Price setting is the process by which an organisation decides the prices it will ask for its products. Clearly, these are critical decisions: if the price asked is too high, sales will be lost because potential buyers will either be discouraged or will buy from a competitor;

if the price is not high enough, the sales will not be profitable.

All price setting decisions are based upon management judgement of two factors both of which are subject to a range of uncertainties:

1. **What the market will bear:** This is a judgement of what willing buyers would be prepared to pay for the product or service offered.

    The uncertainties here are related to the perception that potential buyers have of their wants. The seller may be able to narrow the uncertainty by careful analyses of what motivates buying decisions in general and for the product being offered in particular. However, buying decisions are not always rational and subjective judgement is often difficult to predict.

    The uncertainty will also reflect the nature of the transaction. For example, when offering a product in a mass market where similar products are already selling, the market price is likely to be related to that being paid for current products. However, if the product is unique, other indicators of demand strength have to be sought.

    Products designed to the buyer's specification include a wide range of goods and services including construction contracts, packaging, 'own label' consumer products, professional services, etc. The uncertainty about what is an acceptable price for such products relates to the strength of the competition because buyers will usually seek quotations from more than one supplier. The right price is thus the buyer's perception of the value of the work to be done including assurances of quality, service and reliability.

2. **Profitability:** This is the profit contribution required from sales of the product to satisfy corporate objectives. The uncertainty about profitability relates essentially to the double impact of sales volume. It will influence unit costs and the resultant unit profit margin. It is also the factor which determines the total amount of profit.

    It is first necessary to make an assessment of the volume of sales – preferably a range of possible achievement. It is then feasible to assess the costs of production and distribution and to add the margin of profit necessary to fulfil corporate objectives for return on capital. This computation gives target selling prices at progressive volume levels to compare with the assessment of what the market will bear as a test of viability.

Cost estimates compiled to assist pricing decisions can often provide the basis for controlling production costs for subsequent orders received. Whenever it is feasible, the same standard cost elements should be used for both purposes. The effect is to apply the sanction of market forces to achieve production efficiency.

Price structure

There are many ways in which sales transactions may differ and the price has to reflect the differences. For example:

1. **Unique products:** These are products designed to buyers' specifications. In this case an individual price will be negotiated for each sales contract.
2. **Standard products:** These are often branded products produced to a standard specification and offered in the same form to all buyers in the market. In these cases:

   (a) it is usual to publish a standard price list;
   (b) products may be offered in more than one quality or finish, with premium prices for the up-market editions or models;
   (c) separate prices may be quoted for collected and for delivered orders;
   (d) there may also be a published schedule of discounts for quantity applicable to each separate order;
   (e) discounts are then negotiated with individual buyers, recognising their purchasing power. Suppliers generally negotiate from an undisclosed scale of customer classification discounts ranking customers according to their buying potential for the product.
   (f) in some cases part of the discount is conditional upon the volume of orders placed and

is withheld to be repaid retrospectively to the buyer as a rebate.

Having determined a pricing policy, assessment of the price the market will bear may appear complex because different buyers are able to exert different buying power which has to be recognised in the pricing structure. However, the mix of customers of any organisation will almost invariably be found to follow a Pareto pattern of distribution. That is to say that around 20 per cent of all customers will account for around 80 per cent of total turnover. This means that 80 per cent of all sales are likely to qualify for the highest rate of customer classification discount. This statistical relationship serves to simplify the process of setting list prices at an appropriate level.

The process of price negotiation with customers is critical to profitability and must be firmly controlled. There is little point in establishing list prices to satisfy all the criteria of a well-thought-out pricing policy if customer discounts are not subjected to the same consideration. Those authorised to negotiate prices and discounts with customers must always do so from a clear brief with defined limits which may not be exceeded without further consultation.

Credit policy

Credit is an element of the price structure which may be used as a separate marketing tool. Deferred payment terms may be a valuable concession to offer in negotiating a bulk sales contract or it may be a condition requested by the buyer in consideration for forward commitments to buy. Extended credit is often offered as part of a package of promotional incentives to encourage distributors to stock up in advance of a peak selling season.

Credit on favourable terms is frequently offered to individual consumers as a promotional incentive in marketing high-value consumer products such as motor cars, double glazing, fitted kitchens, etc. In these cases the credit is normally arranged through a finance house as a service to the supplier.

Granting credit involves financial risks and must be properly controlled. These issues are discussed in the section of this chapter on financial management.

Credit approval and debt collection procedures

are generally devised and applied by the finance function in consultation with sales staff. However, it is important that sales staff recognise that the sales they have secured are not complete until payment has been received. When remuneration is related to sales orders it should be forfeited for any orders which become bad debts.

Distribution

Distribution is the marketing tool concerned with customer service. This means ensuring that the product is in the market place and available to meet consumers' needs when and where they occur. It is dependent upon effective communication systems and efficient mechanical handling. It always requires transport and investment in stock and it may require dispersed facilities for production, or for warehousing and selling points.

Customer service is a critical feature of every buying decision ranking with price and quality to be evaluated against competition. Unless buyer and seller have identical perceptions of 'the right time and the right place' for delivery there will be no sale. Where there is no negotiation of terms of sale as in most retail selling, the buyer's perception prevails: the customer is always right.

Good distribution adds value to the product. For most products, few if any consumers are prepared to collect from the factory or to wait for them to be produced, especially if there are alternatives readily available in the high street shops, or which the seller will deliver. In all such cases the product has no value without distribution.

Distribution also adds cost. The extent of the distribution cost element depends upon the nature of the product and on the level of customer service necessary to secure the target sales level. For many industrial products, bulk delivery from factory direct to customer provides a satisfactory customer service at relatively low cost. For most consumer products, however, a significant proportion of the price paid by the consumer is absorbed by distribution costs, and in many cases this is the largest element of total cost.

The added value and added cost attributable to distribution have an important impact on profitability. Consequently, a clearly defined distribution strategy is an essential element of corporate planning. For this it is necessary to define and quantify the customer service objective and then to evaluate all the feasible options for achieving it.

The customer service objective may be quantified in terms of a target service level. This is a measure of the proportion of all demands for the product which can be satisfied on the spot immediately. Ideally, the target would be 100 per cent but the cost may be prohibitive. When raising the service level requirement, distribution costs tend to increase disproportionately. Increasing the service level from 70 per cent to 80 per cent could require a five to tenfold increase in cost.

This cost-to-benefit relationship needs very careful consideration in setting both the target service level and the volume of sales achievable. It could well be that the extra cost of maintaining very high service levels is not justified by the sales potential at risk. Much will depend on the nature of the product, its status in the market segment and the strength of competition.

The distribution options available to a manufacturer of consumer products may include the following:

1. **Direct delivery** (to consumers as direct customers): This may be mail order business promoted through a catalogue or through press advertising or it may be promoted and delivered through door-to-door selling.

   The advantages are:

   (a) customers are able to make the buying decision at home in their own time;
   (b) there are no intermediaries to take a share of profit;
   (c) it is usual to provide the service from a single warehouse, saving the cost of dispersed stock holding.

   The disadvantages are:

   (a) there is often a delay of up to one month between payment with order and delivery;

(b) in mail order business the buyer does not see the goods before ordering, but usually has a right of rejection;

(c) the productivity of door-to-door selling is unlikely to match that of other forms such as trade selling and retail stores and so may cost more.

2. **Own retail outlets:** The best known example is probably Boots the Chemist, and there are others offering specialist products like footwear. In some cases the retail outlets are serviced from a network of regional distribution warehouses.

The advantages are:

(a) there are no intermediaries to take a profit on distribution;

(b) the retail outlets concentrate on promoting the interests of the organisation;

(c) when additional products are offered they may attract buyers into the retail stores and also contribute a retailing margin.

Few organisations have a sufficiently extensive product range or sufficiently specialist product to support a national retail chain. Some augment the range with own-branded bought-in merchandise and other nationally branded products.

Organisations which distribute through their own retail outlets often adopt a policy of exclusivity: their branded products are not available from any other source. The impact of such a policy is far reaching. It avoids the problems of downstream competition which could seriously inhibit profit margins and market share. However, it imposes the burden of financing two distinct strategies: as a national retailer concentrating on ubiquitous market presence and as a manufacturer of consumer goods concentrating on dominant market shares.

3. **Independent distribution:** Many manufacturers' branded products reach the consumer through a spreading network of independent merchants, wholesalers and retailers. There is, however, a very substantial volume of direct buying by national retail chains from manufacturers. Retailers' branded products, on the other hand, are funnelled from the appointed manufacturers direct to the retailer concerned.

Major national supermarket retailers have massive buying power and are well organised to receive bulk supplies from manufacturers. All have developed own-brand products which are offered alongside manufacturers' brands. Distribution through these outlets is crucial for manufacturers' branded products to maintain brand share.

The advantage of using independent distributors is that it provides ready access to the national market for consumer goods.

The disadvantage is that the objectives pursued by distributors are different from those of the manufacturer and may often conflict. For example:

(a) manufacturers seek market dominance and premium pricing for their brands to earn an acceptable return on investment. If they controlled their own distribution they would aim for high stock support to ensure maximum service levels;

(b) distributors seek high stock turn and maximum distribution margin to provide an acceptable return on investment.

These are key features of the scenario in which a distribution strategy must be developed.

The practical aspects of directing and controlling distribution activity are discussed in the materials management section of this chapter.

Internal audit considerations

The business objective expressed in marketing terms is the pursuit of profitability by matching endeavour to identified market needs. Everyone in the organisation needs to identify with this objective.

Marketing is a management activity which has a significant influence on all other functions. This is because the identification of market needs for profitable exploitation is crucial to corporate planning, and all operational strategies then developed from it must identify with the marketing policies taking account of the market forecasts.

So much depends on the marketing judgements that it makes sense to review periodically how valid the principles and processes are for collecting and analysing the evidence on which these judgements have to be made. A review would challenge the soundness of the principles adopted and how well they were applied.

One approach is to start the annual planning round with a formal internal audit review of all marketing activities. The work is best undertaken with an audit team augmented by senior line managers from other functions, guided by the internal auditing function. The objective of this internal audit review would be to identify and evaluate strengths and weaknesses, opportunities and threats (the 'SWOT' approach). All of the techniques considered in Chapters 4 and 5 are relevant.

It is then possible for the review team to apply its extensive knowledge and understanding of the impact on the entire organisation to the process of recommending changes. These would focus on using strengths to maximum advantage and ensuring opportunities are fully exploited, whilst reinforcing controls in weak areas and providing suitable protection in areas at risk.

An important benefit from involving line managers is that it enables them to familiarise themselves with processes by which marketing judgements are made and, when appropriate, to contribute to improvements. They will then be more fully aware of the strengths and weaknesses, opportunities and threats inherent in those judgements as a foundation for planning in their own departments.

7 Specialist audits

Section 1. Payroll

Introduction

A payroll is a collection of procedures by which an organisation dispenses the remuneration due to its employees. Employees are persons who have contracted to work for the organisation in return for payment. Most organisations have at least one payroll.

Every organisation is unique in its relationship with its employees and this is likely to be reflected in its payroll procedures which will have been influenced by management philosophy and industrial relations over the years.

The internal auditor must have an understanding of these influences and work within the framework of the organisational culture.

Although organisations tend to develop payroll systems to match their specific needs, the practice of the Inland Revenue to collect income tax and national insurance contributions at source through the PAYE system imposes a degree of uniformity. There is thus sufficient common ground to permit a gereralised approach which can then be tailored to the needs of each particular organisation.

Organisations have various options in settling their liabilities: for example, in cash; by cheque or bill of exchange; by various forms of credit transfer, or through a barter transaction.

All of these forms may have been used at some time for paying employees in particular circumstances. However, in the United Kingdom there is a persistent tradition whereby many employees receive weekly payment of wages in cash.

The effect of this tradition is that the risks associated with recording, controlling and settling multiple liabilities are compounded with the risks of regularly handling large amounts of cash. The payroll is therefore a very high-risk area and calls for special consideration as a subject for internal auditing.

Payroll preparation

In essence, the payroll task is simply to establish the gross pay earned by each employee, to subtract the appropriate deductions and to pay out the net amount due to each. In practice both the gross pay and the deductions are likely to be comprised of a number of items each requiring a complex calculation determined by fixed and variable criteria. There may also be a range of options for the method of payment. Thus, payroll administration involves a complex pattern of procedures which have to be completed for each individual employee at regular intervals and within strict time constraints.

Whether the payroll is prepared by computer or by clerical routines, it is very responsible work for those entrusted with it. It demands the employment of mature and honest staff. When recruiting staff for this work it is essential that previous references are taken up and approved before any appointment is confirmed.

Payroll administration is frequently supported by a computerised processing system. Organisations which have no computer hardware of their own often use the services of computer bureaux for payroll preparation. It is an operation which is well suited to electronic data processing:

1. A large volume of calculations has to be made with speed and accuracy.
2. A legible detailed payslip is required for each employee.
3. The calculations must take account of elements of permanent data which have to be referred to for subsequent calculations indefinitely and with absolute reliability.
4. The calculations must take account of variable data which have to be introduced for the preparation of each successive payroll. Strict disciplines are critical in the collection and preparation of these data to secure the accuracy of the payroll.
5. Much of the data used in payroll preparation is sensitive personal information for which the organisation has a confidentiality obligation to each employee. It is advisable to record this data in coded form so restricting knowledge of it to those with access to the code.
6. It is feasible to build security checks and convenience facilities into a computer program (such as 'flagging' when predetermined parameters are exceeded or 'rounding up' and carrying balances forward to avoid the need for coin in pay packets.

In payroll preparation there has to be strong internal control involving effective division of duties and integrated internal checks at every stage. Control disciplines must be clearly defined and applied with absolute strictness, for the following reasons:

1. To safeguard the interests of the organisation.
2. To safeguard the interests of employees generally.
3. To protect the payroll staff against the risk of violence in the course of dealing with cash on behalf of the organisation.

4. To protect the payroll staff against wrongful accusation if anything goes wrong.

Elements of pay

Gross pay

The contract of employment for each employee should define the basis for arriving at that employee's gross pay entitlement in return for working for the organisation. It may be related to time or to some measure of the work done: in many cases it includes elements of both. The contract should also specify the frequency of payment.

Remuneration paid by reference to time may be expressed as an hourly rate with or without overtime, a daily rate, a weekly rate or an annual rate.

1. **An hourly rate** There may be an individual rate for each employee based upon skills and seniority, or employees may be graded to qualify for an appropriate rate from a published agreed range of rates. Alternatively, the hourly rate may be determined by the specific work the employee is engaged upon for the time being. It is, however, usual to combine both objectives so that the employee is paid at his individual rate or the rate for the work if it is higher. A detailed record of hours worked is usually essential. It may take the form of clock cards or time sheets, a timekeeper's record book or an automatic time-recording device. Employees whose pay is calculated on hourly rates are normally paid in cash at weekly intervals.
2. **Overtime** Work required to be done outside normal working hours is usually remunerated as overtime at an enhanced hourly rate or a series of progressively enhanced hourly rates, depending on exactly when the work is done, to compensate for the inconvenience of working unsocial hours.
3. **A daily rate** A detailed record of daily attendance at work is usually required. Overtime pay may also be earned. These employees are normally paid in cash at weekly intervals.
4. **A weekly rate** Payment for overtime work may apply in some cases, but not necessarily at enhanced rates. These employees are usually paid in cash at weekly intervals.

5. **An annual rate** Contracts of employment which provide for an annual rate of remuneration will specify the normal hours of work. Some also add that the employee is expected to work such hours as are necessary to discharge the responsibilities of the job. This effectively precludes payment for any overtime worked. However, many annual rate-of-pay contracts do provide for overtime payments and, in these cases, a time record has to be maintained. Employees on annual rates of pay are normally paid at monthly intervals by credit transfer through the banking system.

Remuneration paid by reference to a measure of the work done can take a number of different forms:

6. **Piece work** A range of piece work rates to be applied by reference to the number of units completed of particular products or related to completion of specific tasks.
7. **Productivity bonus** An amount of money calculated according to a formula which takes into account agreed indicators of productivity or production efficiency: these calculations may be specific for each individual, for select groups or for the whole workforce of a production plant. The formula is usually designed to encourage improvements in performance beyond a defined norm.
8. **Commission** A commission calculated as a percentage of the value of the product, output or sales which the employee's work has contributed to directly. Sales commission is probably the most common form.
9. **Profit sharing** A share of the profit earned on operations for which the employee held significant responsibility and power to influence profitability. This may be calculated as a predetermined percentage of the actual profit achieved as reported in audited accounts. Alternatively, it can be calculated as a percentage of the employee's annual salary: the percentage rate being determined by formula from the profit reported in the audited accounts.

Payroll deductions

There are five main categories of deductions:

1. **Statutory** Employers are required by law to withhold income tax and employees' national insurance contributions from the remuneration payable to their employees and to pay over the total of amounts so withheld, along with the employer's national insurance contributions, to the Inland Revenue.
2. **Judicial** A court of law may make an order requiring an employer to make specified deductions from the earnings of an adjudged debtor and to pay the amounts into court.
3. **Pension schemes** Many employers have established contributory superannuation schemes to provide retirement benefits for their employees. Employees' contributions are then collected through payroll deductions.
4. **Discretionary** There is often a range of discretionary payroll deductions by which the employer has undertaken to collect monies from employees and to pay them out on their behalf. This group may include:

   (a) various forms of savings;
   (b) membership contributions to employment-related associations such as trade unions and sports clubs;
   (c) employer-sponsored group schemes such as private medical insurance and contributions to charities.

5. **Special** This group covers all special arrangements agreed with individual employees such as advances of pay, loan repayments or an agreed contribution for a benefit in kind such as a company car.

Control principles

Effective internal control in payroll administration is dependent upon the existence of adequate arrangements for authorisation, well planned segregation of duties, a comprehensive system of internal checks, and strict adherence to disciplines.

Authority

Authorisation should always be in writing and signed. The guiding principle is that every employee's remuneration terms should be authorised by that person's immediate superior and confirmed by the superior's superior. Remuneration for two levels at the top of the organisation should be determined by an independent committee such as a committee of non-executive directors.

This principle should be applied equally to fixed and variable elements of pay, although the practice will differ. Fixed elements are determined on engagement, promotion or at a general review; formal procedures and documentation should provide for the necessary authorising signatures on these occasions. Variable elements are generally the product of a measure of work done and a predetermined rate of pay in accordance with a duly authorised contract of employment. The obligation to pay is then contractual and requires no further authorisation. The measure of work done is often an established fact requiring confirmation by management for any non-standard element such as overtime or piece work.

Authority for all deductions other than those which are statutory or judicial should be in writing signed by the employee.

Segration of duties

The purpose of segregating duties is to ensure that no one person deals with every aspect of an individual transaction so as to be in a position to manipulate the record of it.

Payroll preparation normally consists of a series of repetitive tasks, for example: preparation of time records; preparation of production records; calculation of gross pay; calculation of PAYE income tax; computation of net pay; making up pay packets, etc. For a clerical operation, this pattern of work lends itself to effective segregation. For computer operations, similar consideration should be given to the allocation of responsibility for each stage of processing.

Whenever practical, segregated duties should be rotated from time to time among the payroll staff.

This practice has a number of advantages:

1. It deters manipulation or error due to over-familiarity.
2. It motivates by relieving the tedium of repetitive work.
3. It ensures that the payroll staff become competent in all routine tasks and can provide cover when required.

Internal checks

Integrated internal checks at every stage constitute a critical element in all payroll procedures. Absolute accuracy is of paramount importance in the interests of both security and efficiency: an inefficient pay office can adversely affect the morale of the workforce. If a mistake occurs in payroll preparation it must be promptly identified and corrected before proceeding with the next stage. Thus every stage in the process starts with a series of input validation checks:

1. Total hours extracted from clock cards should be agreed with one or more alternative records such as a pre-list, time sheets, production records. Performance data for output-related elements of pay should be similarly checked.
2. All calculations performed as a clerical operation should be independently checked by another clerk using duplicate data.
3. Individual recorded hours, output-related pay, total gross pay, tax deducted and net pay should all be screened to identify, for detailed examination, those that fall outside defined parameters.
4. Total numbers on the payroll should be reconciled from each pay day to the next, accounting for all starters and leavers with a value reconciliation for totals of all fixed elements of gross pay and all standard deductions. The total of amounts paid out each week or month as appropriate for net pay and all deductions should be agreed with total gross pay.

Compliance

All procedures for payroll preparation need to be clearly defined and strict discipline is absolutely essential in complying with the defined procedures. There are a number of reasons for this:

1. The payroll programme has to be scheduled to complete a complex structure of many calculations accurately to a critical time schedule.
2. A payroll comprises many transactions, each for a relatively small amount of money. It is feasible for small errors to pass unnoticed and to accumulate to a significant total.
3. The process involves dealing with large amounts of cash, the most vulnerable of all forms of property because it is the most difficult to trace if it is misappropriated.
4. In payroll work the risks to which the organisation and its payroll staff are exposed are significant. Effective control procedures provide a measure of protection for both, but only when they are strictly applied.

Standing data

Payroll standing data is of two kinds:

1. That which is specific to each individual employee, such as name and employee code number, date of commencement, department, rate of pay or grading, tax coding, national insurance information, pension information, discretionary deductions, pay instructions (cash, cheque, bank giro etc.).
2. That which applies to all employees, such as standard rates of pay to be selected according to employee grading, formulae for calculating performance-related pay, PAYE tax tables, formulae for calculating national insurance and pension contributions

These are examples only; they are not intended to be exhaustive. Every organisation will have its own lists according to how it administers its payroll.

Maintaining the specific employee standing data should be the responsibility of a personnel function which should be completely independent from the payroll department. Effectively this means that only a duly authorised personnel officer may make additions, deletions and other changes to specific employee standing data.

All information maintained on standing data files is personal and confidential between the employee and the organisation as employer. This confidentiality must be respected at all times. Access to the information should be restricted to those who need to know in the course of their work in the personnel department and in the payroll department. Each should be specifically reminded of their confidentiality obligations.

All changes to standing data must be subject to strict control. Failure to maintain adequate control could provide opportunities for the creation of ghost employees. Other possibilities include situations where employees are listed more than once, where leavers do not get removed from the payroll, or where amendments such as pay increases can be applied without proper authority. Every amendment must be supported by appropriate documentation signed to confirm due authorisation.

Each payroll run should incorporate a procedure for confirming that the standing data used takes account of all amendments since the previous run. This is achieved by using the payroll summary as a control account to reconcile the totals for each element from one payroll to the next by reference to a separate schedule summarising the amendments which should have been made.

The personnel department may also have responsibility for maintaining the general standing data files for payroll preparation. When this is so it is more likely to be for convenience rather than as a control feature. The key consideration is that responsibility for controlling and updating these files must be clearly assigned, preferably to someone independent of the payroll department.

In all these areas the payroll department must act only on instructions received via the department which has the responsibility for maintaining the appropriate standing data. This arrangement enables effective control measures to be applied to all standing data amendments.

When the payroll is computerised, further control checks may be feasible:

1. Access to all master files should be password protected.

2. Access for amendment should be restricted to those responsible for maintaining each file.
3. The payroll department should have 'read only' access.
4. The computer should be programmed to produce serially numbered print-outs reporting all amendments made.

It is especially important that password disciplines are strictly enforced for payroll master files. Passwords should be changed regularly and there should be sound and logical access controls.

Personal information maintained on computer files must be registered under the Data Protection Act 1984 for purposes other than payroll.

Variable data

This refers to information specific to the week or month for which the payroll is being prepared. It includes hours worked for time-related elements of pay and measures of work done for performance-related elements. It is a management responsibility to provide the information and to confirm that it is authentic and correct.

Various forms of automatic recording devices may be used in the collection of this input information, ranging from clocking machines for time cards and automatic time recorders to computerised automatic process control systems which also generate a suitable record of work done for payroll purposes.

Written information should be provided in a standard format and signed as confirmed by the appropriate departmental manager. Any unused lines on the form should be crossed through before it is signed to prevent further information being added.

In all cases it is important that the information used for the payroll is tested for reasonableness and checked against alternative information sources. Validation checks on variable data constitute a critical element of the payroll procedures.

Most payrolls need to have a controlled degree of flexibility by allowing discretionary adjustments to be introduced as variable data to meet exceptional circumstances. It may be payment of a special allowance in recognition of unusual working cond-

itions or a bonus for particular achievement. Discretionary adjustments should always be supported by proper documentation with due authorising signatures.

Deductions

All amounts collected by employers by way of deduction from employees' pay are held in trust for those employees.

The employer is under obligation to pay over these monies to the rightful recipient and they may not be applied for any other purpose. It is then essential to have control procedures which ensure these obligations are properly discharged.

When paying over payroll deductions the employer has to provide information on who contributed and how much. This information should be produced as an integral part of the payroll procedures.

The essence of control for all deductions is in verifying that total paid over for each equals total collected. These totals should be reconciled from each payroll to the next, taking account of starts and stops as recorded in amendments to standing data.

Tax to be deducted under the PAYE system is determined from 'look-up' tables provided by the Inland Revenue. A personal tax code is notified by the Inspector of Taxes. The tax is calculated by reference to taxable pay, which is gross pay less tax-deductible superannuation contributions.

National Insurance contributions for each employee are also determined from 'look-up' tables.

The total of PAYE tax deductions and employer's and employees' national insurance contributions must be paid over to the Inland Revenue at the end of each month. At the end of each tax year the employer is required to give each employee a certificate of total taxable pay and total tax deducted. At the same time the employer must send the Inland Revenue a statement listing for each employee: taxable pay, PAYE tax paid and national insurance. There are appropriate arrangements to account for starters and leavers as part-year employees. This statement should confirm that the correct amount has been paid over in monthly cheques. This is a control which should be maintained by the employer on a progressive basis through the year as an element of internal check.

The arrangements for complying with statutory sick pay legislation are sometimes complex and require special consideration. There is a legal requirement to maintain proper sickness records. For employees who are paid weekly or monthly salaries it is necessary to make a deduction from gross pay for sickness absence. The amount deducted should be matched with the statutory sickness pay entitlement taking due account of 'waiting days' and 'linked days'. To avoid any oversight in this field it is necessary for the management of every department to send regular sickness returns including nil returns to the payroll office.

Timing differences between payroll preparation and paying over some amounts collected by payroll deduction are unavoidable. For example, income tax collected by deduction from weekly payrolls has to be paid over monthly. When timing differences occur the amounts collected are held in suspense. It is most important to ensure that all suspense items are examined and cleared regularly.

Control parameters

A payroll usually deals with a particular category of employee whose remuneration can be expected to fall within a band which can be defined. Parameters can then be selected to cover the expected range. Any case which occurs outside this range is likely to contain unusual elements and should be isolated for close examination.

This principle can be applied to the variable input data such as hours worked and measured work done. It is usually applied to gross pay and to net pay. It may also be applied to individual deductions such as tax or superannuation contributions.

Parameters should be chosen at practical levels and should be reviewed regularly. Parameter tests should be applied to the payroll data to identify exceptions, examine them and, if necessary, correct them before payroll calculation starts. The abnormality could be due to falsified information, genuine mistake or unusual circumstances correctly accounted for.

It is usual for parameter controls to be written into the program for computerised payroll procedures. The system then normally provides a print-out report scheduling the items identified as outside the set parameters. It is important that 'nil reports' are provided for areas tested and found to be all within normal limits.

Paying employees

After completing the work of calculating the net amount of pay due to each of the employees, arrangements have to be made for actually paying them. The key stages are as follows:

1. **Payroll approval**   The payroll is often one of the largest disbursements of an organisation. It is normally prepared by relatively junior staff in the payroll office on the basis of instructions issued at various management levels throughout the organisation which are co-ordinated through the personnel function. There is then a very heavy burden of responsibility which it is appropriate for a senior executive to underwrite by examining and signing approval of the payroll before any payment is made.

2. **Organising funds**   It is not uncommon practice to transfer the total funds needed for pay, deductions and employer's contributions into a separate bank account to meet the payroll disbursements when due. Alternatively, the payroll office may requisition cheques on the main bank account for each separate disbursement to be made. When the employees are to be paid by cheque or bank transfer it is a case of ensuring that the necessary funds are in the bank account on which the salary cheques are drawn.

   When the employees are to be paid in cash some additional procedures are called for:

   (a) it is advisable to have arranged local drawing facilities at a branch of the bank near to the location of pay-out;
   (b) the paying branch of the bank will need early warning of the amount required in cash so that it can ensure that it will be available when required;

(c) it will be necessary to assess the total number of notes and coin of each denomination required to make up the individual pay packets and to request the bank to supply in these denominations.

3. **Distributing pay** The task of distributing pay to employees, whether by bank transfer, cheque or cash, should not be a duty of the payroll office staff. They may however prepare all the document-ation for completion by someone else.

When payment is made by cheque the cheques may well be prepared at the same time as the payroll using the same information sources. This is also applicable to payment by bank giro where further standing information is required for the bank name and address, sort code and account number. In these cases the payroll office may prepare the cheques and giro payment lists and pass them with supporting documents to the cashier to arrange signature and despatch. This division of responsibility is critical when the payroll is computerised.

Handling cash

When the payroll entails handling large amounts of cash, special consideration must be given to the risks involved. They include misappropriation and robbery with violence.

The risk of misappropriation can be minimised through good staff selection and management and sound control systems which are strictly enforced.

Payroll robbery with violence is, however, a sufficiently common occurrence to have to be considered as an inevitable feature of the payroll scene. Every appropriate precaution must be taken firstly to protect payroll staff and secondly to safeguard the cash whenever this is feasible without prejudicing personal safety.

It is important that all payroll staff receive training and clear instruction in how to act in an emergency. In general, it must be assumed that anyone participating in a payroll robbery is prepared to be violent and is probably armed. Consequently, an inexperienced person attempting to stop him is unlikely to succeed and could sustain serious personal injury. It is therefore wise to avoid resisting such threatening demands for the money.

Protection for the cash is best achieved with theft deterrent devices as part of the procedures for handling payroll monies:

1. Using security cash-carrying bags which are available with a range of options, but usually incorporate reinforced construction with security combination locking and an audible alarm signal which starts automatically if the bag is 'snatched' and which cannot then be suppressed.

   Some versions have a time-delayed facility before emitting dense coloured smoke giving a visual alarm, obscuring visibility for the 'get away' and indelibly staining the skin and clothing of persons in close proximity.

2. Using trained and fully equipped security guards for delivering cash over public highways in an armoured van.

3. Adopting random timing for cash collection and pay-out so far as this can be accommodated within the payroll constraints. A rigid time schedule leaves the process vulnerable to a carefully planned attack at its weakest point.

The task of collecting the payroll cash from the bank is normally entrusted to a specialist security firm. Particular care is necessary at the point of collection at the bank and at the point of handing over at the payroll office.

The payroll office must be in a secure location within the site and reasonably protected against forced entry. An alarm button should be provided for use in emergency and the payroll staff should be instructed on when and how to use it.

Whilst making up pay packets the payroll staff should lock themselves in the payroll office with the sole key on the inside. The door should then only be opened when the task is completed and they have confirmation that it is safe to do so.

It is a key element of segregation of duties that pay packets should not be handed to individual employees by payroll staff. Departmental super-visors should collect the pay packets from the payroll office for distribution to their subordinates.

In doing so they should always be accompanied by another person.

All employees who receive their pay in cash should always be required to give a signed receipt for it. The signature is sometimes given on the back of the clock card for the week being paid.

Audit objectives

There are a number of critical aspects of payroll preparation which should be addressed by every payroll audit even though the the audit brief may require concentration on a particular aspect.

1. **Authority** It is necessary to confirm that due authority for all pay entitlement is clearly defined and effectively exercised.

2. **System evaluation** The detailed procedures of the payroll system must be analysed to judge whether it meets the needs of the organisation and any legal requirements and whether it provides a sound basis for effective control.

   It is then necessary to perform a programme of compliance testing to establish whether or not the procedures are being applied as prescribed, and substantive testing to establish whether or not the payroll information is being processed accurately and completely.

3. **Staff suitability** An organisation places much confidence and trust in its payroll staff. They are required to do an exacting job of work which is critical to the organisation, they are entrusted to deal with significant amounts of cash belonging to the organisation, and they are entrusted to use sensitive and confidential information in the course of their work. The organisation should have firm rules for vetting and monitoring these employees to confirm that they are of suitable character for these responsibilities and are not exposed to circumstances or involved in activities which could give rise to a conflict of interest. The audit should examine the recruitment, vetting and monitoring procedures to judge whether they are effective in maintaining the necessary standards for payroll staff.

4. **Protection** Payroll is a high-risk area. The risks include:

   (a) failure to pay wages when due;
   (b) losses through misappropriation or external theft;
   (c) physical injury to payroll staff;
   (d) misuse of confidential information about employees.

The organisation should have soundly constructed contingency plans, firstly to prevent these risks materialising, and secondly to contain the damage if it should happen. The audit should seek evidence that such plans do exist and are kept alive and up to date.

5. **Efficiency** As with all other organisational activity, payroll preparation must be performed efficiently. It must achieve its purpose without waste of resources. It is of course important to avoid compromising essential control in pursuit of economies.

   Requirements change continuously and new techniques become available from time to time. All administrative systems should be subject to regular review with the objective of improving efficiency. The audit should identify with this objective.

Section 2.   Value Added Tax (VAT)

The nature of VAT

Value Added Tax is an indirect tax, which means that it is not paid directly to the state by individual consumers. It is collected by taxable persons supplying goods and services in the United Kingdom in the course of carrying on any business: this includes the importation of goods.

VAT is administered by Her Majesty's Customs and Excise (C & E). C & E officials have wider powers in some respects than those given to the police: they may seize property, search premises and require the provision of information from the public. These powers are granted, and limited, by the Customs and Excise Management Act 1979.

The United Kingdom introduced VAT in 1973 after joining the European Community (EC). EC law on VAT is prescribed in the Sixth Directive.

In those of its provisions which are mandatory, EC VAT law overrides UK VAT law. UK legislation has been consolidated into the Value Added Tax Act 1983 (VATA). It applies to the UK mainland, Northern Ireland, the Scottish off-shore islands and by agreement the Isle of Man. It does not apply to the Channel Islands.

The EC Sixth Directive also defines the mechanism for the collection of VAT. It is a multistage tax imposed on the value added to goods or services at each stage of their supply. It is added to the price charged for supply at each stage, calculated at the appropriate rate of tax. For the supplier, this is referred to as **output** tax. The supplier is then entitled to claim credit for tax paid on goods and services supplied to the business in the course of providing the goods or services it supplies. This is known as **input** tax.

Registration

UK VAT regulations provide for persons carrying on a business of providing goods or services in the United Kingdom to register with Her Majesty's Customs and Excise. Registration is mandatory when a prescribed level of taxable turnover is achieved. In certain circumstances traders whose level of taxable turnover is less than the prescribed level may apply for registration which is then at the discretion of Her Majesty's Customs and Excise. The prescribed level of taxable turnover applies to historic annual turnover, based on calendar quarters to 31 March, 30 June, 30 September and 31 December.

An unregistered trader who foresees his taxable turnover reaching the registration threshold in a period longer than one year may apply to Her Majesty's Customs and Excise for **intending trader registration.**

It is important for unregistered traders to monitor taxable turnover and, if registration becomes necessary, to make the appropriate notification within time. There are heavy penalties for late notification.

Application for registration is made on VAT registration form VAT 1 or form VAT 20 in the Welsh language. A partnership must also complete form VAT 2. Completed application forms must be sent to the nearest VAT Office of Her Majesty's Customs & Excise whose address is to be found in the local telephone directory.
(VAT (General) Regulations 1985.)

Accounting

Her Majesty's Customs and Excise requires that:
1. A person must register for VAT when certain prescribed levels of turnover are achieved or forecast.
2. A VAT account must be kept showing a summary of all output and input tax for each VAT accounting period (normally one month).
3. Records relating to VAT must be kept for six years, subject to a penalty for failure to do so.

In general, registered traders must account to Her Majesty's Customs and Excise for VAT on goods and services supplied by them at quarterly intervals. Quarterly accounting dates are allocated to each trader at the time of registration.

VAT becomes due and chargeable on goods and services supplied by reference to a tax point for each taxable transaction:

1. The tax point is usually specified on the face of a tax invoice which must then be issued either before delivery of the goods or performance of the services or within fourteen days after the tax point.
2. If payment is made before delivery, the date of payment establishes the tax point.
3. In the absence of a valid tax invoice or prepayment a basic tax point applies. For goods, the basic tax point is the point in time at which they are removed by the customer or, if not removed when they are made available to him; for services, the tax point is the point in time at which they are performed.

Definitions

Supply
For VAT purposes a supply is more than a sale. A number of transactions are specifically defined as being supplies for VAT purposes, but there is also a 'catch-all' provision which states that 'anything done for a consideration is to be regarded as a supply'.

Consideration
If there is a contract (written or unwritten, implicit or explicit), then it is likely that there is a consideration of some sort.

Zero-rated supply
Some taxable supplies are taxable at a rate of nought per cent (0%) and are known as 'zero-rated' supplies. These supplies count in determining liability to register for VAT. The supplier also qualifies for refund of input tax. Exports of goods are zero-rated. Other zero-rated supplies are listed in VATA 1983 Sch. 5.

Exempt supply
Certain supplies of goods and services are exempt from VAT (VATA 1983 Sch 6). This means that no tax is charged on such supplies to customers. However, there can be no input tax credit for a business whose entire turnover is in exempt supplies. The VAT suffered becomes a cost to the business.

Business
VAT affects supplies only when they are made in the course or furtherance of a business. 'Business activity' is a term not exclusively defined but examples are listed in VATA 1983.

Person
VAT applies to supplies made in the course of business, but the taxable unit is not the business as such: it is the **person** carrying on the business. 'Person' is taken to include any individual or a body having a separate legal personality such as a company, a trust or a charity; it may also include a partnership or an unincorporated association such as a club.

Contentious items

The interpretation of VAT regulations concerning the following items calls for special care and it may be advisable to consult a VAT specialist.

Management services
This term is used to describe a wide range of support services within an organisation such as:

1. Use of labour, equipment or accommodation.
2. Heating and lighting.
3. Cleaning.
4. Repairs and maintenance.
5. Accounting services.
6. Secretarial services.

Property and construction
This is an area fraught with problems, with a considerable history of case law.

Finance
Traditional financial services such as those provided by banks are exempt in the United Kingdom under the provision of VATA 1983 Sch. 6 Gp 5.

Dealings in money are exempt, including coins and banknotes, except where these are supplied as collector's pieces or investment articles: such supplies are taxable at the standard rate. Dealings in gold coin, whether legal tender or not, are taxable.

The making of loans and the granting of credit are exempt supplies. The value for VAT purposes is the gross interest or other sum received by the person making the loan or granting the credit.

The following supplies are not exempt and attract tax at the standard rate:

1. Debt collection and credit control.
2. Leasing facilities.
3. Investment, finance and taxation advice.
4. Merger and take-over advice.
5. Nominee services.
6. Portfolio management.

International services
Problems can arise in the interpretation of where a service is given or a supply made. Similarly,

apportionment of expenses between the United Kingdom and overseas activities can give rise to difficulty.

Retail organisations

Her Majesty's Customs and Excise have produced nine retail schemes from which an organisation can select the one best suited to its operations.

Second-hand goods

Generally, VAT is calculated on the full selling price of goods. However, provided certain conditions are met, a taxable person dealing in the defined categories of qualifying second-hand goods may account for VAT on the gross margin only.

There are specific regulations and requirements for particular schemes.

Unusual transactions

This speaks for itself. If the organisation is venturing into an area of supply or service which is not part of its normal business, it is wise to consider carefully any VAT implications.

Bad debt relief

A registered trader is generally liable to account for output tax which he has charged to customers by reference to invoices that he has issued. Bad debt relief is now available where the debtor becomes formally insolvent, or for debts over one year old which have been written off in the supplier's books of account.

VAT audit

Objectives

A VAT audit should seek to ensure the following:

1. Registration has been effected where required.
2. VAT on all sales, purchases and expenses is properly accounted for.
3. VAT outputs and inputs are correctly calculated from reliable accounting records.
4. The records comply with the accounting requirements of VATA 1983.
5. Contentious items are identified and their treatment is considered for a ruling by a VAT specialist.
6. Amounts recorded as VAT payable or receivable at the balance sheet date represent the total outstanding for VAT collections and payments.
7. VAT is properly classified, described and disclosed in the financial statements.
8. The amounts reported in the financial statements are in agreement with the accounting records.

Audit of VAT control

The following points need to be considered:

1. The auditor should confirm that the organisation has in place adequate VAT controls as well as sound general accounting controls and that all control procedures are being applied effectively.
2. One member of staff or, if appropriate, a section within the organisation should be assigned the specific responsibility to develop expertise in VAT matters, to be the VAT specialist and to monitor VAT compliance and accounting. This person or section should maintain all contact with Her Majesty's Customs and Excise. All correspondence with Customs and Excise should be dealt with by VAT specialists except such routine activities as may be specifically delegated.
3. Within each accounting unit one person should be given specific responsibility for VAT matters. This person should have a functional reporting relationship to the VAT specialist.
4. The VAT specialist should ensure that arrangements are made to receive all VAT notices, rulings, etc. Copies of such notices and rulings should be disseminated to the VAT persons in the accounting units as necessary.
5. All price lists should clearly indicate whether the price is inclusive or exclusive of VAT.
6. Input tax: the VAT accounting officer in each unit should ensure that all VAT incurred in expenses is identified and accounted for. VAT invoices should be received to support all payments. Reconciliation should be made monthly between VAT recoverable and eligible expenses.
7. Output tax: all liabilities on supplies and services

should be identified, charged out and accounted for in the proper VAT period. All invoices for despatch should be properly authorised. Exempt supplies should be separately recorded. Reconciliations should be made monthly between output tax charged and relevant supplies.

8. Special attention should be given to registration and to contentious items.

Section 3.   Value for money

The essentials of value for money auditing

The concept of value for money is perceived from different viewpoints in the private and public sectors, but the principles involved are identical.

In the private sector, the success of an organisation is measured in terms of profitability. Generally, the more profitable the organisation is, the greater the value for money being achieved. The profitability of an organisation in the private sector depends upon how economically, efficiently and effectively it pursues its corporate objectives, particularly in relation to its market competitors.

Organisations in the public sector are required to provide services which are fair, consistent and dependable at minimum cost. Profitability is generally not a factor. To achieve these objectives, public-sector organisations must also operate economically, efficiently and effectively in husbanding the public resources entrusted to them.

The objective of internal auditing is to assist members of the organisation in the effective discharge of their responsibilities. To this end, internal auditing furnishes them with analyses, appraisals, recommendations, counsel and information concerning the activities reviewed. The audit objective includes promoting effective control at reasonable cost.

The scope of internal auditing encompasses the examination and evaluation of the adequacy and effectiveness of the organisation's system of internal control and the quality of performance in carrying out assigned responsibilities.

(Extract from IIA–UK, Statement of Responsibilities of Internal Auditing).

It is a management responsibility to secure good value for money. The auditor's role is to examine independently how well that responsibility is being discharged.

The essential objective of value for money auditing is therefore to verify achievements in:

Economy – doing things cheaply
Efficiency – doing things right and well
Effectiveness – doing the right things

Economy means minimising the cost of resources acquired or used, with due regard to maintaining adequate quality: spending less.

Efficiency means applying the available resources to achieve the optimum output in terms of goods, services or other results: spending well.

Effectiveness means achieving the results intended as specified in properly authorised plans, programmes and targets: spending wisely.

In practice, the boundaries between economy, efficiency and effectiveness are seldom clear-cut. In a value for money audit, all three should be considered as closely linked and complementary aspects of the same examination.

Measuring economy, efficiency and effectiveness

Value for money is measured by reference to:

1. **Input**   The resources consumed in terms of money, materials and human effort.
2. **Output**   The goods produced, services rendered or other results.
3. **Impact**   The ultimate effect in terms of corporate objectives and policies.

Example 7.1

For a programme to build a new health clinic, the input is the cost of constructing and equipping the clinic in terms of money spent to procure and apply land, materials, services, equipment and manpower. The output is the completed building, fully equipped as a new clinic. The impact is the effect that it has on the health care of the community.

Economy is related entirely to inputs, whether expressed in terms of money, manpower, commodities or services. It is concerned with the acquisition of resources at the lowest acceptable cost. It must be remembered however that economy is something more than mere cost cutting. The organisation has to decide first what standards of quality are necessary, and then to ensure that these standards are maintained at minimum cost. It would be false economy to aim to achieve cost savings by accepting substandard quality.

Efficiency is measured by comparing input and output. The aim must be either to achieve maximum output from a given input or to consume minimum resources in achieving a given output.

Effectiveness is doing the right things: that is, those intended things which have been properly planned. It is ineffective and indeed a waste of resources to do things, which, in the view of those who have provided those resources, do not need to be done. This is so, irrespective of how economically or efficiently the wrong things have been done.

To determine whether the right things are being done, it is necessary to move away from direct outputs and examine closely the ultimate effect or impact of the activity. The auditor must make a judgement as to how far the results of the activity achieve the effects that were intended and whether they are fulfilling corporate objectives and policies. There may be a degree of merit in doing the right things poorly, but there is no merit whatsoever in doing the wrong things, however well they are done.

Assessing performance in terms of economy, efficiency and effectiveness may vary considerably for different categories of organisation or activity. The feasibility of measurement is also significantly different for each of these performance criteria. Input is often easier to identify and value than output and output is almost always more readily measurable than impact. For example: whilst a completed new motorway and its construction cost may be readily established, the economic and social benefits of the project will be much more difficult to ascertain with any degree of certainty. The fulfil-ment of corporate objectives and policy will usually be long-term expectations and likely to involve qualitative as well as quantitative factors. Consequently, the measurement of effectiveness may not be feasible in the short term. In some cases it may have to be confined to determining whether the intended output has been achieved, because no feasible measure of impact could be meaningful.

Performance of audit work

Audit work should include planning the audit, examining and evaluating information, communicating results and follow up.

(IIA–UK General Standard 400)

Planning
A general overview is the first essential in planning a value for money audit. This should be designed to provide an understanding of the organisation and the environment in which it operates and so to facilitate the identification of major risks.

The overview should comprise four main activities:

1. Collecting information;
2. Analysing the information collected;
3. Assessing the risks;
4. Presenting findings and proposals for the detailed audit.

Collecting information
The information needed to complete the overview should include the items listed below:

1. **Background:**

    (a) organisational structure, divisions, branches, local offices, factories, distribution network;
    (b) corporate plan;
    (c) financial information, budgets, management accounts, assets.

2. **Objectives:**

    (a) corporate objectives and policies with their relative priorities;
    (b) operational objectives generally.

3. **Activities:**

Particular activities aimed at fulfilling corporate objectives and policies.

4. **Resources:**

Premises, plant and equipment, working capital, borrowing powers, investments, intellectual property, technology, manpower.

5. **Control systems:**

(a) systems and controls in operation to pursue corporate objectives with due regard for securing value for money;

(b) arrangements for planning activities and allocating resources;

(c) management information systems for monitoring and controlling activities and the use of resources, and for measuring success in achieving objectives.

6. **Personnel management:**

Arrangements for staff recruitment and training.

7. **Other information:**

(a) areas of public interest or sensitivity;

(b) areas of particular interest or concern to shareholders or investors;

(c) areas with inherent risk in the context of value for money;

(d) previous investigations including reviews by internal audit, external audit and consultants.

Analysing the information

The information collected in the overview should enable preliminary assessments to be made for each main activity or function identifying those factors likely to have a significant value for money impact and where it could be at risk. These include:

1. Adequacy and clarity of operational objectives.
2. Adequacy of control systems in terms of securing economy, efficiency and effectiveness.
3. Areas and processes in which value for money is subject to high risk.
4. Strengths and weaknesses apparent in management performance.

5. Effectiveness of the activity in fulfilling corporate objectives and policies.

Risk assessment

1. The organisation should apply sound management principles whatever the operation or activity. For example:

(a) it should set firm objectives and monitor performance as a critical part of its endeavours to achieve them;

(b) it should make the most economic, efficient and effective use of its resources;

(c) it should exercise effective control over all its activities.

2. The auditor should have a thorough understanding of the organisation based upon accumulated knowledge and experience and previous audit findings which should be documented.

3. Priority should be given to areas and processes which attract a high risk in terms of value for money:

(a) activities involving major expenditure categories incurred through numerous small transactions so that decisions are necessarily delegated to a low level;

(b) major fluctuations in programme expenditure;

(c) large one-off projects;

(d) highly technical projects;

(e) projects involving new technology or techniques;

(f) complex organisational structures;

(g) projects where there is pressure for quick results;

(h) expenditure dependent on subjective judgement;

(i) activities which are subject to ambiguous regulations or specifications.

Presenting the findings

The purpose of the overview is to collect and evaluate information to enable the auditor to prepare an audit programme and assign priorities to the tasks of examining areas which have been identified as inherently at risk in terms of value for money. The most suitable form for the overview report is likely to be a concise commentary bringing together views formed on each constituent activity or operational area of the organisation, supported by detailed appendices scheduling the findings and proposals for further detailed examination.

Conducting the detailed audit

The internal auditor is responsible for planning and conducting the audit assignment, subject to supervisory review and approval.

(IIA–UK Internal Auditing Guideline 400.01)

The auditor should adequately plan, control and record his work.

(APC, The Auditor's Operational Standard)

In general, value for money audits should be planned, controlled and recorded similarly to any other internal audit assignment as described elsewhere in this manual. However, the following key considerations call for particular care to be exercised:

1. The overview should have identified areas of inherent risk in terms of value for money and they should have been allocated a priority ranking.
2. Specific objectives should be set for the examination of critical activities established as a result of the overview.
3. The main objectives should be subdivided into specific aims, with targets related to the size and complexity of each area to be examined.
4. The audit techniques to be used should be specified, for example: standard questionnaires, interviews and meetings, transaction testing, visual inspection, taking expert opinion, etc.
5. The necessary resources for conducting the detailed audit examination should be defined and the effect on other audit work considered.
6. A timetable should be established with target dates for progress reports and meetings, completion of key tasks and identifiable stages and for drafting and completion of the final report.

Section 4. Acquisitions

Introduction

The objective of acquisition is the pursuit of growth. Growth is essential to the continuing success of every commercial undertaking. If an organisation is to prosper and increase its profitability, and at the same time protect its shareholders' investment, it must seek constantly to improve its products and enlarge its markets.

Growth may be achieved in two ways:

1. Through self-development: this usually involves substantial capital investment in product development and market expansion over a long period with no guarantee of eventual success – the risks are often great but, when successful, the rewards can be very high.
2. Through acquisition: this is the process by which one organisation secures a material ownership interest in another or gains control of that other as a going concern. It is frequently a take-over transaction by which one organisation acquires the entire equity capital of another, and their two businesses are then merged into a single combined organisation. Acquisition of an established business offers a suitable alternative basis for the pursuit of growth, through the product range and market presence of the acquired business. The capital cost is normally very high in relation to the earnings record of the acquired business, but these earnings are immediately available and there may be opportunities to improve combined profitability. However, a suitable acquisition which matches the perceived need will not necessarily be available at the right time and at the right price.

Many major corporations have adopted growth strategies which incorporate a combination of both policies: self-development and acquisition.

The policy of growth through acquisition must be fully integrated with the plans being pursued for long-term investment in developing new products and new markets. Progressive growth by acquisition may be achieved in various ways:

1. Extending the product range.
2. Extending market presence.
3. Acquiring production or distribution facilities.
4. Acquiring technology or intellectual property.
5. Acquiring management strength.
6. Acquiring a skilled workforce.

The benefits of progressive growth through acquisition are likely to be enhanced by opportunities for growth in other dimensions:

1. Horizontal integration – securing synergy in production, distribution and administration.
2. Vertical integration – securing a strategic source of supplies or a captive market.
3. Diversification – broadening the industrial base.

Governmental control

Although a proposed merger may be of benefit to those directly involved, it may adversely affect the interests of other sections of the community, or indeed may threaten the country's national interest. Consequently an element of official constraint applies in most developed countries. There are two important controls in the United Kingdom:

1. The Monopolies and Mergers Commission, a government-appointed quango which may be called upon to investigate a planned merger if large asset values are involved or if the combined organisation to emerge would be holding a substantial share of the market in its products. The decision as to whether or not the Commission is asked to investigate is a matter for the government of the day. For example, it could favour concentrating industrial resources to protect key industries, or it could seek to discourage mergers with a view to preserving competition.
2. The City Code on Take-overs and Mergers for companies listed on the London Stock Exchange. The Code is enforced by the Panel on Take-overs and Mergers which consists of a chairman and vice-chairman appointed by the Governor of the Bank of England together with representatives of professional bodies involved in investment, banking, accountancy and insurance.

The Code is not concerned with the merits of particular mergers but with ensuring that all the parties involved act honestly and fairly in their relations with each other.

Restrictions on mergers may also be imposed by the European Commission in Europe and by anti-trust legislation in the United States.

Preliminary studies

Once a company has identified a suitable acquisition target, it is necessary to collect sufficient information to form a reasonable opinion as to its value before making an offer to open negotiations. The process of seeking out a company suitable for acquisition will usually have produced some of this background information already, but further preliminary studies are usually necessary and will have to be made with discretion.

Acquisition is likely to have been identified as a major risk area in a company committed to this form of growth. The internal auditing resource should then focus a significant share of attention on this risk area. Much of the preliminary study work can be undertaken by internal audit and this should help to achieve the necessary objective quality in the judgements to be made.

A major reason for acquiring another business is to improve, or at least to protect, existing profitability. Audited financial statements for the business to be acquired are an obvious starting point, but they provide only a limited amount of information. It will be necessary to examine the underlying activities in some detail, for which information on the following points will be needed:

1. The history of the business, including changes in its nature and its ownership throughout its existence.
2. The names of major shareholders.
3. The corporate structure of the business entity and any subsidiaries and associates.
4. The management structure, with personal profiles of key executives.
5. The scale, skills and distribution of the workforce and trade union representation.

6. Names of principal customers and main suppliers.
7. Marketing and technical profiles.
8. Asset profile, including technical specification, location, age and condition of plants, capital commitments, and intellectual property.
9. Potential synergy.
10. Significant agreements, for example: leases, licences, joint ventures, borrowings, guarantees, constraints.
11. Monopolies or antitrust considerations.
12. Financial viability.
13. Pension fund deficiency or surplus.

Frequently, some of these details cannot be obtained without the full knowledge and co-operation of the company being examined. Then, the opening bid needs to leave room for negotiation to reflect the facts if and when they are disclosed subsequently.

Whilst collecting preliminary information of this kind, an experienced internal auditor should at the same time be challenging the objectives and rationale for each proposed acquisition. For example:

1. How does this proposed acquisition match the strategic objectives for growth by acquisition?
2. Why is it proposed to acquire this particular business and what benefits are expected to arise?
3. Precisely what is to be acquired? Shares? Assets? What sort of business is it?
4. Are there any parts not to be acquired and if so, why?
5. Is it currently successful?
6. Why is it available at the present time?

Expected benefits

A wide range of benefits may be expected to arise from taking over or merging with another business. Some of these benefits may be long term and difficult to quantify immediately including, for example, the acquisition of management and staff with new skills and expertise, an extended product range, new markets, new technology, and so on. More immediate advantages may flow from economies of scale through the rationalisation of production and distribution and savings in administration. More intensive use of manufacturing plant, motor vehicles and the like may lead to economies in capital expenditure; stock investment may show savings and lower prices may be achieved from bulk buying.

On the other hand, the process of merging may itself generate considerable expense and inconvenience. Rationalisation will mean fewer jobs, resulting in redundancy for some, promotion for others. It will mean reorientation of attitudes and learning and applying new skills. All this will be traumatic for employees and costly for the employer.

A detailed evaluation of the gains and losses expected to arise from the merger is clearly of vital importance.

Defining the target

When first contemplating growth through acquisition, it is usual to prepare a profile of the sort of company which is being sought for acquisition, much as a prospective employer prepares a job description and person specification to define the sort of person required.

Testing a particular acquisition candidate against this profile will consequently entail checking these points:

1. Precisely what is being bought in terms of both tangible and intangible assets? Tangible assets may include land, buildings, plant, machinery and equipment, and working capital in the form of stock, debtors and cash. Intangible assets may include brand names, trade marks, patent rights, copyrights, etc.
2. Is the company in the right industry, with the right markets and with the sort of technology or management expertise required?
3. Are the size of the company and the price about right?
4. Is the company's level of profitability acceptable?
5. If the company matches up well to this review, what are the reasons for the company's success or lack of it, and why has it come up for sale at this particular time?

As in personnel selection, the perfect candidate will rarely be found and it will usually be necessary to balance strengths against weaknesses in reaching a conclusion about a particular company. The feasibility of bringing a candidate company into line with the profile by correcting or eliminating known weaknesses should be considered.

Accountant's report

It is a common practice to agree terms of acquisition subject to a detailed examination and report by independent accountants. The statutory auditors of the acquiring company will often be commissioned to undertake this work. It will entail a comprehensive examination of the company to be acquired which evaluates its entire operations and activities in terms of policies, procedures and control systems. The accountant's report would cover:

1. Finance, including capital investment, profitability, cash flow.
2. Accounting arrangements and information management.
3. Personnel, including organisation, management, employee numbers and skills and industrial relations.
4. Product range and technological know-how.
5. Sources of supply.
6. Manufacturing processes.
7. Marketing, selling and distribution.

Documents to be inspected

Detailed information collected about the activities of the company to be acquired should be verified by reference to formal documentary evidence where appropriate:

1. Legal existence, from the Memorandum and Articles of Association.
2. Financial performance and status from audited accounts for the last few years and relevant management accounting information.
3. Assets from title deeds, leases, investment share certificates, letters patent, trade mark and brand name registration certificates, licence agreements.

4. Actual and potential liabilities, including capital commitments, past and present tax liabilities, guarantees, warranties, indemnities, debentures, mortgages, hire purchase, rental agreements and any recent, current or pending litigation.
5. Agreements with employees including service agreements, trade union agreements, pension schemes.

Post-acquisition procedures

Responsibility for control passes to the acquiring company on completion of the acquisition transaction. New group reporting procedures will be necessary and should be established immediately after completion.

Two important safeguard measures are necessary immediately following completion of every acquisition.

1. It is necessary to verify that the terms of the acquisition agreement have been met. All the assets assigned in the acquisition agreement should be checked to ensure that full and fair value has been transferred, and the arrangements for security of these assets should be seen to be effective. The status of all issues on which a warranty has been given in the acquisition agreement should be identified, and monitoring procedures established.
2. There should be an early internal audit examination of the newly acquired company. The purpose of this examination would be to evaluate and document every system of internal control in operation in the company, to determine whether each is adequate and being properly applied, and to recommend changes where necessary to bring the quality of control up to group standards.

If the objective of the acquisition is to secure benefits from reorganisation or rationalisation, the changes will need to be introduced as soon as possible after acquisition. Delaying this action will not only delay the expected benefits but it may also exacerbate the trauma suffered by employees and put their loyalty unduly at risk. If management changes have been planned, they should be implemented immediately after completion.

Post-acquisition review

Acquisition is a high-risk activity which often commits very substantial amounts of a company's resources. The directors of the company, being accountable for the proper use of the resources entrusted to them, need to know how well each acquisition they complete fulfils the strategic objectives adopted. The results of each completed acquisition should be evaluated in terms of both financial and practical achievement.

The financial assessment should be based upon the results of a full year following acquisition: any shorter period is unlikely to give a fair view. Results attributable to the acquired business may be difficult or impossible to identify if significant reorganisation or rationalisation followed the acquisition. In such cases it is most important to have evaluated the options before the acquisition. The achieved performance can then be measured against the expected performance with and without the acquired business.

One of the benefits from post-acquisition reviews is the learning process which can be applied for subsequent projects, both in terms of mistakes to be avoided and unexpected successes to be repeated.

Section 5. Contract audit

Introduction

Contract audit tends to be viewed as a specialist area. Certainly it is a field in which an auditor can develop considerable expertise over the years. It is also one where a background in a related discipline such as quantity surveying is a distinct advantage. However, in many respects the audit of a capital contract is no different from any other audit. The auditor requires the same skills: a systematic approach, perseverance, attention to detail and the ability to interpret evidence intelligently and make sound impartial judgements.

Originally, contract audit was synonymous with final account audit. The auditor's role was restricted to carrying out arithmetical checks on final accounts. Subsequently however, there has been an increasing awareness of the need for a 'current approach' to contract audit in which the audit of the final account is just one aspect.

Current contract audit recognises the need for audit involvement from initial planning of each capital development project through to completion and post-project review.

Capital development risks

Entering a commitment for a major capital development project is an expression of mutual confidence between employer and contractor. If either party eventually proves unable to fulfil its commitment, the other is left with the burden of its own commitment without the benefit of receiving full consideration. When the contract is frustrated by the contractor going into liquidation, it is likely to prove costly for the employer, even with the protection of a performance bond.

Depending on the stage reached in the contract when the liquidation occurs, the employer will be in an extremely vulnerable position. He will be left with part-completed works which already represent a substantial investment of resources, but which are effectively useless, and the prospect of further substantial investment to complete the project.

This burden is exacerbated by a weak negotiating position from which to appoint a new contractor to complete the project, and the pressure of time to minimise losses through inevitably delayed completion. Additional costs will have to be incurred to secure the part-finished works after the failed contractor has left the site. There will be extra consultants' fees for additional work on valuation of work done and preparing bills for completing the work.

A performance bond might provide indemnity for certain of the losses which can be quantified at the time of entering the contract, but a major part of the damage caused by the contractor's liquidation cannot be so quantified and the burden falls fully on the employer.

For these reasons, being involved with a contractor who goes into liquidation is a major risk, and every endeavour must be made to avoid it. The objective of every organisation contemplating a major capital development contract should be to investigate thoroughly the financial strength of all tenderers and not to enter any commitment unless and until reliable positive assurance has been received on this score.

Audit considerations

Risk is an inevitable ingredient of all operational activity and it is a fundamental responsibility of management to identify the risk and protect the organisation against its impact.

The objective of internal auditing is to assist management to discharge this responsibility effectively. In the field of capital development, the contract auditor is in a unique position to assist management by appraising the risk exposure and offering an impartial view on the effectiveness of the procedures in place for protecting the organisation against its impact.

This is an important area for the contract auditor to examine, and it raises a number of questions:

1. What standard procedures does the organisation use for collecting information from which to judge the financial strength of potential contractors?
2. Are these procedures adequate and are they always strictly followed?
3. What information is collected on the financial status of potential contractors? Is it relevant? Is it kept up to date? Is the source reliable? Is any of the information confirmed from more than one source?
4. At what level in the organisation are potential contractors approved for financial strength?
5. What assurances on financial strength are sought from potential contractors? What assurances are received? Is there continuous monitoring throughout the currency of the contract?
6. Is any form of financial guarantee required and if so does it have substance and is it commensurate with the risk?

The public and the private sectors both invest vast sums of money each year as capital expenditure. To protect the interests of the taxpayer and the private investor, this expenditure has to be controlled effectively to prevent loss through waste, inefficiency or fraud. The auditor's role is to ensure that the procedures and systems for controlling this expenditure are adequate so that the risk of loss from any cause is minimised. The principal tasks in an audit of a capital contract are:

1. Appraising and reporting on the adequacy of the organisation's standing orders and financial regulations relating to contracts.
2. Reviewing the adequacy of systems for controlling the scheme from the initial planning stage to post-completion review.
3. Assessing the arrangements for security of the organisation's assets.
4. Preventing and detecting fraud, error and impropriety.
5. Identifying losses due to waste and inefficiency.

A capital contract can be considered in three stages: pre-contract, currency of contract, and post-contract. In each of these stages there are areas of particular concern to the auditor:

Pre-contract

1. The system for project appraisal within the organisation.
2. The system for selecting contractors invited to tender.
3. The procedures for tendering and letting contracts.
4. The suitability of contract conditions and tender documents.
5. The adequacy of arrangements for insurance, retention sums, liquidated damages and performance bonds.

Currency of contract

1. The systems and documentation for controlling costs and providing financial information.
2. The adequacy of on-site control including site records.
3. The procedure for carrying out interim valuations.

4. The system for issuing variation orders.
5. The system for examining price fluctuations.
6. The procedure for examining contractual claims.

Post-contract

1. The correctness of the final account.
2. Payment of accounts for consultants' fees.
3. The system for ensuring that the contract was completed on schedule and, if not, that either an extension of time was granted or liquidated damages were deducted.
4. The system for post-project appraisal.

Contract audit procedures

There are a number of differences between ICE conditions of contract (engineering contracts) and RIBA conditions of contract (building contracts). It is therefore necessary to refer to the particular conditions of the contract under examination to ascertain the precise terms for such items as release of retention, extension of time and payment of interim certificates.

Areas requiring detailed examination are listed below under Pre-contract, Currency of contract, and Post-contract headings.

Pre-contract

Project appraisal system

1. How is the need for the project identified?
2. What is the project intended to achieve?
3. How is the cost of the project estimated?
4. How are the merits of each option evaluated and compared?

Contractor selection system

1. Does the organisation maintain a select list of tenderers?
2. Is it reviewed at regular intervals? (e.g. every two years)
3. Does the procedure ensure that new contractors have an opportunity to get on the list?
4. Is there a satisfactory procedure for vetting contractors before inclusion on the list?

5. Are references obtained from bankers and previous customers?
6. How are contractors selected from the list? Are all tenderers given an equal opportunity?

Tendering procedures

1. What is the procedure for the receipt of tenders? Are they received in plain envelopes and opened together in the presence of more than one authorised employee?
2. What is the procedure for correcting Bills of Tender? Is a contractor allowed to amend his tender if arithmetical or technical mistakes are found when the tenders are examined by the technical officers? Whatever procedure for checking tenders is adopted by the organisation, the auditor must be satisfied that it reduces the opportunity for fraud to a minimum, whilst giving each tendering contractor a reasonable opportunity to correct genuine mistakes.

Example 7.2
A contractor adopted the practice of showing a percentage added to his tender to cover his profit. The percentage shown in the bill was 10 per cent, but it had been extended at 5 per cent and this tender was the lowest. It was conceivable that this contractor had deliberately written this error into his tender to give him the option of claiming that either the 5 per cent or the 10 per cent was what he intended, depending upon later knowledge of how close the competition was. In this case the tenders were close and no adjustment was made for mistake, leaving the profit addition at 5 per cent.

Suitability of conditions

1. Do the tender documents refer to a standard form of contract or, if not, were the tenderers supplied with a full set of contract conditions when tenders were invited?
2. Do the documents clearly define the terms under which the work is to be undertaken?
3. Has a formal contract been entered into, signed and, if appropriate, sealed by both parties?

Performance safeguards

1. Does the contractor have adequate insurance cover for employer's liability, public liability, fire and employer's all risks?
2. Does the contract provide for retention money at an adequate level?
3. Is the level of liquidated damages commensurate with the loss that the organisation would suffer in the event of delay rather than just a penalty on the contractor?
4. Has a properly executed bond of sufficient value been entered into with a bank, insurance company or other reputable institution?

Currency of contract

The advantages of audit involvement during the currency of the contract are as follows:

1. The auditor becomes familiar with all aspects of the work as it proceeds, for example site conditions.
2. Queries can be resolved with the technical officers as they arise.
3. Effective control procedures can be designed with audit support and established from the start of the contract: this is particularly important for approving variations, agreeing claims, dealing with time extensions and maintaining records.
4. The final account should be easier to follow and should then take less time to agree.

The auditor should prepare a programme for each individual contract. The audit work will vary depending on both the contract value and its time-span, but the programme should aim to cover the following key aspects during the currency of the contract.

Examination of contract documents

This aspect may be covered in part during the pre-contract audit. The documents to be examined include the contract, bills of quantities, tender documents, insurance policies, performance bond and terms of liquidated damages.

Examination of files

This should include correspondence files, variation orders, appointment of nominated subcontractors and suppliers, site instructions, minutes of site meetings and daywork sheets. The auditor should consider a number of key questions:

1. Did work start on the date specified in the contract?
2. Have all architect's instructions and variation orders been signed by the appropriate supervising officer?
3. Do the minutes of site meetings indicate any delays, potential areas of conflict or other problems?
4. Have dayworks been properly authorised by the supervising officer?
5. Have standing orders been followed in the appointment of nominated subcontractors and suppliers?

Valuations

The auditor should aim to examine several valuations in detail, primarily to establish that interim valuations are carried out in a professional manner and to ensure that payments are not simply agreed over a cup of tea in the site hut. The value and nature of the work included in the valuation should be verified as being commensurate with the stage reached in the contract: for example, if the construction is still at ground level the valuation should not include roofing work.

Increased costs and claims

Calculations and documentation relating to increased costs and claims should be examined to ensure that they have been allowed in accordance with the terms of the contract and are substantiated by invoices, wage awards and price indices.

Time extensions and liquidated damages

The auditor should ascertain whether the contract is behind schedule and, if so, whether either an extension of time has been granted or liquidated damages deducted. If the contractor has submitted a claim for loss and expense, the supporting documentation should be examined and the auditor should consult the supervising officer about the background to the claim.

Site visits

The auditor should aim to visit the site with either the architect or the quantity surveyor at least three times during the currency of the contract: at the start, midway through and at practical completion. It is important to check insurance cover for such visits and the recommended protective clothing should be worn. Opportunity should be taken of the visits to make notes of any problems encountered that could affect completion time or the contract cost. Note should also be taken of the conditions on site including the stage of construction reached, the number of men on site, materials on site, contractor's plant, subcontractor's vans, etc.

Post-contract

Final account

Errors may occur in the final account which would not have been uncovered by audit tests in the course of the contract; arithmetical errors or a failure to adjust for P.C. sums are common examples. Audit examination of the contract during its currency should nevertheless have reduced significantly the degree of checking necessary at the final account stage.

Here is a final account checklist:

Documentation:

Consult the contract, bills of quantities, variation orders, correspondence files and audit notes.

Prime cost sums:

1. Verify that all P.C. sums have been adjusted in the final account.
2. Verify that the additions are supported by quotations or tenders and invoices.
3. Examine the forms of tender to ensure that standing orders were complied with.
4. Check that the correct percentage for profit and attendance has been allowed to the contractor.
5. Verify that the employer has received the full benefit of all due discounts.

Provisional sums:

1. Verify that all provisional sums have been excluded from the final account.
2. Check that all additions are supported by quotations or tenders and invoices.
3. If the additional work was undertaken by the main contractor, check that it is supported by bill rates or agreed rates.
4. Check that the correct percentage for profit and attendance has been allowed to the contractor.

Variation orders and architect's instructions:

1. Verify that every variation order is supported by a properly authorised formal document.
2. Check that all variation orders are priced.

Dayworks:

Daywork rates are expensive and should only be used as a last resort when there is no suitable rate in the bill or other method of pricing the work.

1. Verify that the works were authorised by the architect or engineer in writing.
2. Verify that the hourly rates are correct and that materials are supported by invoices.
3. Verify that the percentage oncosts agree with the percentages priced by the contractor in the bill.
4. Check that the work has not been duplicated elsewhere in the account as a measured item.

Contingencies:

Verify that all amounts included in the bills for contingencies have been omitted from the final account.

Fluctuations:

Contractors can be expected to claim for all increases but may forget to make adjustment for reductions.

1. Check whether the contract provides for full fluctuations in the price of labour and materials or limited fluctuations arising from these changes.
2. Verify that adjustments for fluctuations are supported by detailed documentation: this may be time sheets and invoices or calculations based upon price indices.
3. When fluctuations are calculated using indices,

ensure that they do not include work already in the final account at current rates: for example, nominated subcontractors and suppliers, provisional sum items and dayworks. The indices to be used are those for the month which is midway between valuations.

4. Verify that the non-adjustable element has not been overlooked.

Remeasurement:

1. Test check rates for remeasured items against the bill. If there are significant variations in quantities, test check to the dimension books.

2. Compare related items: for example, topsoil excavated with the quantity of topsoil deposited on spoil heaps or removed from the site.

3. Check that additional items not found in bills are supported by variation orders or architect's instructions. Ensure that the rates used are either pro rata to bill rates or are quantity surveyor agreed rates.

Claims and extension of time:

1. Verify whether the contract was completed on time. If not, ascertain whether liquidated damages were deducted.

2. If the contractor was allowed an extension of time, ascertain under which clause of the contract it was granted and whether or not the contractor is entitled to claim for loss and expense. Extension of time does not necessarily entitle the contractor to additional payment.

3. If a claim is payable, examine the calculations supporting the claim to ensure that it is reasonable. Verify that additional amounts included for preliminaries do not include items which are not time sensitive: for example, site set up and site clean up costs.

Final payment:

1. Verify that the contract is outside of the defects liability period, that all defects have been rectified and that a certificate of completion of making good defects has been issued.

2. Verify that the final certificate takes into account previous payments to the contractor.

Post-contract appraisal

Due to pressures to proceed with the next project, there is often little time to reflect on the one just completed and, if it was overspent, there is often a reluctance to devote further resources to it. A proper post-contract appraisal is nevertheless an important element in the control and audit procedures. The organisation should have a system of post completion appraisal to assess whether the project was completed on time and within budget: if it was not, the reasons should be clarified and recorded. This record may be helpful in planning subsequent similar projects.

The appraisal should also evaluate the success of the project in meeting its original objectives.

Here are some key questions for post-contract appraisal:

1. Did the contract overspend and, if so, was the necessary approval given in accordance with the organisation's standing orders?

2. Were there an exceptional number of variation orders issued and, if so, were they due to flaws in the original design?

3. Was there excessive use of daywork and, if so, was it due to poor design or failure on the part of the quantity surveyor to measure the work by a more efficient method?

4. Was the contractor allowed an extension of time and, if so, was the delay the fault of the supervising officer? For example, the contractor did not receive instructions and drawings in due time.

5. Were extra costs incurred due to design faults by consultant architects and, if so, has the additional expenditure been recovered by deduction from their fee accounts?

6. Were extra costs incurred due to errors by consultant quantity surveyors and, if so, has the additional expenditure been recovered by deduction from their fee accounts?

7. Do the correspondence files provide evidence that the customer is satisfied or not satisfied with the completed project?

8. Have any latent defects become apparent to be taken up with the contractor? For example ceiling tiles at a swimming pool began to fall off when it

was closed for maintenance. The fixing was faulty and it was only condensation from the pool which had prevented them from falling earlier.

9. Has the project achieved its objectives?
10. Can the performances of contractor, subcontractors and consultants involved in this project be considered satisfactory in every respect to justify retaining them on the select list for future projects?

Contract register

The purpose of the contract register is to provide a single comprehensive record of the progress of all capital projects undertaken by the corporation. It should be kept up to date to serve as the authentic source of reference to commitments entered and expenditure incurred.

It used to be traditional in public-sector organisations for the contract auditor to be responsible for maintaining the contract register. This practice ensured that the auditor was kept fully aware of progress on all the projects on hand. Maintaining this register is, however, a management function and responsibility is now normally placed with the accounting department.

Here are some periodical audit checks which may be made on the contract register:

1. Verify selected entries in the register for a sample of payments made to ensure that they are appropriately supported, either by properly certified contract certificates, or by a detailed valuation prepared by the quantity surveyor, or by a detailed payment claim submitted by the contractor and checked by the engineer.
2. Verify that payments are being made within the period allowed in the contract: the periods allowed are not the same in ICE and RIBA contracts. Payments made against capital development contracts are likely to have significant impact on cash flow for both contractor and employer. Consequently, failure to adhere to the contracted timing for payments can have serious repercussions for both parties and may put strain on the relationship between them.

3. Verify that VAT has been properly charged on invoices where it applies and that it has been properly accounted for.
4. Verify that provisions for retention monies in the contracts are being observed and that deductions are made in accordance with the terms of the contracts.
5. Verify that correct procedures are being applied in accordance with contract terms for dealing with settlement where contracts have overrun or been overspent.

    This will involve establishing the reasons for delay or extra cost and checking that appropriate action was taken. For example: authority to overspend, agreed extension of time granted, deduction of liquidated damages.
6. Verify that contractors hold valid 714 Tax Exemption Certificates or that income tax is deducted in paying the labour element of the contract work.

Fee accounts

The procedures for appointing consultants and for determining and settling their charges should be examined at each appropriate stage of the audit of each capital development project: pre-contract, currency of contract, and post-contract.

Appointment of consultants

1. How are consultants appointed? Is a select list used or are the same consultants appointed time after time?
2. Has the cost effectiveness of appointing independent consultants been evaluated and compared with maintaining appropriately staffed in-house facilities for providing technical and professional services?
3. Are consultants' fees negotiated for each appointment or is their remuneration determined from fixed fee scales?
4. Has competitive tendering for consultants' services been considered?

Documentation and payment

1. Examine letters of appointment and the standard forms of agreement, if these are used, and ascertain the principal terms including the basis for payment.
2. Examine the fee account and verify that payments have been in accordance with agreed terms.
3. Verify that amounts claimed as out of pocket expenses are reasonable and admissible under the terms of appointment, substantiated by vouchers or other evidence as appropriate, and have been properly approved.
4. Examine the time records for work charged on a time basis.
5. Check that fee charges are rendered on bona fide VAT invoices to enable the VAT input to be recovered.
6. Verify that the total fees charged and accepted accord with the tender and the contractor's final account.
7. Verify that any additional costs incurred as a result of consultant's errors have been recovered by deduction from their fees.

Examples of contract weaknesses

1. Under the terms of a contract for the construction of 320 two-storey houses, the contractor was entitled to price fluctuations on materials and labour. On examination, the fluctuations claim was found to include increased costs on over 600 staircases.
2. A contract was let to refurbish 60 dwellings, but later amended to omit one of them. The quantity surveyor failed to deduct this property from the final account.
3. A local authority had a policy of bonding internally, through its insurance fund, contracts up to a certain value. This policy was applied at no cost to the contractor. The standard tender documents, however, required contractors to include in their tenders the cost of providing their own performance bonds. On a number of occasions the architect failed to issue an instruction that no contractor's bond was required and consequently the quantity surveyor did not omit the cost of the bond from the final account.
4. A contract for the construction of a sports centre and swimming pool complex involved a considerable amount of dayworks. In the final account it was found that workmen engaged on dayworks, for which the contractor had been paid current daywork rates, had also been included in the contractor's claim for increased costs of labour.
5. A main contractor submitted a claim for increased costs from his plumbing subcontractor. The subcontractor's claim was based on the difference between the list prices of materials at the time of tender and those at the time of supply. When tendering, the subcontractor had quoted substantial discounts off list prices and had in fact received these discounts when purchasing the materials. The main contractor, eventually conceded after much discussion, that the claim should be based upon the difference between tender prices less discount and invoiced prices less discount.
6. An organisation let a contract for the refurbishment of a number of dwellings. It was the policy of the organisation not to modernise a house unless the tenant agreed. Problems arose decanting the tenants to temporary accommodation, partly because some tenants who had originally agreed to participate in the scheme subsequently changed their minds, and the organisation was, therefore, unable to make the houses available to the contractor in accordance with the contract.

   The contractor submitted a claim for additional preliminaries because the contract was overrunning. The contract was eventually completed over a year late and was overspent by more than £100,000. The documentation to substantiate the delays was inadequate and the management of the scheme had been generally unsatisfactory. Early audit involvement should have highlighted the problems and might have resulted in a review of the management policy on modernisation.
7. An organisation invited consultant architects to produce designs for accommodation for elderly

persons. One of the designs submitted incorporated a spiral staircase. The scheme was eventually aborted as no satisfactory design was submitted but the organisation incurred substantial fees. Audit involvement at the project appraisal stage might have identified weaknesses in the design brief given to the consultants.

Section 6. Joint ventures

The nature of joint ventures

A joint venture is an arrangement between two or more organisations to undertake a specific project jointly. This normally means that each participant contributes a share of the capital investment, and each shares in the returns generated. Operational management of the project is usually entrusted to one of the participants who then becomes the operator. Frequently, operators perform this function on a 'no gain, no loss' basis but in some cases a consideration is specified for providing the expertise required.

The contractual relationship between the participants provides for the employment of resources for joint account. This does not constitute a business entity, and it must be clearly differentiated from a corporate entity or a partnership.

The exploitation of natural resources such as oil and other mineral deposits, afforestation and agricultural potential, or the development of national public services such as transport, communications or energy all involve major capital development projects. Such projects require very large capital investment in very long-term development. There is also often a basis for local public interest in all such developments because of their potential to contribute to the local domestic economy and also, in some cases, their potential impact on the environment.

Developments of this kind are often undertaken as joint ventures between a multinational commercial organisation and the local government. The local government's aim will be to ensure that the local population benefits fairly from the exploitation of local resources and to safeguard the environment. The commercial organisation will usually be in a position to contribute well developed access to the appropriate world markets and extensive international experience in the relevant technology.

A joint venture, then, may be comprised of an operator and one or more non-operators, possibly including the local government, all committed to a specific project and bound by a set of rules specified in an operating agreement. Often there is a separate administration or accounting agreement which defines how financing and operating costs are to be shared. In most cases non-operators are able to influence joint venture operations through participation in an operating committee.

A unitisation agreement covers a particular form of joint venture which is appropriate when the separate concessions of the participants overlay the same reservoir. It is particularly relevant to the oil industry. The working interests are pooled so that each participant acquires an undivided interest in the total unit.

Operating agreement

Terms and conditions normally specified are:

1. Scope and duration of the agreement.
2. Participating interest of each party.
3. Ownership of assets and rights to production.
4. Statement that the rights, duties, obligations and liabilities of the parties shall be several and not joint or collective, so that each party will be responsible for his share only of the costs and expenses.
5. The designated operator, with details of the rights and responsibilities.
6. Appointment of an operating committee to direct operations, its role and responsibilities and the voting procedure.
7. Rules for the preparation and approval of a programme of work and budget and performance reporting requirements.
8. Financing arrangements.
9. Right of audit, amplified in the accounting agreement.
10. Terms and conditions for surrender, withdrawal and transfer of interests in the venture.
11. Disposal of production: it is necessary for each

participant to dispose of its own share of production separately to avoid the joint venture being classified as a partnership and a legal entity for tax purposes. The operating agreement should have a clause stating categorically that the joint venture is not a partnership.

Accounting agreement

This would normally cover the following items:

1. Accounting records.
2. Main cost headings.
3. Cash advances by the participants: the procedure by which the operator notifies cash requirements in advance with a due date and non-operators provide funds.
4. Statements and billings: normally, the operator bills non-operators for their shares of costs monthly in arrears.
5. Audit: authority should be given for annual audit by the non-operators of the accounts of the joint venture maintained by the operator. Audits should be conducted with minimum inconvenience to the operator and preferably on a joint basis. The cost should be borne by the non-operators.
6. Charges to the joint account: classifications of all charges admissible against the joint account should be specified and the basis of charging defined. For example: labour costs, contract services, materials, transportation. Frequently the operator will be conducting his own business with activities in common, perhaps, on an adjacent site. Combined ordering and stocking, shared services and the like may be economically beneficial for both the operator's own business and the joint venture. In such cases special care is necessary in specifying how costs are to be segregated.
7. Credits to the joint account.
8. Several responsibility: the accounting agreement should contain a statement that each participant is responsible for maintaining its own accounting records to comply with legal requirements and to support its own tax returns in respect of its interest in the joint operations.

9. Reference to industry guidelines where appropriate.

Operating committee

This is the forum through which non-operators are able to monitor progress of the venture and exercise control. Its functions are as follows:

1. To approve original budgets and programmes and all subsequent variations.
2. To verify that billings are accurate and in line with budgets.
3. To verify that cash calls are fair and in line with budgets and billings.
4. To verify that legal and commercial requirements are being met.
5. To consider any external audit reports received.
6. To exercise the right to audit the operator's records of the venture. When there is more than one non-operator, consideration should be given to establishing an audit committee with duties:
   (a) to approve the audit plan;
   (b) to approve specific audit objectives and scope;
   (c) to schedule audit work in liaison with the operator;
   (d) to agree the constitution of the audit team and to nominate the lead auditor;
   (e) to review the audit report;
   (f) to support the recommendations made to the operating committee;
   (g) to monitor action on agreed audit recommendations.

Audit of joint ventures

Objectives

The primary purpose of an examination of the operator's activities on behalf of the non-operators is to confirm that the joint venture operations are legitimate and properly accounted for. This means verifying two things:

1. That operations have been carried out in the most efficient way for the benefit of all participants and in accordance with the terms of the

operating agreement and the directions of the operating committee.

2. That all revenue and expenditure has been fairly allocated in accordance with the terms of the operating and accounting agreements.

The audit will not be concerned to verify that the operator has charged to joint account all the amounts he could justify under the agreements. However, any errors discovered to the disadvantage of the operator should be reported to him.

Although it is not the principal objective of the non-operators' audit brief to evaluate the effectiveness of control procedures, any weakness in internal control uncovered in the course of the audit examination should always be reported.

The operator may well maintain an internal auditing function as a management service within his own organisation. If so, it is likely he would extend its services to assist in fulfilling his responsibility for management of the joint venture.

In view of the audit objective, some emphasis has to be placed on identifying any expenditure misallocated to non-operators. In some cases this could generate a climate of restricted co-operation and the selection of the audit team needs to take account of this possibility.

A written audit report should always be produced, signed by all the members of the audit team. Whenever possible, the content of the report should be cleared for factual accuracy with responsible executives of the operator before the report is issued. It should be addressed to the chairman of the operating committee and when there is a non-operators' audit committee each member of that committee should receive a copy.

Follow-up of the audit report should be the responsibility of the non-operators' audit committee through the operating committee.

Audit planning

The scope of the audit examination should be defined by the non-operators' audit committee when there is one. Failing this, a meeting of the heads of internal audit for each non-operator should prepare a plan for approval by the operating committee. The audit plan should cover these points:

1. Nomination of the person to take charge of the audit assignment as lead auditor. It may be appropriate for this role to be changed annually on a rotational basis.

2. The period to be subject to audit, usually one year.

3. Arrangements for liaison with other auditors involved, such as the operator's internal auditors and external auditors, if any, appointed for the joint venture. Liaison with other auditors may influence the audit scope selected. However, the objectives of the other auditors are quite different in some important aspects. The non-operator's audit brief for joint venture operations may provide little opportunity for using other auditors' work, but liaison is likely to provide indications as to where attention needs to be focused.

4. Definition of the areas to be examined.

5. Composition of the audit team: this should incorporate a mixture of skills pertinent to the areas to be examined and a fair representation from each non-operator.

Audit programme

On major joint venture operations it may be feasible for the audit scope to be selected by rotation to cover the entire range over a period of two to three years. A detailed programme of audit work should then be prepared for all the areas selected for examination. For example:

Preparatory review

1. Review the operating agreement and the accounting agreement and all amendments.

2. Review minutes of operating committee meetings and related correspondence.

3. Review previous audit reports issued by non-operators and external auditors, if any.

   If the operator has received internal audit reports on the joint venture, sight of them should be requested but the operator may not be prepared to release them.

4. List all cash calls and billings for the period under review and check the correlation.

5. Review organisation charts, authority lists and procedure manuals to ascertain whether there is satisfactory segregation of duties.
6. Establish what operations of his own, if any, the operator has adjacent to the joint venture.
7. Find out what local legislation (including taxation) applies to the joint venture and to the category of business involved and review the requirements.
8. List any significant concerns identified in these enquiries to be followed up as the audit proceeds.

Budget

1. Confirm that all budgets and subsequent amendments have been agreed by the operating committee.
2. Confirm that all overexpenditure and significant time overruns have been reported to the operating committee and received retrospective approval.
3. Investigate the explanations for overspending and significant overruns.

Billings to non-operators

1. Confirm that billings match the operator's record of costs.
2. Check the exchange rates used for currency conversions.
3. Confirm that revenue and expense allocations to non-operators accord with the terms of the operating agreement.
4. Verify that only revenue received and expenses paid in cash have been included in billings: accruals for services rendered should not be included.

Production

1. Examine the production planning and recording procedures and verify that effective control is being exercised.
2. Identify those processes where waste is likely to occur and verify that there are adequate procedures to ensure that wastage is properly controlled and that scrapped materials are recovered and accounted for.

3. Examine the methods adopted for measuring production and the procedures used for reconciling production, sales and stock. Check that any significant discrepancies are investigated and reported to the operating committee.
4. Verify that all sales are properly invoiced and confirm the allocation of production volumes to each participant in the joint venture. When the operator prepares documentation on behalf of non-operators, the procedures should be examined to verify that the documents are being properly drawn up in accordance with the contracts.
5. If royalty is paid by the operator on behalf of the joint venture, verify that liability has been calculated strictly in line with the terms of the licence agreement, that it is fully supported by documentation, and that the amounts are paid when due and accounted for through the joint account in accordance with the operating agreement.
6. Confirm that all safety and environmental obligations are being properly discharged in all activities of the joint venture.

Materials

1. Verify that the operator applies adequate procedures for efficient and economic procurement of materials.
2. Test check suppliers' invoices to confirm that price, quantity and quality accord with purchase notes, contracts and receipt documentation.
3. Verify that suppliers are paid on due date and that all applicable discounts are taken and credited to the joint account.
4. Examine freight and transport invoices to confirm that they accord with receiving documentation and bills of lading. Check that there are no separate freight invoices in respect of goods invoiced cif.
5. Test quantities purchased against quantities used in operations.
6. Confirm that stock pricing accords with the terms of the operating agreement.
7. Examine warehouse security and evaluate the effectiveness of protection against fire and theft.

8. Examine the stock management procedures for regular stock inventories, independent stock checking and proper authorisation of inventory adjustments.
9. Carry out sample physical stock checks.
10. Examine the stock inventory to confirm that it does not contain dead or obsolete items.
11. Examine and test the system for maintaining stocks at the appropriate economic level to avoid stock-outs with minimum investment.
12. If stock for the joint venture is warehoused with other stocks, it is necessary to ensure that stock management costs are fairly apportioned.
13. Check that appropriate documentation is generated for all materials issued.
14. Examine procedures for the disposal of surplus materials and scrap.
15. When the operator has provided materials to be used on the joint venture, the amounts charged should be verified as being fair and reasonable and the transaction should accord with the terms of the operating agreement.

Employment

Since the joint venture is not a legal entity it has no contractual capacity. Those employed on the joint venture operation are likely to have contracts of employment with the operator. Care is therefore necessary to differentiate between the costs of employment for joint venture operations and those for the operator's own operations:

1. Verify that there are effective control procedures to ensure that all employees charged to the joint venture payroll are in fact working exclusively for the joint venture.
2. Verify that a fair and reasonable basis of apportionment is used for the allocation of employment costs of any employees whose work is shared between the joint venture and other operations.
3. Check that any employment costs charged directly to the joint venture have not also been included in the operator's service or overhead charges.

4. Review personnel turnover and recruitment costs.
5. Verify that all subcontract employees have signed confidentiality documents.
6. Perform selected payroll audit tests to verify that:
   (a) all employment costs relate to bona fide employees;
   (b) all rates of pay accord with the terms of employment and are properly authorised;
   (c) hours worked and work done are fully documented;
   (d) all extra payments are fully documented and properly approved;
   (e) the payroll disciplines are well designed to provide an effective basis for control and they are strictly enforced.

Subcontract work

Contracting with specialist organisations to undertake key elements of the work is a normal feature of most major development projects including joint venture operations. Contracts may be awarded for civil engineering, construction, drilling and so on.

The operator may consider it appropriate to apply contract audit techniques as part of the management process. The non-operators' audit should however apply a measure of testing to confirm that joint venture resources have been properly and efficiently used. The following checks are examples of such testing:

1. Verify that all contracted out work has been provided for in the operating agreement and approved by the operating committee.
2. Verify that the operator maintains adequate procedures for controlling contracted-out work, particularly in selecting suitable contractors and securing competitive prices.
3. Review the operator's system for monitoring and controlling progress, efficiency and costs, to confirm that it is adequate.
4. Review all extras relating to contracts to confirm that they have been properly authorised.
5. Test to confirm that the operator's standards of safety and security and those prescribed in the operating agreement are also applied in the work contracted out.

6. Test to confirm that contractors' charges accord with the contract and supporting documentation, including extras and escalation clauses.
7. Verify that all allowable discounts are taken and credited to the joint account.
8. Confirm that payments are made to contractors on the due date as prescribed in the contract.
9. Examine the procedures for controlling expenditure on any variable price contracts.

Operator's charges

1. Confirm that the technical services and other facilities provided and charged for by the operator accord with the terms of the operating agreement.
2. Check the computation of the amounts charged for services and facilities and verify them against operational records. The charges have to be fair and reasonable and must be fully supported by documentation.
3. Verify that all charges made by the operator for services or facilities are properly attributable to the joint venture and exclude any amounts relating to other operations on the same site or elsewhere.
4. Examine mobilisation and demobilisation fees against the dates of commencement and completion of joint venture operations.
5. Confirm that charges made by the operator for administrative or other overhead costs accord with the terms of the operating agreement.
6. Examine the operator's method of accounting for overheads in order to verify that the basis of attributing a share to joint venture operations is fair and reasonable.
7. Check that amounts charged specifically for overheads have not also been included in amounts directly charged to the joint account for services or facilities provided by the operator.
8. In any case where agreement cannot be reached on what constitutes a fair basis for allocating overhead costs the differences should be scheduled in the audit report for resolution by the operating committee.

Insurance

1. Ascertain whether any categories of insurance are required by the law of the country and verify that any such requirement is met.
2. Confirm that the requirements of the operating agreement concerning insurance cover have been met.
3. Verify that any insurance cover underwritten by the operator or arranged on a group basis has been approved by the operating committee and that the premium charges are fair and reasonable.
4. Review the insurable risks and verify that adequate protection has been arranged particularly for those areas where the joint venture operations are most vulnerable. For example: workmen's compensation, damages inflicted on third parties, seepage or pollution, storm damage, accidents and consequential loss.
5. Verify that whenever an insured hazard has materialised, a legitimate claim has been made and actively pursued.

Taxes and grants

1. Verify that all returns required by fiscal legislation have been rendered in good time and are accurate.
2. Verify that all taxes paid by the operator on behalf of the joint venture were correctly assessed and that optimum use has been made of available exemptions, allowances, reliefs and other deductions or concessions.
3. Ascertain what subsidies or grants are available from public funds and verify that advantage is being taken of any such assistance for which the joint venture operations qualify.

Fixed assets

1. Confirm that all capital expenditure projects have been approved by the operating committee.
2. Confirm that the methods adopted for financing capital expenditure are as required by the operating agreement and the operating committee.
3. Verify that proper detailed records are main-

tained for fixed assets and that the assets are inspected periodically for comparison with the record.

4. Verify that depreciation is provided for in accordance with the terms of the operating agreement.

5. Confirm that retirements and disposals of fixed assets have been approved by the operating committee and that sale proceeds have been duly accounted for through the joint account.

6. If fixed assets have been transferred between the operator and the joint venture, the transaction should have been specifically approved by the operating committee and the consideration determined on a fair basis.

Cash

1. Review the cash management systems and practices to verify that the non-operators' funds are not being used to finance the operator's share of the joint venture.

2. Examine the organisation and the internal control procedures applicable to all individuals involved in handling or accounting for cash on behalf of the joint venture.

3. Verify that the safeguards and security procedures are adequate and that the control disciplines are strictly adhered to.

4. Verify that all bank accounts are regularly reconciled with the bank statements.

5. Verify that all petty cash floats are subjected to frequent independent cash counts.

Section 7.   Health and safety

Introduction

Over five hundred people die each year at work and several hundred thousand lose time through injury or illness. (C. M. Thomas, Health and Safety Commission, 1988)

This statement gives some indication of the scale of the burden on society in general and on industry in particular attributable to accidents and health hazards at work in the United Kingdom. The general public are also exposed to the risk of injury and health hazards from environmental pollution, defective public services and other perils.

In humanitarian terms, any human suffering caused in the pursuit of economic objectives is intolerable. Consequently, the onus is on the management of every organisation to give priority to health and safety considerations and to foster an active policy of accident prevention in all industrial activities.

It is primarily the duty of every person responsible for managing an industrial activity to ensure that effective control mechanisms are in place to prevent accidents and health hazards at work. In this area, effective control demands an open commitment from the most senior management of every organisation to maintain the highest safety standards and to promote a positive attitude towards accident prevention to be adopted by every individual working in the organisation.

The primary objective of investment in measures to reduce accidents and health hazards must be to avoid or reduce human suffering. If it is effective it will also contribute to economic objectives by yielding benefits in the form of improved productivity and fewer claims for injury compensation.

Health and safety and the law

Health and safety legislation in the United Kingdom has been enacted for the protection of the public in general and people at work in particular. It defines the respective responsibilities of employers and people at work. Its main aim however is the promotion of safety awareness with the philosophy that employers should be self-monitoring.

The main legislation comprises:

1. The Factories Act 1961
2. The Offices, Shops and Railway Premises Act 1963
3. The Health and Safety at Work Act 1974

In addition, there are specific regulations for particular operations such as radiation equipment in hospitals, agricultural machinery on farms, and the storage and use of explosives or dangerous substances in industry.

The Health and Safety Commission is in effect the

custodian of legislation in this field. It is an official monitoring and advisory body comprising representatives of employers and employees in industry and local authorities. Its main purpose is to promote arrangements for the following:

1. Securing the health, safety and welfare of people at work.
2. Protecting the public against risks arising from work activities.
3. Controlling the keeping and use of explosives, highly flammable or other dangerous substances.

The Commission proposes legislation, provides relevant information, advice and guidance and carries out and sponsors research.

The Commission also appoints the Health and Safety Executive which is a separate statutory body. The Executive's function is to ensure that the legal requirements are observed and to provide an advisory service to employers and employees. The activities of all the major inspectorates in the health and safety field are now controlled and co-ordinated by the Executive.

The Health and Safety at Work Act 1974

This Act establishes ways of securing the health and safety of people at work and the protection of the public affected by work activities. Its principal effects are listed below:

1. Its main aim is the promotion of safety awareness.
2. It provides a basis for encouraging effective safety arrangements both in organisation and in performance by means of schemes designed to suit particular undertakings or industries.
3. It specifies the relevant responsibilities of employers and of people at work.
4. It specifies duties for employers, the self-employed, employees, controllers of premises, designers, manufacturers, importers and suppliers.
5. It requires that, so far as is reasonably practicable, premises, equipment, systems of work and articles for use at work are all safe and do not constitute a health hazard.

The health and safety provisions of the Factories Act, the Offices, Shops and Railway Premises Act and the Mines and Quarries Act remain in force to supplement the provisions of the Health and Safety at Work Act of 1974.

The 1974 Act deals with health and safety under four headings:

1. **Employers' duties to employees**
   Employers have a duty to ensure the health, safety and welfare of all employees and in particular:

   (a) to provide and maintain in good order all plant (including machinery, equipment and appliances) and systems of work;
   (b) to ensure safe arrangements for the use, handling, storage and transport of all articles and substances used at work;
   (c) to provide information, instruction, training and supervision;
   (d) to maintain the workplace in a safe condition and to provide and maintain safe means of access and egress;
   (e) to provide and maintain a safe working environment with adequate arrangements for welfare.

2. **Written statement of safety policy**
   (a) Every employer must prepare and revise as necessary, a written statement of general policy with respect to the health and safety at work of his employees.
   (b) The statement must specify the organisation and arrangements for the time being in force for carrying out the policy.
   (c) The employer must bring the statement and any revision of it to the notice of all of his employees.

3. **Safety committees**
   The Health and Safety Commission considers it advisable for employers to set up a safety committee consisting of members drawn from both management and employees.

4. **Employers' duties to other persons**
   Every employer has duties to other persons, for example to members of the public:
   (a) to conduct his undertakings, so far as is reasonably practicable, in a way which en-

sures that the health and safety of persons who are not in his employment but who may be affected by such undertakings are not put at risk;

(b) to give information to persons who are not in his employment about such aspects of the way he conducts his undertaking as might affect their health and safety.

Inspection and enforcement

Inspectors, under the Health and Safety Executive, have powers to enter premises, to examine, to sample, to dismantle, to test and to question. An inspector who discovers a contravention may:

1. Issue a prohibition notice to stop an activity.
2. Issue an improvement notice to require the fault to be remedied within a specified time.
3. Prosecute instead of, or in addition to, serving a notice; this may lead to a fine or imprisonment.
4. Seize, render harmless or destroy any dangerous substance.

Notwithstanding these powers of enforcement the expressed view of the Executive is that employers should be self-monitoring.

A health and safety control programme

Development and operation of an effective control system will depend on six vital factors:

1. **Statement of policy on health and safety**
   This allows a clearly defined common attitude towards health and safety issues to be adopted by all employees throughout the organisation.
2. **Knowledge of statutory obligations**
   When applying practices designed for safety, their effectiveness is dependent upon those who have to apply them having a full understanding of their purpose. It is necessary to ensure that the legal requirements are identified and made known throughout the organisation.
3. **Safe working methods**
   A sense of shared responsibility for safety needs to be encouraged in every employee. It is a key aspect of the management culture and management training programmes should should take

account of this. Advice on safe working procedures should form an essential element of job training for all employees.

4. **Appointment of safety officers**
   This is a specialist advisory and training role. The safety officer should be an expert in interpretation of safety law and experienced in safe working methods to give guidance and advice to operational managers. Designing and administering the safety element of job training is also a key part of the safety officer's work. In certain work activities, there may be a need to give a specific individual responsibility for monitoring safety compliance in the work section.
5. **Training**
   Every employee needs to know and understand all the hazards likely to be encountered in the work place. He or she should be trained in working procedures which are safe, and should be armed with the knowledge and equipment to deal with any emergency.
6. **Monitoring**
   A full record must be made of every accident and every injury or illness caused by the activities of the organisation. The accident record book must be kept up to date and reviewed regularly by management to identify particular problems or trends and to guide further action to prevent recurrence.

Health and safety audit

Responsibilities

Internal auditors should review the systems established to ensure compliance with those policies, plans, procedures, laws and regulations which could have a significant impact on operations and reports, and should determine whether the organisation is in compliance.

(IIA–UK Specific Standard 320)

Management is responsible for establishing the systems designed to ensure compliance with such requirements as policies, plans, procedures and applicable laws and regulations. Internal auditors are responsible for determining whether the systems are adequate and effective and whether the activities are complying with the appropriate requirements.

(IIA–UK Guideline 320.01)

Internal audit assurance

The internal auditor must examine the control systems established by management:

1. To verify that the systems provide a sound basis for effective control in accord with established policy and within the constraints of the law.
2. To check the degree and quality of compliance with the procedures prescribed for these systems.
3. To consider whether changes in procedures or practices could bring about improvements in efficiency or effectiveness.

To provide this service in the field of health and safety, the internal auditor must become familiar with the policies, procedures, laws and regulations relating to health and safety at work. As in other specialist areas, expert advice must be sought for particular problems identified.

The auditor should examine statements of policy, accident records, minutes, correspondence and notices. He needs to make visits to examine working practices, hazardous material stores, fire escapes, alarms, hydrants, entrances and exits, etc.

Audit questions on health and safety

Written statement of safety policy

1. Has the written statement of safety policy, organisation and arrangements been prepared in accordance with the Act?
2. Have measures been adopted to ensure that employees at all levels are aware of the safety policy and to encourage them actively to apply it in their work?

Employers' duties to employees

1. When new plant is installed, has latest good practice been taken into account? Have factory inspectors' recommendations always been implemented?
2. Is there provision by regular inspection and, where necessary, testing to ensure that plant and its safety devices are being maintained to the proper standard? Is all equipment safely stored?

3. Are all lifts, lifting machinery and pressure vessels subjected to regular expert inspection and certification?
4. Have arrangements been made for regular maintenance and testing of electrical installations and equipment?
5. What attention has been paid to the safety of cleaning, repair and maintenance operations?
6. What personal protective equipment and clothing is required? Has it been issued? Have those who need it been trained in its use?
7. Are the containers of all substances correctly labelled? Are there appropriate hazard warnings on dangerous substances both in store and in use?
8. Are there effective arrangements in place for secure storage of explosives and other dangerous substances and is access to them restricted and properly controlled?
9. If there is mechanical transport on the premises, have the operational procedures been critically appraised? Are the transport rules adequate and are they properly enforced?
10. If subcontractors are employed such as for maintenance services or on a construction project, are there safe working conditions written into the contract?
11. Is there a code of rules for use of the organisation's road vehicles including regular servicing and safety checks? Is safe driving actively encouraged?
12. Is adequate provision made for the protection of employees against the risks to which they may be exposed in handling cash or other valuables in the course of their work?
13. Is adequate information and guidance given to all employees on the hazards of the work activities and the methods for avoiding them and on any other matters affecting health and safety?
14. Has every employee exposed to a health hazard been informed of the risks and the necessary precautions? Have arrangements been made for each to be told the results of any relevant monitoring carried out?
15. Has adequate consideration been given to

special safety requirements of all buildings, such as fire escapes, fixture points for window cleaners' harnesses, and adequate preparation and safety arrangements for building maintenance?

16. Are fire exits prominently identified and are they checked to ensure that they are maintained free from obstructions?

17. Is fire fighting equipment provided and properly maintained? Are there employees who are adequately trained in its use?

18. Is there a fire certificate for the premises and are its conditions being observed?

19. Are the fire alarms regularly tested? Are fire drills held?

20. Are the welfare arrangements satisfactory, including seating accommodation, protective clothing, washing facilities, and lavatories?

21. Are the first aid arrangements satisfactory?

Employers' duties to other persons

1. Is all machinery and plant adequately protected against risks to the public including, for example, children even when trespassing?

2. Could any activities undertaken cause danger, injury or a health hazard to members of the public or workpeople other than employees?

3. Are toxic gases or dust emitted into the atmosphere from the premises?

4. Is effluent discharged into public sewers or natural drainage courses?

5. Is there any other potential cause of environmental pollution such as noise, radiation or biological hazards?

6. Have effective systems been installed for atmospheric emissions, effluent and environmental pollution to be monitored and are effective control devices in operation?

7. Could there be danger to the public from any conveyance of toxic or otherwise dangerous substances?

8. If the business of the organisation involves providing a public service such as transport, is there a system in force for monitoring the service and controlling it effectively within the safety standards prescribed as a condition of the operat-

ing licence or concession or the relevant legislation or other regulations?

These are examples of the questions the auditor would ask in order to verify management's systems of control. There would be more in a full audit and the emphasis of these would be tailored to the nature of the organisation involved.

Section 8.   Social audit

The nature of social audit

The concept of social audit is relatively new. It is a development which reflects world-wide trends in social attitudes, firstly in the importance attached to human rights and secondly in growing concern for the environment. These trends have been recognised in the pronouncements of leading international organisations such as the United Nations, the British Commonwealth and the European Commission.

A social audit reviews the activities of an organisation with the objective of ensuring that they are directed with due consideration for the social and environmental consequences.

This concept recognises that there are social and environmental responsibilities to be satisfied in the pursuit of business or service related objectives. Some of these responsibilities are enforceable by law, others may involve risks of serious personal injury which could lead to costly claims for damages, whilst some of the organisation's activities may just be socially or environmentally undesirable and even unacceptable.

The management of the organisation must of course ensure that all its activities are lawful. A responsible management will also take care to minimise the risks of personal injury resulting from the organisation's activities. However, it is often a matter of subjective judgement to decide whether or not an activity is socially undesirable. It is thus a top management responsibility to establish a social policy for determining how operational decisions are to be influenced by consideration of the social and environmental consequences. An audit is thus appropriate to examine and report on compliance with the social policy.

In this context, social audit may be perceived as a facet of operational auditing. It requires similar skills, employs the same techniques and its effectiveness depends upon a thorough knowledge and a sound understanding of the activities to be audited. Indeed, the concept of internal auditing as a service to management involves examining the entire range of an organisation's activities in the context of the objectives being pursued by its management. Since the management objectives need to have social and environmental perspectives, so should the internal audit scope.

The term is sometimes used to describe an external review of an organisation, measuring its performance against an independent view of what is socially desirable. This kind of audit serves a purpose beyond the usual scope of the internal audit role.

The internal auditor has to identify with the objectives of the management being served, and to examine and report on how well those objectives are being achieved. The objective of an external social audit is to serve a public interest within the perception that every organisation is socially accountable to the community in which it operates. The external review would be primarily concerned with evaluating the social and environmental policies adopted by the management of the organisation with particular emphasis on issues which are not being addressed.

Social and environmental hazards

Some achievements in improving the quality of life have produced unacceptable social consequences, which have not been recognised until long afterwards. An example has been the development of energy generation and consumption.

In the nineteenth century, Britain led the world with its industrial revolution; great advances in productivity resulted from burning coal as a source of energy and employing human beings under conditions now universally recognised as intolerable. Progress towards reasonable working conditions was painfully slow and it also took us many years to acknowledge a direct connection between coal burning and the ill health of the nation.

Meanwhile, ever increasing energy demands continued to be met by extracting more and more coal from the earth and burning it. Winning this useful fuel was also hazardous and over the years has claimed many lives both from pit accidents and from diseases caused by prolonged exposure to coal dust.

Clean air legislation in the mid-twentieth century addressed the health hazard of a soot-laden atmosphere. It took another quarter of a century to recognise that this source of readily available and seemingly limitless energy has been contributing to the desolation of extensive forest areas in Europe through acid rain. Even later came some consensus understanding of a much greater threat to the environment: the contribution to global warming attributable to increased atmospheric carbon dioxide generated from fossil fuel combustion.

The invention of the internal combustion engine facilitated great achievements in transport by exploiting oil as a source of energy. As with coal, winning oil from the earth has cost lives and its use involves threats to the environment in atmospheric and oceanic pollution.

Many of the manifestations of modern civilisation involve a high demand for energy for which fossil fuels have provided the main source of supply. The accumulating environmental costs of using this source of energy are now threatening to overtake the advantages achieved. Pressure to resolve this global social dilemma now places a heavy burden of responsibility on us all as energy consumers.

The agrochemical industry has enabled farmers to promote crop growth with fertilisers whilst suppressing or eliminating its competitors and enemies with pesticides and herbicides. This requires powerful chemicals: sometimes they have been too powerful or used without a full understanding of all the consequences, and have caused damage to the environment.

Productivity has increased enormously, but it is a social tragedy that the human race has failed to overcome barriers to distribution which leave significant numbers of the increasing world population to survive on the threshold of starvation; many fail to survive.

Medical research sponsored by the pharmaceutical industry has made a significant contribution to improving the quality of life. Penicillin and other antibiotics, for example, have provided the means of eliminating a number of diseases which were once considered serious and even fatal. However, with some developments unforeseen side effects have emerged to mar the progress achieved. Thalidomide was a particularly tragic example. It offered relief for nausea in pregnancy. Too late it was discovered also to cause congenital deformity of the unborn child: much damage had already been done. This example demonstrates the enormous responsibility for ensuring that utmost care and indeed caution are applied in all health care developments.

A code of behaviour

The history of mankind is a continuum of changing social attitudes in the pursuit of fundamental liberties and improved quality of life. Every individual develops a social conscience which is shaped by experience of life and inevitably influenced by cultural, political and moral considerations. Consequently, attitudes will vary significantly across the social spectrum.

The changes in social attitudes have been significantly greater in the twentieth century than at any previous time. The pace of change adds emphasis to differences in individual opinions as to what is socially desirable and what is unacceptable at any point in time.

Nevertheless, the acceptance of a code of basic concepts where there is a consensus view of what is socially acceptable and what is not, is a fundamental feature of society. A balance has to be maintained between the aims of individuals or groups and the interests of society as a whole. Social auditing can contribute to clarification of the code of socially acceptable behaviour in the course of examining compliance with it.

A generally accepted view of human rights provides the criteria for judging whether or not social behaviour is acceptable. In some cases the law intervenes to define and protect the rights of those at risk or to protect social amenities. There are for example, constraints on the activities of organisations prescribed by UK legislation:

1. Sale of goods which must be of merchantable quality, trade descriptions, restrictive practices, abuse of monopoly, consumer credit protection.
2. Regulations covering safe and hygienic production of food and catering, control and disclosure of food additives and humane slaughter of animals for food.
3. Regulations controlling the testing, production and prescription of drugs used for medical treatment.
4. Health and safety at work, protection of employment, protection against racial and sexual discrimination.
5. Control of the location of industry and construction developments, constraints on the use of premises; preservation of structures, sites and natural features, conservation of natural amenities.
6. Restrictions on effluent and waste disposal and atmospheric pollution.
7. Restrictions on the extraction of minerals including water. Some activities, like advertising, financial services, and the press are subject to self-regulation in the public interest.

Within the European Community the Convention of Human Rights is administered through the Court of the Human Rights Commission. In other parts of the world notably the United States of America the rights of the citizen are enshrined in the written constitution.

Sensitive areas

Socially and environmentally sensitive activities or products may include:

1. Consumer products which can damage health such as tobacco, leaded petrol, asbestos.
2. Consumer products which can cause accidental injury or death such as foam vinyl.
3. Lethal horticultural pesticides and herbicides which can contaminate food or damage the environment such as DDT.

4. Industrial processes with particular health hazards such as silicosis in mining.
5. Operations which are noisy such as aircraft, pneumatic drilling, heavy machinery.
6. Operations which can cause radio interference in communications, control systems, medical equipment, etc.
7. Manufacturing processes which pollute the atmosphere such as fossil fuels, solvents, CFCs.
8. Operations where a risk of fire or explosion could have catastrophic consequences: Bhopal and Chernobyl serve as grim reminders.
9. Discharge of hazardous or toxic waste products into the sea such as untreated domestic sewage, radioactive waste, crude oil sludge.
10. Contamination of fresh-water sources by discharge of toxic industrial effluent into the soil or direct into rivers or lakes. There are extensive antipollution laws for protection against this hazard in the United States.
11. Contamination of water supplies through leaching of residual chemicals applied to the soil as agricultural fertilisers.
12. Unauthorised tipping, especially of dangerous or toxic waste.
13. Extravagant depletion of natural resources.
14. Exploitation of underprivileged peoples.
15. Trade which involves unnecessary slaughter of wild animals especially endangered species such as elephants and whales.

These are examples of undesirable social consequences. The list is not intended to be exhaustive.

Further activities, perhaps more contentious in nature, might be added, depending on the purpose and viewpoint of the social audit. For example:

1. Activities where there are risks of radiation leakage or nuclear contamination.
2. Involvement in international arms trade.
3. Involvement in trade with South Africa.

There are also positive social objectives which an organisation may actively pursue whether or not they are related to its principal activities:

1. A programme of measures to conserve energy.
2. Active involvement in the development of or application of processes for recycling scarce resources.
3. A declared policy of avoiding materials, products and activities which involve specified elements of social injustice or threats to the environment. For example: South African produce, ivory, intensively farmed produce.
4. Encouragement of cultural interests through sponsorship of education, arts or sports.
5. Support for community projects, such as leisure complexes, libraries, health care, medical research.
6. Economic support or other forms of aid for third-world countries.

Responsibilities

When the activities of an organisation involve some risk of unacceptable social consequences the responsibility for avoiding those consequences rests primarily with the management.

Every organisation will have a social profile reflecting the social and environmental policies adopted by its top management. The policies will inevitably be influenced by the primary objectives of the organisation. Firstly, because the organisation's main activities may be socially or environmentally sensitive, as with power generation or the manufacture of agricultural chemicals. Secondly, because supporting social or environmental causes usually involves cost.

Cost has to be justified either as allowing a private-sector organisation to remain efficient and competitive or as proper use of taxpayers' money in the public sector. Often the justification includes an improved public image which the organisation earns from giving due attention to the social consequences of its activities. In the long term a favourable public image can be expected to bestow commercial advantages.

Having established a social and environmental policy, the top management must then make it work throughout the organisation. A well-considered social and environmental policy is likely to be perceived as a cause worthy of support by most of the executives who will have to make it work. However, it is important to secure the commitment of them all to the precise terms of the policy adopted.

Different individuals are likely to have differing preferences in ranking social obligations. Consequently, the priorities chosen in formulating the policy may not be the choices each individual would have preferred. It is therefore necessary to communicate the rationale adopted for the policy very clearly to ensure that it will be implemented coherently in the interests of the organisation rather than fragmentally as each individual perceives the need.

Internal audit confirmation of adherence to the policy is particularly helpful in these circumstances. It helps to ensure that the resources applied are not dissipated, with no real benefits to the organisation, the public or the environment.

It may be appropriate to present the policy in terms of a social and environmental development programme:

1. Continuous review of the use of energy to explore every opportunity for energy conservation.
2. Enlightened personnel management with training programmes for all employees, including the disabled and disadvantaged, genuine concern for health and safety at work; fair rewards and incentives; sound retirement plans; and a commitment to security of employment.
3. Research for new product development, with emphasis on health and safety factors and giving special consideration to waste disposal and emissions and the use of recycled materials.
4. Continuous review of all materials used, and all products, with a view to eliminating any which are the result of socially undesirable activity.
5. A procedure to be followed when considering every new development to ensure proper consideration of all environmental issues raised.
6. An allocation of funds for sponsorship of specific cultural or community activities.
7. Provision for internal audit examination of compliance with the policy.

Audit programme

In an organisation which has a defined social and environmental policy the internal auditing function should have a clear brief to examine and report on implementation of the policy.

The general scope should be covered in the internal audit charter, but it is advisable to have a specific brief from top management which should be made known to all executives involved in implementing the policy.

Ideally, the statement of social policy should state that compliance is to be subject to internal audit examination. This precaution is necessary because the term social audit can mean different things to different people from checking the social club accounts to a political witch-hunt.

It is important for a constructive audit that there are no misconceptions from the start and that all involved know what it is about. The social audit programme should cover:

1. Consideration of the statement of social and environmental policy as determined by the top management of the organisation. It would normally be established as a board minute but the full details and explanations should be available to all executives throughout the organisation.
2. Examination of the social and environmental programme for putting the policy into effect and verifying that effective systems are in place to implement the programme.
3. Verification that budgets have been established with appropriate authority and accountability for the resources allocated to social or environmental causes in the policy statement or programme.
4. A detailed programme of tests to confirm that the procedures established for implementation of the social policy are being properly applied.
5. A programme of tests to confirm that all requirements of the law affecting activities in socially or environmentally sensitive areas are being strictly observed.
6. A review of the detailed plans for approved projects to verify that full effect has been given to the requirements of the social and environmental policy.

7. A review of progress on all aspects of the social and environmental programme.

8. An appraisal of the information used for monitoring progress towards the objectives defined in the policy.

9. Evaluation of the degree of compliance with the policy and reporting to the top management.

8 Prevention and detection of fraud

The nature of fraud

Fraud is any act of intentional deception to obtain benefit or to gain an advantage. It often involves theft.

A person is guilty of theft if he dishonestly appropriates property belonging to another with the intention of permanently depriving the other of it.

(Theft Act 1968, s. 1)

The Theft Acts 1968 and 1978 also specify a range of acts of deception which are unlawful in the United Kingdom:

1. Obtaining property by deception (Theft Act 1968, s. 15)
2. Obtaining pecuniary advantage by deception; (Theft Act 1968, s. 16)
3. False accounting (Theft Act 1968, s. 17)
4. Liability of company officers for certain offences by the company (Theft Act 1968, s. 18)
5. False statements by company directors, etc. (Theft Act 1968, s. 19)
6. Suppression, etc. of documents (Theft Act 1968, s. 20)
7. Obtaining services by deception (Theft Act 1978, s.1)
8. Evasion of liability by deception (Theft Act 1978, s.2)

Causes of fraud

The proliferation of fraud is closely related to the history of business development. With growth in scale and complexity, relationships between people within organisations have expanded nationally and internationally to allow greatly increased distance between the defrauder and the defrauded.

Population growth and increased living standards in industrial communities have placed increased pressures on individuals and resulted in greater temptations. Elliot and Willingham analyse the psychological process of how people get involved in fraud in three stages:

1. A feeling that a personal financial problem is unsharable.
2. Knowledge how to solve the problem, but doubts about violating a position of trust.
3. Verbalisation – the ability to find a formula to describe the act in terms compatible with one's image as a trusted person. At this stage the potential defrauder can convince himself that the violation of trust is not really a violation.

A feeling that a problem is unsharable may be related to both the real and the perceived needs of the individual including, possibly, needs related to drinking, to drug addiction, to gambling or to marital stress. However, people with unsharable problems do not necessarily turn to a life of crime.

White-collar fraud

The American criminologist, Edwin O. Sutherland, coined the expression white-collar fraud to describe

233

crimes committed against an organisation by those employed in it in a managerial or supervisory capacity. The basic ingredients are:

1. **Motive** This may be a personal need or the result of bribery, coercion or even blackmail.
2. **Attraction**   A desirable target must be available: it may be cash or readily convertible goods or knowledge.
3. **Opportunity** The perpetrator must have the opportunity both to gain possession of the target and to dispose of it.
4. **Concealment** Concealing the act may reduce the chance of detection: certainty of detection is a major deterrent.

Comer (1987) explains the theory compounded by Sutherland as follows:

where a company condones crime, its action and the action of the criminals working within and against it encourage others to follow. Where the senior management of an organisation engages in unethical conduct, accepts sloppy controls, wastes assets and talents, then it encourages crime at all levels within its structure. Crime is contagious. Conversely, and this is probably the greatest value of Sutherland's work, the company that creates the right climate of honesty can reduce crime. It can ensure that the factors unfavourable to crime exceed those favourable to it.

Examples of fraud

A person taking goods from a shop, intending to avoid paying for them, is committing theft. However, if that person offers, by way of payment, a cheque, knowing it will not be honoured on presentation, or a cheque with a forged signature, or a stolen credit card, these are all dishonest acts intended to deceive and therefore essentially fraudulent.

Misappropriation occurs when a person entrusted with the custody of funds or other property belonging to another uses them or allows them to be used in any way which is contrary to the owner's interests or instructions, usually with wrongful or dishonest intent. It becomes embezzlement when any attempt is made to conceal such misuse by giving false explanations or by falsifying records. These offences may be committed against individuals or organisations.

When a person misuses a position of trust for personal gain it is defalcation. It applies to employees who commit theft, misappropriation or embezzlement against their employers. Defalcation by employees is one of the possible causes for losses, excess costs or inefficiency within an organisation.

On the other hand, management fraud may be perpetrated for the benefit of an organisation by a representative misusing ostensive authority. The organisation is then exposed to risks of damage to its reputation and probably prosecution for unlawful activity.

Staff defalcation

Defalcation by employees against their employers may include theft or misappropriation of the employer's cash, goods or other assets in the employee's custody. This would also include selling or misusing confidential information.

Cash appears prominently in the list of defalcations: this is because it is relatively easy to obtain by misrepresentation, readily usable and difficult to trace.

This is not necessarily true, however, of a bank-type fraud involving misappropriation of cash through high-speed transfer technology. Here the sheer volume of transactions and the large values may be perceived as providing a screen for misdirecting a single item so that it may escape detection.

Staff defalcation may include the following:

1. Teeming and lading cash receipts.
2. Pocketing cash received from credit customers, cash sales, sales of scrap, unauthorised sales of assets.
3. Pocketing cash received from realisation of unrecorded assets such as consumable tools or spares, bad debts written off, obsolete stock, fully depreciated equipment.
4. Stealing goods, returnable packaging or other assets.
5. Diverting cash or goods to a fictitious third party.

Attempts to conceal, which will make the offence embezzlement, include:

1. Altering vouchers, dockets or other records.
2. Suppressing sales invoices, raising false sales invoices or credit notes.

3. Creating ghost supplier accounts.
4. Generating dummy purchase invoices, suppressing supplier's credit notes.
5. Purchasing goods or services for personal use on the employer's credit including wrongful use of company credit cards.
6. Submitting false expense claims.
7. Creating ghost employees on the payroll.
8. Providing wage payments for overtime not worked, or unearned bonuses.
9. Falsifying bills of lading.
10. Allowing unauthorised price concessions or special services to favoured customers for a personal consideration.
11. Permitting unauthorised despatches of goods.
12. Accepting bribes from favoured suppliers.
13. Diverting the proceeds of special discounts from suppliers.
14. Forging signatures on cheques, bills of lading, documentary credits for external commitments.
15. Forging signatures on purchase invoices, expense claims, sales credits for internal approval.
16. Using the organisation's contacts or information in carrying on a competitive business.

Improper acts by managers for the benefit of the organisation as opposed to the individual may include:

1. Paying inducements to customers' staff to place preferential orders with the organisation.
2. Making false claims on suppliers for alleged deficiencies in delivery, quality or service.
3. Making false charges to customers for work not done or goods not supplied.
4. Deliberate short delivery of goods or services to customers in terms of quantity or quality against specification, sample or advertised description.
5. Deliberate overcharging for goods or services against published or displayed prices.
6. Making false returns to H.M. Customs and Excise or the Inland Revenue with intent to evade payment of VAT, Corporation Tax, PAYE or National Insurance due.
7. Making false insurance claims.
8. Unauthorised use of intellectual property belonging to other parties.

External fraud

Every organisation may be vulnerable to fraud which could be perpetrated against it by persons outside the organisation. Such persons are those who need to have some knowledge of the organisation's control systems and procedures or access to its property in the course of a normal business relationship. This includes suppliers and customers and their staff.

These offences may also be perpetrated by the organisation's own employees against other organisations with which the employer has dealings such as customers and suppliers. There may also be collusion between the staff of separate organisations in pursuing improper gains from their mutual transactions.

Depending on the scale of risk, measures designed to safeguard the organisation against these risks may include personal vetting and requiring adherence to specific disciplinary procedures. Such measures should be seen to provide equivalent safeguards for the organisation and for the individuals by providing protection against wrongful accusation when something has gone wrong.

External fraud may, however, also be perpetrated by persons who may have some knowledge of the organisation but no direct connection with it. This category includes competitors and past employees: both could, on occasion, be strongly motivated to take advantage of weaknesses in the organisation's defences. Protection against risks of this kind needs to be pursued with particular vigilance in the absence of any disciplinary authority over those in a position to perpetrate such offences.

Risks attributable to external fraud may include:

1. Short delivery by a supplier's van driver where control of goods inwards is known to be weak.
2. Supply of inferior quality material where quality testing is known to be weak.
3. Presentation of false statements of work done on construction, maintenance or servicing contracts where contract control is known to be weak.
4. 'Cube cutting' by a freight agency handling export shipping requirements. By falsifying the

documents, the agency collects at a higher tariff from its client than it pays to the shipper.

5. Theft of merchandise from retail stores, euphemistically described as stock shrinkage.

6. Procurement of goods or services on credit by a business entity which has been set up for the purpose of a specific fraudulent activity such as long-term fraud.

7. Procurement by a customer of goods or services against a stolen credit card or a forged or worthless cheque.

8. Submission of false claims by a customer for short delivery, inferior quality or damaged merchandise.

9. Misuse of privileged information against the organisation by persons entrusted with knowledge to be used for its benefit. This may include passing commercially sensitive information to competitors, using financially sensitive information for private gain or maliciously misusing computer access codes.

10. Misuse of stolen information against the organisation. The risks are similar to those for privileged information, but less controllable.

Management fraud

The expression management fraud is generally used in relation to deliberate distortion of financial statements and other reports which are intended to mislead recipients about management performance.

Motivation for management fraud may be personal gain such as a bonus incentive, promotion prospects, or simply to avoid the opprobrium of unsatisfactory performance. In other cases there may be corporate motivation such as evading tax liabilities or concealing corporate activities which may be irregular, unauthorised or unlawful.

Serious corporate fraud also includes dishonestly issuing a false financial statement or a false prospectus with intention to mislead in order to maintain a share price, avoid take-over threats, attract new capital, etc. The Companies Acts provide severe penalties for these serious criminal offences. Dishonest falsification of records or reports by persons entrusted with the responsibility for managing an organisation is an example

of serious fraud which may be particularly difficult to detect.

It represents a breach of trust in which the perpetrator is usually in a position to manipulate records by altering, removing or destroying all evidence likely to conflict with the false position presented.

The reasons for dishonest misrepresentation of the organisation's activities or performance could be:

1. To avoid criticism for unsatisfactory performance.

2. To influence performance-related management remuneration.

3. To secure benefits or advantageous consideration for the organisation or its management which might not be forthcoming if the true position were disclosed. The incentive could be benefits such as bank facilities, supplier credit, sales contracts, prestigious awards or grants from public funds.

4. To mislead by denying the true facts to other parties perceived as being in a position to misuse them to the disadvantage of the organisation. It could be competitors, creditors, take-over predators, customers or even employees.

5. To hide unlawful, unauthorised or otherwise unacceptable activity.

Examples of management fraud include the following:

1. Suppression or destruction of documents which would provide evidence of activity different from that recorded or reported.

2. Falsification of documents or other evidence to support fictitious records or reports.

3. Collusion with third parties to generate documentation which provides misleading or false evidence to support fictitious records or reports.

4. Overstating reported profitability. This may be accomplished by:
   (a) suppressing purchase invoices to understate costs;
   (b) taking credit for fictitious sales;
   (c) overstating or overvaluing stock;
   (d) underestimating accruing liabilities or pro-

visions for losses such as bad debts or obsolescence of stock or equipment;

(e) manipulation of accounting cut-off procedures so that income and expenditure are not matched. For instance: taking credit for sales delivered around the end of the accounting period, for which the related costs are left to be accounted for after the period end; or taking raw materials into stock but omitting the liability to pay for them. Continuous distortion of profitability by such practices is likely to result in some form of teeming and lading on a progressively increasing scale.

Such distortions should be clearly distinguished from soundly based accounting practices such as taking credit in monthly accounts for accruing profits on uncompleted long-term contracts, which may be necessary to present fair and reasonable reports of the progress of profitability where the reporting cycle is materially shorter than that of the business activity.

5. Issuing false financial statements with intent to mislead shareholders, Inland Revenue and anyone entitled to receive copies or to inspect such statements on public record. This entitlement is in many cases prescribed by the law applicable to companies, building societies, charities, trusts, public bodies, etc. In some cases the law also provides some protection for the recipient by requiring the statements to be accompanied by an independent audit certificate.

6. Issuing a false prospectus. This is a serious criminal offence: anyone committing it is also exposed to claims for damages from those who have incurred losses as a result of being misled by the prospectus. Special care must be taken to ensure that all statements made in a prospectus inviting public subscription of capital for the organisation are not only accurate but that they are also presented fairly and unambiguously. This applies equally to the record of past performance and the current financial status, to any estimates given for future performance, and to all details published about the organisation and its management and how the new capital is to

be used. Failure to take all reasonable steps to ensure that all the information given is true and fair will leave those responsible for issuing the prospectus at risk.

Criminal fraud

Criminal fraud is that which is punishable by conviction in a criminal court.

There are a number of criminal frauds which particularly concern business operations. These include the following:

1. **Fraudulent trading** It is a criminal offence to continue to trade and incur debts after the trader or the directors of the trading company have become aware that the business is insolvent: that is to say, when it is unable to meet its liabilities as they fall due.

2. **Long-term fraud** This is a form of fraud where credit is the essence of the activity. Complex schemes of deception are devised to obtain goods on credit with no real intention of paying for them. When the maximum quantity of goods has been taken, the perpetrator absconds without paying and disposes of the goods through obscure outlets from whence they are unlikely to be traced.

3. **Investment fraud** This involves dishonestly inducing individuals to part with money for investment on false promises of attractive returns which never materialise.

4. **Insider dealing** This involves using privileged information about a company for personal gain derived from dealing in the company's shares. The information concerned has to be in the price-sensitive category and may be within the privileged knowledge of directors, employees, auditors, bankers and advisors of the company.

Computer fraud

A distinction needs to be made between those common frauds which may be computer-assisted and true computer frauds in which programs or computer-stored data are manipulated to misappropriate funds or other resources. It is most likely to be users who perpetrate computer-assisted fraud, whereas specialist computer staff skills are necessary for true computer fraud.

A survey conducted by BIS Computer Systems Ltd and reported in 1984 found that most perpetrators of computer fraud were users rather than computer staff. The most common frauds were:

1. Fraudulent adjustments to transactions.
2. Adding bogus transactions.
3. Unauthorised changes to records.
4. Granting unauthorised discounts.
5. Creating bogus suppliers.
6. Creating ghost employees.
7. Charging for fictitious services.
8. Extracting money from customer accounts.

A survey by the UK government audit inspectorate reported in 1984 found only one true computer fraud in 77 cases examined; the remainder were computer-assisted frauds.

Michael Cowen in *Professional Administration*, June 1979, listed, in descending order of probability, the eight main ways in which computers might be used to perpetrate or conceal fraudulent acts. The first five are computer-assisted frauds; the last three are true computer frauds:

Computer-assisted frauds

1. False input of transaction data, transaction entry codes or communication transfers.
2. Failures, errors and delays in reconciling listings and balances.
3. False amendments to master files.
4. Manipulation of data into suspense accounts, exceptions and errors.
5. Manipulation, diversion or destruction of output.

True computer frauds

6. Diversion of processing to a false program or false data source by the use of irregular job control instructions or language.
7. Unauthorised amendment to an application program or the procedure for transaction processing.
8. Unauthorised amendment to computer operating system or hardware.

Falsification of input data or transaction codes is probably the simplest computer-assisted fraud to perpetrate; it is likely to be concealed in loosely controlled income and expenditure accounts.

Falsification of master file amendments is a more serious risk because the processing control totals will not be distorted and the amendment will continue to misdirect transaction processing without further intervention until discovered and corrected.

Unauthorised program patching is the most likely method for perpetrating true computer fraud. It would normally require advanced technical skill and it is quite possible that the motivation is the technical challenge rather than material gain.

One other type of computer-related fraud is unauthorised use or sale of computer time. In addition to the leakage of resources, this practice could impose restrictions on the organisation's computing capacity. Since it is not visible it may be difficult to detect.

The defence against computer fraud has to be constructed on the basis of a comprehensive system of sound control procedures and firmly applied disciplines to ensure that they are strictly observed. The control procedures should incorporate rules for preparation and validation of input data and safeguards for access to input devices, access to applications, access to master files and distribution of output.

At the same time it is necessary to ensure that all users are properly trained in the operation of the systems they use and are fully aware of what is expected of them. They need to be properly motivated in the use of these systems and their controls, and all controls should be properly policed. The principles of segregation of duties and internal checking remain valid for computerised systems.

Responsibilities

General management

Primary responsibility for prevention and detection of fraud within an organisation rests firmly with the management. This responsibility has to be addressed by establishing and maintaining effective control systems and procedures and by cultivating an environment of fraud prevention. Internal audit is a key management tool for achieving this aim.

Internal audit

The objective of internal auditing is to assist members of the organisation in the effective discharge of their responsibilities. . . . (Extract from IIA–UK Statement of Responsibilities of Internal Auditing.)

The internal auditor must evaluate fraud in terms of the measures necessary to safeguard the organisation against all risks, including fraud, whether criminal or otherwise. The Institute of Internal Auditors has issued extensive guidance on the responsibilities of internal auditors in relation to fraud and other irregularities:

Fraud encompasses an array of irregularities and illegal acts characterised by intentional deception. It can be perpetrated for the benefit of or to the detriment of the organisation and by persons outside as well as inside the organisation.

Fraud designed to benefit the organisation generally produces such benefit by exploiting an unfair or dishonest advantage that also may deceive an outside party. Perpetrators of such frauds usually benefit indirectly, since personal benefit usually accrues when the organisation is aided by the act.

Fraud perpetrated to the detriment of the organisation generally is for the direct or indirect benefit of an employee, outside individual or another firm.
(Extracts from IIA–UK Guideline 280.01)

Due professional care

In exercising due professional care, internal auditors should be alert to the possibility of intentional wrongdoing, errors and omissions, inefficiency, waste, ineffectiveness and conflicts of interest.

They should also be alert to those conditions and activities where irregularities are most likely to occur. In addition they should identify inadequate controls and recommend improvements to promote compliance with acceptable procedures and practices.
(Extracts from IIA–UK Guideline 280.01)

Due care implies reasonable care and competence, not infallibility or extraordinary performance. Due care requires the auditor to conduct examinations and verifications to a reasonable extent, but does not require detailed audits of all transactions. Accordingly the auditor cannot give absolute assurance that non-compliance or irregularities do not exist. Nevertheless, the possibility of material irregularities or non-compliance should be considered whenever the internal auditor undertakes an internal auditing assignment.

Detection of fraud consists of identifying indicators sufficient to warrant recommending an investigation. These indicators may arise as a result of controls established by management, tests conducted by auditors, and other sources both within and outside the organisation.

In conducting audit assignments, the internal auditor's responsibilities for detecting fraud are:

(a) To have sufficient knowledge of fraud to be able to identify indicators that fraud might have been committed. This knowledge includes the need to know the characteristics of fraud, the techniques used to commit fraud and the types of fraud associated with the activities audited.

(b) To be alert to opportunities, such as control weaknesses, that could allow fraud. If significant control weaknesses are detected, additional tests conducted by internal auditors should include tests directed towards identification of other indicators of frauds. Some examples of indicators are: unauthorised transactions, override of controls, unexplained pricing exceptions and unusually large product losses. Internal auditors should recognise that the presence of more than one indicator at any one time increases the probability that fraud might have occurred.

(c) To evaluate the indicators that fraud might have been committed and decide whether any further action is necessary or whether an investigation should be recommended.

(d) To notify the appropriate authorities within the organisation if a determination is made that there are sufficient indicators of the commission of a fraud to recommend an investigation.

Internal auditors are not expected to have knowledge equivalent to that of a person whose primary responsibility is detecting and investigating fraud. Also, audit procedures alone, even when carried out with due professional care, do not guarantee that fraud will be detected.
(IIA–UK Guideline 280.02)

When an internal auditor suspects wrongdoing, the appropriate authorities within the organisation should be informed. The internal auditor may recommend whatever investigation is considered necessary in the circumstances. Thereafter the auditor should follow up to see that the internal auditing department's responsibility has been met.
(IIA–UK Guideline 280.03)

Safeguarding assets

Internal auditors are responsible for assisting in the deterrence of fraud by examining and evaluating the adequacy and effectiveness of control, commensurate with the extent of the potential exposure/risk in the various segments of the organisation's operations. In carrying out this responsibility, internal auditors should, for example determine whether:

(a) The organisational environment fosters control consciousness;
(b) Realistic organisational goals and objectives are set;
(c) Written policies (e.g. code of conduct) exist that describe prohibited activities and the action required whenever violations are discovered;
(d) Appropriate authorisation policies for transactions are established and maintained;
(e) Policies, practices, procedures, reports and other mechanisms are developed to monitor activities and safeguard assets, particularly in high-risk areas;
(f) Communication channels provide management with adequate and reliable information;
(g) Recommendations need to be made for the establishment or enhancement of cost-effective controls to help deter fraud.

(Extract from IIA–UK Guideline 330.01)

Once a fraud investigation is concluded, internal auditors should assess the facts known in order to:

(a) Determine if controls need to be implemented or strengthened to reduce future vulnerability;
(b) Design audit tests to help disclose the existence of similar frauds in future;
(c) Help meet the internal auditor's responsibility to maintain sufficient knowledge of fraud and thereby be able to identify future indicators of fraud.

(Extract from IIA–UK Guideline 330.02)

Internal audit planning

When conducting fraud investigations, internal auditors should:

(a) Assess the probable level and the extent of complicity in the fraud within the organisation. This can be critical to ensure that the internal auditor avoids providing information to, or obtaining misleading information from, persons who may be involved.
(b) Determine the knowledge, skills, and disciplines needed to carry out the investigation effectively. Assess the qualifications and the skills of the internal auditors and of the specialists available to participate in the investigation to ensure it is conducted by individuals having the appropriate type and level of technical expertise. This should include assurances on such matters as professional certifications, licences, reputation and that there is no relationship to those being investigated or to any of the employees or management of the organisation.
(c) Design procedures to follow in attempting to identify the perpetrators, extent of the fraud, techniques used and cause of the fraud.

(d) Co-ordinate activities with management personnel, legal counsel and other specialists as appropriate throughout the investigation.
(e) Be cognisant of the rights of alleged perpetrators and personnel within the scope of the investigation and the reputation of the organisation itself.

(IIA–UK Guideline 410.02)

Internal audit reporting

An interim or final report may be desirable at the conclusion of the detection phase of a fraud. The report should include the internal auditor's conclusion as to whether sufficient information exists to conduct an investigation. It should also summarise findings that serve as the basis for such decision.

(a) When the incidence of significant fraud has been established to a reasonable certainty, management or the board should be notified immediately.
(b) The results of a fraud investigation may indicate that fraud has had a previously undiscovered materially adverse effect on the financial position and results of operations for one or more years on which financial statements have already been issued. Internal audit should inform appropriate management and the board of directors of such discovery.
(c) A written report should be issued at the conclusion of the investigation phase. It should include all findings, conclusions, recommendations and corrective action taken.
(d) A draft of the proposed report on fraud should be submitted to legal counsel for review.

(IIA–UK Guideline 430.01.3)

Fraud prevention

Climate of honesty

Crime is contagious. . . . The company that creates the right climate of honesty can reduce crime. It can ensure that the factors unfavourable to crime exceed those favourable to it. (Comer, 1987)

Crime will flourish in a climate in which it is condoned, but it will quickly come to be perceived as repugnant in a climate where honesty and probity are actively encouraged as an integral feature of the pursuit of efficiency.

A climate of honesty reflects the leadership quality of top management in setting the tone and encouraging exemplary standards of probity throughout the organisation. It is the first essential in fraud prevention. The top management must make it absolutely clear that fraud will not be tolerated under any circumstances and that any cases discovered will be prosecuted with the utmost severity.

Sound internal control procedures which are properly maintained and applied effectively will then provide the necessary foundation from which to cultivate an environment which discourages wrongdoing.

This will minimise opportunities for fraudulent activity and limit the extent of any which occurs. It must be supported by effective measures for fraud detection and for dealing fairly but firmly with any culprits when caught.

It is a responsibility of managers to be aware of particular problems of their subordinates. If a person has personal problems in the family with drink, gambling, taking drugs, etc., he or she may be at risk or a hazard for others with whom they work. In these circumstances a person under stress is likely to become more prone to temptation and may drift into the fraud syndrome.

It should be an essential element in the training of all managers to acknowledge the importance of knowing their subordinates as people so that they are aware of individual characteristics and able to recognise changes which could signal problems. A known open door policy is likely to encourage problem sharing.

Essential controls

Fraud prevention is a management responsibility. In discharging this responsibility the management can be greatly assisted through continuous evaluation of the organisation's control procedures by a competent, properly resourced internal audit department.

There is no ultimate secure system, but if all controls are sound, the chance of concealing a fraudulent act is low and there will be a high possibility of detection. Maintaining stringent controls in key areas may be costly and this has to be weighed against the scale of the risk. There are however some basic rules which can be applied to most organisations.

Rules for internal control

1. There should be a proper segregation of duties throughout the organisation.

2. There should be an independent complaints review procedure which should be designed to ensure that complaints from suppliers or customers do not automatically find their way to the clerical person dealing with that account. They should go, first, either to that person's superior or to a higher level of management.

3. There must be regular reconciliation of all suppliers' accounts with statements received and agreement with control accounts.

4. There must be regular agreement of all customers' accounts with control accounts, and reconciliation of statements sent out with remittances received.

5. All stock accounts should be reconciled regularly with control accounts and agreed with actual quantities.

6. All receipts of money in cash or cheques must be banked intact on the day of receipt. The cash book records of every bank account must be reconciled regularly with the bank statements. Petty cash records should be examined regularly and the cash balance counted by the cashier's superior.

7. Cashiers should never be in a position to record any aspect of transactions other than the receipt or payment of cash for which they are responsible. A cashier should not have access to more than one cash fund.

8. There should be a formal system which ensures that all purchases are properly approved in all respects before commitment and that the receipt and acceptance of goods and acceptance of invoices are independently matched against the approved purchase orders before paying the supplier.

9. There should be a formal system which ensures that every delivery of goods or service to a customer causes a sales invoice to be raised for the correct sales value so that it is properly accounted for as a sale and settled in due time.

10. There should be clear rules for hiring and firing

employees and for determining the remuneration paid to employees. Ideally this should be co-ordinated through a professionally staffed personnel function which maintains the detailed records of all employees independently from the pay office. Rules for recruitment should include taking up references and proof of qualifications. See Chapter 6, section 4.

11. There must be a clear policy for information management; and for every centralised data processing system, responsibility for use and authority for data input and access must be clearly defined.

12. Access to computer master files and their control and maintenance must be strictly regulated because of the critical information these files contain such as price lists, customer terms, individual rates of pay and so on. There should be formal procedures for the proper control of all master file amendments which ensure that no amendment can be made without proper authority and which provide proof listing of all amendments made so that if any unauthorised change slipped through the net, it could be traced.

Fraud detection

Detection of fraud is simply the process of exploring symptoms until sufficient evidence is uncovered to establish that fraud has been perpetrated and further investigation is seen to be necessary.

The objectives of the statutory auditor and the internal auditor are likely to differ in relation to fraud detection.

To the statutory auditor, the possibility of fraud imposes a threat to the truth and fairness of the view given by the financial statements on which he is required to express an opinion. He thus has a clear responsibility to apply due professional care in directing his audit examination to detect any errors or irregularities which might impair the truth and fairness of the view given by the financial statements.

The internal auditor's role is to assist management to achieve its targets economically, efficiently and effectively. The possibility of fraud is one of many potential causes of waste, inefficiency or frustration. The primary objective of internal auditing must be to identify weakness in management control systems where such leakage or losses could occur and to recommend means for reinforcement. This means being fully aware of fraud risks and keeping an alert mind for symptoms.

There are two important characteristics of fraud which help recognition of the symptoms. Firstly, fraud is fact and once perpetrated cannot be undone, nor can the record of it be expunged, however effectively it may be concealed. Secondly, fraud is aimed at achieving financial benefit and consequently it will have an impact on financial controls. Listed below are some common symptoms that may suggest irregular activity.

Performance symptoms

1. Declining profit margins.
2. High level of sales credits.
3. High bad debt experience.
4. Exceptional stock discrepancies.
5. Low material yields and high wastage.
6. Exceptional adverse cost variances.
7. Asset losses.
8. Unrecorded assets.

Accounting procedure symptoms

1. Breaches of the control systems – a matter for particular concern.
2. Failure to correct system deficiencies.
3. Evidence of unauthorised transactions.
4. Unusual recording of transactions.
5. Exceptional year-end transactions.
6. Documentary discrepancies.
7. Loosely controlled suspense accounts.
8. Numerous correcting entries.
9. Many altered, missing or destroyed records.
10. Many customer or supplier complaints.
11. Problems repeatedly passed to the same employee to resolve.
12. Lack of co-operation and difficulties in extracting audit information.
13. Glib or guarded replies.

Documentary symptoms

1. Photocopies in place of lost originals.
2. Inconsistency in authorising signatures.
3. Customer or supplier correspondence.
4. Altered documents which are not properly authorised.
5. Documents frequently missing from files.

Employee symptoms

1. Rewriting records.
2. Excessive overtime working.
3. Not taking full holidays.
4. Regular borrowing.
5. Cashing post-dated cheques.
6. Personal cheques dishonoured.
7. Living beyond means.
8. Regular gambler, heavy drinker, drug addict or known marital problems.
9. Personal visits from creditors or debtors.

Management fraud symptoms

1. Working capital shortage may be due to diversion of funds.
2. High staff turnover in financial and other key positions may lead to lack of continuity in control practices so that irregularities can escape detection.
3. When key material requirements are always procured from the same supplier, the reasons call for close scrutiny.
4. Exceptionally high levels of travelling and entertainment costs should be examined to verify that they are both fully justified and properly approved.
5. Maintaining a complex pattern of separate bank accounts, or generating excessive movement of funds between subsidiary or associated organisations, may be symptoms of some sophisticated form of teeming and lading or 'window dressing'.
6. Debt collection problems could be a symptom that the organisation is not receiving all the monies paid by its customers. Consideration should be given to the methods by which it

may be possible for debtors' settlements to be diverted.

7. Downward trends in performance may be a symptom of misappropriation of resources. It will also signify that the management is under pressure to improve performance. The temptation to present results in a better light than they really are should not be overlooked.
8. Delayed reporting is often a sign that all is not well.
9. Unexplained asset losses should always be a cause for concern. Whether the loss is attributable to theft, misappropriation or fraudulent conversion, it is a manifestation of inadequate safeguarding.
10. Effective team management based upon shared responsibility and mutual trust among the team members provides an element of insurance against management fraud. The risk is greater in organisations where the management is dominated by one individual.
11. Operational audit techniques can be very effective in detecting misleading information caused by management fraud.

Fraud detection enquiries

1. Good working relationships are especially critical to successful enquiries when there is any suspicion of irregularity.
2. Take due note of the moral climate of the organisation as a whole. Its success depends upon good team work within a fabric of trust.
3. Beware of paranoia. Whilst it is necessary to be fully alert to the possibilities of irregular activity, it is also important to keep an open mind. The internal auditor must be on guard against any tendency to disbelieve automatically everyone who indulges in gambling or drinking or who appears to have an extravagant life-style.
4. The rules of interviewing are particularly important when pursuing enquiries which could lead to disclosure of irregular activities. All questions should be so framed that they require something more than a 'yes' or 'no' answer. Never accept the first glib answer. Clarify any

ambiguity before going on. When something looks wrong, persist until a satisfactory answer is obtained.

5. The internal auditor must protect the identity of his information sources. Do not trust uncorroborated information volunteered by an informer, but do not ignore it.

6. Fraud is often perpetrated by the person with the most obvious credentials. When concealment is suspected, consider first the person with best access to a course of concealment and whose guilt would have been obvious without concealment.

7. Concentrate on the weakest point in the possible fraud chain.

8. Many frauds are simple and often obvious. Consider first the easiest path of the steal – convert – conceal theme. Do not overlook the obvious opportunities. Start with the simplest solution and, if that does not succeed, progress to the next most simple and so on, step by step.

9. Keep a sharp look-out for irregular entries and be particularly wary of altered entries, amended documents, photocopies and duplicate documents and especially addresses with only a post office box number.

10. Do not overlook unrecorded funds such as staff clubs. These could be serving as a reservoir for sustaining teeming and lading activity.

11. Consider carefully the audit sampling techniques to be used. It may be necessary to choose a very much larger sample if a fraud investigation proves to be necessary. Special care is necessary in selecting the population so that it can be stratified to isolate the probable area of defalcation.

Fraud investigation

Once the internal auditor has established that there is a fraud to be investigated, he must report at the earliest opportunity to the most senior executive of the organisation. It is then necessary to agree the level of investigation to be undertaken and the resources to be applied to it. These are issues to be resolved by senior management. Detailed fraud investigation is painstaking, time-consuming work which may require special technical knowledge or experience of the area involved. In most cases some internal auditing involvement will be appropriate.

There is a legal requirement to inform the police in the United Kingdom when evidence of fraud has been uncovered. The police will probably wish to initiate their own investigation and it is therefore important that enquiries are properly co-ordinated.

The aim of the investigation is to determine the extent of the fraud, how it was perpetrated, and by whom. The internal auditor will have three specific goals:

1. To ensure that the perpetrator is caught.
2. To ensure that the evidence necessary to prove the charges is collected and verified.
3. To ensure that the method used to perpetrate the offence is exposed and clearly understood so that safeguards can be implemented to ensure that it cannot be repeated.

Investigation techniques

1. Trend analysis

This is a diagnostic tool of operational auditing. Projections of future performance are analysed and compared with previous performance. The technique is to chart the operating data for the period under examination against that for the control period. Individual items of cost are compared and all variances investigated. It often reveals the first indication of inflated or depressed figures. It is important when using this tool that all evidence is fully corroborated by testing and inspection. This technique is particularly useful when applied to short periods of risk such as holiday periods and when applied to periods of high activity when controls would normally be expected to be under strain.

2. Proportional analysis

This is also a tool of operational auditing. The auditor seeks to establish the relationship between one set of costs and another, for example: between freight and shipment of products, or between material used and product produced.

The technique is to compare the relationship for the period under examination with that for a selected control period. It can also be used to examine the relationship of what is happening with what should be happening, calculated on a standard basis.

The technique can also be used to measure performance in the period under examination against that of comparable organisations in the same sector. This is a basic requirement where unfair trading is suspected from outside parties or by employees of the organisation.

3. Critical point auditing

This is a process of isolating for detailed examination those transactions most vulnerable to fraud or manipulation. The technique is to filter out from the transactions passing through the organisation, those with characteristics which identify them as being most vulnerable to irregularities so that these can be re-examined in detail. The filtration process examines all information in monetary or statistical terms and looks at particular risk areas. The technique examines specifically those areas of account differences which could be expected to arise from incorrectly handled or suppressed debits or credits and the areas where these would show discrepancies in the individual account statements.

4. Spot checking

This is a technique which can be used for both detection testing and investigation. The main financial institutions have used spot checking of cash balances as a method of satisfying themselves that their systems of control over cash are operating properly. There have nevertheless been many successful misappropriations from banks. The spot check is more a deterrent than a detection technique. It does, however, help to identify weak controls in cash management.

5. Invigilation and created checks

With this technique a current performance standard is established for the suspect area by applying such tight control for a test period that no irregularity could pass undetected.

Performance for previous periods is then measured against this standard and deviations investigated for evidence of irregularity. Surveillance of the area should continue after relaxing the test period controls.

6. Observation

The objective of any surveillance is to report precisely what happens and to catch the culprits in the act, if possible. It may be tedious or boring and, very occasionally, dangerous.

There are many techniqes available to match varying surveillance requirements. Most of the basic techniques are simple and can be adopted without specific training or prior experience. The more sophisticated devices, however, such as remotely controlled video recorders, infra-red cameras, etc., may require specialist skills.

It is critical to select observers for surveillance with great care for their suitability for the particular investigation.

It is important to obtain prior agreement of the management to carry out the surveillance work and to define precisely the area to be covered. It should be restricted to as small an area of the organisation as possible which should be self-contained.

7. Undercover investigation

This is specialised surveillance which should not be attempted by an amateur. It should only be adopted when there are well-founded suspicions of a major fraud involving a number of people and significant risk to the organisation. The specialist investigator's terms as to anonymity and the length of the surveillance period must be scrupulously observed. Any departure from the agreed terms or any attempt to make contact with the investigator may frustrate the investigation and could endanger the investigator.

8. Technical and forensic examinations

These may be necessary for proving the method by which loss has been sustained. They often require access to laboratory facilities. They would be appropriate where stolen product has been used by competitors in their own production, or repackaged. In some computer fraud cases forensic evidence may be required from expert witnesses in testifying to the operation of the hardware or software.

Conduct of investigations

1. Objectives

Objectives should be determined by the organisation in consultation with professional advisors. Four issues must be addressed:

(a) criminal prosecution;
(b) civil recovery of losses;
(c) dismissal of employees;
(d) preventive action.

2. Secrecy

When a fraud has been detected, the specific facts must be kept secret until an arrest can be made. All knowledge of it must be strictly limited to the top management and those directly involved in the investigation.

Suspicions must be treated with the utmost discretion to avoid the risk of libel action and the possibility of the culprit absconding.

3. Immediate action

It may be necessary to make some guesses in the early stages of an investigation in order to get it started off in a reasonable direction. It is most important, however, not to prejudge guilt by attempting to make the facts fit a predetermined crime theory.

Arrangements may well have to be made for documents and other records to be secured or for employees' duties to be suspended, and dealings with customers or suppliers may have to be rearranged in some way so as to conceal the investigation.

4. Police involvement

There is a legal requirement to inform the police whenever evidence of a criminal act is discovered. If the main objective is to obtain a conviction, it is wise to inform the police as soon as there is sufficient evidence that a fraud has been perpetrated so that an early arrest can be made. However, if the co-operation of the culprit is

needed to arrive at an accurate assessment of the loss for an insurance claim, there may be a case for delaying the arrest.

If the sum involved exceeds £1m, the Serious Fraud Office has a statutory right to take over the investigation.

5. Analysing documents

An investigation requires a thorough professional examination and analysis of all records and other documents associated with the suspected fraud. The purpose is:

(a) to prove the extent of the loss;
(b) to establish the cause of the loss and the methods used;
(c) to identify responsibility and possible guilty knowledge.

This analysis should cover:

(a) all records of movement of assets or information during the period under investigation;
(b) all the correspondence relating to these movements;
(c) all formal records handled by suspects;
(d) all private or informal records within the control of suspects.

A search of a suspect's desk, files or other records often uncovers useful information which can shorten the investigative work.

The process of analysis of the relevant documents and records should focus on possible evidence of manipulation. This may include erased or crossed out figures, inconsistent inks, typefaces, handwriting and evidence of old documents being re-used or duplicated.

6. Interviews with witnesses

The whole of the evidence needed to prove that a fraud has been perpetrated will not necessarily be in recorded or documentary form. Verbal evidence frequently contributes essential elements of the case and corroborative details will usually be required from witnesses to place documentary evidence in an appropriate perspective.

Verbal evidence from witnesses may be necessary for a number of reasons:

(a) to prove loss;
(b) to establish responsibility;

(c) to confirm the method of the fraud;

(d) to establish the guilty intent of the suspect;

(e) to establish the basic credentials of witnesses;

(f) to reveal areas of discrepancy affecting other witnesses' statements and documentary evidence.

The skilled interviewer will get to know the witness over one or more interviews and will be able to assess the reliability of that witness and of the evidence in terms of a possible prosecution. A note of personal views added after closing the record of the interview as to character, reliability, likely performance in the witness box, may assist counsel who will present the case in court.

Witnesses should be interviewed away from fellow employees. If possible, interviewer and interviewee should both be positioned so that there is no likelihood of distraction for either of them from the windows. Care must be taken to ensure that the interview is not likely to be interrupted. A quiet place away from all distracting sounds of normal business activity is essential and telephones should be disconnected.

The interviewer must maintain control throughout the interview to obtain the information required. The witness must have the opportunity to tell his own story in his own way.

The investigator must be alert to the possibility of distorted or false evidence from a witness with a prejudiced viewpoint due to jealousy, spite or some other vendetta. It is not unknown for a witness to perceive the interview as an opportunity for a vindictive attack or to promote his own sense of self-importance.

It is wise to have the witness's statement vetted by the legal advisor before it is signed.

7. Interviews with suspects

The rules of evidence as prescribed in Sections 68 to 82 of the Police and Criminal Evidence Act 1984 apply to the questioning of all persons suspected of having committed a criminal offence. There are also guidelines which the courts will apply in determining the admissibility of oral or written statements made by witnesses. It is wise for the fraud investigator to be guided by competent legal advice on the conduct of any interview with a person suspected of involvement in fraudulent activity.

Conditions for interviewing a suspect should be the same as those described for interviewing a witness. It is particularly important to ensure privacy, absence of distractions and interruptions and to maintain control of the interview.

All admissions must be freely made, with no indication of coercion, pressure or threats.

Subsidiary aims when interviewing a suspect may include establishing the method used and identifying accomplices and the part played by them or the receivers of stolen property.

(a) Preliminary interview

There will usually be a preliminary interview with any suspected party, conducted as for interviewing a witness. At this interview, the activities for which the interviewee is responsible should be identified. The interviewer should seek to obtain an original explanation of events for comparison with known facts and subsequent statements.

(b) Final interview

The purpose of this interview is to obtain admission of guilt or proof of the guilty action. It is particularly advisable to conduct this interview on a one to one basis. A witness may be present but should remain outside the suspect's angle of vision. The interviewer must remain in control throughout, conducting the interview at his pace and on his terms.

The interviewer must remember that the interviewee has a common law right to leave the interview at any time and if restrained, could bring an action for wrongful arrest even if guilty. The question of arrest should be left to the police.

The whole interview should be private: the interviewer should sit as close as possible to the suspect. Notes should not be taken during the interview unless a warning has been given. It is likely to be distracting to both the interviewer and the suspect, and the notes so taken may not be admissible evidence. In many cases the evidence needed for prosecution will already be available by this stage.

The interviewer must emphasise that his sole objective is to discover the truth. He must remain calm and polite at all times and avoid any manifestation of emotion, sarcasm or humour. He must be particularly careful to use language which is simple, direct and unambiguous. He must take care to ensure that what he says is understood by the suspect. It is especially important not to use emotive words or phrases. Provocative words like lie, steal or thief are likely to be perceived as assertions of guilt and all such words must be avoided. The interviewer should instead use words indicating his disbelief.

8. Documentation

Every investigation eventually results in a written report. It may be a report to management on the causes and methodology of the fraud with recommendations for preventing recurrence.

Alternatively, it may a statement of the evidence uncovered supporting a full and detailed description of what happened, intended as a brief for legal representation in criminal proceedings or in support of an insurance claim.

It is essential, both for the security of the investigation and for a successful outcome, that full and proper records are maintained in an orderly and sequential fashion. This will facilitate preparation of the final report and ensure that nothing of importance gets left out. It also enables the work to continue if for any reason there has to be a change of investigator.

Spiral-bound index books are suitable for making a permanent record of all interviews in sequence as they occur, with appropriate references to all relevant documentary evidence. Loose-leaf note books in which pages can be changed are not acceptable for providing evidence in court.

(a) Collecting and examining documents

The first rule must be to obtain all documents that might possibly be relevant. Any subsequently found not to be required can be returned, whereas documents not collected but later found to be needed may by then have been destroyed, mutilated or removed, and evidence lost.

All documents collected should be listed, stating the place where the document was found, the name of the person who removed it, and the date of removal.

Documents already bound in binders or bundles should not be separated, but the contents of each bundle should be listed identifying each separate document.

All documents collected should be copied front and back and only the copies used as working documents. The originals should not be marked or written on or fastened together. They should be kept secure and separate from the copies and beyond the reach of suspects.

One individual should carry out the examination of all documents so that there can be no conflict of opinion at a later stage. Detailed notes of the examination should be made for permanent record in the investigation note book.

No original document which is relevant to the investigation should be returned to the custody of the suspects until after the investigation and after the resulting proceedings have been completed.

(b) Interview reports

A standard report format for interviewing witnesses will assist analysis and collation of verbal evidence.

9 External audit

The nature of external audit

There is an important conceptual difference between internal auditing and most external auditing. Whereas internal auditing may be concerned with the efficiency and effectiveness of management activity and operations, external auditing concentrates on the truth and fairness of financial reporting.

This difference is reflected in the definition of audit developed by the Auditing Practices Committee (APC) and approved and adopted by the Councils of the governing bodies of the Consultative Council of Accountancy Bodies (CCAB). The role of APC is to develop standards and guidelines for the practice of auditing by professionally qualified accountants who are collectively represented by CCAB.

An audit is the independent examination of, and expression of opinion on, the financial statements of an enterprise. (When reading Auditing Standards and Guidelines, the term 'enterprise' should be read as embracing any form of entity, whether profit oriented or not.)

Unless the relevant Auditing Standard or Auditing Guideline indicates to the contrary, the term 'audit' applies:

(a) where there is a statutory requirement for the auditor to express an opinion in terms of whether the financial statements give a true and fair view (for example, audits under the Companies Acts or the Industrial and Provident Societies Acts);
(b) Where there is a statutory requirement for the auditor to express an opinion in terms other than whether the

financial statements give a true and fair view (for example audits of government departments or local authorities); and
(c) Where the terms and scope of the engagement are agreed between the auditor and his client (for example, the audit of a sole trader or partnership) or where they are specified in a legal document (for example, a trust deed).

(Extract from Explanatory Foreword to Auditing Standards and Guidelines approved by CCAB governing bodies; all other quotations in this chapter are taken from these Standards and Guidelines)

Independence is an essential condition in all auditing. In those cases where external auditing is a statutory requirement the law generally specifies the conditions to be met to ensure the necessary degree of independence. In some cases an acceptable level of competence and degree of professional integrity are also implied by requiring the office of auditor to be held only by members of specified professional bodies.

Categories of external audit

UK Companies Acts

Audit of the statutory accounts of companies incorporated under the UK Companies Acts accounts for a major part of external audit work in the United Kingdom.

The directors of UK companies are required to prepare and submit to members an annual report and accounts. The accounts have to be examined by an independent auditor appointed by the members in general meeting who is required to report to the members and express an opinion on the truth and fairness of the accounts.

The qualification required for appointment as auditor of a UK registered company is membership of one of four accountancy bodies specified in the Companies Act 1985; these are:

1. The Institute of Chartered Accountants in England and Wales.
2. The Institute of Chartered Accountants of Scotland.
3. The Chartered Association of Certified Accountants.
4. The Institute of Chartered Accountants in Ireland.

None of the following persons is qualified for appointment as auditor of a company:

1. An officer or servant of the company.
2. A person who is a partner of or in the employment of an officer of the company.
3. A body corporate. But following the EC Eighth Directive on company law, the Companies Act 1989 permits the appointment of a body corporate as auditor provided that body satisfies defined conditions of ownership and control to ensure independence and competence.

The financial statements or annual accounts of companies on which the auditor has to express an opinion are required to give a true and fair view of the profit or loss and in some cases of the source and application of funds of the company for a specified accounting period and of the state of its affairs at the end of the period. The Companies Acts specify a limited range of options for the format of the annual accounts and detailed disclosure requirements.

Most of the Statements of Standard Accounting Practice issued by the Accounting Standards Committee of CCAB have direct relevance to the content and presentation of the annual accounts of companies. There are also International Accounting Standards to be considered.

Companies with capital traded on the International Stock Exchange must complete a listing agreement which also imposes conditions on the content and publication of audited annual accounts. Other conditions apply if the capital is traded on other stock exchanges.

In fulfilling his primary duty to examine the annual accounts and express an opinion as to truth and fairness, the auditor must take account of compliance with all relevant requirements on form and content, accounting principles and listing conditions.

Building societies

Building societies are established to raise a fund by members' subscriptions for making advances to members upon security by way of mortgage of freehold or leasehold estate. They are subject to regulation under the Building Societies Act 1986 which provides for the appointment of auditors and sets out their statutory duties and rights. The duties are more extensive than those placed on auditors appointed under the Companies Act 1985. The Act requires building societies to establish and maintain systems of control, supervision and inspection and the directors must take the necessary steps to secure compliance.

The building society auditor is required to form an opinion on systems of control, supervision and inspection. In addition to expressing his opinion on these issues and on the truth and fairness of the annual accounts, the auditor is required to express an opinion on certain parts of the annual return to the Chief Registrar.

Charities

The Charities Act 1960 defines a charity as any institution, corporate or not, which is established exclusively for charitable purposes according to the laws of England and Wales and is subject to the control of the High Court.

The Act imposes a requirement on a charity to keep proper books of account and to prepare consecutive statements of account to account for stewardship of the funds entrusted to it by the public. An audit of these statements may be required by statute, by the charity itself or by the Charity Commissioners. In many cases an audit is not required.

The scope of the audit and the form of report to be given will depend on how the charity is constituted, for example:

1. By trust deed.
2. As an unincorporated association.
3. As a company limited by guarantee under the Companies Acts.
4. Under the Acts relating to friendly, industrial and provident societies.
5. By Royal Charter.
6. By special Act of Parliament.

The Charity Commissioners maintain the central register of charities. The Commissioners can request accounts of registered charities to be filed and they can also require the accounts to be audited.

For charities constituted under the Companies Acts, the Friendly, Industrial and Provident Societies Acts, and most special Acts of Parliament, minimum audit requirements are laid down by statute. In other cases the instrument constituting the charity will specify audit requirements, if any.

Housing associations
A housing association is a society established for the purpose of encouraging the construction or improvement of houses or hostels. Alternatively, it may be a body of trustees or a company. It may not trade for profit and its constitution should impose specific restrictions on its ability to raise capital and to pay interest or dividends. This description covers housing associations registered under the Housing Act 1964 and societies registered under the Friendly Societies Act 1965.

All are required by the relevant legislation to publish annual financial statements which disclose prescribed categories of information and generally give a true and fair view. All are subject to independent audit, and the specific audit requirements for each are laid down in the respective statutes.

Charitable housing associations registered under the Charities Act 1960 may also be required to publish annual accounts which are subject to independent audit.

Trade unions and employers' associations
The Trade Union and Labour Relations Act 1974 defines both trade unions and employers' associations and imposes obligations on them to prepare, and issue annually, audited financial statements.

Trade unions or employers' associations may be constituted under the provisions of the Companies Acts or of the Friendly Societies Act and will then have specific obligations to satisfy the accounting and audit requirements of the appropriate statutes.

In general, these organisations will be governed according to their respective rules. The accounting and audit requirements are prescribed by law.

Each must have a satisfactory system of accounting control, from which it prepares an annual statement of accounts in prescribed format presenting a true and fair view and forming part of the annual return to be filed with the Certification Officer.

Each must appoint an auditor who should report whether, in his opinion, the accounts give a true and fair view of the matters to which they relate. The auditor is required to report any case where, in his opinion, there has been a failure to satisfy the statutory requirements.

The 1974 Act requires each trade union or employers' association to file a copy of its rules annually with the Certification Officer for Trade Unions and Employers' Associations. One of the responsibilities of the Certification Officer is to see that trade unions and employers' associations keep accounting records, have their accounts properly audited, and submit annual returns.

Local government audit
The Audit Commission has been established as a central government service function to examine and report on the administrative activities of local government. This is external auditing but the role differs from most other external auditing: it is not confined to examination and reporting on prescribed financial statements where the prescriptive requirements for financial reporting define the audit scope.

The function of local authorities is to provide public services to a local community which are funded partially by raising local taxation but also from some allocation from central taxation. In the context of public accountability, the objective of providing optimum value for the money spent is paramount. Consequently this particular branch of external auditing has become known as value for money auditing.

The Audit Commission has clearly defined objectives and has developed its own strategy and methods for achieving them. In general they are concerned with evaluating the performance of local authorities in terms of economy, efficiency and effectiveness. Many of the auditing practices and techniques used in internal auditing are of course appropriate to this work and the particular elements to be considered are dealt with in more detail in Chapter 7 under the heading Value for money.

Auditing standards

The Auditing Practices Committee has developed two statements of standards for external auditing practice which have been explicitly approved by each of the CCAB governing bodies:

1. The auditor's operational standard.
2. The audit report.

Both of these standards, and the supporting guidelines, are required to be read in conjunction with a common explanatory foreword which includes the definition of an audit quoted above. It also outlines the scope of the standards and guidelines and defines the obligation of members to observe the auditing standards.

Members of the CCAB bodies who assume responsibility as auditors are expected to observe these standards, and apparent failure to do so may be enquired into by the appropriate committee established by the Council of the relevant accountancy body, and disciplinary action may result. Members are also advised that a court of law may, when considering the adequacy of the work of an auditor, take into account any pronouncements or publications which it thinks may be indicative of good practice: these auditing standards and guidelines are likely to be so regarded.

The auditor's operational standard

This auditing standard applies whenever an audit is carried out. It includes the following obligations:

1. The auditor should adequately plan, control and record his work.
2. The auditor should ascertain the enterprise's system of recording and processing transactions and assess its adequacy as a basis for the preparation of financial statements.
3. The auditor should obtain relevant and reliable audit evidence sufficient for him to draw reasonable conclusions therefrom.
4. If the auditor wishes to place reliance on any internal controls, he should ascertain and evaluate those controls and perform compliance tests on their operation.
5. The auditor should carry out such a review of the financial statements as is sufficient, in conjunction with the conclusions drawn from other audit evidence obtained, to give him a reasonable basis for his opinion on the financial statements.

This auditing standard is effective for the audit of financial statements relating to accounting periods starting on or after 1 April 1980.

The audit report

Part 1 – Statement of Auditing Standard
This auditing standard applies to all audit reports issued as a result of audits within the meaning of the Explanatory Foreword to Auditing Standards and Guidelines. Although this standard is not primarily intended to apply to other forms of report provided by auditors, many of the principles of this standard will normally be applicable to such reports.
The audit report should state clearly:
(a) the addressee;
(b) the financial statements audited;
(c) the auditing standards followed;
(d) the audit opinion;
(e) any other information or opinions prescribed by statutory or other requirements;
(f) the identity of the auditor; and
(g) the date of the report.
If the auditor is unable to express an audit opinion without reservation he should qualify his report by referring to all those matters which he considers to be material and about which he has reservations.
This Auditing Standard is effective for audit reports dated on or after 1 September 1989.

Part 2 of this standard consists of explanatory notes covering:

1. Standards followed.
2. The audit opinion.
3. Qualified audit reports.
4. Circumstances giving rise to a qualification.
5. Forms of qualification.
6. Disclosure of reasons for qualification.
7. Uncertainty and management representations.
8. Emphasis of matter.
9. Other information or opinions prescribed by statutory or other requirements.
10. Dating of the audit report.

Qualifications in audit reports

Qualification of the opinion on the financial statements should be expressed in a manner which leaves the reader in no doubt as to its meaning and its implications for an understanding of the financial statements. To promote a more consistent understanding of qualified reports the forms of qualification described in the explanatory notes to the standard should be used unless the auditor considers that to do so would fail to convey clearly the intended meaning.

The nature of the circumstances giving rise to a qualification of opinion will generally fall into one of two categories:

1. Where there is an uncertainty which prevents the auditor from forming an opinion on a matter (uncertainty).
2. Where the auditor is able to form an opinion on the matter but this conflicts with the view given by the financial statements (disagreement).

When the uncertainty or disagreement is material, the auditor must consider whether the effect is fundamental so as to undermine the view given by the financial statements taken as a whole.

The forms of qualification used in different circumstances are as follows:

1. Where there is uncertainty and:

   (a) the effect is material but not fundamental:
   'Subject to' opinion

   (b) the effect is fundamental:
   Disclaimer of opinion

2. Where there is disagreement and:
   (a) the effect is material but not fundamental:
   'Except for' opinion
   (b) the effect is fundamental: *Adverse opinion*

Errors and irregularities

Fraud and other irregularities are potential risks to the achievement of operational objectives to be explored and evaluated in the context of those objectives, so that appropriate safeguards can be applied. This is a responsibility of management.

The techniques are fully described in Chapter 8, which discusses in some detail the nature of fraud in its most common forms, where responsibility lies for fraud prevention and the philosophy and practices for constructing an effective defence against these risks. This chapter addresses the concern of external auditors whose primary responsibility is to make an independent examination of, and to express an opinion on, the financial statements of an enterprise in pursuance of their appointments or in compliance with any relevant statutory obligation.

When an external auditor uncovers evidence of potential errors or irregularity he has to make a judgement as to whether this could materially affect the truth and fairness of the financial statements. He would also normally discuss his findings with the appropriate level of management with a view to supporting management action to strengthen areas of weak control. If he judges the impact on the financial statements to be material and the management is not persuaded of the need for corrective action, his duty is to qualify his opinion on the statements.

An external auditor is not required to report any irregularities he has uncovered to the shareholders or to third parties and normally his duty of confidentiality debars him from so doing. However, there can be circumstances where the auditor is not bound by his duty of confidentiality and he may be legally bound to disclose the commission of a criminal offence if ordered to do so by a court. The auditor has a public duty to disclose information in his possession of any serious criminal offence, whether intended or already committed, if it is likely to cause serious harm to an individual or if it may affect a large number of people.

Reliance on internal audit

Relationships

Internal audit is an element of the internal control system set up by the management of an enterprise to examine, evaluate and report on accounting and other controls on operations. It exists either because of a management decision or in certain circumstances because of a statutory requirement.

Unlike the internal auditor who is an employee of the enterprise or a related enterprise, the external auditor is required to be independent of the enterprise, usually having a statutory responsibility to report on the financial statements giving an account of management's stewardship.
(Extracts from Auditing Guideline: Reliance on Internal Audit)

Although external auditors and internal auditors pursue different objectives, their audit judgements must be based on evidence collected from common sources. These include the auditee organisation's records of its transactions and the explanations given by its executives. There is then a prima-facie case for sharing some of the tasks of collecting and analysing audit evidence.

Co-operation between internal and external auditors depends upon mutual respect and trust. Each must fully understand the other's role and purpose and be in a position to judge fairly the quality standards applied in the other's work. It involves a degree of joint audit planning and regular consultation; and each making available to the other working papers and copies of all audit reports. This is all confidential information and so the arrangements must have full support from management. It is then likely to assist both, and to lead to a more efficient combined audit service for the benefit of the auditee organisation.

Scope for co-operation

Although the extent of the work of the external auditor may be reduced by placing reliance on the work of internal audit, the responsibility to report is that of the external auditor alone, and therefore is indivisible and is not reduced by this reliance.

As a result, all final judgements relating to matters which are material to the financial statements or other matters on which he is reporting, must be made by the external auditor.
(Extracts from Auditing Guideline: Reliance on Internal Audit)

The work of both kinds of auditors must take account of the operational activity of the organisation. Consequently, the greatest benefits from co-operation between auditors are likely to be achieved when audit planning is considered at a joint meeting with the management of the organisation.

1. Each of the auditors is able to take account of the other's audit plans in formulating his or her own, particularly in selecting areas to be examined on a rotational basis: the incidence of audit examination is an important factor in risk assessment.
2. A programme can be agreed for regular consultation to exchange information and monitor progress on common plans.
3. Unnecessary duplication of work in collecting audit evidence can be avoided.
4. In some cases detailed audit programmes may be modified to satisfy the requirements of both when this is feasible without compromising the original purpose.
5. Each auditor is able to take account of evidence uncovered by the other which may have relevance to audit judgements to be made concerning areas other than that for which it was collected.

Systems evaluation

The external auditor's primary interest in systems documentation and testing is to establish the degree of reliance that can be placed on information produced by the systems and its materiality in relation to the financial statements on which he has to express an opinion. In the course of evaluating control systems for this purpose, the external auditor may uncover weakness and he would normally report such findings to the accountable management.

Internal audit work to evaluate accounting systems and internal controls will also involve both documenting the systems and the associated compliance and substantive testing. The purpose of this work is to reassure the accountable management that the systems are sound and being properly used, or to recommend changes to overcome weakness uncovered by the audit.

This difference of focus may be reflected in variations in the audit techniques used and the emphasis given to certain elements of testing. With good co-operation between internal and external auditors, it is normally feasible to design audit tests which will satisfy both objectives without undue difficulty.

Assessing internal audit work

The degree of reliance the external auditor is prepared to place on internal audit work will depend upon his assessment of its effectiveness and relevance.

The external auditor has to be satisfied on these key criteria:

1. **Independence** This is established through organisational status and reporting responsibilities. Any constraints placed on the chief internal auditor or his staff need very careful consideration.
2. **Objective and scope** This is determined by the internal audit charter which should be confirmed by the highest level of management (for example a board resolution) and by the chief internal auditor's job description.
3. **Professional care** This is a reflection of how well the internal audit work is planned, controlled, recorded and reviewed.
4. **Technical competence** The work must be done by persons who have adequate training and experience in audit work.
5. **Reports** The test of effectiveness is whether or not management considers and acts upon internal audit reports.
6. **Resources** The internal audit function should be adequately staffed to fulfil its objectives.

Before placing reliance on internal audit work the external auditor must review the work and satisfy himself that the necessary standards are being maintained and that the work is being adequately controlled and recorded.

10 Audit committees

Introduction

An audit committee is a subcommittee of selected members of the board of directors of an organisation and answerable to that board. Its function normally includes assisting the board in the effective discharge of its responsibilities for public accountability, financial reporting and corporate control; it should have neither executive powers nor a supervisory role.

Although currently not prescribed by law, there is growing interest in the use of audit committees in the United Kingdom. This is due to two main factors:

1. The personal responsibilities of company directors and members of executive boards have been significantly extended by each successive Companies Act, by the Financial Services Act 1986, the Building Societies Act 1986 and the Banking Act 1987. There has also been growing concern about the accuracy and credibility of financial reporting and concern to ensure that management implementation of approved policies is properly controlled. These developments have led to increased pressures on directors to discharge their personal responsibilities effectively.
2. Financial services and activities have been expanding rapidly. There is significant growth in new financial markets and financial activities are being deregulated and becoming increasingly international. There is concern over 'insider dealing' and other irregularities in large organisations. All these developments have led to a greater public interest in propriety in both public and private sector operations.

Development

In the United States of America, a well-known insurance company has had an audit committee for more than one hundred years. The first public recognition of the importance of audit committees came from the Securities and Exchange Commission in 1972.

Then, in 1973, the New York Stock Exchange published a paper illustrating the advantages for a corporation whose stock was quoted on the exchange to have an audit committee. It was made a compulsory condition of listing from 30 June 1978, after the Foreign Corrupt Practices Act 1977 had imposed a statutory responsibility on the directors of publicly quoted corporations to maintain adequate internal control systems. The National Association of Securities Dealers Annotated Questions also introduced the obligation, for every corporation wishing to have its stock quoted nationally, to appoint an audit committee as a condition.

The National Commission on Fraudulent Financial Reporting (Treadway Commission) reporting in October 1987 expressed the opinion that the board of directors of each US corporation should be assisted by an appropriate organ in fulfilling its responsibilities as controller of the corporation's activities.

The Canadian Business Corporations Act requires every Canadian corporation which accepts deposits from the public to set up an audit committee.

In the United Kingdom a code of recommended practice for non-executive directors was published in April 1987 by PRO-NED, an organisation for the promotion of non-executive directors set up in 1982 by the Stock Exchange, CBI, The Bank of England and other financial institutions. The code suggests that the boards of quoted companies are most likely to be effective when comprised of able executive directors and strong independent non-executive directors and that the non-executive directors' task will be facilitated by the establishment of an audit committee.

The Bank of England published a consultative paper in January 1987 entitled 'The role of audit committees in banks'. It recommended that every bank should have an audit committee. The Financial Services Act 1986 and the Building Societies Act 1986 have assigned increased duties and responsibilities to boards of directors, particularly in relation to financial reporting and internal control. It is generally accepted that an audit committee can greatly assist in the discharge of these responsibilities.

A private member's bill requiring large public companies to consider, at their annual general meetings, the appointment of an audit committee was passed through the House of Commons in 1988, but foundered in the House of Lords.

Function

The ultimate responsibility for proper direction of the activities of a corporate organisation rests with its board of directors. It involves the determination and implementation of policies and monitoring performance to ensure that the policy objectives are achieved within the law.

It also involves serving the interests of those to whom the board may be accountable, such as shareholders, creditors and the public and reporting to them on its stewardship.

In fulfilling these responsibilities, the board of directors must rely upon the systems of internal control and will need to be assured that these are adequate and effective. Internal auditing is a management tool for giving this assurance and its activity should be properly focused to serve the requirements of the board. External audit involves verifying both effective control and true and fair reporting on behalf of external interests such as shareholders, creditors and the public. The board needs to liaise closely with the external auditors to facilitate the audit examination and to establish the principles upon which true and fair reporting is to be based.

Audit committees have come into being to assist boards of directors to address these special responsibilities. The audit committee, as a subcommittee of selected directors, becomes the focus of control and provides a forum for liaison between the board and the external auditors. Its aim should be to promote an environment of effective control and meaningful reporting. It is normally comprised of non-executive directors to ensure objectivity.

Whilst the objectivity of a subcommittee of non-executive directors is crucial to the role of an audit committee, there are also other reasons which justify it.

Effective monitoring of internal control, steering internal audit activity and liaison in external audit planning and reporting all require time for detailed consideration of the facts as well as unrestrained opportunities for collecting them. Such activity cannot normally be accommodated within the time frame of regular meetings of the full board. This is work which should be delegated to a subcommittee.

In order to demonstrate that the audit committee is acting on behalf of the board and has no executive or supervisory role, its terms of reference need to be defined by the board and formally recorded. Similarly, its deliberations should be formally recorded and reported for the information of all members of the board with recommendations for the board to consider and implement.

Duties

The terms of reference for the audit committee can vary from one organisation to another depending on how the board perceives the need for specific assistance in discharging collective and individual responsibilities, the circumstances of the particular organisation, and the constitution of the board. In some cases additional functions are assigned to the audit committee because of its unique position as an impartial organ of the organisation. Such functions might include reviewing directors' remuneration and monitoring the activities of the executive directors.

Some or all of the following duties will normally be included:

1. Reviewing the organisation's compliance with the law, official regulations and ethical standards and arrangements for avoiding conflicts of interest.
2. Reviewing the appointment and remuneration of external auditors and making recommendations for board consideration.
3. Concurring in the appointment or removal of the chief internal auditor.
4. Reviewing with the external auditors the accounting policies and reporting standards adopted by the organisation.
5. Reviewing, with the chief internal auditor and the external auditors, the adequacy and effectiveness of the organisation's systems of internal control.
6. Reviewing with the chief internal auditor:
   (a) the relevance of the terms of reference for internal auditing;
   (b) the adequacy of the resources provided for internal auditing;
   (c) whether there are any limiting circumstances imposed by management or otherwise which may restrict the scope of internal audit enquiries;
   (d) the appropriateness of the plans for internal auditing;
   (e) the quality of the internal auditing service in terms of the standards adopted for practice and review;
   (f) the significance of internal audit findings;
   (g) the extent to which internal audit recommendations are acted upon by management;
   (h) the incidence of fraud and other irregularity within the organisation and how it has been addressed.
7. Considering with the external auditors:
   (a) the strategic objectives being pursued by the board and the policies adopted to achieve them;
   (b) the audit scope in terms of plans prepared by the auditors for their examination of the organisation's records, control systems and reporting procedures;
   (c) arrangements for co-operation between internal and external auditors and the extent of reliance to be placed on internal audit work.
8. Reviewing with the external auditors:
   (a) proposed interim statements before publication;
   (b) the annual report and accounts including the auditors' report on the accounts before adoption by the board for publication;
   (c) all issues which are material to the presentation of the annual report and accounts, on which the auditors are seeking confirmation of expert judgements from the board;
   (d) the form and content, before publication, of all statements and reports concerning the organisation to be issued by the directors or the auditors, in connection with any proposed merger, acquisition or divestment or the raising of funds.

The requirements of every organisation will reflect the organisational structure, the personalities of its directors and the management culture. For example, in a company which has appointed an audit committee but has no internal auditing function, it may be considered necessary for the audit committee to take on some of the responsibilities normally assigned to the internal auditing function such as verifying the security and protection of assets.

Similarly, the nature of consultations with external auditors are likely to take a significantly different form in an organisation which is a single legal entity compared with a group of separately registered companies, particularly when some are incorporated overseas. The audit committee of the main board will be concerned not only with the investment in subsidiaries, but also with the true and fair reporting of consolidated assets, liabilities and revenue and with propriety in the activities of subsidiaries.

The scope for variation is very wide and the needs of each organisation are likely to be unique. Consequently, there is no common list of duties applicable to all audit committees and it may well be best to specify them in very broad terms. This enables the members to exercise responsibility from their independent viewpoints for the maximum benefit of the organisation and its board.

Meetings

When the audit committee is comprised of strong independent non-executive directors as recommended by PRO-NED, they are likely to be busy people with crowded diaries. Consequently, the calendar for both board meetings and audit committee meetings needs to be fixed well in advance to ensure that all members can attend and contribute.

Practice varies in the frequency of audit committee meetings, from meeting only once a year to consider the annual report and accounts before presentation to the board for adoption, to meeting regularly at quarterly or even monthly intervals. Clearly, a restricted programme of meetings limits the influence the audit committee can have and consequently its effectiveness. In some cases definite dates are fixed for specific tasks related to the organisation's programme for planning, monitoring progress and reporting. In many organisations the full range of duties can be accommodated by the audit committee meeting on four occasions in each financial year:

1. Meeting to consider all aspects of audit planning, to be attended by the external auditors and the chief internal auditor.
2. Meeting to review audit progress and to consider the quality of internal control, compliance with

the law and other obligations, to be attended by the external auditors and the chief internal auditor. This meeting may be so timed as to facilitate consideration of the interim statement.
3. Meeting to consider the annual report and accounts before presentation to the board for adoption, to be attended by the external auditors. This meeting should also address those issues on which the auditors, in forming an opinion on the accounts, rely on the expert judgement of the directors.
4. Post-audit meeting to review matters arising from the audit, post-balance sheet events and possible questions to be dealt with at the annual general meeting. This meeting would be held immediately before the AGM and would be attended by the external auditors.

Meetings may often be attended by one or more executive directors at the specific invitation of the chairman of the audit committee. In particular, the chief executive and the finance director may be required to assist the audit committee when further explanations are required and when work has to be commissioned to collect additional information needed by the committee.

Relationship with internal auditing

The objectives of internal auditing and audit committees are identical in many respects. Internal auditing is a tool to assist management to achieve its objectives through proper control. The audit committee is a device to assist the board to achieve corporate objectives through sound internal control. An effective audit committee will make full use of the internal auditing function to secure assurance that internal control is adequate. The internal audit reporting line through the audit committee to top management will be strengthened and its independence will be enhanced.

The Institute of Internal Auditors Inc. has issued a statement summarising its views concerning the appropriate relationship between audit committees and internal auditing.

Internal auditing and the audit committee

The Institute of Internal Auditors recommends that every public company have an audit committee organized as a standing committee of the board of directors. The Institute also encourages the establishment of audit committees in other organizations, including not-for-profit and governmental bodies. The audit committee should consist solely of outside directors, independent of management.

The primary responsibilities of the audit committee should involve assisting the board of directors in carrying out their responsibilities as they relate to the organization's accounting policies, internal control and financial reporting practices. The audit committee should establish and maintain lines of communication between the board and the company's independent auditors, internal auditors and financial management.

The audit committee should expect internal auditing to examine and evaluate the adequacy and effectiveness of the organization's system of internal control and the quality of performance in carrying out assigned responsibilities. Internal auditing may be used as a source of information to the audit committee on major frauds or irregularities as well as company compliance with laws and regulations.

To ensure that internal auditors carry out their responsibilities, the audit committee should approve and periodically review the internal audit charter, a management approved document which states internal audit's purpose, authority and responsibility. The audit committee should review annually the internal audit department's objectives and goals, audit schedules, staffing plans and financial budgets. The director of internal auditing should inform the audit committee of the results of audits, highlighting significant audit findings and recommendations. The audit committee should also determine whether internal audit activities are being carried out in accordance with the Standards for the Professional Practice of Internal Auditing adopted by the Institute of Internal Auditors.

To help assure independence, the director of internal auditing should have direct communication with the audit committee. The director should attend audit committee meetings and meet privately with the audit committee at least annually. Independence is further enhanced when the audit committee concurs in the appointment or removal of the director of internal auditing.

(IIA Inc., Internal Auditing and the Audit Committee)

Appendix 1
Specimen internal audit charter

Management and internal audit

It is the responsibility of management to establish a control environment which is both efficient and effective. Internal audit is one element of the control environment.

The control environment also depends upon the system of internal control the objectives of which are to ensure that:

(a) operations are conducted in an efficient and well ordered manner to fulfil defined management objectives;

(b) assets are safeguarded; and

(c) reliable information is available on which sound decisions can be made by those authorised to do so.

Internal audit does not relieve management of its responsibility for maintaining effective control. It is, however, that element of the control environment specifically set up by management to appraise the effectiveness of control. It can then reassure management when control is adequate, and identify and report inadequate control to enable the accountable management to strengthen it before any serious breakdown occurs.

Company law does not require a company to establish an internal audit function, and there is no universal specification for such a function. The format depends upon how the directors perceive the role and the resources they are prepared to invest in it.

Organisational status and relationships

The internal audit unit is responsible to the director of corporate control. This reporting line enables it to examine all functions objectively without being constrained by line management. Internal audit programmes are set up and reports are cleared with the accountable management and issued without reference to the director of corporate control, thus achieving reasonable independence.

The internal audit unit's effectiveness is critically dependent on maintaining credibility with management. This in turn depends upon building and maintaining a reputation for contributing constructively and adopting an objective professional approach. The internal audit unit and management share a common aim to achieve effective internal control. The internal auditor endeavours to establish a partnership with the auditee for a joint operation to improve conditions.

Whereas the aim of the internal audit unit is to assist management, the external auditors fulfil a statutory duty for which they are responsible to the shareholders.

The objectives differ, but in practice much of the evidence each collects as the basis for audit judgements may be common to both purposes. Effective liaison between internal auditors and external auditors is necessary to avoid duplication of work and clashing timetables. The internal audit unit consults regularly with the external auditors in the process of planning audit assignments and coverage. Internal audit plans and copies of agreed programmes of work are sent to the external auditors. They also receive copies of all internal audit reports issued and working papers are made available to them for examination.

Objectives

The internal audit unit is required to reassure the board through its audit committee as follows:

1. That there is adequate surveillance of internal control throughout the organisation so that serious breakdowns are avoided.
2. That the organisation's system of internal control is both sound and effective so that its assets are safeguarded and its performance reporting can be accepted with confidence.

The internal audit unit meets these requirements through the following procedures:

1. Establishing and maintaining standards for the practice of effective internal auditing throughout the organisation.
2. Assisting management throughout the organisation to undertake regular internal control reviews.
3. Testing the organisation's control systems for adequate effectiveness and compliance.
4. Liaising with the external auditors to avoid duplication or gaps in cover.
5. Disseminating throughout the organisation the lessons learned through internal audit findings.
6. Reporting to the audit committee on the adequacy of internal control throughout the organisation and on the internal audit work planned for each ensuing year.

Responsibilities

The internal audit unit is authorised to examine all activities throughout the organisation for the purpose of evaluating internal control, with specific responsibilities:

1. To reassure the accountable managements that their arrangements for internal control are adequate and efficient and that they are being properly complied with.
2. To identify and report to the accountable management any weakness in control and any procedures that are commercially unsound.
3. To offer feasible recommendations for improving performance and preventing future shortcomings.

Internal auditors are concerned to preserve their independence from the operations they examine. They are not empowered to make changes in systems, methods or staffing, and may not undertake to do so: their role is to act as agents for change by making recommendations to the accountable management from an impartial viewpoint.

Services

The internal audit service is in three parts:

1. **Internal control reviews**
   Internal control reviews are in-depth examinations of all the control systems of every management unit.

   Each review is undertaken by the accountable management assisted by the internal audit unit which also determines the review method and coordinates the annual review programme.

   The review evaluates whether the environment of control developed by management is adequate and whether the detailed control systems give reasonable assurance that control objectives will be attained. Any significant control weaknesses are recorded and are then monitored until eliminated.
2. **Compliance audit**
   The internal audit unit carries out compliance audit tests to establish whether operational staff are complying with the procedures and authority structures of the internal control systems. This is achieved by regularly testing samples of all transactions on both random and structured bases.

All divergence found is reported to the accountable management and monitored until rectified.

3. Operational audit

'Operational audit' is the term used to describe all other internal audit activity.

An operational audit is a complete review of a particular activity at the specific request of management. It involves evaluation of the control system including testing both for effectiveness and compliance. It may also include appraisal of the technical or commercial validity of activities.

The internal audit unit undertakes operational audit assignments, with assistance from line management, when it lacks a particular skill which is vital to the audit.

Working practices

For those operations where the management or the circumstances have changed significantly since the last internal audit visit and for all operations not previously visited, the internal auditor initially approaches the accountable management to explain the concept of internal auditing and to talk over possible areas where it could assist the management task.

For other operations there will be an established pattern of annual internal audit visits planned in consultation with the accountable managements when the programme for the annual review of internal control is prepared.

Before the internal audit examination starts, the internal auditor and the accountable management identify those areas which they jointly consider to involve the highest risk. These areas will then be assigned priority attention in the plan for the internal audit examination.

The internal auditor will prepare for approval a draft internal audit plan giving the proposed scope, approximate commencement date and duration. The accountable management then has the opportunity to accept it or to propose changes in the process of establishing an agreed internal audit plan.

Accountable managers need to allow internal auditors unrestricted access to interview staff, observe operations and examine records to enable them to fulfil their responsibilities.

Internal auditors have an obligation to respect the confidentiality of information to which they are privileged to have access in the course of their work.

Internal auditors will discuss their findings and the conclusions they draw from them with the accountable management at the time of the internal audit examination. A course of action to achieve operational improvements or to rectify control weaknesses may then be resolved jointly, to form the basis of the internal audit recommendations. This practice helps to ensure that the recommended course of action is feasible.

Reports

A formal report, written by the internal auditor who has done the examination work, is to be issued promptly after each internal audit assignment.

On completion of the internal audit examination, and before the formal report is issued, every effort is made to ensure that the accountable management agrees that its factual content is accurate, presented in appropriate context, and with proper emphasis.

The accountable management is given an opportunity to comment on the internal audit findings as stated in a draft report. The comments are then incorporated into the final report.

Internal audit reports are acknowledged to be confidential documents and are addressed to the accountable manager of the operations which have been examined. Copies are sent to those other executives only who, by virtue of their position in the organisation, need to know, and to the external auditors.

Internal auditors are entitled to expect those managers to whom their internal audit reports are addressed to respond to them formally, either (a) confirming acceptance of each internal audit recommendation or (b) stating that the case has been fully considered and that the course of action recommended has been positively set aside.

Accountable managers will be concerned to implement each internal audit recommendation which has been accepted and to monitor progress. The progress will be reviewed at subsequent internal audit visits.

Appendix 2
Specimen job description
for an internal auditor

Purpose

To provide an internal audit service to management as defined in the internal audit charter which was confirmed by board resolution on —:—:—; and in particular:

1. To give reassurance to management:
    (a) where the system of internal control is found to be adequate for achieving management objectives in an efficient and orderly manner and where the established procedures are being properly followed;
    (b) where assets are found to be adequately safeguarded and properly protected;
    (c) where the management information available is found to be sound and adequate for proper control.

2. To identify and report to the accountable management actual or potential weakness in control where it exists, and to recommend feasible ways to remedy it so that breakdown can be avoided.

3. To recommend to the accountable management feasible ways of improving the economy, efficiency or effectiveness of operations based upon findings from an impartial and objective examination.

Authority

The head of internal audit reports directly to the director of internal control and has unrestricted right of access to all levels of management, to the board of directors, and in particular to the audit committee.

All activities of the organisation are to be subject to regular internal audit examination and the head of internal audit is free to plan and direct the work of the internal audit unit in consultation with management within the parameters defined in the internal audit charter.

On every internal audit assignment, the accountable management is expected to allow the internal auditors involved unrestricted right of access:

1. To interview staff.
2. To observe operations.
3. To examine records and other documents.

Internal auditors have no authority to change staff, systems or methods of work; their role is to examine and make recommendations to the accountable management.

Responsibilities

Internal auditors are expected to perform their duties in a professional way and in particular:

1. To foster constructive working relationships with

accountable managements and their staff and with external auditors.

2. To plan, control and record their work to facilitate subsequent review and meaningful reference.

3. To exercise due care in the collection and interpretation of evidence and in the presentation of internal audit findings, conclusions and recommendations.

4. To respect the confidentiality of all information they are privileged to examine in the course of their work.

Internal auditors must be free of all responsibility for, or any other involvement in, every operational activity which they may be required to examine.

It is the responsibility of the head of internal audit to delegate specific internal audit assignments to individual internal auditors.

Duties

Internal auditors to whom internal audit assignments have been delegated are required to perform the following duties:

1. Generally to apply a sound understanding of internal auditing techniques to a thorough knowledge of the organisation and its system of internal control involving all functions: marketing, production, material management, personnel management, financial management, information management, etc.

2. To agree with the accountable management on either:
   (a) the timing and duration of the regular annual internal audit visit and any modifications to the proposed scope to accommodate specific management requirements;
   or
   (b) a programme for examining and reporting on particular areas of activity for a defined purpose at the specific request of management;
   and then, as appropriate:

3. To survey operations and functions in order to identify and record the nature of the activities,

the management objectives and the organisational structure.

4. In consultation with management to identify, assess and rank the risks to which the unit is exposed.

5. To identify the key control points of the system of internal control.

6. To plan and organise the detailed examination work for the internal audit assignment, including, when appropriate, consultation with the external auditors for the purpose of avoiding duplication of effort or clashing timetables.

7. To evaluate the adequacy and effectiveness of the system of internal control for achieving the management objectives.

8. To test compliance with the system of internal control.

9. To analyse the evidence collected and to interpret it objectively in the context of both management objectives and the purpose of the internal audit assignment.

10. To keep the accountable management informed about the progress of the internal audit assignment so as to allow significant findings to be discussed as they arise.

11. To present the findings and conclusions verbally to the accountable management at the end of the internal audit examination and to take due note of management comments.

12. To consider, with the accountable management, a feasible course of appropriate action when the audit examination has uncovered control weakness, or opportunities for improving performance.

13. To submit a draft written report to the accountable management promptly after the internal audit examination, requesting a prompt response confirming or correcting factual accuracy, appropriate context and proper emphasis.

14. To arrange to issue, with the approval of the head of internal audit and without undue delay, a formal internal audit report:

   (a) stating succinctly what has been examined and the internal auditor's conclusions arising from that examination, supported by a record of the detailed findings and recommendations and the management comments;

(b) addressed to the accountable management with copies to only those other executives who, by virtue of their position in the organisation, have a right to know, and to the external auditors;

(c) formally requesting a written response from the accountable management.

15. To monitor management responses and send a reminder if there is delay.

16. To follow up by reviewing progress in implementing internal audit recommendations which have been confirmed as accepted by management (normally at the next internal audit visit).

References

Chapter 1

IIA–UK (1988) *Standards and guidelines for the Professional Practice of Internal Auditing,* Institute of Internal Auditors–United Kingdom.

Chapter 2

Chambers, A., Selim, G. and Vinten, G. (1987) *Internal Auditing,* 2nd edn, Pitman.

Child, John (1977) *Organisation – A Guide to Problems and Practice,* Harper and Row.

Heeschen, P. and Sawyer, L. B. (1984) *Internal Auditor's Handbook,* IIA Inc.

ICAEW (1984) *Reliance on internal audit: Auditing guideline,* Institute of Chartered Accountants in England and Wales, Chartac.

IIA Inc. (1985) *The Institute of Internal Auditors: Position on audit committees statement,* Institute of Internal Auditors, Inc., USA.

IIA–UK (1988) *Standards and Guidelines for the Professional Practice of Internal Auditing,* Institute of Internal Auditors–United Kingdom.

Jay, Anthony (1970) *Effective Presentation,* Lewis Reprints.

Koontz, H., O'Donnell, C. and Weihrich, H. (1984) *Management,* McGraw-Hill.

Perry, W. E. (1984) *Improving Audit Productivity,* John Wiley.

Peters, Tom and Austin, Nancy (1985) *A Passion for Excellence,* Collins.

Rose, T. G. (1932) *The Management Audit,* Gee and Co.

Sawyer, L. B. (1981) *The Practice of Modern Internal Auditing,* expanded edition, IIA Inc.

Tanenbaum, R. and Schmidt, W. H. (1973), 'How to choose a leadership pattern', *Harvard Business Review,* May/June.

US Exposure Draft Report of the National Commission on Fraudulent Financial Reporting (April 1987).

Chapter 3

IIA–UK (1988) Standards and Guidelines for the Professional Practice of Internal Auditing (1988), The Institute of Internal Auditors–United Kingdom.

Chapter 4

Bromage, M. C. (1984) *Writing Audit Reports,* McGraw-Hill.

Currie, R. M. (1981) *Work Study,* 4th edn, Pitman.

Gowers, Sir Ernest, Greenbaum, S. and Whitcut, J. (1986) *The Complete Plain Words,* HMSO.

H. M. Treasury (1983) *Government Internal Audit Manual,* HMSO.

Lockheed Aircraft Corporation (1966) *Sampling Manual for auditors,* IIA Inc.

Maniak, A. J. (1985) *Presenting Audit Results, Logic, Content and Form,* IIA Inc.

Patton, J. M., Evans, J. H. and Lewis, B. L. (1986) *A Framework for Evaluating Internal Audit Risk: Research Report No. 25,* IIA Inc.

Rutteman, P. J. (1976) *Accountants' Digest No. 32: Flowcharting for auditors,* ICAEW.

Skinner, R. M. and Anderson, R. J. (1966), *Analytical Auditing: An Outline of the Flow Chart Approach to Audits,* Canada Pitman (out of print).

Chapter 5

Chambers, A. D. and Court, J. M. (1986) *Computer Auditing,* Pitman.

Kelman, A. (1985)*Computer Fraud in Small Businesses: Special report for the Economist Intelligence Unit,* Economist Intelligence Unit.

268　References

Mair, W. C., Wood, D. R. and Davies, R. W. (1978) *Computer Control and Audit*, 3rd edn, IIA Inc.

Travis, B. J. (1987) *Auditing the Development of Computing Systems*, Butterworth.

Chapter 6

Accounting Standards Steering Committee (1975) *The Corporate Report*, ICAEW.

CIMA (1982) *Management Accounting Official Terminology*, first edn, The Chartered Institute of Management Accountants.

Datta, A. K. *Rationalising Materials Management*, World Press.

Doyle, P. (1984) 'Marketing management' in J. F. Pickering and T. A. J. Cockerill (eds) *The Economic Management of the Firm*, Philip Allan.

Harris, N. D. and Skedd, A. (1980) *Materials Management*, ICAEW.

Herzberg, F., (1974) *Work and the Nature of Man*, Granada.

ICAEW, (1989), *Making the Most of Marketing*, Chartac.

Institute of Materials Handling (February 1965) *Introduction to Materials Handling*, Institute of Materials Handling.

McClelland, D. C. (1961) *The Achieving Society*, Van Nostrand Reinhold.

McGregor, D. M. (1960) *The Human Side of Enterprise*, McGraw-Hill.

Maslow, A. H. (1943) *A Theory of Human Motivation*, Psychological Review 50, July.

Solomon, E. (1963) *The Theory of Financial Management*, Colombia University Press.

Stelzer, W. R. *Materials Handling*, Prentice Hall.

Travis, B. J. (1987) *Auditing the Development of Computing Systems,* Butterworth.

Wilmshurst John, (1984) *The Fundamentals and Practice of Marketing,* second edn, Insitute of Marketing.

Chapter 7

Allen, M., Hodgkinson, R. and Arthur Anderson and Co. *Buying a Business: A guide to the decisions*, Graham and Trotman.

Lindberg, R. A. and Cohn, Theodore (1972) *Operations Auditing*, American Management Association.

Moon, R. W. (1976) *Business Mergers and Take-over Bids*, Gee and Co.

Narvaez, C. R., Campbell, T. I. and Savage, L. (1984) *A Model for Preacquisition Audits of Financial Institutions*, IIA Inc.

Panel on Take-overs and Mergers (April 1985) *The City Code on Take-overs and Mergers and the Rules Governing Substantial Acquisitions of Shares*, The Stock Exchange, London.

Venables, J. S. R. and Impey, K. W. (1988) *Internal Audit*, 2nd edn, Butterworth.

Williams, J. G. (1980) *Acquisitions and Mergers*, ICAEW.

Chapter 8

Comer, M. J. (1987) *Corporate Fraud*, 2nd edn, McGraw-Hill.

Elliot, R. K. and Willingham, John J. *Management Fraud, Detection and Deterrence*. PBI Books.

Chapter 9

ICAEW (1987) *Auditing Guidelines ed Explanatory Foreword to Auditing Standards and Guidelines and Review of Reporting Guidance*, ICAEW.

ICAEW (1988) 'Auditing and reporting' in *UK Auditing Standards, Guidelines and Exposure Drafts*, ICAEW.

Chapter 10

Ernst & Whinney (1987) *Audit Committees*, Ernst and Whinney.

IIA Inc. (1985) *Internal Auditing and the Audit Committee, Working Together Toward Common Goals*, The Institute of Internal Auditors Inc.

Index